Patricia Kennedy Grimsted

Archives and Manuscript Repositories in the USSR

Moscow and Leningrad

Studies of the Russian Institute | Columbia University

D0209626

Princeton University Press
Princeton, New Jersey

This book has been composed in Press Roman
by the Peterson Research Group.
Printed in the United States of America
by Princeton University Press, Princeton, New Jersey

This volume is dedicated to the many individuals and institutions in the USSR who did so much to assist its preparation, with the hope that its publication may serve as an example of the possibilities of international scholarly cooperation and promote more fruitful scientific and cultural exchange.

ARCHIVES AND MANUSCRIPT REPOSITORIES IN THE USSR
Moscow and Leningrad

The Russian Institute of Columbia University sponsors the *Studies of the Russian Institute* in the belief that their publication contributes to scholarly research and public understanding. In this way the Institute, while not necessarily endorsing their conclusions, is pleased to make available the results of some of the research conducted under its auspices. A list of the *Studies of the Russian Institute* appears at the back of the book.

PREFACE

The impressive wealth of manuscript and archival holdings in the Soviet Union lures researchers in many fields from all over the world. But too easily the foreigner can be overwhelmed by the number and variety of repositories, by the complexities of archival organization and procedures, by documentary migrations, by the many changes of name or location of different archives and collections, and by the bulk of published literature in the archival realm. The increased opportunity for foreigners to obtain archival access in recent years heightens the need for organizational, procedural, and bibliographical information.

Over half a century ago the American historian Frank Golder visited imperial Russia and gathered the data for his helpful reference work on materials for American history in Russian archives. Golder's work, as far as it went, has retained its usefulness, although the materials he cataloged are now located in different repositories. When Golder was working he could turn for general reference and specific bibliographical data to the exhaustive survey of Russian archives and manuscript holdings by V. S. Ikonnikov, which forms the first part of his never-completed *Opyt russkoi istoriografii* (2 vols. in 4; Kiev, 1891-1908).

In the succeeding half-century, the archives Golder and Ikonnikov described have been completely transformed into one of the most extensive state-controlled archival systems in the world. At the same time, the information needs of foreign scholars have increased many times with the blossoming of interest in the Soviet Union and its prerevolutionary society and culture. The extensive Soviet archival development and the multidimensional nature of scholarly investigations in the field now call for a more comprehensive approach to a directory of archival resources. Yet, despite the unusual facilities for centralized bibliographic and reference work in the Soviet Union, and a number of helpful publications in the field, Ikonnikov's monumental work has never been updated or surpassed.

A single individual is hardly equal to such a project today, and indeed it would be impossible to attempt in any but preliminary form. For a foreign scholar to undertake such a task is even more presumptuous, but I felt that the dearth of procedural and bibliographic information available abroad was so great that a preliminary effort would prove of value to growing number of researchers concerned with Soviet archives. In its conception as a basic research manual, the present volume is an outgrowth of a short article, "Soviet Archives and Manuscript Collections: A Bibliographic Introduction," *Slavic Review* 24 (March 1965): 105-20, which I prepared as an offshoot of my own historical research experience in the Soviet Union in 1964.

The current kaleidoscopic volume is accordingly intended first to serve as a starting point for the foreigner planning research in the Soviet Union. The importance of advance preparation and detailed arrangements for those contemplating archival research can hardly be overemphasized, but the information required has hitherto been extremely inadequate abroad. With better preparation at home and more extensive knowledge of the resources, a scholar's efforts might be more fruitful and his time in the Soviet Union more efficiently spent than has been possible in the past.

Second, the volume is intended for the scholar who may not be planning research in the Soviet Union himself but who may need to know more about the holdings and existing published finding aids. He may want to ascertain the existence of a particular manuscript or group of records or to verify the contents of a certain archive or name of its predecessors.

It is intended, third, to acquaint foreigners—potential researchers, archivists, librarians, and other area specialists—with some of the features of the development and overall organization of archives and manuscript repositories in the Soviet Union. Archival affairs is a field in which the Soviet Union has effected revolutionary conceptual and organizational innovations, all of which have attracted only fleeting attention abroad. Except for specialized guides to catalogs in the field of medieval Slavic, Latin, and Greek manuscripts, and those in various oriental language groups, where the Soviet Union has been covered in more general bibliographic compendia, scant data are available about the nature and range of manuscript repositories in the Soviet Union. A brief sketch of the history and present organizational aspects of Soviet developments in the archival field may serve to orient users, to help explain some of the general characteristics of the system, and to acquaint researchers with sources of further information.

Finally, the present volume is intended as an aid for research libraries in keeping their reference holdings abreast of the literature in the field. I would also hope that reprint organizations will find the bibliographic sections helpful in determining key reference materials which should be more widely available to the scholarly public. Because of the importance of careful research planning and detailed applications prior to departure, and of relating research and writing to extant documents, the availability of bibliographic data about published archival finding aids and manuscript catalogs is a crucial prerequisite for modern research libraries. Lester Born recognized this need in his article some years ago, "A Universal Guide to Catalogues of Manuscripts and Inventories of Archival Collections: A Proposal for Cooperative Listing," in *College and Research Libraries* 17 (1956):322-29, but his proposals for centralized reference work in this area have gone largely unheeded except for some specialized types of manuscript coverage.

As to the organization of this volume, the introductory historical survey provides brief general orientation and background information on the development of the Soviet archival system. An additional introductory section gives procedural information about the technicalities of archival arrangement and reference publications in the Soviet Union, problems of access, working conditions, and related information for potential researchers. The general bibliographic introduction (Part A) covers comprehensive archival literature (including bibliographies and periodicals), specialized reference aids covering holdings in two or more repositories, and directories or catalogs of specific types of manuscript collections or archival materials.

As will be apparent from the table of contents, the directory itself is organized by institutions, grouped in broad administrative categories. The eleven central state archives under the control of the Main Archival Administration are presented in Part B, followed in Part C by the archives and other manuscript repositories under libraries and institutes of the Academy of Sciences of the USSR. Part D covers special archives, including the archival system of the Communist Party, the archives under the ministries of Foreign Affairs and Defense, and the comprehensive state film archive, Gosfil'mofond. Manuscript divisions of state libraries, museums, and other institutions are grouped by city: those in Moscow in Part E, starting with the extensive manuscript divisions of the Lenin Library and the State Historical Museum; those in Leningrad in Part F, headed by the equally distinguished Manuscript Division of the Saltykov-Shchedrin State Public Library. Finally, Part G covers republic-, oblast-, and city-level state archives located in Moscow and Leningrad. Appendix 1 gives information about research facilities in major libraries in Moscow and Leningrad and bibliographical data about more extensive library guides; and Appendix 2 gives introductory bibliographical information about paleography and the ancillary disciplines relating to research in medieval Slavic manuscripts. A glossary at the end of the volume includes important Russian archival terms that might prove confusing to foreign researchers, and explains peculiarities of usage in the Soviet Union.

Although coverage of individual institutions varies according to the nature of the holdings and other available reference aids, I have adopted a fairly standard format starting with a brief historical survey and a general characterization of the nature and extent of the holdings. Because of the difficulties that arise from the many changes of institutional names and resulting shifts or reorganization of holdings, I have made an effort to list, with dates, all the previous official names and acronyms of the institutions covered and, where possible, to coordinate this information with previously published finding aids covering the holdings involved. For larger institutions, a separate section gives pertinent details about working conditions for foreign scholars, including specific problems of access and the availability of catalogs and other finding aids. A bibliographical compendium of finding aids for each institution includes general descriptions, guides, inventories or catalogs, and other more specialized types of reference publications.

The extent of bibliographic coverage for given repositories generally varies according to the availability of other bibliographical data, or to the nature and completeness of published finding aids. I have made no effort to include all published descriptions for large repositories when these are listed in other available sources. Most particularly because of the large volume of publications involved, catalogs of different Slavic manuscript collections are not included when they are listed in the general directory of catalogs compiled by Iu. K. Begunov et al., *Spravochnik-ukazatel' pechatnykh opisanii slaviano-russkikh rukopisei* (Moscow/Leningrad, 1963) (see A-14); I have cited appropriate pages of this volume under individual repositories.

Since I am confining my bibliographical coverage to *finding aids* for archives or other manuscript repositories, I have generally excluded the following types of items: documentary publications or descriptions of published sources; items presenting more substantive or historical analysis than external description; studies of single manuscripts; textual criticism, i.e., philological, paleographic, or technical analyses of manuscripts, and comparisons of texts; catalogs of printed books, including incunabula, unless such publications also cover manuscripts in the same repository or collection; items of extremely limited scope; popularized or newspaper descriptions; typed or manuscript catalogs of individual fonds or collections unless available in mimeographed format (mimeographed or *rotoprint* publications are always so indicated, because usually they are not available for export); and items that could not be located for perusal.

I have included only selected survey *(obzor)* or generalized descriptive articles that cover limited groups of materials. Because of the great quantity of this type of publication and the difficulties of thorough bibiliographic control, I have given preference to items published more recently than the available archival guides, and to items covering holdings about which adequate descriptions are lacking. I have generally not included survey articles for repositories under the Academy of Sciences for which more comprehensive bibliographical data is available, but I have tried to include the more comprehensive or substantial ones for many of the state archives in Parts B and G. But in all cases coverage of this type of item remains highly selective.

Selected studies of the history and organization of individual repositories are included in introductory notes, but these are not assigned code numbers unless they contain significant information about the nature of the holdings not otherwise available or substantial bibliographies of finding aids.

For bibliographic purposes, I have observed the end of 1970 as a cutoff date for publications included, except for a few key 1971 imprints which I was able to add at the last moment, and forthcoming publications for which I was able to consult a typescript or to find detailed information about the contents.

The information presented varies considerably from one institution to another, as do the nature and adequacy of published finding aids. I made a concerted attempt to verify and expand my initial findings through personal visits to as many of the repositories as possible and through consultations with specialists in the Soviet Union and abroad. Unfortunately, however, my coverage of a number of institutions is less extensive or authoritative than I would have liked. Although in certain cases I have excluded reference to some holdings and reports that I was unable to verify, I have tried to extend my treatment of lesser-known repositiories when reliable information was available to me.

I had initially intended to cover repositories in the union republics and regions outside Moscow and Leningrad in the present volume. However, the extent and complexity of this information dictated its exclusion. A grant from the National Endowment for the Humanities made possible by matching funds from the Council on Library Resources is now enabling me to extend my treatment of regional archives; the resultant directory and bibliography is being prepared for later publication under the sponsorship of the Russian Institute at Columbia University. In the meantime, interested scholars can refer to the preliminary bibliographic coverage of state archives in my article "Regional State Archives in the USSR: Some Notes and a Bibliography of Published Guides," *Slavic Review* 28 (March 1969):92-115.

My attempt to accomplish so many purposes and to include all types of repositories within the framework of a single volume has naturally resulted in unevenness and the need for selectivity. But I hope that the broader perspective and general orientation gained from more comprehensive coverage will compensate for the drawbacks of the regrettably sketchy presentation in some sections. I hope, too, that the gaps and shortcomings of this volume will provide incentive for further publications by many of the institutions not covered by adequate finding aids, and for the preparation of specialized reference aids for archival research in many fields. And since I am only too well aware that the extent and complexity of this project are bound to result in errors and omissions, and that subsequent changes and publications are bound to necessitate periodic updatings or revision, I would be most appreciative of corrections, additions, or further suggestions that readers might be able to furnish me.

December, 1970

ACKNOWLEDGMENTS

So many individuals and institutions have contributed so much to this volume that I can hardly begin to thank them all adequately. I started the project during a year at Harvard University as an Associate of the Russian Research Center and a Fellow of the Radcliffe Institute; the Radcliffe Institute continued to provide fellowship support during a subsequent year in Washington, D.C. The exceptionally rich resources and congenial working conditions at Widener Library were particularly helpful; I am very much indebted to the Slavic Division director, Charles Gredler, and his staff for assistance at various stages of my enterprise, and especially for the final verification of my bibliographical entries against the Harvard holdings.

From its beginnings my work has been associated with the Russian Institute at Columbia University, which provided for many of the research and secretarial expenses, gave me fellowship support as a Research Associate, and sponsored the project for publication. I feel special gratitude to the former director, Professor Alexander Dallin, who initially encouraged me to expand my earlier article for reference publication, to the current director, Professor Marshall Shulman, and to Professors Loren Graham, Leopold Haimson, and Robert Maguire. Constance Bezer's efficient attention to so many editorial and procedural details was invaluable, and Mildred O'Brien transformed the unwieldy text into a final typescript with special care.

Much of the American library work for the project has been carried out at the Library of Congress, and I am grateful for the assistance of the staff of the Slavic and Central European Division, headed until recently by Dr. Sergius Yakobson; Dr. Paul Horecky and Dr. Robert Allen were always on hand to respond to my countless queries and assist my location of materials. I also appreciate the assistance of Laurence Miller, of the Library of the University of Illinois, for arranging to have bibliographical entries checked against library holdings there.

The American Council of Learned Societies and the International Research and Exchanges Board, through their sponsorship and generous financial support, made possible my research visits to the Soviet Union. For their assistance and encouragement at so many stages of my work, as well as the arrangements for my travels to the Soviet Union, I am particularly grateful to Dr. Frederick Burkhardt, President of the ACLS, and Dr. Gordon Turner, vice-president, and to Professor Allen Kassof, Executive Director of IREX, and his assistant Daniel Matuszewski.

The gracious reception and extended assistance which the Academy of Sciences of the USSR and the Main Archival Administration of the Council of Ministers of the USSR gave to the project were crucial to its completion. Through their auspices and special arrangements I was able to spend both the fall of 1969 and the summer of 1970 visiting archives and other repositories in

Moscow, Leningrad, and the capitals of many union republics. The opportunity for this research and for consultation with scholars, archivists, and officials gave me the chance to expand my coverage, to correct numerous errors, and to benefit from the criticism, suggestions, and general expertise of many Soviet specialists. I wish especially to thank the staffs of the foreign divisions of the Main Archival Administration and the Academy of Sciences who so kindly assisted me with the complicated arrangements for my research.

The Ministry of Foreign Affairs of the USSR arranged for my visit to the Archive of Russian Foreign Policy (AVPR), and its director, V. I. Mazaev, kindly assisted with my coverage of Foreign Ministry holdings. Many staff members of the Manuscript Division of the Lenin Library in Moscow and of the Saltykov-Shchedrin State Public Library in Leningrad assisted me in many aspects of my work as well as advised me about my coverage of their own institutions. I appreciate the extensive efforts of my colleagues at the Moscow State Historical-Archival Institute who read over several parts of my manuscript and contributed a number of helpful suggestions.

My coverage of medieval Slavic manuscript holdings and the bibliography in that field was aided by the advice of A. I. Rogov at the Institute of Slavic and Balkan Studies and S. O. Shmidt of the Archeographical Commission of the Academy of Sciences in Moscow, and most especially by the knowledgeable tutelage of V. I. Malyshev of the Institute of Russian Literature (Pushkinskii Dom) in Leningrad.

My research in the field of oriental manuscripts and bibliography profited greatly from the counsel of Iu. E. Borshchevskii, Librarian of the Leningrad Branch of the Institute of Oriental Studies of the Academy of Sciences; I am immeasurably grateful for his assistance in many phases of my research and his careful scrutiny of my typescript.

Many other persons in Moscow and Leningrad gave generously of their time and expertise and advised me on problems of bibliography and archival holdings. I am particularly grateful to those who read over and verified my preliminary coverage of their institutions. I hope that all who assisted me in the Soviet Union may realize the extent of my appreciation for their contributions and for the many errors they helped me avoid.

I am also indebted to a number of friends and scholars on the home front for their many and varied contributions. I regret that space does not permit me to single out all those who responded to my questionnaires and many queries about specific repositories, or research in specialized fields, and who supplied a variety of bibliographical and procedural suggestions, but I hope that they too realize the measure of my gratitude. I owe special thanks to the following: Professor Terence Emmons of Stanford University and David Shapiro of London who gave assistance during the early stages of my project; J. D. Pearson, Librarian of the School of Oriental and African Studies of the University of London, who advised me on coverage of oriental manuscript holdings and made available to me the results of his own research in that field; and Morris Rieger, Special Assistant to the Archivist of the United States for International Programs and Deputy Director General of the International Council on Archives, who assisted me on numerous occasions.

Professor Walter Pintner of Cornell University and Professor Marc Raeff of Columbia University read significant portions of the typescript and contributed a number of helpful suggestions. Eleanor Buist, formerly of Columbia University Library, contributed much bibliographical expertise and general assistance and scrutinized a preliminary draft. Ernst Posner, Professor Emeritus of History and Archives Administration of American University, gave a most careful and fruitful reading to the historical introduction and often provided me the benefit of his long experience in archival affairs. Professor Fritz Epstein, of Indiana University, diligently went over both a preliminary draft and my final typescript to much profit.

John S. G. Simmons, of All Souls College, Oxford, read early drafts and the final manuscript with utmost care and helped me avoid a number of pitfalls along the way; I am immeasurably indebted to him for his extensive bibliographical, procedural, and editorial guidance, and for his continuing interest in and assistance with my work since its inception.

My hearty appreciation goes out to Robert G. Carlton of the Slavic Bibliographic and Documentation Center for his conscientious assistance in proofreading and most especially in the preparation of the subject index.

Some selections from the introductory historical and procedural sections of this volume appeared in condensed form as an article, "Archives in the Soviet Union: Their Organization and the Problem of Access," in the *American Archivist* 34 (January 1971):27-41.

My husband, David, is undoubtedly much more interested in knowing that this volume is behind me than in any acknowledgment which might associate him with its genesis; yet it goes without saying that he and my children bore much more of the brunt of my work than I would have liked, and were too often ill-compensated by tardy meals or postcards from Moscow.

NOTE ON BIBLIOGRAPHICAL FORMAT

Marginal code numbers have been assigned for each bibliographical entry to aid in cross references and ready identification. The letters A, B, C, etc., refer to the different parts within the volume, and the numbers run consecutively throughout each part. Occasionally items containing descriptions of materials in two or more repositories may be listed more than once; however, usually only brief titles or authors' names plus cross reference numbers are given for subsequent references. Historical and supplementary materials cited in annotations, footnotes, or introductory remarks do not bear code numbers.

The first line of each bibliographical item gives the appropriate "author" or "main entry" as used by the Library of Congress for its catalog and printed cards. The entry is enclosed in square brackets when it is an institutional or "corporate entry," or when it does not provide the main author or compiler as indicated on the title page. Although the use of these forms leads to many inconsistencies, their inclusion should make it easier to locate materials in American libraries and union catalogs. Otherwise, it is very difficult for a researcher to know whether a given volume is cataloged under the author, editor, or a corporate entry such as "Akademiia nauk SSSR" (followed by a sub-entry such as "Biblioteka," etc.). Furthermore, some items are cataloged under the city in which the described institution is located, as in the case of the Lenin Library's listing under "Moscow. Publichnaia biblioteka." (part of its prerevolutionary name), or under the country and an administrative agency; for example, many publications of state archives are found under "Russia (1923-USSR). Glavnoe arkhivnoe upravlenie." (or its earlier variants). The problem is further complicated by the frequent changes Soviet institutions have undergone; the Library of Congress has not always kept up with the changes, and itself has changed the cataloging rules under which it operates; as a result, different volumes in the same series sometimes end up cataloged under two or three different main entries. Accordingly, mistakes and inconsistencies in the Library of Congress official catalog as they existed at the time of checking have been recorded here to assist in the retrieval of the items listed. While future changes in the Library of Congress catalogs may retrospectively affect some entries, cross references will presumably be provided in the catalogs to the entries recorded here. Widener Library entries have occasionally been given as alternates, especially for items not held by the Library of Congress.

The full title as it appears on the title page (even if this involves repetition of part of the corporate entry) starts a new bibliographical line following the appropriate author entry. The title is followed by the compiler and editor, if these are not given as the author entry; when there are more than three compilers, etc., all names are usually not given. The place of publication is given according to the established English name of the city at the time of publication. The total pagination is included to indicate the extent of the work and to aid in the estimation of reproduction costs.

As a further aid to researchers and libraries, call numbers have been furnished in square brackets for volumes available in the Library of Congress (DLC) and the Harvard University Library (MH; or MH-L for the Law Library), as verified in their own catalogs. For volumes not available in either of these two libraries, other American locations—but not call numbers—are furnished if they are available in the Cyrillic Union catalog in the Library of Congress or other sources, but this coverage is not complete and most particularly is not up-to-date. Processing delays, cataloging backlogs, and the difficulty of locating certain volumes reported to be in the library undoubtedly makes for errors in this compilation. It should also be pointed out that Harvard University Library, on the basis of a typescript of this volume, has put on order microfilms or other form of copies of all items not in its possession at the time of checking; many of these may be available there by the time of publication, so that it will provide a center for the accumulation of these materials.

Locations and call numbers are not given for articles, except when they are published in relatively obscure or lesser-known serials. Serial titles and locations in the United States are now easily available in the invaluable reference volumes prepared by Rudolf Smits, *Half a Century of Soviet Serials, 1917-1968: A Bibliography and Union List of Serials Published in the USSR*, 2 vols. (Washington: Library of Congress, 1968).

Annotations for many entries provide additional information, such as scope and limitations, the present status of the records or manuscripts described, the current name of the institution housing them, and the relationship to earlier guides or catalogs. Regrettably, it has been impossible to provide this type of information for all entries.

The author-title index includes all titles of books and articles listed in the coded bibliographical entries, together with their authors, compilers, and/or editors. The subject matter, persons, and institutions covered by the entries are covered in the separate subject index.

TRANSLITERATION TABLE

As indicated in the table below, the Library of Congress system of transliteration has been used throughout, with such slight modifications as the omission of ligatures. Orthography in the Russian language has been modernized to conform with current Soviet usage. Proper names of authors or editors of books published in the USSR are transliterated from their Soviet Russian form, even though they may be of non-Russian origin. Capitalization in institutional and book titles also follows current Soviet usage, as does the use of periods in book titles to separate titles from subtitles.

А а	A a		Р р	R r		
Б б	B b		С с	S s		
В в	V v		Т т	T t		
Г г	G g		У у	U u		
Д д	D d		Ф ф	F f		
Е е	E e		Х х	Kh kh		
Ж ж	Zh zh		Ц ц	Ts ts		
З з	Z z		Ч ч	Ch ch		
И и	I i		Ш ш	Sh sh		
I i	I i		Щ щ	Shch shch		
Й й	I i		— ъ	— "		
К к	K k		— ы	— y		
Л л	L l		— ь	— '		
М м	M m		Ѣ ѣ	E e		
Н н	N n		Э э	E e		
О о	O o		Ю ю	Iu iu		
П п	P p		Я я	Ia ia		

ABBREVIATIONS AND ACRONYMS

Abbreviations or acronyms that are given only once in the text in connection with the full official name of an institution are not included in the list below. The forms given are the official ones used most frequently in Soviet publications, although readers should be aware of occasional variations. The designation "SSSR" [USSR] is frequently used along with and hence forms part of the official acronym of all-union archival institutions, such as TsGAOR SSSR, thus permitting clear distinction between all-union and individual republic institutions. However, it is often dropped when the context makes the all-union reference apparent without it; hence some variation will be found in this usage.

For a full list of Soviet abbreviations and acronyms, see the most recent dictionary, *Slovar' sokrashchenii russkogo iazyka,* compiled by D. I. Alekseev, I. G. Gozman, and G. V. Sakharov (Moscow, 1963; 486 p.). Historians will also want to consult the short pamphlet prepared by N. A. Samorukova, *Spravochnik sokrashchenii, priniatykh v istoricheskoi literature* (Moscow, 1964; 59 p.). See also the Library of Congress publication, *Glossary of Russian Abbreviations and Acronyms* (Washington, D.C., 1967; 806 p.), which includes English translations.

AN SSSR	–	Akademiia nauk SSSR [Academy of Sciences of the USSR]
AVPR	–	Arkhiv vneshnei politiki Rossii [Archive of Russian Foreign Policy]
BAN	–	Biblioteka Akademii nauk SSSR [Library of the Academy of Sciences of the USSR] , Leningrad
BMM	–	Gosudarstvennaia biblioteka-muzei V. V. Maiakov-skogo [V. V. Maiakovskii State Library and Museum]
CStH	–	Stanford University, Library of the Hoover Institution on War, Revolution, and Peace
DDO	–	Dumbarton Oaks Library, Washington, D. C.
DLC	–	Library of Congress, Washington, D. C.
EGAF	–	Edinyi gosudarstvennyi arkhivnyi fond [Single State Archival Fond] , later GAF
GAF	–	Gosudarstvennyi arkhivnyi fond [State Archival Fond]
GAFKE	–	Gosudarstvennyi arkhiv feodal'no-krepostnicheskoi epokhi [State Archive of the Feudal-Serfdom Epoch] ; now essentially TsGADA
GAMO	–	Gosudarstvennyi arkhiv Moskovskoi oblasti [State Archive of Moscow Oblast] , formerly GAORMO

GAORLO — Gosudarstvennyi arkhiv Oktiabr'skoi revoliutsii Leningradskoi oblasti [State Archive of the October Revolution of Leningrad Oblast] , now LGAORSS

GAORMO — Gosudarstvennyi arkhiv Oktiabr'skoi revoliutsii Moskovskoi oblasti [State Archive of the October Revolution of Moscow Oblast] , now GAMO

GAORSS LO — Gosudarstvennyi arkhiv Oktiabr'skoi revoliutsii i sotsialisticheskogo stroitel'stva Leningradskoi oblasti [State Archive of the October Revolution and Socialist Development of Leningrad Oblast] , now LGAORSS

GAORSS MO — Gosudarstvennyi arkhiv Oktiabr'skoi revoliutsii i sotsialisticheskogo stroitel'stva Moskovskoi oblasti [State Archive of the October Revolution and Socialist Development of Moscow Oblast] , now GAMO

GAU — Glavnoe arkhivnoe upravlenie pri Sovete ministrov SSSR [Main Archival Administration of the Council of Ministers of the USSR]

GBL — Gosudarstvennaia ordena Lenina Biblioteka SSSR imeni V. I. Lenina [V. I. Lenin State Library with the Order of Lenin]

GIALO — Gosudarstvennyi istoricheskii arkhiv Leningradskoi oblasti [State Historical Archive of Leningrad Oblast] , now LGIA

GIAMO — Gosudarstvennyi istoricheskii arkhiv Moskovskoi oblasti [State Historical Archive of Moscow Oblast] , now part of TsGAgM

GIM — Gosudarstvennyi istoricheskii muzei [State Historical Museum]

Glavarkhiv — Glavnoe upravlenie arkhivnym delom (Main Administration of Archival Affairs), later Tsentrarkhiv and GAU

GLM — Gosudarstvennyi literaturnyi muzei [State Literary Museum]

Gosarkhiv — Gosudarstvennyi arkhiv RSFSR [State Archive of the RSFSR] ; also used as an abbreviation for the former Gosudarstvennyi arkhiv Rossiiskoi imperii [State Archive of the Russian Empire] , now housed in TsGADA

GPB — Gosudarstvennaia ordena Trudovogo Krasnogo Znameni Publichnaia biblioteka imeni M. E. Saltykova-Shchedrina [M. E. Saltykov-Shchedrin State Public Library with the Order of the

Red Banner of Labor]

ICA — International Council on Archives

IMLI — Institut mirovoi literatury imeni A. M. Gor'kogo Akademii nauk SSSR [Institute of World Literature in the name of A. M. Gor'kii of the Academy of Sciences of the USSR]

Istpart — Komissiia dlia sobiraniia i izucheniia materialov po istorii Oktiabr'skoi revoliutsii i RKP(b) [Commission for the Gathering and Study of Materials for the History of the October Revolution and the Russian Communist Party]

IU — University of Illinois Library

izd-vo — izdatel'stvo [publishing house]

LGAORSS — Leningradskii gosudarstvennyi arkhiv Oktiabr'skoi revoliutsii i sotsialisticheskogo stroitel'stva [Leningrad State Archive of the October Revolution and Socialist Development], formerly GAORSS LO, or GAORLO

LGIA — Leningradskii gosudarstvennyi istoricheskii arkhiv [Leningrad State Historical Archive], formerly GIALO

LGU — Leningradskii gosudarstvennyi universitet imeni A. A. Zhdanova [Leningrad State University in the name of A. A. Zhdanov]

LIIZhT — Leningradskii institut inzhenerov zheleznodo-rozhnogo transporta imeni akademika V. N. Obraztsova [Leningrad Institute of Railroad Transport Engineers in the name of Academician V. N. Obraztsov]

LOII — Leningradskoe otdelenie Instituta istorii SSSR AN SSSR [Leningrad Branch of the Institute of the History of the USSR of the Academy of Sciences of the USSR]

LOIV AN — Leningradskoe otdelenie Instituta vostokovedeniia AN SSSR [Leningrad Branch of the Institute of Oriental Studies of the Academy of Sciences of the USSR]

LOTsIA — Leningradskoe otdelenie Tsentral'nogo istoricheskogo arkhiva [Leningrad Branch of the Central Historical Archive], now mostly in TsGIA SSSR

MAMIu — Moskovskii arkhiv Ministerstva iustitsii [Moscow Archive of the Ministry of Justice], now absorbed by TsGADA

MGIAI — Moskovskii gosudarstvennyi istoriko-arkhivnyi institut [Moscow State Historico-Archival Institute]

xxiii

MGU	—	Moskovskii gosudarstvennyi universitet imeni M. V. Lomonosova [Moscow State University in the name of M. V. Lomonosov]
MH	—	Harvard University Library
MH-L	—	Harvard University Law Library
MID	—	Ministerstvo inostrannykh del [Ministry of Foreign Affairs]
NN	—	New York Public Library
PD	—	Institut russkoi literatury (Pushkinskii dom) Akademii nauk SSSR [Institute of Russian Literature (Pushkin House) of the Academy of Sciences of the USSR]
TsAOR	—	Tsentral'nyi arkhiv Oktiabr'skoi revoliutsii [Central Archive of the October Revolution], later TsGAOR
Tsentrarkhiv	—	Tsentral'nyi arkhiv RSFSR [Central Archive of the RSFSR]
TsGADA	—	Tsentral'nyi gosudarstvennyi arkhiv drevnikh aktov [Central State Archive of Ancient Acts]
TsGAKA	—	Tsentral'nyi gosudarstvennyi arkhiv Krasnoi Armii [Central State Archive of the Red Army], now TsGASA
TsGAKFD SSSR	—	Tsentral'nyi gosudarstvennyi arkhiv kinofoto-dokumentov SSSR [Central State Archive of Film and Photographic Documents of the USSR], formerly TsGAKFFD
TsGAKFFD SSSR–		Tsentral'nyi gosudarstvennyi arkhiv kino-foto-fonodokumentov SSSR [Central State Archive of Film, Photo, and Phonographic Documents of the USSR], now TsGAKFD and TsGAZ
TsGALI SSSR	—	Tsentral'nyi gosudarstvennyi arkhiv literatury i iskusstva SSSR [Central State Archive of Literature and Art of the USSR]
TsGAgM	—	Tsentral'nyi gosudarstvennyi arkhiv goroda Moskvy [Central State Archive of the City of Moscow], formerly GIAMO
TsGANKh	—	Tsentral'nyi gosudarstvennyi arkhiv narodnogo khoziaistva SSSR [Central State Archive of the National Economy of the USSR]
TsGANTD	—	Tsentral'nyi gosudarstvennyi arkhiv nauchno-tekh-nicheskoi dokumentatsii SSSR [Central State Archive of Scientific and Technical Documentation of the USSR]

TsGAOR SSSR	—	Tsentral'nyi gosudarstvennyi arkhiv Oktiabr'skoi revoliutsii, vysshikh organov gosudarstvennoi vlasti i organov gosudarstvennogo upravleniia SSSR [Central State Archive of the October Revolution, High Organs of State Government, and Organs of State Administration of the USSR]
TsGASA	—	Tsentral'nyi gosudarstvennyi arkhiv Sovetskoi Armii [Central State Archive of the Soviet Army]
TsGAVMF	—	Tsentral'nyi gosudarstvennyi arkhiv Voenno-Morskogo Flota SSSR [Central State Archive of the Navy of the USSR]
TsGAZ SSSR	—	Tsentral'nyi gosudarstvennyi arkhiv zvukozapisei SSSR [Central State Archive of Sound Recordings of the USSR], formerly part of TsGAKFFD
TsGIA SSSR	—	Tsentral'nyi gosudarstvennyi istoricheskii arkhiv SSSR [Central State Historical Archive of the USSR], formerly TsGIAL
TsGIAL	—	Tsentral'nyi gosudarstvennyi istoricheskii arkhiv SSSR v Leningrade [Central State Historical Archive of the USSR in Leningrad], now TsGIA SSSR
TsGIAM	—	Tsentral'nyi gosudarstvennyi istoricheskii arkhiv SSSR v Moskve [Central State Historical Archive of the USSR in Moscow], now mostly part of TsGAOR SSSR
TsGLA	—	Tsentral'nyi gosudarstvennyi literaturnyi arkhiv [Central State Literary Archive], now TsGALI
TsGVIA	—	Tsentral'nyi gosudarstvennyi voenno-istoricheskii arkhiv SSSR [Central State Military History Archive of the USSR]
TsPA IML	—	Tsentral'nyi partiinyi arkhiv Instituta Marksizma-Leninizma pri Tsentral'nom komitete KPSS [Central Party Archive of the Institute of Marxism-Leninism of the Central Committee of the Communist Party of the Soviet Union]
VNIIDAD	—	Vsesoiuznyi nauchno-issledovatel'skii institut dokumentovedeniia i arkhivnogo dela [All-Union Scientific Research Institute for Documentation and Archival Affairs]

TABLE OF CONTENTS

ARCHIVES AND MANUSCRIPT REPOSITORIES IN THE USSR
Moscow and Leningrad

HISTORICAL SURVEY

1. PREREVOLUTIONARY ARCHIVES AND MANUSCRIPT COLLECTIONS

The impressive archival development in the USSR since 1917 should not obscure the long, variegated history of prerevolutionary archives. Soviet archives would hardly be so rich today had it not been for the early development of manuscript repositories in Russia and the large-scale preservation of documentary records through the ages. Despite the high degree of centralization and state control which distinguishes the Soviet archival system, some seemingly typical features of Soviet archives have strong prerevolutionary roots. Many archive-related institutions have prerevolutionary antecedents; many repositories themselves are the direct heirs of earlier institutions; many early collections have survived intact and have served as nuclei for current archival holdings. The prerevolutionary history of archives and manuscript collections in the Russian Empire has a direct bearing on some of the current administrative and institutional diversity; it further helps to explain the characteristics and current location of documentary materials and underscores the Soviet heritage and achievement in the realm of archival management.

Since various types of record-keeping procedures were known to the ancient world, it is not surprising to find examples among the early cultures which took root in several parts of the present-day Soviet Union, especially in Armenia and along the northern shore of the Black Sea. There is no evidence, however, that these early developments had any carry-over or direct impact on subsequent archives. Likewise in Central Asia, although few documents have survived, there is evidence of early conscious preservation of state records as well as private manuscript collections. The oldest library in the Soviet Union with a continuous history was founded in Armenia in fifth-century Echmiadzin; its monastic library collection still survives, forming the basis for the rich state manuscript repository, the Matenadaran, now located in near-by Erevan.

State documents were consciously preserved during the Kievan era, principally through the church, which, after the acceptance of Christianity in the ninth century, supported learning and scholarship and encouraged the preservation of documentary records. Early chronicles indicate that in Kiev, as in many parts of medieval Christendom, state and princely documents were preserved in a central location, such as the library of the Saint Sophia Church or the Kievo-Pecherskii monastery. However, virtually no documents from this period have survived, so that our knowledge of them now comes chiefly through much later chronicles in which they were quoted or described. The earliest extant manuscripts from Kiev itself, almost entirely of a religious character, date back to the late eleventh century; but the earliest surviving Russian handwritten book, the so-called "Ostromir Gospel" dating from 1056-1057, comes from Novgorod.

The great commercial republic of Novgorod, which reached its zenith in the thirteenth and fourteenth centuries, had more organized record-keeping for state and private documents. The Saint Sophia cathedral within the Novgorod citadel and the church of John on the Rock [Ioanna na Opokakh], apparently were the most important of many public, religious, and even private manuscript repositories.

Archeological excavations have unearthed extensive documents written on birch-bark, the earliest of which go back to the eleventh century.

As appanage principalities developed in other areas of medieval Russia from the twelfth to the fifteenth centuries, archival or library collections grew step by step. Centrally located churches and important monasteries, usually the centers of learning for their localities, became the most significant manuscript repositories. As it was often in the monasteries that chronicles were prepared, state documents, charters, and other written records were accordingly collected there. Surviving records suggest that usually these were not systematic archives, but rather haphazard collections of important state charters, documents, or manuscript books.[1] Particularly notable libraries grew up in Rostov and Vladimir, the latter containing over one thousand Greek manuscript books as well as other manuscripts. The libraries of the Troitsko-Sergievskii, Chudovskii, Solovetskii, Kirillo-Belozerskii, and Iosifo-Volokolamskii monasteries were also noted in this period for their rich collections of manuscript books.

As the principality of Moscow developed, princely records took on new significance in the struggle for the unification of the Russian lands. The process of archival centralization at the court of the Grand Prince of Moscow developed in part from the political need to establish territorial claims; as rival principalities were brought under Muscovite control, their archives were often confiscated and held by the Moscow rulers. Various treaties and charters took on great importance, and as the writing of chronicles acquired a political purpose, documentation was safeguarded to establish particular claims. With the complicated system of feudal land tenure, records of holdings and of family descent were needed. Such forces led to systematic record-keeping activities by the fifteenth century. State archival practices in Moscow were further promoted by the end of the century, particularly through the efforts of Ivan III, who reportedly instituted the so-called stone vault, where records were kept in the Kremlin in the 1480's.[2] Documentary storage chests, called *kazny* or *kazenki,* were the repositories for copies of treaties, charters, state correspondence, edicts, military and genealogical record books, and other documents of importance. Such is the origin of the state archive of the early rulers of Moscow, which had even greater political importance as it became further institutionalized under Ivan IV in the sixteenth century. A partial inventory of this "Tsar's Archive" preserved from the late sixteenth century suggests its contents and organization. It included documents from the various principalities collected in the course of Muscovite consolidation along with those relating to the princely family

---

[1] For the types of documents preserved and archival remains of that period, see L. B. Cherepnin, *Russkie feodal'nye arkhivy XIV-XV vekov,* 2 vols. (Moscow, 1948-1951), esp. vol. 2. A selected list of general studies pertaining to the history and development of archives in the USSR that were used in the preparation of this survey is included at the end of the general bibliography below, Part A, section 20.

[2] For details of the remains of princely archives in Moscow through the reign of Ivan III, see the first four chapters of Cherepnin, *Russkie feodal'nye arkhivy XIV-XV vekov,* 1:10-220.

and the internal development of the state.[3] Unfortunately, large portions of that collection were looted or destroyed with the burning of Moscow during the Time of Troubles in the early seventeenth century, after which it ceased to exist as a central state archive.

Aside from this central collection, documentary materials of the Muscovite state between the sixteenth and eighteenth centuries were retained in the separate and rather haphazard archives of the *prikazy*, the departments or bureaus charged with the administration of various aspects of state affairs. Some of the prikazy were established as early as the fifteenth century under Ivan III; they multiplied in the course of the sixteenth and seventeenth centuries. At the beginning of the eighteenth century they numbered around fifty when Peter the Great, following the Swedish model, reorganized their functions in the administrative *kollegii*, or colleges, with the result that the prikazy were gradually superseded. Although some documents from a number of the early prikazy found their way into the central state archive in the fifteenth and sixteenth centuries, the bulk of them remained separate.

As was true in most European nations, documents in this period were not kept systematically for their historical value so much as for their possible political usefulness. So it came about that when storage space became limited and the chests full, the older documents, adjudged to be of less current importance, were often discarded. Since no pains were taken to protect documents as permanent records, fire, flood, and the ravages of war and climatic variations took heavy toll. It is small wonder that there are now so few surviving sections.

The archive of the Posol'skii Prikaz, or Ambassadorial Prikaz, was the best-known early repository of the Moscow state. Its records, many of which survive today in the Central State Archive of Ancient Acts (TsGADA), go back to its foundation in the fifteenth century under Ivan III. Not only was it the repository of treaties and documents relating to the early political and commercial relations of Russia with foreign powers, but it also kept the records of relations between the various Russian principalities and cities and the Grand Duke of Moscow. Many of these records became part of the "Tsar's Archive" in the sixteenth century, but subsequently the documents from that collection that survived the Time of Troubles came into the custody of the Posol'skii Prikaz later

---

[3] This inventory, dating from the period 1575-1584, was recently published in a new edition by S. O. Shmidt, *Opisi Tsarskogo arkhiva XVI veka i arkhiva Posol'skogo prikaza 1614 goda* (Moscow, 1960), pp. 15-44. It was first published soon after its discovery in the early nineteenth century, as "Opis' Tsarskogo arkhiva," in *Akty, sobrannye v bibliotekakh i arkhivakh Rossiiskoi imperii Arkheograficheskoi ekspeditsii imperatorskoi Akademii nauk,* vol. 1: *1294-1598* (St. Petersburg, 1836), pp. 333-55 (no. 289). Shmidt has also published a series of scholarly articles on this early archive which fill in many details regarding its nature and extent: "Tsarskii arkhiv serediny XVI v. i arkhivy pravitel'stvennykh uchrezhdenii (Opyt izucheniia opisi Tsarskogo arkhiva)," *Trudy MGIAI* 8 (1957):260-78; "K istorii Tsarskogo arkhiva serediny XVI v.," *Trudy MGIAI* 11 (1958):364-407; and "K istorii sostavleniia opisei Tsarskogo arkhiva XVI veka," *Arkheograficheskii ezhegodnik za 1958 god,* pp. 54-65.

in the seventeenth century. Thus, its archive became the repository for many of the earliest existing records of the Moscow state, covering internal development, inter-princely relations, foreign embassies, commercial enterprises, peace treaties, and other aspects of diplomacy and foreign trade.[4]

The archive of the Pomestnyi Prikaz, or the Prikaz of Domains, which held the records of land grants and land holding in the Moscow state, was one of the most significant in the period. The court rolls registered information about personal non-inheritable land-grants [*pomest'ia*] given to individuals in exchange for state service. Various records of taxation, peasant problems, and boundary and other land-related information were systematically kept, but as fire destroyed most of the records in 1626 the most extensive surviving parts date only from the seventeenth century. Because of fire damage in the 1730's, almost nothing remains of the related archive of the Votchinnyi Prikaz which held the records of the patrimonial estates [*votchiny*].

Detailed record-keeping was started as early as the fifteenth century by the Razriadnyi Prikaz. Its archive retained the service records of the upper classes of the Moscow state, most particularly those of the boyars.[5] It accordingly received the most extensive military records, along with many records of local administration, since the appointed *voevody*, or generals in charge of different military districts, took on significant judicial and administrative powers.

The Siberian [Sibirskii] Prikaz, which was established for the administration of the eastern parts of the Russian Empire in 1637, retained especially rich archival records, many of which have survived. Since this archive took over most of the documentary legacy of earlier prikazy that functioned in the East, its holdings date back to the end of the sixteenth century and include many materials relating to the early history of the peoples of Siberia and Central Asia and to the early Russian penetration of the area. The Siberian Prikaz itself functioned until 1765, at which time its records became part of the Razriad-Senate archive.

Other archives of special importance included those with records of the court, of court estates, the court armory, and of coinage and other monetary affairs. The Prikaz of the Court of Kazan [Kazanskii dvor] retained records dating from the time when that area came under Russian rule in the sixteenth century, since it also had administrative functions in the eastern areas of the empire before the foundation of the separate Siberian Prikaz in 1637. On the local level, by the beginning of the seventeenth century many regional governors started keeping records which became permanent archives of local administration.

The general cultural flowering in the Moscow state in the sixteenth and

---

[4] The 1614 inventory of this archive, which shows the extent of the holdings in the early seventeenth century, is now preserved in TsGADA; see the recent edition by S. O. Shmidt, *Opisi Tsarskogo arkhiva XVI veka i arkhiva Posol'skogo prikaza 1614 goda*, pp. 45-195.

[5] On the early razriadnye record books, see Viktor Ivanovich Buganov, *Razriadnye knigi poslednei chetverti XV-nachala XVII v.* (Moscow, 1962), and additional information in the descriptive literature about present holdings in TsGADA in Part B, below.

seventeenth centuries also saw the growth of libraries with rich collections of hand-copied books, incunabula, and some miscellaneous manuscripts. Monastery collections and other ecclesiastical libraries grew apace, and started to include printed works after printing began in Russia in the mid-sixteenth century; some were particularly rich in early Slavic and Greek manuscripts, mostly of a religious character. The library and archive of Patriarch Nikon, with some thirteen hundred books and other documents, is an example of a private collection within the religious establishment; it later became the basis for the Moscow Synod library. The library of Ivan IV, which has stimulated vain investigations in the Kremlin, was allegedly one of the earliest Russian court collections. Private collections also became important in this period; for example, the collection of the Stroganov family came to include some records of their own activities in Siberia, along with many chronicles and other manuscripts gathered in the course of their travels.[6]

The reforms during the reign of Peter the Great which brought a complete reorganization of administrative structure to the Russian Empire had more than the expected repercussions in the archival realm. Peter recognized the need for the systematic preservation of historical records and in his "General Regulation" [General'nyi reglament] of 1720 he devoted a special section to archives.[7] The newly formed administrative kollegii were required to preserve and register their records and deposit them periodically in centralized state archives. Peter further ordered the collection of historical books and manuscripts from monasteries and other outlying institutions. Although these decrees were never fully implemented, Peter's plans show the developing interest in state preservation of historical documents, and an early concern for the centralization and systematic management of government records.

Following its formation in 1720, the College of Foreign Affairs took over the archival records of its predecessor, the Ambassadorial Prikaz, as well as the archives of some of the other dissolved prikazy, notably that of Smolensk and parts of the Prikaz for Little Russia.[8] Its legacy from the Ambassadorial Prikaz gave it a wide range of materials on internal as well as external aspects of Russian history which might have formed the nucleus of the more comprehensive archive envisaged in

[6] For more details on these developments, with rich bibliographical footnotes, see the article by Iu. F. Kononov, "Chastnye kollektsii rukopisnykh materialov v tsentralizovannom russkom gosudarstve (konets XV-XIX vv.)," *Trudy MGIAI* 15 (1962):405-18. The most important earlier treatment of this subject, with extensive descriptions of library contents, is the volume by S. A. Belokurov, *O biblioteke moskovskikh gosudarei v XVI stoletii* (Moscow, 1898). See the additional information presented in S. P. Luppov, *Kniga v Rossii v XVII veke. Knigoizdatel'stvo. Knigotorgovlia. Rasprostranenie knig sredi razlichnykh sloev naseleniia. Knizhnye sobraniia chastnykh lits. Biblioteki* (Leningrad, 1970), and in the general history of pre-eighteenth-century libraries by M. I. Slukhovskii (A-89).

[7] The paragraph on archives is reprinted in *Sbornik materialov, otnosiashchikhsia do arkhivnoi chasti v Rossii* (Petrograd, 1916-1917) (A-87) 1:76-77.

[8] A detailed scholarly reconstruction of the formation and development of this archive in the eighteenth century is presented by G. A. Dremina, "Moskovskii arkhiv Kollegii inostrannykh del," in G. A. Dremina, *Iz istorii Tsentral'nogo gosudarstvennogo arkhiva drevnikh aktov* (Moscow, 1959) (B-75), pp. 23-68.

Peter's decree. Throughout the eighteenth century, however, this archive remained—in administration, contents, and customary nomenclature—largely a repository for the College of Foreign Affairs alone, rather than becoming the general historical record office Peter had planned. The German scholar Gerhard Friedrich Müller, who came to Russia in 1725 and became so closely associated with the growing historical interests of the eighteenth century, was appointed director of the archive by Catherine the Great in 1766, and did much to increase its riches and organization; he was particularly active in developing the extensive library manuscript collections and in starting the early historical publication projects which came to be associated with the archive. This work was continued under the successors whom he trained, most notably N. N. Bantysh-Kamenskii, in the early nineteenth century. In 1781 the organization of the archive was changed somewhat when it became officially what it had been commonly called all along, the Moscow Archive of the College of Foreign Affairs. It remained the official depository for all the papers of the college, which were transferred to it from St. Petersburg. After the bureaucratic reorganization of the early nineteenth century in which ministries replaced colleges, the Moscow Archive—known after 1832 as the Moscow Main Archive of the Ministry of Foreign Affairs [Moskovskii glavnyi arkhiv Ministerstva inostrannykh del] —ceased adding new material. The records postdating the formation of the ministry were retained in the ministry itself or its archive in St. Petersburg, although a few sections of the ministry sent their papers to the Moscow archive through the 1830's.

Although the archive of the College of Foreign Affairs was undoubtedly one of the richest diplomatic, and indeed broadly historical, archives in Europe of the period, it never came to have the comprehensive centralizing character Peter had outlined. In fact a trend which persisted in Russia until 1917 was already noticeable in the early eighteenth century: documentary records commonly remained in the custody of their issuing agency, with resultant fragmentation and dispersion of archival sources. As Peter the Great had ordered, the administrative colleges did tend to preserve their records, but this was done on an individual basis without any standardized storage procedures. The documentary legacy of the defunct prikazy initially either came under the control of the Senate repository or came into the custody of the colleges that succeeded them; only gradually were more comprehensive state archives formed for these earlier historical records.

From the time of its establishment in 1711 as the highest and most important state institution, the Governing Senate made provisions for storing its documentary records and became a centralizing administration for earlier historical records. The large volume of manuscript materials from the Razriadnyi Prikaz came into its custody in Moscow, as did the documentary legacy of several other defunct organs of central administration. For the most part, however, materials remained in diverse storage places and were not amalgamated with the more current Senate records. When the headquarters of most departments of the Senate were moved to St. Petersburg, a second Senate archive was established in the new capital, but the two sets of records, though they involved much duplication, were never amalgamated.

Archival consolidation of the documents in the custody of the Senate in Moscow, through the establishment of the Razriad-Senate Archive [Razriadno-senatskii arkhiv], accompanied the 1763 reorganization of the Senate; in subsequent decades after the various original holdings had been gathered in a single location, the archival remains of the Siberian Prikaz, the Heraldry Office, and the records of some additional Senate offices were transferred there and kept together under the control of the archive office of the Senate.

Other formal state archives were established in Moscow during the reign of Catherine II, whose interest in scholarship and culture coincided with a developing consciousness of the Russian historical past in the late eighteenth century. These included the Central (later Main) Land Survey Archive [Tsentral'nyi mezhevoi arkhiv], which remained an independent archive with the function of a title record office until after 1939. Also in this period, the extensive Pomestno-votchinnyi Archive [Gosudarstvennyi arkhiv prezhnikh votchinnykh del] was founded in 1786, inheriting the legacy of the earlier Pomestnyi Prikaz as well as the records of the Votchinnyi College, or College (later, Department) of Domains. Most significant and extensive in its holdings was the Moscow State Archive of Ancient Records [Gosudarstvennyi Moskovskii arkhiv starykh del] created in 1782, following Catherine's administrative reforms, to bring together documents from about forty defunct administrative organs. A corresponding State Archive of Ancient Records had already been established in 1780 in St. Petersburg [Gosudarstvennyi Sankt-Peterburgskii arkhiv starykh del] to house the records of an additional fifty administrative agencies liquidated in the course of reforms; its holdings, however, never became as extensive as those of its Moscow counterpart.

Thus in the same period in which revolutionary France was establishing its epoch-making Archives Nationales, Russia was taking constructive steps towards the organized retention of historical records. The Russian developments, however, involved provision only for the records of defunct governmental organs. And despite the efforts of Catherine the Great, by the beginning of the nineteenth century the storage of historical records still remained highly decentralized. There were none of the provisions for their overall organization and administration that were developing in other European countries. Some improvements did come about by mid-century with the establishment in 1852 of the Moscow Archive of the Ministry of Justice [Moskovskii arkhiv Ministerstva iustitsii—MAMIu]. The earlier plan of Peter the Great for a centralized historical archive may not have been the motivating factor, but the consolidation of the three principal historical archives in Moscow had the same effect. Bringing together under one centralized admin-istration the former Razriad-Senate Archive, the Pomestno-votchinnyi Archive, and the Moscow State Archive of Ancient Records, the Moscow Archive of the Ministry of Justice quickly developed into the single most important and richest state historical archive of prerevolutionary Russia.[9]

---

[9] A general description of this archive at the end of the nineteenth century is available in the prerevolutionary guide, *Pamiatnaia knizhka Moskovskogo arkhiva*

In the era of the Great Reforms of the 1860's and 1870's, a decree established this archive as the central repository for all pre-nineteenth-century state records and those of state institutions that were liquidated in the course of reforms, thus officially signifying its preeminence as the major historical archive for the earliest documents of the empire. Many of its files extended up through the middle of the nineteenth century as well, because following the liquidation of the Moscow Department of the Senate in 1872, all the Senate records hitherto stored in Moscow were transferred to its jurisdiction. However, like its heir, the present-day Central State Archive of Ancient Acts (TsGADA), it never succeeded in becoming a fully centralized storage place for all early records, particularly since it never consolidated the holdings of the Foreign Ministry archives or the various repositories of military records. Nor did it control any of the materials stored in St. Petersburg, and even in Moscow in the nineteenth century there were other archives that also housed rich groups of pre-nineteenth-century records.

Whatever its shortcomings, the Moscow Archive of the Ministry of Justice nevertheless became the focal point of archival development in Russia in the late nineteenth and early twentieth centuries. Particularly under the enlightened directorship of N. V. Kalachov and later D. Ia. Samokvasov, it developed into one of the most progressive archival institutions on the Continent, engaging in extensive cataloging and documentary publication projects, initiating a training program for archivists, as well as attempting to plan a centralized archival system for the Russian Empire.[10] A special building constructed for the archive near the Novodevichii monastery further symbolized the importance of the institution, which by the end of the nineteenth century contained over two and a half million storage units dating from the fourteenth through the nineteenth century.

Despite the gradual consolidation of historical records which had developed during the eighteenth and nineteenth centuries, centrifugal tendencies remained strong. Consolidation and management of state archival holdings proved easier and more successful for ancient documents and the records of the defunct prikazy and colleges than they did for the more current records of the ministries after their establishment in the early nineteenth century. This tendency coincided with the usual and customary practice in many other countries in which the lack of centralized archival management went hand in hand with the lack of centralized state political power and planning.

Ministerstva iustitsii (Moscow, 1890) (B-78). Detailed historical accounts of several earlier archives which were amalgamated into this repository were published in the inventory series: *Opisanie dokumentov i bumag khrania-shchikhsia v Moskovskom arkhive Ministerstva iustitsii,* 21 vols. (St. Petersburg/Moscow, 1869-1921) (B-79), vols. 5-9. See also the summary description of this archive by J.-J. Chimko and L. M. Batiffol, "Les Archives de l'Empire russe à Moscou," *Revue historique* 44 (1890): 56-68.

[10] A summary of the early reform proposals is given by D. Ia. Samokvasov, *Arkhivnoe delo v Rossii,* 2 vols. (Moscow, 1902) (A-88), 1:95-114, and appendix, 11-15, 23-27. The same director's own 1902 proposal is published separately as *Proekt arkhivnoi reformy i sovremennoe sostoianie okonchatel'nykh arkhivov v Rossii* (Moscow, 1902).

In the course of the nineteenth century, in Russia, almost all the documentary records of defunct organs of government—and with the reorganization in the early nineteenth century many earlier organs of central administration had become superseded—found their way into organized state archival repositories. The newly created ministries and other organs of state administration and justice, on the other hand, all retained their own records, usually within their own buildings, with varying degrees of care and organization. Unlike the situation in France and other European countries, which at the time were developing systems of state archival administration, there was neither a central archive to which these more current records could be transferred for safer preservation, nor an agency for records management, nor yet any set standards for deciding which merited preservation or for organizing and cataloging those which were retained.

The Archive of the Ministry of the Navy [Arkhiv Morskogo ministerstva] was the only ministerial repository that established its own separate building, constructed for that purpose in St. Petersburg in the 1880's. The naval records housed there were continuous from the time of the foundation of the Russian navy by Peter the Great. Because of their great volume and adequate housing, these records have retained their prerevolutionary location and today form a separate central state archive (TsGAVMF). Typical of the splintering organization, the archive of the Hydrographic Section of the ministry, although located in the same building, was always kept separate.

Unlike that of the Ministry of the Navy, the other military archives were never consolidated before the Revolution. In part this may be attributable to the sheer bulk of documentation involved as well as the complex and diverse military organization in imperial Russia. The army's Archive of the Inspectors' Department of the General Staff [Arkhiv Inspektorskogo departamenta Glavnogo shtaba] was formally established in St. Petersburg in 1819, and became the central repository for army records and many military documents originating in the St. Petersburg area. After the liquidation of the Inspectors' Department in 1865, it was called the General Archive of the General Staff, with another slight modification in name after 1906 [Obshchii arkhiv Glavnogo shtaba; after 1906, Obshchii arkhiv Glavnogo upravleniia General'nogo shtaba].

Military records, however, were not centralized; the Ministry of War continued to keep many of its own records in separate storage areas, and the records of the different armies, military districts, and related military institutions remained dispersed. The Imperial Map Depot originated by Paul I at the end of the eighteenth century had traditionally been a separate repository for military maps and plans, many of which dated back to the sixteenth century. After 1812, the Ministry of War took over this collection as part of the archive of its newly established Military Topographical Depot [Voenno-topograficheskoe depo]. In 1863 this archive became part of the Military History Archive [Voenno-istoricheskii arkhiv]; later, in 1867, it came under the administration of the General Staff and became part of the newly formed Military Science Archive [Voenno-uchenyi arkhiv-VUA], but was never consolidated with the General Archive of the General Staff.

The Moscow division of the main army archive (Moskovskoe otdelenie Arkhiva Inspektorskogo departamenta Glavnogo shtaba), established under the Inspectors' Department in 1819, came into prominence as the central repository for documents of Russian military history because it took over the most important pre-nineteenth-century army records and other military collections. Renamed the Moscow Division of the General Archive of the General Staff [Moskovskoe otdelenie Obshchego arkhiva Glavnogo shtaba] in 1865, it was more commonly known as the Lefort Archive, since it was housed in the famous Lefort Palace; its contents remain in the same place today as the nucleus of the centralized state military history archive (TsGVIA).

Of the various ministerial archives, the St. Petersburg Main Archive of the Ministry of Foreign Affairs [Sankt-Peterburgskii glavnyi arkhiv Ministerstva inostrannykh del] had the most prominence. Although it had really been in existence since the beginning of the century, collecting the diplomatic documents which had not been transferred to Moscow, it was not established as a formal archive until 1834 within the ministry building.[11] The pre-nineteenth-century foreign department papers, however, always remained in the Moscow archive of the ministry, and many of the later chancellery files were never transferred to the archive. After 1864 the St. Petersburg archive was administratively united with the State Archive of the Russian Empire although, in fact, many of the papers in this latter repository had been part of the Foreign Ministry archive much earlier.

The State Archive of the Russian Empire [Gosudarstvennyi arkhiv Rossiiskoi imperii], formally established in St. Petersburg in 1834, had the explicit function of preserving high-level state papers and those relating to the imperial family. Somewhat similar to its Austrian counterpart, such an archive had been projected as early as 1809, but had made no progress until a commission was set up with the purpose of developing it in 1830. With the bureaucratic reforms of Nicholas I, which resulted in the liquidation of the vestiges of the College of Foreign Affairs in the early 1830's, some of the most important imperial papers were separated from the Foreign Ministry files, along with other documents from the ministry chancellery. Since these papers were then housed in the Foreign Ministry building, the archive itself was established there, but for administrative purposes remained distinct from the main diplomatic archive. As the archive developed, it took over most of the contents of the early St. Petersburg Archive of Ancient Records, which had been formed during the reign of Catherine II, as well as various imperial papers from the Winter Palace and other sources, and files from several sections of the Senate archive. It gathered the records of imperial investigating commissions concerned with various phases of social and cultural unrest, such as the Pugachev rebellion, masonic activities, and the Decembrist movement, and also miscellaneous

---

[11] A brief but elaborately illustrated description of this archive was published in both the Russian and French editions: *Moskovskii glavnyi arkhiv Ministerstva inostrannykh del. Vidy arkhiva i snimki khraniashchikhsia v nem dokumentov, rukopisei i pechatei* (Moscow, 1898); *Les Archives principales de Moscou du Ministère des affaires étrangères* (Moscow, 1898).

groups of papers relating to important diplomatic developments. From the start, however, its contents were marked by their heterogeneity; its haphazard development precluded its becoming a systematic or regularized ongoing central archive. It continued to acquire various important documents and even personal papers of high officials, mostly dating from the first half of the nineteenth century, but after its administrative merger with the Foreign Ministry Archive in 1864 it became a purely historical repository.[12]

As was the case with the various ministerial archives, diversity and splintering of holdings characterized the records of all ongoing state organs. The Senate, the Council of State, and later the Duma, all maintained their own records separately in St. Petersburg. The Senate archive [Arkhiv Pravitel'stvuiushchego senata] was the richest and most extensive of these repositories, since it had fallen heir to a variety of earlier historical records along with those of its own departments going back to the reign of Peter the Great.[13] In Moscow, it was only after the liquidation of the Moscow departments of the Senate that their records were incorporated into the historical archive of the Ministry of Justice. The archives of various imperial palaces, with many of the documents dating back to the sixteenth century, were only gradually incorporated into historical archives, and the most important ones, such as the Court Armory Archive [Arkhiv Oruzheinoi palaty] retained their own separate depositories, as did most of the records of the imperial chancellery and other important court agencies, estates, and enterprises.

Side by side with the growth of and interest in the archives of central state administration went the development of repositories in many outlying parts of the empire. As early as the sixteenth and seventeenth centuries some organs of local administration were making an attempt to preserve their papers. Many important medieval documents which had not been transferred to Moscow or St. Petersburg remained in local hands, but these had often suffered from severe neglect.

As local administration became better organized toward the end of the eighteenth century and as interest in the preservation of historical documents grew, provincial administrative centers, following the directives of St. Petersburg, started to retain their records. Thoroughness and care in retention and storage varied considerably. During the nineteenth century, with increased interest in historical materials for their own sake, sizeable local archives developed on the guberniia, and in some cases on the city, level.

In the 1880's provincial archive commissions were set up to check over materials destined for destruction by their creating agencies and arrange the retention of those worthy of preservation. These efforts considerably raised the standards of local archives and resulted in the retention of a much more significant body of

---

[12] The development of this archive during the nineteenth century is described by Iu. F. Kononov, "Iz istorii organizatsii i komplektovaniia b. Gosudarstvennogo arkhiva Rossiiskoi imperii," *Trudy MGIAI* 8(1957):279-354.

[13] See the general guide to this archive published on the eve of the First World War, *Pamiatnaia knizhka Senatskogo arkhiva,* ed. I. A. Blinov (St. Petersburg, 1913) (B-109).

documents from subsequent years, but the powers of the commissions remained extremely limited.[14]

Many non-Russian areas which came under imperial authority as the Russian Empire enlarged its boundaries westward and eastward already had large established documentary records. There is good evidence of continuing interest in many of these holdings, and further efforts were made to set up or consolidate archival records in other areas. For example, archeographical commissions were established in Kiev (1843), in Vilna (1842), and in the Caucasus (1864). In 1852, a decree provided for the establishment of central historical archives in Kiev for the Ukraine, Vilna for Lithuania, and Vitebsk for Belorussia, first under the control of the local governor-general, and later under the Ministry of the Interior.

In a country where the church had as important a role as it did in prerevolutionary Russia, church archives naturally touched on widespread aspects of state and society. Since its establishment by Peter the Great in 1721, the Holy Synod, the governing body of the Russian Orthodox Church, retained its increasingly rich archive with many manuscript holdings dating back to the sixteenth century in its St. Petersburg headquarters [Arkhiv Sviateishego pravitel'stvuiushchego sinoda]. Because the chancellery of the Procurator of the Synod was at some distance from the main Synod offices, there was a tendency for those files to be kept separately and only subsequently to be transferred to the main Synod archive. During the last half of the nineteenth century an extensive cataloging project was undertaken, but published volumes of archival inventories never got beyond the eighteenth century.[15]

Although the Synod archive was considered the most important archive retaining papers relating to religious affairs, many documents from areas outside St. Petersburg never reached it. Various church officials maintained their own private records, as did churches, dioceses, monasteries, and other religious establishments throughout the empire. Some of the early diocesan, consistory, monastic, and other church records were gathered and described by commissions or historical groups active in the course of the nineteenth century, but there was never any real attempt to centralize or systematize the holdings.

Aside from actual archival records, many official church institutions maintained extremely rich libraries with extensive collections of early books and other

[14] Details about these commissions and a complete bibliography of their publications have been published by O. I. Shvedova, "Ukazatel' 'trudov' gubernskikh uchenykh arkhivnykh komissii i otdel'nykh ikh izdanii," *Arkheograficheskii ezhegodnik za 1957 god,* pp. 377-433. See the article by N. V. Brzostovska, "Deiatel'nost gubernskikh arkhivnykh komissii po sozdaniiu istoricheskikh arkhivov," *Trudy MGIAI* 5(1954):79-118. See also the detailed descriptions and extensive bibliographical footnotes regarding major local archives in V. S. Ikonnikov, *Opyt russkoi istoriografii,* 2 vols. in 4 (Kiev, 1891-1908) (A-83), vol. 1, pt. 1:518-77.

[15] See the description of this enterprise in *Piatidesiatiletie vysochaishe utverzhdennoi Komissii po razboru i opisaniiu Arkhiva Sviateishego Sinoda, 1865-1915. Istoricheskaia zapiska* (Petrograd, 1915), pp. 172-77, and in B-114 below.

miscellaneous manuscripts. Most important, undoubtedly, were the collections of the Synod Library [Sinodal'naia biblioteka], the former Patriarchal library located in the Synod Palace in the Kremlin, and the library of the Moscow Synod Press [Moskovskaia sinodal'naia tipografskaia biblioteka], which was the descendant of Russia's earliest, and for many years only, printing office. The Moscow Ecclesiastical Academy Library [Biblioteka Moskovskoi dukhovnoi akademii], originally based on the library of the early Slavonic-Greco-Latin Academy [Slaviano-greko-latinskaia akademiia], also developed a significant collection of manuscripts, as did the other highest-level ecclesiastical academies in St. Petersburg, Kiev, and Kazan. In other regions, many local seminaries also gathered sizeable collections, some of which overlapped with some of the oldest and most important monastic and church libraries.[16]

Since so much of the written culture of pre-Petrine Russia had been a church monopoly, with the church playing the leading role in education, printing, and hence most of the written legacy of the past, it is small wonder that many of the most important libraries before the eighteenth century were attached to religious institutions. The further back into the Middle Ages these institutions dated, the richer were their manuscript holdings. As some monasteries disbanded through the centuries, their collections were usually transferred to other libraries in the region. Although many regional institutions continued to guard jealously their precious written relics through the ages, some were turned over to major repositories in Moscow and St. Petersburg; requests for the centralization of manuscripts, such as those made in the early eighteenth century by Peter the Great, were occasionally heeded, particularly in the case of some of the earliest and historically most valuable manuscripts. Later, as early manuscripts gained monetary value as collectors' items, many were sold to private or museum collections.

The development of libraries in the Russian Empire has significant bearing for the present study, because from their very outset almost all the important libraries were repositories for manuscript collections. Before the introduction of printing in the mid-sixteenth century, of course, the great libraries of the empire were in fact collections of manuscript books. And as has already been seen, these libraries were often centers for preserving local historical documents. Later, as state and private libraries grew up apart from religious institutions, manuscript collections were usually an integral part of their holdings, as was the case of the Academy of Sciences library in the eighteenth century.[17]

In fact, the most important library of the empire, the Imperial Public Library [Imperatorskaia publichnaia biblioteka] in St. Petersburg, was initially based on the

---

[16] Ikonnikov surveys the most important local religious archives and manuscript collections and provides a bibliography of publications relating to them, *Opyt russkoi istoriografii* (A-83), vol. 1, pt. 1:578-686.

[17] Details about the development of manuscript collections in libraries and museums are to be found in the mimeographed booklet by Iu. F. Kononov, "Komplektovanie rukopisnykh otdelov bibliotek i muzeev v dorevoliutsionnoi Rossii (Uchebnoe posobie)" (1961), from lectures at MGIAI, available in the Manuscript Division of the Lenin Library.

major manuscript and book collection of the Zaluski brothers. Even before the library's official opening in 1814, its manuscript division had acquired the rich collection of Western manuscripts and documents (including some from the Bastille archive) gathered by P. P. Dubrovski in France during the revolutionary years.[18] As was the case of many major libraries, this manuscript depository came to receive a variety of archival fonds and collections of historical documents from private individuals and institutions throughout the years, in addition to its more traditional manuscript acquisitions.

The library and museum manuscript holdings of the Imperial Hermitage [Imperatorskii Ermitazh], which owed many of its riches to the cultural and literary efforts of Catherine the Great, remained one of the most significant collections of the nineteenth century, until it was gradually transferred to the Imperial Public Library in the 1850's and 60's.

Coming into special prominence as a manuscript repository after its formal establishment in Moscow in 1862, the Moscow Public and Rumiantsev Museum [Moskovskii publichnyi i Rumiantsevskii muzei] never equalled its St. Petersburg counterpart before the Revolution in overall size and riches. Its manuscript holdings, nevertheless, which had started with the collection of early Russian, Slavic, and other foreign materials gathered in the late eighteenth and early nineteenth centuries by N. P. Rumiantsev, made it one of the most important repositories in the country. It was more fully recognized and its position improved after the Revolution; when the capital was moved to Moscow it became the basis for the present-day Lenin Library.[19]

Museum manuscript collections, such as those of the Imperial Historical Museum and the smaller Bakhrushin Theatrical Museum, also had their origins in the late nineteenth century, in a period when historical and general cultural interests led to large expenditures for preservation and display.

From its foundation by Peter the Great in 1725 the Imperial Academy of Sciences had a significant influence on the development of Russian archives, both from the standpoint of repositories which developed under its auspices, and from the activities of its members or commissions under its auspices in the area of cataloging, collecting, and publishing. The Academy archive proper, which is today one of the most important archives in the Soviet Union, was founded in St. Petersburg in 1734. As it developed during the subsequent centuries, it amassed not only the institutional records of the Academy and its many varied scientific and cultural projects and activities, but also the personal papers of many Academy members.[20]

[18] See especially the section "Nachal'nyi period sobiraniia rukopisnykh fondov," in *Istoriia Gosudarstvennoi ordena Trudovogo Krasnogo Znameni Publichnoi biblioteki imeni M. E. Saltykova-Shchedrina,* ed. V. M. Barashenkov et al. (Leningrad, 1963) (F-2), pp. 18-20.

[19] See the chapter by V. G. Zimina, "Otdel rukopisei za 100 let," in *Istoriia Gosudarstvennoi ordena Lenina biblioteki SSSR imeni V. I. Lenina za 100 let, 1862-1962,* ed. F. S. Abrikosova et al. (Moscow, 1962) (E-2), pp. 246-71.

[20] The early history of the Academy archive is included in the introductory

The Academy library in St. Petersburg, which dates its foundation to 1714—even before the establishment of the Academy itself—developed in the eighteenth century into one of the most important libraries in the empire. In contrast to archives as such, the Academy library from its origin became noted for its rich collections of manuscripts, particularly early manuscript books. The original basis for its holdings, first housed in the Winter Palace, was the personal library of Peter the Great and that of his immediate family, as well as collections gathered from other parts of the empire and abroad.[21]

Various sections or institutions under the Academy of Sciences had a tendency to develop independent archives and manuscript holdings. One of its oldest and most famous was the Asiatic Museum, founded in St. Petersburg in 1818. During the nineteenth century it came to rank as one of the most valuable repositories of oriental manuscripts and one of the important centers for oriental studies in the world. Early in the twentieth century, Pushkin House [Pushkinskii Dom] was opened to house the library and manuscripts of Pushkin and was soon to become a great center for literary studies.

Several other learned and cultural societies also spread the tradition of collecting and displaying manuscripts. For example, the Imperial Archeological Society developed its own sizeable manuscript collection, as did the Moscow Archeological Society. The archive and library of the Imperial Geographical Society were also of special note, as they continue today under the Geographical Society of the Academy of Sciences. The same tradition extended to various provincial centers and brought the rise of many significant local library or museum manuscript collections in this period.

The growth of major universities in the late eighteenth and the nineteenth centuries brought with it additional library centers which in all cases included some important manuscript riches, along with the archives of the universities themselves. Apart from the centers in Moscow and St. Petersburg, manuscript holdings of some importance grew up in the university libraries of Kazan, Kiev, Kharkov, Odessa, Dorpat, and Vilna. In some cases learned societies attached to particular universities established their own separate libraries or museums. Such was the case of the Society for Russian History and Antiquities in Moscow in the early nineteenth century, the Historical Society of Odessa, the Society of Archeology, History, and Ethnography in the last quarter of the century at Kazan University, and the Historico-Philological Society at Kharkov.[22]

In an epoch when so much of the material and cultural wealth of the nation was

---

section of the first volume of *Arkhiv Akademii nauk SSSR. Obozrenie arkhivnykh materialov,* 6 vols. (Leningrad, 1933-1971) (C-3).

[21] See the early sections of *Istoriia Biblioteki Akademii nauk SSSR, 1714-1964,* by S. P. Luppov et al. (Moscow/Leningrad, 1964), and the more detailed description in *Istoricheskii ocherk i obzor fondov rukopisnogo otdela Biblioteki Akademii nauk,* 2 vols. (Moscow/Leningrad, 1956-1958) (C-21).

[22] Ikonnikov surveys the manuscript collections in the libraries and museums of universities and other learned societies with detailed bibliographical notes, *Opyt russkoi istoriografii* (A-83), vol. 1, pt. 2:916-1071.

concentrated in the hands of a tiny segment of the elite, and when the state assumed such a minor role in the cultural development of the nation, much of the impetus and financial backing for manuscript-collecting came from wealthy individuals. Many private family collections were as extensive and valuable as those of many museums, libraries, or other public institutions.[23] In fact, many of the most important museum and library collections were started or—as time went on—enriched by bequests from private sources.

In the realm of archives, too, the importance of family holdings is no less great in Russia than it is elsewhere. Particularly in a period when there were no regularized procedures for the retention of state files, many important state records found their way into the papers of individual office-holders; since it was often a standard practice for individuals in high governmental positions to retain correspondence, reports, and other papers from the period of their own service, private family archives preserved many important records which might otherwise have been lost. Although some families were notoriously uninterested in their family papers, others took great pains to have them bound for preservation; several important families even underwrote multi-volume publications from their family archives. Preservation was even more haphazard in the economic sphere, where most enterprises were in private hands. And since so many aspects of the cultural, economic, and general social life of the country developed outside the immediate control of the state, these private archives, to the extent that they have been preserved, rank high among the national archival treasures.

The growing interest in the manuscript riches of early history and culture, which had been encouraged by Peter the Great and Catherine II in the eighteenth century, blossomed in many forms in the early nineteenth century. But nowhere did it have more effect on the development of archives and the specific interest in Russian historical manuscripts than in the efforts of the Archeographical Commission. Although not formally established until 1834, the commission really grew out of the interest in archeographical expeditions and documentary publication projects which dates back well into the eighteenth-century work of G. F. Müller, V. N. Tatishchev, M. M. Shcherbatov, and N. I. Novikov. During his term as Russian foreign minister prior to the 1812 war, N. P. Rumiantsev gave much impetus and financial encouragement to these activities. He financed the first large-scale documentary-publication project, undertaken by the director of the archive of the College of Foreign Affairs, N. N. Bantysh-Kamenskii, underwrote several small

---

[23] Ikonnikov gives extensive coverage of some of the most significant private collections, *Opyt russkoi istoriografii* (A-83), vol. 1, pt. 2:1072-1349. On private collections started before the nineteenth century, see the mimeographed booklet by Iu. F. Kononov, "Chastnye kollektsii rukopisnykh materialov v Rossii do XIX veka (Uchebnoe posobie)" (Moscow, 1961), available in the Manuscript Division of the Lenin Library. See also the article by M. P. Alekseev, "Iz istorii russkikh rukopisnykh sobranii," in *Neizdannye pis'ma inostrannykh pisatelei XVIII-XIX vekov iz Leningradskikh rukopisnykh sobranii* (Moscow/Leningrad, 1960) (A-36), pp. 7-122, which makes particular reference to collections of foreign literary materials.

expeditions for gathering historical materials, and encouraged the Moscow Society for Russian History and Antiquities.

P. M. Stroev had been an early member of that group, but turned to the Imperial Academy of Sciences in St. Petersburg for support and encouragement of his more extensive enterprise, the first important archeographical expedition of this period. Starting in 1829, this expedition spent six years in various parts of the empire collecting manuscripts that were not being looked after and gathering information about collections of historical documents. Their findings were published as the first report of the newly established Archeographical Commission, which continued expeditions and publication efforts in subsequent years.[24] Some of the provincial commissions, established in the 1840's and later, made considerable progress in the publication of documents and in descriptions of archives and manuscript collections, and there was evidence of coordinating efforts of different provincial commissions under the auspices of the Imperial Commission in St. Petersburg.

While interest in and information about early manuscripts and provincial collections developed and were encouraged through the efforts of the Imperial Archeographical Commission, the most promising projects for reform and centralization of a state archival system came from the archives themselves, and most particularly from the successive directors of the Moscow Archive of the Ministry of Justice. However, several far-reaching proposals for reform found no more favor with the government than did proposals for basic reform in the social and political realm. The only tangible result of this movement was the initiation of an archival training program in the Archeological Institutes in St. Petersburg in 1877 and in Moscow in 1907. Despite government intransigence and opposition to basic change and administrative reorganization, the fundamental work of cataloging and publishing descriptions of manuscripts and archival holdings continued with tremendous zeal, and the fact that many of these prerevolutionary inventories and catalogs remain in use today as the major finding aids for the fonds or collections to which they relate, attests to the high standards of scholarly work undertaken in that period.[25]

Although such developments are evidence of the hightened interest and scholarly concern about archives and manuscript collections in the last decades of prerevolutionary Russia, the general development of state archives lagged considerably behind that of the more advanced nations of Western Europe. The trend for centralized state archival repositories that had been developing in Europe in the

---

[24] For a list of the publications of the Archeographical Commission, see [Russia. Arkheograficheskaia komisiia.], *Podrobnyi katalog izdanii Arkheograficheskoi komissii, vyshedshikh v svet s 1836 po 1918 god,* 6th ed. (Petrograd: 1918). The commission's work is discussed by Ikonnikov, *Opyt russkoi istoriografii* (A-83), vol. 1, pt. 1:244-89; see also items A-84 and A-90.

[25] M. N. Shobukhov's pamphlet critically surveys the prerevolutionary work in inventorying documents in state archives: *Opisanie dokumental'nykh materialov v arkhivakh dorevoliutsionnoi Rossii* (Moscow, 1955).

nineteenth century, especially after the example France initiated at the time of the French Revolution, had seen some manifestations in Russia, but had not adequately taken root. To be sure, pre-nineteenth century records were finding their way into a variety of public repositories, but there were no provisions whatsoever for the retention and centralization of documentation from ongoing governmental offices. The tremendous cultural interest and concern that motivated the blossoming of private, academic, and religious collections was also motivating scholars and archival directors to demand archival reform and to make extensive plans for more comprehensive and coordinated record-keeping efforts, but such demands fell on deaf ears.

The state interest in systematic record-keeping which had been manifested under Ivan III, Peter the Great, Catherine II, and Nicholas I had seen the development of a major tradition and the establishment of important historical repositories. However, toward the end of the Romanov empire, the state itself—particularly in the persons of the last few emperors— took little interest in and paid little attention to this problem. As a result, much of the growth of state archives was due to the efforts of a cultured and scholarly elite working in opposition to rather than in cooperation with ruling governmental circles. Hence, archival efforts tended to be fragmentary, compartmentalized, and lacking in overall planning. Yet the tremendous manuscript wealth that was being carefully and systematically preserved in a variety of repositories is the real basis for the historical riches of Soviet collections today. And, as will be seen in subsequent pages, many of those institutions themselves which had taken such pains in collecting and preserving manuscript materials survived the Revolution in one way or another, and, although with transformed nomenclature, exist today either as separate repositories or as divisions of more centralized archives.

2. THE DEVELOPMENT AND ORGANIZATION OF ARCHIVES SINCE 1917

The October Revolution of 1917 had as great an impact on archives in the Soviet Union as it did on most other aspects of society and culture. The establishment of Bolshevik power stands as the single most important turning-point in the history and organization of Soviet archives, for it brought to Russia the most highly centralized state archival system and the most highly state-directed principles of preservation and management of documentary records which the world had seen. Deeply grounded in historical theory and completely committed to the necessity of historical interpretation, Marxism-Leninism as an ideology gave both extensive philosophical justification and crucial political importance to documentary control. This in turn brought innovations in archival management, as the Communist Party and the highly centralized political system encouraged firm control over all archival records at the same time that they developed the bureaucratic machinery for insuring that control.

The immediate social and political dislocations of revolution and civil war initially had a very detrimental effect on archives, and the ravages of war and social dislocation naturally wreaked havoc and incalculable damage. Potentially incriminating records or those of hated agencies of the past became targets for intentional destruction or defacement in response to continued political purges. Wide-scale emigration resulted in the loss of a number of important documentary collections and personal archives and in the loss of a number of individuals who possessed the knowledge and experience to deal with the papers left behind. The severe paper shortage of the early postrevolutionary period saw a large volume of irreplaceable records sacrificed for reprocessed pulp. Even after the new government took moves to prevent further destruction of records, the dearth of trained staff, the lack of adequate techniques for preservation, and the frequent or ill-planned transfers of records resulted in disarrangement of files and inestimable physical and organizational damage. Even among those records that escaped damage or destruction, the hasty imposition of new schemes for arrangement and classification and the frequent changes of administrative units and institutional names has made it hard to trace specific files or to reestablish the original natural arrangement of records in their creating agency.

These negative factors were, however, offset and in some measure soon overshadowed by the positive measures taken to avert destruction and insure centralized governmental control. Less than a year after its seizure of power, and in the midst of a brutal civil war, the new Bolshevik government took immediate action to insure the preservation of records through the now famous decree of 1 June 1918.[1] Issued over Lenin's signature, this regulation calling for the total

[1] "O reorganizatsii i tsentralizatsii arkhivnogo dela," *Sbornik rukovodiashchikh materialov po arkhivnomu delu (1917–iiun' 1941 gg.)* (Moscow, 1961) (A-99), pp. 12-13; reprinted in *K 50-letiiu sovetskogo arkhivnogo dela* (Moscow, 1968), pp. 10-12. The radical innovation of this concept and its significance in the

23

reorganization of state archives provided the basis for the extension of state control to all the records of the prerevolutionary state and of the new regime, and for their systematic retention under a coordinated and highly centralized administrative system. The revolutionary importance of this Bolshevik move, made sixteen years before the much less extensive National Archives Act in the United States, has not always commanded the attention it deserves. The most innovative archival reform yet enacted in the twentieth century, it resulted in the most extensive state control and centralized management of all national records that had been instituted in any major country at that time.

Its political and intellectual roots still require further exploration. To a certain extent its origins can be sought in some of the reform projects developed in Russia on the eve of the Revolution. Indigenous roots can be traced back further, to the unfulfilled plans of Peter the Great, and other influences and precedents can be seen in the archival developments on the Continent during the nineteenth century.

The early Soviet reform also has some antecedents in the centralizing archival innovations in France at the time of the French Revolution, and in the concern of an historically conscious government, imposed by revolution, with the records of its predecessors and its own achievements. However, centralization and control of archives went much further in the Soviet Union than they ever did in France, or in other continental nations that followed the French model. And so to a large extent their background should be sought in the theoretical tenets of Marxism-Leninism. Its unreconciled combination of historical determinism and centralized state political and ideological control gave unprecedented importance to the national documentary legacy and to the revolutionary reorganization of a comprehensive state archival system.

Yet there was continuity as well as change between the archival systems of Imperial Russia and the Soviet Union. There was much institutional continuity in manuscript repositories and in certain elements of over-all organization, despite the great innovations in centralization and modernization of management techniques. A nation in so deep a state of economic and social crisis as existed in the years of civil

---

historical development of archival administration is suggested by Ernst Posner, "Some Aspects of Archival Development since the French Revolution," *American Archivist* 3 (1940):171, reprinted in *Archives and the Public Interest: Selected Essays by Ernst Posner,* ed. Ken Munden (Washington, 1967), pp. 34-35. For the best discussion of the background of Lenin's decree see the recent article by S. O. Shmidt, "K istorii arkhivnogo stroitel'stva v pervye gody sovetskoi vlasti," in *Problemy arkhivovedeniia i istorii arkhivnykh uchrezhdenii. Materialy iubileinoi nauchnoi konferentsii arkhivistov Leningrada, 13-14 iiunia 1968 g.,* ed. I. N. Solov'ev, et al. (Leningrad, 1970) (A-82), pp. 19-35. For an appraisal of the immediate difficulties experienced by the archives as a result of the revolutionary upheaval, see the article by the noted Russian historian, A. Presniakov, "Historical Research in Russia during the Revolutionary Crisis," *American Historical Review,* 28 (January 1923): 248-57; Presniakov goes on to emphasize the values of the sweeping archival reform; compare the earlier Russian version of this article, "Reforma arkhivnogo dela," *Russkii istoricheskii zhurnal* 5 (1918): 205-22. For additional studies pertaining to the development of Soviet archives used in the preparation of this survey, see the general bibliography below, Part A, section 20.

war had to preserve what it could from the past. It is not surprising that the early organization of storage areas for the newly centralized state archival records was structured around existing archives. And since Soviet archival theory had for a cardinal principle the preservation of records in the original organization of their creating agency, it is not surprising that the restructured archives preserved to the maximum possible extent their original internal arrangement. In other words, the forms were new, but much of the contents, as well as their storage areas, were old. It is significant that the present-day central executive offices of the Main Archival Administration occupy the building that was built in the 1880's to house the Moscow Archive of the Ministry of Justice, the best-established and most reform-oriented state archival institution of the Russian Empire.

In characterizing the development of the highly complex Soviet archival system, three main aspects stand out, not only from the point of view of archival administration, but for the effects they have on the facilitation of research: 1) the extension of state proprietorship to all documentary records of the nation through the concept of a unified State Archival Fond; 2) the formation of an independent central agency charged with overall archival planning, archives administration, and records management; and 3) the actual organization of repositories, with their highly complex and relatively decentralized administrative ties.

The highly centralized, bureaucratized tendencies in Soviet archival management are manifested most extensively in the first two aspects. The next few pages will attempt to characterize their current situation, which now appears more or less stabilized after considerable modifications during the first fifty years of Soviet power. The third aspect, the actual organization of manuscript repositories, is naturally of most concern to those doing research in the USSR and will accordingly occupy the major portion of this survey; but it is the most difficult to characterize because of the extent and diversity of the current picture and even more because of its complex fifty-year evolution. Although decentralizing forces have come to predominate in this third area, as will be seen in subsequent pages, they are held in check, if not counteracted, by the centralizing effects of state proprietorship and state management and planning; hence a brief review of these first two aspects will set the stage for the more complex problems of actual institutional organization.

The State Archival Fond

Certainly one of the most significant Soviet innovations in the archival field has been the state appropriation of all archival records regardless of their institutional or family origin, a principle established through the archival regulations promulgated during the first year of Bolshevik power. Most significantly, the decree of 1 June 1918 on the reorganization and centralization of archival affairs provided for the formation of a Single State Archival Fond [Edinyi Gosudarstvennyi arkhivnyi fond—EGAF], comprising all the existing documentary legacy of liquidated agencies and institutions. During the 1920's it came to be called simply the State Archival Fond [Gosudarstvennyi arkhivnyi fond—GAF], and this was adopted as the official name in 1929.

In 1919 the state claim over archives was extended to all the military records of World War I and to the papers of deceased scientific and cultural figures in libraries and museums, as well as to the files of trade unions and cooperative organizations. In subsequent years other categories of papers were added by decree, including papers of counterrevolutionary participants, nationalized or municipalized industrial and commercial concerns, religious institutions, and family papers of the Romanovs and others in high governmental positions. Films and photographs of sociopolitical significance were later brought under state archival control. In 1941 decrees extended state custody to the records of scientific, cultural, and technical institutions and organizations, to the papers of important political, cultural, and scientific leaders, and to all historical documentary and manuscript collections in libraries, museums, or other institutions. Further refinements were developed in the course of later archival legislation; most recently the regulation of 13 August 1958 fully describes the so-called State Archival Fond of the USSR, defining its contents to include virtually all records of all types of institutions and organizations of state and society as well as the manuscripts of all cultural and scientific works and the papers of all important personalities.[2]

Regulations not only provided for state custody and control of all existing archives, manuscript collections, and records of defunct institutions, but also extended the State Archival Fond to include the files of current record-producing agencies. Thus archival authorities were granted broad powers in the field of records management both for the appropriation of non-current records and for work with the offices themselves in determining guidelines for disposal and for the sorting and retention of permanent files. Initially papers were to remain in their issuing agency for five years, but after several fluctuations in this time-span, the normal period of retention came to be ten or fifteen years, depending on the nature of the documentation involved.[3] In some cases local or intermediate storage areas have been established for longer temporary storage, with further provisions for re-sorting records designated for more permanent archival retention. Such provisions have naturally developed the concept of total state control over the documentary records of all segments of society.

Proprietorship on paper or in law, however, has naturally not always meant immediate expropriation in fact, nor has it meant the deposit of all records in state archives. Although such records are technically still part of the State Archival Fond (GAF), there are some ongoing organizations which have been able to justify the long-term retention of their own records. And going a step further, the Communist Party, the Foreign Ministry, and the Academy of Sciences, for example, have

---

[2] "Polozhenie o gosudarstvennom arkhivnom fonde Soiuza SSR," 13 August 1958, in *K 50-letiiu sovetskogo arkhivnogo dela,* pp. 26-41. This regulation is summarized by the Director General of GAU, G.A. Belov, in a French translation, "Nouveau statut du fonds des archives d'état de l'URSS." in *Mélanges offerts par ses confrères étrangers à Charles Braibant* (Brussels, 1959), pp. 43-49;

[3] The current regulations for these retention periods are detailed in the preceding regulation of 13 August 1958, in *K 50-letiiu sovetskogo arkhivnogo dela,* pp. 34-36.

established their own archival systems and retain their own records completely independent of the state archival system. Manuscript holdings of numerous libraries and museums and of many cultural organizations, all considered part of the GAF, have likewise not been brought under centralized administration. Although the state has no legal authority to force individuals to surrender family papers, significant progress has been made in bringing noteworthy materials into state institutions through purchase or other types of pressure, and through guarantees of restricted access. Great efforts on the part of numerous manuscript repositories have also brought about the influx of former private or church manuscript collections, with the result that many formerly dispersed cultural treasures are being inventoried and preserved.

The current relatively enlightened efforts in this respect, however, will never be able to compensate for the many losses inflicted by earlier, less fortunate cultural policies. Manuscript librarians have reason to bemoan the number of medieval manuscripts that found their way to foreign auction sales or that were lost or damaged in social upheaval or religious persecution. Archivists today also regret the large numbers of personal papers and other records that were removed from the country in the course of wide-scale emigration; numerous efforts have been made abroad in recent years to recover historical and cultural records either in the original or copy.

Despite some delays and exceptions, and despite the continuing dispersal of many cultural materials, the achievement of bringing important personal and institutional papers as well as early manuscript treasures under state archival control remains highly significant. The resulting value to researchers can hardly be overemphasized. Anyone who has tried to locate and tap personal family papers in a country such as France or Spain—notorious for the long-term private retention of family papers and the high price of famous historical autographs—can appreciate the value to scholars of the Soviet innovation, particularly since it has usually been accompanied by the development of centralized cataloging techniques. Central storage areas for cultural, labor, and business records are other examples of progressive archival practices in this realm; no other country in the world has established such extensive collections of feature films, documentary films, sound recordings, and photographs in special central repositories.

The State Agency for Archival Administration

Another major innovation in the Soviet Union has been the establishment of an independent agency charged with the management of all of the State Archival Fond. The existence of such an agency has permitted the centralization and planning that has undergirded the great archival achievement in the past fifty years and that has made possible the total state control of the historically valuable and politically sensitive records of state and society.

The actual name and placement of this agency within the Soviet bureaucratic hierarchy has been subject to characteristically shifting patterns, but its actual existence and general function has been fairly constant. By the decree that created it in 1918, the management of the so-called Single State Archival Fond (EGAF) was initially entrusted to the Main Administration of Archival Affairs [Glavnoe upravlenie arkhivnym delom-GUAD], or Glavarkhiv, which was under the People's Commissariat of Education of the Russian SFSR. Similar decrees were issued for the other five Soviet republics of the Ukraine, Belorussia, Armenia, Azerbaijan, and Georgia, which nationalized their republic-level archival materials and placed their administration under the control of the local commissariats of education.

Among his many positions in the early Soviet organization of scholarship, the noted historian Mikhail Nikolaevich Pokrovskii served as the first director of the archive administration until his death in 1932. Working with him during this period as assistant directors were V. V. Adoratskii and V. V. Maksakov, and Maksakov also served as the editor of the professional journal of the archival administration, *Arkhivnoe delo* [Archival Affairs] (A-70) started in 1923.

The archives did not long remain under the rather loose control of the Ministry of Education. With the adoption of the new constitution in 1922 and the official formation of the Soviet Union the following year, the archival administration was raised to a position directly subordinate to the Central Executive Committee of the Russian Federation. With the formation of the Central Archive of the RSFSR [Tsentral'nyi arkhiv RSFSR], or Tsentrarkhiv, in 1922, the administrative functions of Glavarkhiv were taken over by the directorate of Tsentrarkhiv (Upravlenie Tsentral'nym arkhivom RSFSR). Its duties included the direction and planning of all archives in the Russian Federation, the direct management of all archives in Moscow and Petrograd, the control of record-keeping functions in all governmental offices, and the general coordination of archival administration throughout the country. Similar central archival organizations were set up in the other Soviet republics in subsequent years under Moscow's guidance and coordination. All-union records as well as those of the Russian Federation remained under the management of Tsentrarkhiv until further administrative changes took place in 1929.

In 1929 an all-union Central Archival Administration [Tsentral'noe arkhivnoe upravlenie Soiuza SSR], directly subordinate to the Central Executive Committee of the USSR, was established with broader supervision over archives throughout the USSR. At this time archives of the Russian Federation were distinguished from those of all-union importance, and a separate subordinate administration was set up for the RSFSR, similar in pattern to those in other republics. This structure was maintained until after the new constitution of 1936, when general administrative changes and tightening of state security again brought reorganization in archival administration.

Most important at this point, the archival administration lost a degree of its independent status, when in 1938 it was subordinated to the powerful security-minded Peoples' Commissariat (later Ministry) of Internal Affairs, and renamed the Main Archival Administration of the NKVD [Glavnoe arkhivnoe upravlenie pri NKVD (later MVD) SSSR]. Similarly, the archival administrations on republic and autonomous republic levels, as well as those of lower administrative units, were shifted to the control of the local ministries of internal affairs. On the whole, however, these shifts did not result in any basic changes in the function of the archival administration, despite the strong political and attitudinal effects of its close association with organs of police and state security. This bureaucratic arrangement under the NKVD and later MVD lasted for twenty-two years. Only in 1960 was the Main Archival Administration once again made independent of the Ministry of Internal Affairs and attached directly to the Council of Ministers of the USSR [Glavnoe arkhivnoe upravlenie pri Sovete ministrov SSSR-GAU].[4]

Currently, the Main Archival Administration, or GAU, has eight separate divisions, a form that suggests its manifold functions. The first, or administrative, division handles the general problems of state archival administration and records management, and supervises directly the all-union central state archives. Individual central state archives have their own directors and internal administrative divisions, but GAU provides overall coordinating management. Similarly, GAU works out the overall organizational patterns for union and autonomous republic archives and for the archives on the oblast, krai, or lower levels; it coordinates and supervises them through the regional archival administrations, which in turn supervise the management of individual archives. GAU further controls the organization of archival files for ministries, and other state institutions, working out their records-management principles and coordinating the eventual transfer of files to state archives.

A second, or information, division handles problems of news about archival developments and activities. It puts out various internal newsletters or directives for archives throughout the country and also publishes the bi-monthly information bulletin, *Sovetskie arkhivy* [Soviet archives] (A-74), which, since it replaced the earlier quarterly *Voprosy arkhivovedeniia* [Problems of archival science] (A-76) in 1966, has been generally available by internal and international subscription.

A third division manages the archives of the Russian Federation, which, because of the complex problems of overlap between Russian and all-union government functions, does not now have its own separate archival administrative agency, although it does have separate republic-level archives. The placement and administration of RSFSR records has been subject to considerable earlier variations. Now the separate republic-level archives of the RSFSR have been brought under the more direct management of GAU, whereas those of other union republics maintain a relatively more independent bureaucratic structure.

A fourth division handles the more technical problems of archival arrangement and storage—problems like the structuring and description of storage groups,

---

[4] The most complete regulation defining the current functions of GAU, "Polozhenie o Glavnom arkhivnom upravlenii pri Sovete ministrov SSSR," 28 July 1961, is printed in *K 50-letiiu sovetskogo arkhivnogo dela*, pp. 42-48; it was published earlier in *Voprosy arkhivovedeniia*, 1961, no. 3, pp. 3-8, followed by an interpretive article, "K novomu pod'emu v arkhivnom stroitel'stve," *ibid.*, pp. 9-20. Further information about the current organization of GAU was furnished me in the course of interviews with GAU officials in Moscow in 1969 and 1970.

favorable storage conditions, restoration and microfilm preservation—and provides instructions on such matters for state and other institutional archives throughout the Soviet Union.

A fifth division is in charge of publications. The systematic publication of selected archival documents is one of the chief aims and constitutes one of the most significant activities of the Soviet archival administration. Actually, each separate central state archive has its own division in charge of publications, but the Main Archival Administration works with them in planning the general format for such projects and carrying out publication details. Most particularly, GAU coordinates the many extensive general documentary series published with the participation of other segments of the scholarly community. Other archival systems such as the Foreign Ministry, the Academy of Sciences, and the Communist Party control their own publication projects, but the Main Archival Administration cooperates with many of these.[5] GAU and its predecessors also published the important journal of documentary publications, *Krasnyi arkhiv* [Red Archives] from 1922 to 1941,[6] and cooperated with the later journal *Istoricheskii arkhiv* [Historical Archives] (A-73), published between 1955 and 1962 by the Institute of History of the Academy of Sciences. Currently there is no similar journal devoted to documentary publications, but there are many multi-volume publication projects underway.

The extent of these projects and of documentary publications in the past underscores the crucial importance of the publication function of Soviet archives. Political considerations are naturally important in the planning and execution of such projects, as they are in most countries that issue official documentary collections. But the requirements of political theory have not prevented a high level of scholarly endeavor on many of the large-scale projects, although theoretical and political considerations naturally have a lot to do with the nature, subject matter, and extent of projects undertaken. Selected publication of the documents judged "most important" has often been viewed as a substitute for open scholarly research in the records from which they were drawn. The type of large-scale microfilm publication of entire runs of complete record groups containing historical materials for scholarly research such as those the United States National Archives has undertaken runs quite contrary to Soviet archival theory.

[5] For a complete bibliography of official publications from state archives since 1917, see *Katalog sbornikov dokumentov, izdannykh arkhivnymi uchrezhdeniiami SSSR 1917-1960 gg.* (Moscow, 1961) (A-65), and the supplements A-2 (Moscow, 1964), pp. 98-117, covering the years 1960-1963, and A-3 (Moscow, 1970), pp. 126-53, covering the years 1964-1967. See also the series *Istoriia sovetskoi arkheografii. Uchebnoe posobie* (A-95).

[6] For details of the contents of this journal, see the two-volume English-language summary, *A Digest of the Krasnyi Arkhiv (Red Archives):* pt. 1 (vols. 1-30), compiled by Leonid S. Rubinchek, ed. Louise M. Boutelle and Gordon W. Thayer (Cleveland, 1947); pt. 2 (vols. 31-106), compiled by Leona W. Eisele under the direction of A. Lobanov-Rostovsky (Ann Arbor, 1955). See also the comprehensive index volume compiled by R. Ia. Zverev, ed. V. V. Maksakov, *Krasnyi arkhiv. Istoricheskii zhurnal, 1922-1941 gg. Annotirovannyi ukazatel' soderzhaniia* (Moscow, 1960).

In addition to historical documents, the publications division is also in charge of the extensive program of producing archival handbooks, inventories, and other directories, location aids, or reference materials for state archives. Individual archives are responsible for the actual preparation of their own guides and catalogs, but the overall planning and the details of publishing are handled by the Main Archival Administration. GAU also puts out technical instructions, administrative manuals, and various other reports or information brochures for archives throughout the country.

A sixth division deals with problems of utilization of archival materials, such as the organization of reading rooms and reader services and facilities, the compilation and location of documentary materials for particular state events such as the anniversary of the Revolution or the centennial of Lenin's birth, and the general problems of catalogs and reference materials. This division is currently planning and developing comprehensive centralized catalogs for information retrieval from state archives throughout the Soviet Union.

The seventh division concerns itself with archival development and new techniques of archival management. In recent years, however, some of the most theoretical or scientific work in this area has been shifted to a newly established semi-independent research institute for archival affairs under GAU (see below).

The eighth division handles foreign relations for the archival administration. Since 1956 the Soviet Union has been actively participating in the International Council on Archives (ICA).[7] The director of GAU, G. A. Belov, was elected in 1968 to a four-year term as the vice-president of the ICA and Moscow plans to be the host of its 1972 international congress. The Soviet Union has also participated in various archival projects sponsored by UNESCO and in the French-inspired "Round Table" of leading international archivists which meets between ICA congresses.

The foreign relations division also carries out various exchange arrangements with foreign countries to gather information about archival techniques and administrative developments and to acquire microfilms of documents from foreign archives of interest to Soviet scholars.[8] Most important to foreign scholars, this division handles all contacts with individual foreign readers for all the state archives in the USSR. Foreigners' requests for archival information, access, or microfilms all go through this office. Its representatives are also in charge of special reading rooms

---

[7] In an earlier period of Soviet nonparticipation, this organization was looked on with disfavor by official circles in the USSR. See the article "Arkhivy," in *Bol'shaia sovetskaia entsiklopediia*, 2nd ed. (1950), 3:177, and the reaction to this statement by Fritz T. Epstein, "Archives Administration in the Soviet Union," *American Archivist* 20 (January 1957): 144.

[8] On these projects of acquiring additional foreign microfilm materials, see G. A. Belov, "Rasshirenie istochnikovedcheskoi bazy istorii narodov SSSR za schet dokumentov, khraniashchikhsia v zarubezhnykh arkhivakh," *Arkheograficheskii ezhegodnik za 1963 god,* pp. 223-40. See also the summary of Soviet archival activities on the international front by M. Ia. Kapran, "Mezhdunarodnoe sotrudnichestvo sovetskikh arkhivistov," *Sovetskie arkhivy,* 1968, no. 3, pp. 32-39.

for foreigners and make all the arrangements for foreign readers using the state archives.

Much of the coordinating work of the Main Archival Administration is handled through the quarterly meetings of the administration's "Learned Council," which includes not only the heads of the several divisions of GAU itself and the directors of its central state archives, but also representatives of other major archives not under its direct management, such as those of the Academy of Sciences, the Party archives of the Institute of Marxism-Leninism, the archival administrations of the ministries of Foreign Affairs and Defense, and the manuscript divisions of major libraries and museums as well as representatives from the archival research and training institutes. Such meetings and discussions do much to coordinate different archival organizations whose actual administration is out of the direct control of GAU. Periodic conferences of archival workers from different parts of the country also aid archival coordination and permit the dissemination of information and the standardization of archival practices; their most important proceedings are usually published, and more general reports about their sessions often appear in the professional archival and disciplinary journals.

Soviet centralized planning and administration in archival affairs, as in many other cultural and political subjects, is strongly supported by research and educational establishments. The Main Archival Administration has accordingly been exceedingly active in both these realms.

During the late 1960's many of the more theoretical or research problems of archival affairs have been turned over to the All-Union Scientific-Research Institute on Documentation and Archival Affairs [Vsesoiuznyi nauchno-issledovatel'skii institut dokumentovedeniia i arkhivnogo dela—VNIIDAD]. Established in 1966 under GAU, VNIIDAD, the only institution of its kind in any country in the world, devotes itself solely to scientific research on archival matters.[9] It currently has five main divisions investigating different types of problems. The documentation division is planning means of systematizing government documentation in an effort to correlate the needs of current record-keeping with the requirements of long-term archival storage. The archival management division is concerned with the organization of the state archival system, organizational problems of individual archives, and cataloging systems.

VNIIDAD's third division deals with such technical problems of archival storage as restoration techniques, the optimal conditions for documentary preservation, and reproduction processes; it has a laboratory with scientific staff for research in these areas. The fourth division deals specifically with mechanization in archives, such as the possibilities of computerization of catalogs and techniques for information retrieval. Finally, the scientific-technical information division handles institute reports and publications, and since 1969 has put out two different

[9] Information about the current organization and activities of VNIIDAD was furnished me in an interview with the director in the fall of 1969. See also the article by A. S. Malitikov, "O rabote metodicheskikh sektsii VNIIDAD," *Sovetskie arkhivy*, 1968, no. 6, pp. 34-41.

monthly journals that abstract all new publications, including journal articles, on all phases of archival matters; the first is devoted to literature on the Soviet Union, and the second covers foreign archival developments from a wide variety of foreign publications.[10]

Through the education of archivists, an area in which the Soviet Union has shown itself to be especially progressive, the Main Archival Administration has sought to recruit well-trained cadres and to achieve standardization of archival procedures and management techniques. The Moscow State Historico-Archival Institute [Moskovskii gosudarstvennyi istoriko-arkhivnyi institut—MGIAI] has prerevolutionary roots in the archival program of the St. Petersburg Archeological Institute started in 1877 and its Moscow counterpart, which began in 1907. These were disbanded soon after the Revolution, but archival training courses continued under the central archival administration and extensive programs went forward in sections of the universities of both Moscow and Leningrad. A full-scale Institute of Archival Affairs was opened in Moscow in 1931 under the auspices of the Main Archival Administration; in 1932 it was renamed the Historico-Archival Institute [Istoriko-arkhivnyi institut], and after the Second World War, the Moscow State Historico-Archival Institute.[11] Currently located in the historic building formerly occupied by the Synod Printing Office, the archival institute has developed into a training school which is coming to rank with its smaller French, Austrian, and West German counterparts in quality.

Now administered by the Ministry of Higher and Specialized Education, its comprehensive programs of study are carefully correlated with archival staff requirements by the Main Archival Administration, and its director or his representative sits on the Learned Council of GAU.[12] Students are admitted for one of three alternative five-year programs, after they have completed their basic ten-year school. The traditional historical archival program combines historical and

[10] The first monthly series, *Bibliograficheskii ukazatel' po otechestvennym materialam. Dokumentovedenie i arkhivnoe delo* (A-17), started with no. 1 in 1969, but apparently twelve earlier issues had been put out in a less widely circulated form. The second series, covering the non-Soviet literature, started in 1969, *Bibliograficheskii ukazatel' po zarubezhnym materialam* (A-72).

[11] The training courses for archivists before 1930 are described in detail by G. A. Dremina, "Iz istorii arkhivnogo obrazovaniia v SSSR (1918-1930 gg.)," in *Trudy MGIAI* 15 (1962):157-71; and more briefly by Inna Lubimenko, "La Science des archives dans la Russie des Sovets," *Nederlandsch Archievenblad* 34(1926-1927): 49-53. For a summary of the first twenty-five years of the institute's development, see A. S. Roslova, "25 let raboty Moskovskogo gosudarstvennogo istoriko-arkhivnogo instituta," *Trudy MGIAI* 11 (1958):3-51. See also Ingo Rösler, "Archivstudien in Moskau und Leningrad," *Archivmitteilungen* 7, no. 2 (1957):45-53, and the earlier article by A. S. Roslova, "Moskovskii gosudarstvennyi istoriko-arkhivnyi institut (K 25-letiiu so dnia osnovaniia)," *Istoricheskii arkhiv*, 1955, no. 5, pp. 160-67, and the German translation in *Archivmitteilungen* 7, no. 1 (1956):11-16.

[12] Information about the institute's program was compiled from the 1969 student prospectus, "Prospekt spravochnika dlia postupaiushchikh v Moskovskii gosudarstvennyi istoriko-arkhivnyi institut," and from the study programs and other data presented in the course of personal interviews in 1969 and 1970.

linguistic studies with special archival subjects to prepare workers for the state historical and cultural archives and various other manuscript repositories. Since 1964 the institute has had a records management program to prepare workers to organize documentation systems in various state establishments, which combines general courses in law and public administration with more specialized studies of documentation procedures. A third program was started in the fall of 1969 to train workers for scientific and technical archives or for management of documentary records in technical or scientific establishments. A graduate program leading to the "candidate" degree has been in existence since 1944 to prepare teachers or more advanced archival research workers. In addition to various text books, the institute puts out its own scholarly serial, *Trudy,* containing articles or monographic contributions of its advanced students and faculty.[13]

The school grew from an enrollment of around two hundred fifty in the early 1930's to about eighteen hundred by the mid-50's, and to approximately three thousand by 1969; about two-thirds of these are regularly employed and follow evening or correspondence courses. Although at present it is the only institute of its kind in the Soviet Union, there are small archival programs in Leningrad and Moscow universities, and a comprehensive one in the Historical Faculty of Kiev University.

Through its various divisions and coordinated institutes, the Main Archival Administration thus serves the Soviet state as a centralized agency for administration and planning of archives and records management. Its operation and leadership have accordingly been largely responsible for the development and implementation of the Soviet archival system. Ostensibly its extent and activities provide the Soviet Union with one of the most highly centralized and bureaucratized archival systems in the world.

Yet, as is so typical of the general pattern in Soviet governmental structure and operation, GAU does not stand alone, nor has it brought a complete centralization. A parallel archival administration has been developed by the Communist Party; independent archival administrations have been organized by the Foreign Ministry and the Academy of Sciences; and manuscript divisions of libraries and museums continue to be administered under the Ministry of Culture. While GAU through its publications, conferences, and the meetings of its Learned Council takes steps to coordinate its efforts with these other administrative organs and provide technical guidelines for their archival operations, its authority and effectiveness are often limited in their jurisdiction. Such bureaucratic complexities must be taken into account in any attempt to understand and appraise the general organization and effectiveness of the overall Soviet archival system.

---

[13] *Trudy MGIAI,* vols. 5-26 (1954-1968) (see A-75); the first four volumes (1939-1948) were entitled *Trudy Istoriko-arkhivnogo instituta.* A summary of MGIAI dissertations on archival subjects is given in the article by V. V. Maksakov, K. G. Mitaev, A. T. Nikolaeva, and M. S. Seleznev, "Razrabotka voprosov arkhivovedeniia i vspomogatel'nykh istoricheskikh distsiplin v Istoriko-arkhivnom istitute," *Istoricheskii arkhiv,* 1956, no. 4, pp. 213-28.

The Organization of Repositories: State Archives

The creation after the Revolution of the Single State Archival Fond and a central agency for its administration and control involved the further and more fundamental problem of organizing actual repositories to house different types of archival and manuscript materials. The location of these materials in archives and other manuscript repositories in the Soviet Union today presents a highly complicated picture of diversity and decentralization, not unlike the situation in many other large countries. Actually, however, there is much more coordination and administrative centralization than exists in countries of comparable size or importance. Particularly when attention centers on the state archival system under the Main Archival Administration, the relatively centralized organization of eleven central state archives and the coordinated system of republic and regional state archives as it exists today contrasts markedly with the relatively chaotic, uncoordinated situation in many large Western nations.

Although this state system is likely to be central to any consideration of Soviet archives, one must remember that it constitutes only a part of the total highly complex, and to the foreigner often bewildering, overall situation. Most important, and often of most interest to foreign scholars, the Communist Party and Foreign Ministry maintain their own archives quite independently of the state archival system, as do the Academy of Sciences and its various institutes. And a great deal of less official documentation, along with many of the country's most impressive manuscript collections, remains concentrated and independently administered by a large number of museums and libraries, most of which fall under the jurisdiction of the Ministry of Culture.

The state archival system remains the most extensive part of the broader complex and includes the greatest concentration of governmental records. As currently organized, that system is relatively easy to understand, but an attempt to trace the genealogy of the central state archives as they exist today involves immense complications. Except for those of most recent formation, not one of the central state archives has escaped at least four or five changes of name since 1918 and an equal number of administrative reorganizations that have directly affected its contents. The complexities of this development, which involved such frequent administrative reshuffling, need to be considered here in some detail because the frequent changes in nomenclature and the equally confusing shifts of archival contents have left permanent marks on the arrangement of materials within different archives as well as on a wide range of archival literature and scholarly publications. Dependent as current research is on earlier catalogs and guides and on monographic publications that have used various documents at different times, it is often crucial to understand the overall organization or the official names of specific repositories at a given time.

The immediate commitment to systematized state control of the documentary heritage of Imperial Russia and to the careful retention of all the records of the new regime in the early years of Soviet power provoked considerable discussion of how best these goals could be accomplished. As in many aspects of economic and political administration, considerable experimentation and organizational re-shuffling ensued as successive plans were put into operation. The establishment of the Single State Archival Fond (EGAF) in 1918 and the creation of Glavarkhiv provided both the legal imperative for the state appropriation of all archival records and a centralized organ for their administration. Even before the end of the Civil War, efforts were under way to protect existing records and consolidate them in rationally organized repositories.

Because of the extent of the state documentary legacy and its prior decentralization in multiple storage areas, it was deemed impractical to attempt the complete physical consolidation of all state records in a single archival complex or institution. The basic principle introduced at the beginning, which has endured with some modifications, called for complete *bureaucratic* centralization under the central archival administrative agency, but for relatively decentralized storage areas. A number of consolidated repositories were structured along subject-matter divisions for the records of central government and along geographical adminis-trative divisions for regional records.

Without further delay, a rational organization was introduced, dividing the State Archival Fond into eight sections in both Moscow and Petrograd: 1) political (legislative and high administrative, and foreign policy); 2) juridical; 3) military-naval; 4) educational; 5) historical-economic; 6) internal administrative; 7) historical-revolutionary; and 8) printed documentary. A ninth section was added to this list for cultural and literary materials in 1921, and the eighth section was expanded to include film and photographic documents.[14] This initial plan had important bearings on all the subsequent rearrangements.

In the official names of the sections and their overall organization there were no apparent traces of prerevolutionary archival arrangements. But in point of fact, the rational plan and overall administrative structure of the repositories had a very direct correspondence to preexisting storage areas, and the actual housing of documents had a firm basis in prerevolutionary locations. From the outset one of the guiding principles was to retain intact the contents of different prerevolutionary archives as well as the archival records of former institutions, preserving them to the extent possible in their original order and arrangement. Only in the case of the historical-revolutionary collection was an "artificial" archive created around a special subject, drawing fonds out of their previous sources.

Each of the sections included the contents of related prerevolutionary archives together with corresponding groups of records that had been stored in their issuing agencies. However, lack of suitable space prevented physical consolidation. The

---

[14] V. V. Maksakov (*Istoriia i organizatsiia arkhivnogo dela v SSSR, 1917-1945* [Moscow, 1969] [A-98], pp. 64-69), describes the organization of these sections, as does his earlier book: *Arkhivnoe delo v pervye gody Sovetskoi vlasti* (Moscow, 1959), pp. 42-54. See also the recent summary by V. I. Vialikov, "Arkhivnoe stroitel'stvo v RSFSR v 1917-1925 godakh," *Sovetskie arkhivy,* 1968, no. 1, pp. 30-38, and the early article in French by Inna Lubimenko, "L'Organisation des archives dans la Russie des Sovets, d'après les données officielles," *Neder-landsch Archievenblad* 33(1925-1926):164-72.

sections were further broken down into different divisions, usually centering on a major preexisting repository where the other fonds in the division could also be stored. Thus in large part the organization proceeded pragmatically to utilize the prerevolutionary archives when their physical location permitted, thereby avoiding the necessity of recataloging or rearranging fonds and moving large quantities of documents.

The first (political) section in Petrograd brought together the State Archive of the Russian Empire, the St. Petersburg Main Archive of the Ministry of Foreign Affairs, the St. Petersburg Archive of the Ministry of the Imperial Court, and the archives of the State Council, the State Duma, and the Committee of Ministers, among others. In Moscow, the first section developed on the basis of the Moscow Main Archive of the Ministry of Foreign Affairs, the Armory Archive, and the Moscow Archive of the Imperial Court.

The second (juridical) section in Petrograd was based on the former St. Petersburg Senate Archive. In Moscow, it was based on the Moscow Archive of the Ministry of Justice (MAMIu), and included various Moscow court records.

The third (military-naval) section in Petrograd centered on the General Archive of the General Staff and the Naval History Archive. In Moscow it was based on the Lefort Archive and absorbed the former Military Science Archive.

The fourth (educational) section in Petrograd was based on the archives of the Ministry of Education, the educational districts, the Holy Synod, and various educational and scientific institutions. In Moscow it included the records of Moscow University and other educational and religious institutions, including the collections of the Synod Press.

The fifth (historical-economic) section in Petrograd comprised the archives of the ministries of finance, trade, and manufacturing, and other business and banking enterprises. In Moscow it included the fonds of similar establishments in that region and the Land Survey Archive.

The sixth (internal administrative) section was based on the Petrograd archive of the Ministry of Internal Affairs and other local government records. In Moscow it centered around the Moscow guberniia Archive of Ancient Records.

The seventh (historical-revolutionary) section in Petrograd collected various police and gendarme records which became the basis for the Petrograd Historical-Revolutionary Archive [Petrogradskii istoriko-revoliutsionnyi arkhiv]. This entire collection was later transferred to Moscow and combined with the police records from the Moscow region which had formed the basis for the seventh section there.

The eighth (printed documentary) section in Petrograd, begun in 1919, collected revolutionary handbills and a variety of other printed materials. The Moscow section collected similar revolutionary documents which in 1920 became the basis for the Archive of the October Revolution, concentrating on materials relating to 1917 and the subsequent Civil War.

The ninth (cultural) sections formed in both Moscow and Petrograd in 1921 gathered various formerly dispersed fonds of individuals and cultural organizations. Initially intended as a centralizing force to bring together the bulk of personal papers in the cultural realm, most of which had been in private hands before the Revolution, special divisions were planned for cultural life, literature and art, education, and church organs. Particularly significant were the plans to concentrate private papers of literary, artistic, and other cultural figures under the literary division, but these plans did not materialize at that time, since no satisfactory repository was set up for them. Instead, many of the most important cultural fonds were taken into the custody of memorial museums or the diverse library and museum manuscript divisions which, having survived the Revolution as separate repositories, were prepared to handle them immediately. Thus it is that many sets of papers remain today in the locations where they ended up in the 1920's, although many other cultural fonds were later brought together when the state literary archive developed in the 1940's.[15]

The establishment of these sections of the EGAF did not immediately result in the rational organization of archives in the Soviet Union. The process of collecting, sorting, organizing, and cataloging the nation's documentary wealth has been an exceedingly slow and tortuous procedure and is still in progress. Things were particularly chaotic in the early years of Soviet power, when civil war and economic collapse diverted state priorities away from elaborate archival arrangements. At the same time the very great volume and variety of documentary materials appropriated by the state put a tremendous burden on the archival administration to the extent that pragmatic considerations had a lot to do with organizational arrangements.

Even with the complete administrative centralization, most of the larger holdings from prerevolutionary state archives and libraries in fact remained for storage purposes in their prerevolutionary storage areas, or in those areas to which they had been removed for safekeeping during revolution and war. Archival records from a wide variety of prerevolutionary organizations, businesses, religious institutions, and private family papers, all of which had been by law appropriated by the state, only gradually found a permanent storage place. A depository for many former private holdings was set up in January 1919 in Moscow in the former mansion of Count Sheremetev (Vozdvizhenka, 8); this was not a permanent archive, however, but rather a center where papers were concentrated and stored until they could be sorted and transferred to the appropriate section of the state archives. Efforts were also made in Petrograd to collect papers from private sources and store them where space could be found. While some large groups of private papers were thus directly appropriated by state archives and stored with the earlier state materials, many others found their way into museums and library manuscript divisions, which continued to function as such, generally independently of the administration of Glavarkhiv.[16]

[15] For details about the early locations of literary fonds after the Revolution, see the article by L. G. Syrchenko, "K istorii komplektovaniia gosudarstvennykh arkhivov SSSR dokumental'nymi materialami deiatelei literatury (1918-1941 gg.)," *Trudy MGIAI* 15 (1962):345-77.

[16] See V. V. Maksakov, "Organizatsiia v SSSR arkhivnykh fondov byvshikh chastnovladel'cheskikh predpriiatii i fondov lichnogo proiskhozhdeniia," *Istoricheskii arkhiv*, 1957, no. 2, pp. 149-54.

Glavarkhiv naturally concentrated its own resources on the largest and politically most important state records and on working out a general administrative system to centralize and control the entire EGAF. In an effort to provide better administrative structure to some of the important state records in Moscow, the State Archive of the Russian Federation [Gosudarstvennyi arkhiv RSFSR], or Gosarkhiv, was established in 1920, drawing holdings from the first, seventh, and eighth sections of the Single State Archival Fond. Gosarkhiv, which as an admininstrative structure lasted only until 1925, had four divisions: 1) the documents dealing with foreign and domestic history of Russia to the end of the eighteenth century; 2) state documents of the nineteenth and early twentieth centuries; 3) documents on the history of revolutionary movements to 1 March 1917; and   4) documents from the Revolution itself and the period immediately following it.[17] Each of these divisions or their subdivisions centered on a major prerevolutionary repository or subsequently established collection. They were not intended as, nor did they become, comprehensive storage centers along strict subject-matter lines because they did not gather all the fonds related to their topics from other sources, nor were their own fonds strictly divided according to their subjects.

The first division, which was drawn entirely from parts of the original first section of EGAF, was divided into internal and external sections: Section A was based on the former State Archive of the Russian Empire from Petrograd, and Section B on the Moscow Main Archive of the Ministry of Foreign Affairs.

The second division, also drawn from parts of the first section of the EGAF, likewise had a Section A for internal affairs, absorbing the collection of important imperial papers from the late nineteenth century that had come to be called the New Romanov Archive [Novoromanovskii arkhiv], and a Section B, consisting of the former St. Petersburg Main Archive of the Ministry of Foreign Affairs.

The third division of Gosarkhiv RSFSR was founded on the Moscow division of the seventh (historical-revolutionary) section of EGAF, and subsequently absorbed the Petrograd Historical-Revolutionary Archive, which was transferred to Moscow. It soon effectively became a separate institution, the Moscow Historical-Revolutionary Archive [Moskovskii istoriko-revoliutsionnyi arkhiv].

The fourth division was also recognized as a separate institution, the Archive of the October Revolution [Arkhiv Oktiabr'skoi revoliutsii—AOR]; it had been officially established by a directive of Lenin in September 1920 to gather all the records of revolutionary events and their aftermath.[18] It grew out of the original eighth section of the EGAF in Moscow, which had been devoted to printed

[17] A detailed account of this archive was published by A. V. Chernov, "Gosudarstvennyi arkhiv RSFSR (1920-1925 gg.)," in *Trudy MGIAI* 4(1948):52-72.

[18] The regulation of 21 September 1920 is printed in *Sbornik rukovodiashchikh materialov* (A-99), p. 242. An early account of this archive is presented by V. Maksakov, "Piat' let Arkhiva Oktiabr'skoi revoliutsii, 1920—sentiabr'—1925," *Arkhivnoe delo* 5-6(1926):3-13. The formation and development of this archive up to 1938 is described by G. Kostomarov, "Tsentral'nyi arkhiv Velikoi Oktiabr'skoi sotsialisticheskoi revoliutsii," *Arkhivnoe delo* 47 (1938, no. 3):30-52.

materials from the period of the Revolution, and expanded to include not only all types of documentary materials on the Revolution, but postrevolutionary records as well. Until the special Communist Party Archive was founded later in the 1920's, it also controlled a large quantity of Party records.

The formation of Gosarkhiv RSFSR did not, however, affect the other sections of the Single State Archival Fond in Moscow, nor the archival arrangements already developing in Petrograd. Although some modifications were gradually being introduced in the original structure in the course of implementation, a new plan was officially adopted in 1922. The formation of the Central Archive of the RSFSR [Tsentral'nyi arkhiv RSFSR], or Tsentrarkhiv, introduced a new and more comprehensive administrative structure for Soviet archives, resulting in a complete reorganization and further centralization of the state archival system. The directorate of Tsentrarkhiv replaced the former administrative agency Glavarkhiv. Fundamental organizational work proceeded throughout the USSR as local divisions of Tsentrarkhiv were established and plans worked out for the systematic organization of repositories to house both prerevolutionary and current records.

At the same time, the principal divisions of the Single State Archival Fond were revamped to constitute five instead of the original nine sections: 1) political; 2) economic; 3) juridical; 4) historical-cultural; and 5) military-naval.[19] This did not, however, change the basic arrangement of storage areas which had been developing in Moscow, nor did it have the effect of regrouping the repositories already in existence. Gosarkhiv RSFSR simply continued as the first (political) section of the Moscow division of Tsentrarkhiv; it had already absorbed the original seventh and eighth sections of EGAF. The reorganization under Tsentrarkhiv did officially recognize some further consolidation which had taken place in other sections in the course of archival organization. The seventh and eighth sections were also liquidated in Leningrad, and further archival consolidation proceeded along the lines of the revised five sections of EGAF. In effect, these sectional divisions determined the basic organizational pattern for the newly constituted Leningrad Branch of the Central Archive of the RSFSR [Leningradskoe otdelenie Tsentral'nogo arkhiva RSFSR].

Tsentrarkhiv as an administrative entity and as a general organizational system lasted until 1929, but it never became the consolidated centralized repository for all state archival records that its name might suggest. The organization of repositories and divisions of the State Archival Fond were again reorganized in 1925, and at that point the tendency to establish a number of separate state archives under the general administration of the central archival agency emerged definitively. The earlier plans, which had sought to centralize all the Single State Archival Fond and organize it in rational sections, were to a certain extent thwarted by centrifugal tendencies reinforced by the established institutional arrangements, many of which had developed before the Revolution.

[19] The decree of 30 January 1922 is printed in *Sbornik rukovodiashchikh materialov* (A-99), pp. 19-21.

The original sectional divisions of the State Archival Fond continued to have an important effect on administrative arrangements for the state archives. But in 1925 the official sections were reduced to four: 1) economic; 2) political and juridical; 3) military-naval; and 4) cultural. The main change resulted from the consolidation of the political and juridical sections which had been separated in the previous divisions.

The most important organizational principle which emerged in 1925 was that of strict chronological divisions which were to dominate the organization and structure of archives in subsequent years. According to the regulation of 3 February 1925, state documents were to be organized into archives distinguished as historical archives for materials predating March 1917, and archives of the October Revolution for later documents. This formal distinction was to apply for all-union central archives as well as republic-level, regional, and other local archives, thus setting up a basic archival blueprint which was to be followed throughout the Soviet Union. At the same time the four subject-matter divisions determined the internal organization within the historical or October Revolution archives.[20] With some modifications and refinements these arrangements have dominated Soviet archival development ever since.

Despite the relatively simple formal pattern for archival organization, the actual arrangement of archival storage areas in Moscow and Leningrad was exceedingly complicated and reflected some basic changes from the situation that had existed earlier. In terms of storage for central governmental records, 1925 brought the formal establishment of a single Central Archive of the October Revolution [Tsentral'nyi arkhiv Oktiabr'skoi revoliutsii—TsAOR] in Moscow and two archives for prerevolutionary records: the Moscow Central Historical Archive [Moskovskii tsentral'nyi istoricheskii arkhiv] to consolidate the prerevolutionary documents that were stored in different Moscow repositories, and the correlated Leningrad Central Historical Archive [Leningradskii tsentral'nyi istoricheskii arkhiv] to bring together all the state documentary records still stored in various centers in the former imperial capital.

The new structural pattern for archives brought centralization of a distinctively Soviet type, but much more comprehensive—by virtue of the extension of state control to all types of records—than the national archives in many other countries. The trend toward a variety of separate archives under centralized bureaucracy, as opposed to a single integrated archive, had already become irreversible in previous institutional patterns, because of the sheer bulk and diversity of materials already well established in different locations and the lack of an adequate central storage area. The "historical" and "October Revolution" archives were established in name, but these names referred principally to an administrative superstructure which controlled materials actually stored in a number of different repositories. In 1925 many of these became in effect separate archives and were generally referred to by

---

[20] The regulation of 3 February 1925 is printed in *Sbornik rukovodiashchikh materialov* (A-99), pp. 109-11. Cf. Maksakov, *Istoriia i organizatsiia* (A-98), pp. 154-56.

their generic names rather than as subject-matter divisions of the central historical or October Revolution archives.

The situation was most complex in the case of the Moscow Central Historical Archive because, whatever may have been the aim of its founders, it remained a formal bureaucratic entity and never became a centralized archive for all prerevolutionary records. With the dissolution of the Gosarkhiv RSFSR as an administrative unit in 1925, there were actually five main storage areas where early documents had been consolidated in the early 1920's. These had grown up around prerevolutionary collections and had formed divisions of the original sections of the State Archival Fond; some had been shifted to the administration of Gosarkhiv RSFSR and others had remained independent sections of the Moscow branch of Tsentrarkhiv. Reorganization in 1925 and 1926 brought some major changes and even transfers of the entire holdings of some of the earlier institutions, reducing their number to the five archives which emerged as formal divisions of the Moscow Central Historical Archive. While they represented the new quadripartite subject-matter sections of the State Archival Fond as organizational divisions of the Central Historical Archive, they had effectively become separate state archives.[21]

The first—and organizationally best established, largely because of their long prerevolutionary history—were the predominantly pre-nineteenth-century historical records which were referred to at the time as the Repository of Earliest Records [Drevlekhranilishche]. Actually the newly combined political-juridical division of the Moscow Central Historical Archive, it was organized in the original building of the former Moscow Archive of the Ministry of Justice (MAMIu). To that distinguished archive, which had been the basis for the original Moscow juridical section of the State Archival Fond, were transferred the entire holdings of the former Moscow Archive of the Ministry of Foreign Affairs and of the former State Archive of the Russian Empire; these latter archives had been combined as Sections A and B of the first (political) division of the Gosarkhiv RSFSR. The contents of the former Moscow court archive were also transferred to this repository. The direct ancestor of the present-day Central State Archive of Ancient Acts, TsGADA [Tsentral'nyi gosudarstvennyi arkhiv drevnikh aktov], the Drevlekhranilishche continued to be a gathering point for additional important collections from disbanded monasteries and for a variety of prerevolutionary personal or family papers.[22]

[21] See Maksakov, *Istoriia i organizatsiia* (A-98), pp. 156-59. The extent to which these were later considered as having existed as separate archives in 1925 is apparent in the literature of the period and in the historical introductions to the published guides to their successor institutions. For a German impression of the Soviet archival organization in the mid-1920's, see the article by Heinrich O. Meisner, "Über das Archivwesen der russischen Sowjet-Republik. Beobachtungen während eines Studienaufenthalts in Moskau und Leningrad," *Archivalische Zeitschrift,* 3rd series, 5(1929):178-96.

[22] For a detailed description of the contents of this archive in the late 1920's together with a brief history of the different component parts, see the article by N. Lapin, "Drevlekhranilishche Moskovskogo Tsentral'nogo istoricheskogo arkhiva," *Arkhivnoe delo* 24-25 (1930, no. 3-4):40-68. For its subsequent development, see the references provided in note 29.

The second archive effectively recognized at that time as a separate institution was the Military History Archive [Voenno-istoricheskii arkhiv]. It grew out of the prerevolutionary Moscow Division of the Archive of the General Staff (the Lefort Archive) and incorporated other pre-1917 military documents including the Military Science Archive and the large group of fonds relating to the First World War, all of which had been brought together for storage purposes in the Lefort Palace as the Military-Naval Section of EGAF.[23]

The third institution came to be known as the Archive of the Revolution and Foreign Policy [Arkhiv revoliutsii i vneshnei politiki]. Combining the second and third sections of the Gosarkhiv RSFSR, this archive brought together the earlier Moscow (formerly Petrograd) Historico-Revolutionary Archive, the Novoromanovskii Archive, and the former St. Petersburg Main Archive of the Ministry of Foreign Affairs. After their transfer to Moscow these records were consolidated in the building which today houses the prerevolutionary division of the Foreign Ministry Archive (AVPR) (Bol'shaia Serpukhovskaia ulitsa, 15).[24]

The fourth division of the Central Historical Archive, effectively founded as a separate repository in 1925 under the name Archive of Economics, Culture, and Life [Arkhiv narodnogo khoziaistva, kul'tury i byta], actually combined the economic and cultural sections of the EGAF. Its contents, stored in the building formerly occupied by the Synod Library, had recently been brought together from a variety of prerevolutionary and predominantly private sources. It lasted as a separate repository only until 1934, when its holdings were all transferred elsewhere.

The Land Survey Archive [Mezhevoi arkhiv] also remained a separate archive in Moscow at this time, continuing with its records intact from the eighteenth century, only later, at the end of the thirties, to be incorporated into TsGADA.[25] It had earlier been the basis of the fifth (economic) section of the EGAF, but had not developed into a gathering point for related fonds.

The historical archive in Leningrad was structurally much more unified than its Moscow counterpart, probably because most of its holdings had been brought together in a single storage area. Called the Leningrad Central Historical Archive from 1925 to 1929, it then became officially the Leningrad Branch of the Central Historical Archive [Leningradskoe otdelenie Tsentral'nogo istoricheskogo arkhiva] until 1934, when it was split into four separate archives.[26] The complex of

[23] The first extensive published description of this repository was provided by I. Khripach, "Moskovskii Tsentral'nyi istoricheskii arkhiv: Voenno-istoricheskii arkhiv," *Arkhivnoe delo* 8-9 (1926):3-25. For later references, see note 30.

[24] See the early description of the organization of this archive by V. Maksakov, "Arkhiv revoliutsii i vneshnei politiki XIX i XX vv.," *Arkhivnoe delo* 13 (1927):27-41.

[25] See V. Gerasimiuk, "Kratkii istoricheskii ocherk Tsentral'nogo mezhevogo arkhiva (byv. Arkhiva Kantseliarii) 1768-1938 gg.," *Arkhivnoe delo* 51 (1939, no. 3): 127-35.

[26] A guide published in 1933 to this archive, the only state archive in Leningrad at that time, gives details of its then current organization and contents, *Arkhivy*

buildings on the Neva embankment facing the Senate Square that had housed the prerevolutionary Senate and Synod and their archives served as headquarters and as the storage area for three of its divisions—political and juridical, economic, and cultural. The Palace Archive [Dvortsovyi arkhiv] was initially housed elsewhere but subsequently consolidated into the central location.

The fonds which comprised the military-naval division, however, were stored in separate repositories. The main Naval Archive [Glavnyi morskoi arkhiv] effectively remained separate, housed in its prerevolutionary building where all the naval records had been consolidated after 1917. The military section, the outgrowth of the prerevolutionary Archive of the General Staff, likewise remained apart, but officially became a separate archive only in 1934.[27]

The 1925 reorganization had less effect on the Archive of the October Revolution, which had been developing as a distinctive institution since its establishment in 1920. It was henceforth called the Central Archive of the October Revolution (TsAOR) and its function was redefined to encompass all categories of revolutionary and postrevolutionary materials; its new subdivisions formally reflected the quadripartite divisions of the State Archival Fond. Although TsAOR remained structurally much more unified than the historical archives at that time, its formal divisions proved to be germs of future separate archival institutions.

The one division to be separated in 1925 and established as a distinct institution was the Archive of the Red Army [Arkhiv krasnoi armii—AKA], which took over all the postrevolutionary military records, including those from Leningrad.[28] A film and photographic archive was also organized in 1926, growing out of the early division devoted to those materials, but it remained under the administration of the central archive.

Some Communist Party files were housed in the Archive of the October Revolution in the early twenties, constituting a special section under the watchful eye of the Institute for the History of the Party and the October Revolution (Istpart). These remained part of the political division of the Central Archive of the October Revolution until, in 1928, they were consolidated with other Party files in the newly established Party archive.

Thus by the late 1920's the basic pattern of all-union central state archives that

---

SSSR. Leningradskoe otdelenie Tsentral'nogo istoricheskogo arkhiva, ed. A. K. Drezen (Leningrad, 1933) (B-103). For more details on the development of state archives in Leningrad before World War II, see I. Maiakovskii, "20-let raboty Leningradskikh tsentral'nykh arkhivov," *Arkhivnoe delo* 47 (1938, no. 3):125-44. See also the pamphlet by G. A. Dremina and T. V. Kuznetsova, *Tsentral'nyi gosudarstvennyi istoricheskii arkhiv SSSR v g. Leningrade. Uchebnoe posobie* (Moscow, 1959).

[27] The military and naval sections are also described in the 1933 guide cited above, note 26 (B-103); see below, B-21 and B-152.

[28] See M. Sokolov, "Tsentral'nyi arkhiv Krasnoi Armii za 20 let," *Arkhivnoe delo* 47 (1938, no. 3):53-68, for its development to 1938. See also the early guide to the holdings, *Arkhiv Krasnoi Armii,* compiled by A. K. Bochkov et al. (Moscow, 1933), which describes the archive as it was then organized.

was to prevail for the next half-century was emerging. The principle of an all-inclusive centralized repository for the different sections of the State Archival Fond had effectively given way to the principle of separate repositories for specific groups of fonds with a centralized administration coordinating them. Subsequent developments brought administrative and organizational changes, institutional name-changes, regrouping of fonds, and the separating of additional archives, but the basic system and principles of archival organization as they had been worked out at that time remained in effect.

The next major administrative reorganization occurred in 1929 with the creation of the Central Archival Administration of the USSR as well as the Central Archival Administration of the RSFSR. This bureaucratic structure resulted in some further reshuffling on the administrative level, and it was some time before the situation became stabilized. Most divisions of the Central Historical Archive remained under the RSFSR administration, but the postrevolutionary repositories under the Central Archive of the October Revolution became subject to the all-union administrative agency. At the same time, in the early thirties, the different divisions of the historical and October Revolution archives, were reorganized as separate archives and underwent some further restructuring; the Moscow and Leningrad Central Historical Archives as organized after 1925 soon ceased to exist as administrative entities.

The earliest historical division (Drevlekhranilishche) of the Moscow Central Historical Archive, which in fact had been a separate archive all along, was formally recognized in 1931 as the State Archive of the Feudal-Serfdom Epoch [Gosudarstvennyi arkhiv feodal'no-krepostnicheskoi epokhi—GAFKE]. This predominantly pre-nineteenth-century archive, which brought together the holdings of several prerevolutionary archives in the building of the former Moscow Archive of the Ministry of Justice, was the direct predecessor of the present-day Central State Archive of Ancient Acts (TsGADA).[29]

The military division in the Lefort Palace had already been recognized as the Military History Archive. In 1933, its name was officially changed to the Central Military History Archive [Tsentral'nyi voenno-istoricheskii arkhiv] and it came under the administration of the all-union Central Archival Administration.[30]

The Archive of the Revolution and Foreign Policy, which had also officially been a division of the Moscow Central Historical Archive, was split into its two

[29] A. Birze, "Gosudarstvennyi arkhiv feodal'no-krepostnicheskoi epokhi. K dvadtsatiletiiu leninskogo dekreta," *Arkhivnoe delo* 47 (1938, no. 3): 110-15, describes its formation and predecessors. See also the general summary of the history and development of the archive by G. A. Dremina, "Tsentral'nyi gosudarstvennyi arkhiv drevnikh aktov SSSR (K istorii obrazovaniia arkhiva)," in *Trudy MGIAI* 11 (1958):297-363, and in the pamphlet by G. A. Dremina, E. V. Kraiskaia, and Iu. F. Kononov, "Tsentral'nyi gosudarstvennyi arkhiv drevnikh aktov SSSR," in *Gosudarstvennye arkhivy SSSR. Uchebnoe posobie* (Moscow, 1959) (B-75).

[30] See I. Nazin and M. Semin, "Tsentral'nyi voenno-istoricheskii arkhiv," *Arkhivnoe delo* 47 (1938, no. 3): 85-99, for the development of this archive through the 1930's.

earlier components in 1933. The holdings from the former St. Petersburg Foreign Ministry Archive were established as the separate State Archive of Foreign Policy [Gosudarstvennyi arkhiv vneshnei politiki] under the direction of the archival administration of the USSR.[31] The historical-revolutionary division became the separate State Archive of the Revolution [Gosudarstvennyi arkhiv revoliutsii].[32] Both archives remained housed in the same building and used a common reading room; in 1941 they were reconsolidated into a single archival institution.

In this same period, the economic and cultural divisions of the Central Historical Archive in Moscow were effectively eliminated as separate institutions. In 1934 the Archive of Economics, Culture, and Life in Moscow was liquidated and many of its most important economic sections were transferred to the new economic archive in Leningrad. Other fonds that had been stored there were transferred either to the State Archive of the Feudal-Serfdom Epoch or to the Moscow oblast archive. The Land Survey Archive, however, remained as a separate institution until 1939, when it was amalgamated into the State Archive of the Feudal-Serfdom Epoch.

The same pattern of archival divisions was carried out in Leningrad. In 1934 the Leningrad Branch of the Central Historical Archive was reorganized to form four separate archives: the Archive of National Economy [Arkhiv narodnogo khoziaistva]; the Archive of Internal Policy, Culture, and Life [Arkhiv vnutrennei politiki, kul'tury i byta]; the Naval History Archive [Morskoi-istoricheskii arkhiv]; and the Leningrad Branch of the Military History Archive [Voenno-istoricheskii arkhiv]. Of these, however, only the Naval History Archive has endured as a separate institution, because in 1941 the first two were reunited (they had remained in the same storage area all along), and the fourth became a branch of the Central Military History Archive in Moscow and later was completely absorbed by that institution.

Some organizational changes also took place in the Central Archive of the October Revolution (TsAOR) in Moscow, but these were mostly related to the internal structure of the archive and the arrangement of fonds. The Archive of the Red Army, already established in 1925, became the Central Archive of the Red Army [Tsentral'nyi arkhiv Krasnoi armii] in 1933; it remained distinct from TsAOR throughout the 1930's and, under the archival administration of the USSR, continued to gather postrevolutionary military materials.

A separate repository for documentary films and photographs had been formed in 1926 as a division of TsAOR, and an all-union archive for sound recordings was established in 1932. These were combined in 1935 to form the administratively distinct Central Photo, Phonographic, and Film Archive of the USSR [Tsentral'nyi foto-, fono-, kinoarkhiv SSSR].

Also during this period a separate archive for trade union materials was established. Formed in 1930, the Central Archive of the Trade-Union Movement

---

[31] A. Iur'ev, "Gosudarstvennyi arkhiv vneshnei politiki i ego politicheskoe znachenie," *Arkhivnoe delo* 47 (1938, no. 3):116-24, describes the administration of this institution since the Revolution.

[32] See the short history of the location and administration of these materials in V. Dalago, "Arkhiv revoliutsii za 20 let," *Arkhivnoe delo* 47 (1938, no 3):79-87.

and Labor Organizations [Tsentral'nyi arkhiv profdvizheniia i organizatsii truda],
was administered independently of TsAOR until 1941, when its holdings were
transferred to the jurisdiction of the reorganized Central State Archive of the
October Revolution (TsGAOR).[33] The trade-union archive itself was subsequently
reorganized as a temporary repository where records are kept until consolidation
with the more permanent TsGAOR fonds.

Following the subordination of the Central Archival Administration to the
Commissariat of Internal Affairs and its reorganization as the Main Archival
Administration [Glavnoe arkhivnoe upravlenie NKVD] in 1938, there were again
administrative and structural changes in the organization of central state archives.
The reorganization of 1941 was most important in establishing the new system and
in setting up the basic nomenclature and organization of these institutions, which
have endured with relatively few subsequent modifications. According to the 1941
arrangement there were ten all-union central state archives, seven in Moscow and
three in Leningrad, all of which were directly under the Main Archival
Administration of the USSR. Of these ten, eight still exist today although there
have been several changes of name and some rearrangements of fonds.[34]

1) The Archive of the October Revolution had adopted the name of Central
State Archive of the October Revolution, with the acronym TsGAOR, in the late
1930's. In 1941 it was renamed the Central State Archive of the October
Revolution and Socialist Development [Tsentral'nyi gosudarstvennyi arkhiv
Oktiabr'skoi revoliutsii i sotsialisticheskogo stroitel'stva—TsGAOR]. This main
repository for postrevolutionary materials was reorganized into five divisions:
a) high organs of state power of the USSR and the RSFSR; b) courts and procura-
tors of the USSR and the RSFSR; c) economics; d) culture and life; and e) trade
unions, which took over the then liquidated Central Archive of the Trade-Union
Movement and Labor Organizations. It had subsections including materials regarding
the Provisional Government and the October Revolution which had been transferred
from Leningrad in the 1920's. In 1945 it absorbed the rich holdings of the émigré
Russian archive in Prague [Russkii zagranichnyi istoricheskii arkhiv], which was
transferred to Moscow after Communist rule was established in Czechoslovakia.

2) The Central State Archive of the Red Army [Tsentral'nyi gosudarstvennyi
arkhiv Krasnoi Armii—TsGAKA] continued to be the repository for postrevolutionary military documents, especially those relating to the Civil War.

3) The Naval History Archive in Leningrad, which had been reorganized as a
separate institution in 1934, was renamed the Central State Archive of the Navy
[Tsentral'nyi gosudarstvennyi arkhiv Voenno-Morskogo Flota—TsGAVMF] and
contained documents from the eighteenth century through the Soviet period.

---

[33] See T. Illeritskaia, "Sozdanie i deiatel'nost' Tsentral'nogo arkhiva profdvizheniia i organizatsii truda," *Arkhivnoe delo* 47 (1938, no. 3):69-78, and the
more recent article by N. A. Orlova, "Tsentral'nyi arkhiv profdvizheniia i
organizatsii truda (1930-1941 gg.)," *Trudy MGIAI* 15 (1962):199-228.

[34] The guides and descriptions of these archives published since 1941 are listed
in full in Part B and hence are not repeated here.

4) The Central State Historical Archive in Leningrad [Tsentral'nyi gosudarstvennyi istoricheskii arkhiv v Leningrade—TsGIAL], the principal repository for nineteenth- and early twentieth-century records, reconsolidated the holdings of the Archive of National Economy and the Archive of Internal Policy, Culture, and Life, which had been organized as two separate archives in 1934 but had remained together in the same building.

5) Its Moscow counterpart, the Central State Historical Archive in Moscow [Tsentral'nyi gosudarstvennyi istoricheskii arkhiv v Moskve—TsGIAM] reconsolidated the Central Archive of the Revolution and the Archive of Foreign Policy, much as had its predecessor before the 1934 split, and added a large section of private family papers, mostly of the nineteenth and early twentieth centuries, that had remained from the former Moscow Central Historical Archive. The foreign policy section was, however, separated from TsGIAM in 1946 and transferred to the jurisdiction of the Foreign Ministry to form the Archive of Russian Foreign Policy [Arkhiv vneshnei politiki Rossii—AVPR].

6) The Military History Archive remained essentially unchanged under its new name of the Central State Military History Archive [Tsentral'nyi gosudarstvennyi voenno-istoricheskii arkhiv—TsGVIA].

7) The former Leningrad Military History Archive officially became a branch of the Moscow archive [Filial Tsentral'nogo gosudarstvennogo voenno-istoricheskogo arkhiva]; it was later totally merged with TsGVIA in the 1950's, at which time its holdings were all transferred to Moscow.

8) The Central State Archive of Ancient Acts [Tsentral'nyi gosudarstvennyi arkhiv drevnikh aktov—TsGADA] was the new name given to the former State Archive of the Feudal-Serfdom Epoch (GAFKE). This principal repository for pre-nineteenth-century historical materials had recently incorporated the Central Land Survey Archive [Mezhevoi arkhiv] in 1939. In 1946 the post-1720 diplomatic records from the former Moscow Archive of the Ministry of Foreign Affairs were transferred to the newly established Archive of Russian Foreign Policy under the Foreign Ministry (AVPR), and some of the post-1775 records of local administration were transferred to regional archives.

9) A new Central State Literary Archive [Tsentral'nyi gosudarstvennyi literaturnyi arkhiv—TsGLA] was founded in Moscow in 1941; it combined the rich collection of literary manuscripts and personal papers gathered since the 1920's by the State Literary Museum [Gosudarstvennyi literaturnyi muzei], augmented by important holdings gathered from other state archives, libraries, and museums.

10) The Central State Archive of Film, Photo, and Phonographic Documents [Tsentral'nyi gosudarstvennyi arkhiv kino-, foto-, fono-dokumentov—TsGAKFFD] remained essentially unchanged after its establishment in 1935.

In addition to these ten central state archives, the 1941 regulations also brought the reorganization of state archives on the regional and republic levels which had been developing during the preceding two decades. The state archives of the Russian Federated Republic were under the direct administration of the all-union Main Archival Administration. Each oblast and krai had its own state archive, with

48

some branches in major administrative centers; for the RSFSR these totaled one hundred two state archives. These all combined pre- and postrevolutionary divisions in a single institution, except for the Moscow and Leningrad oblasti, where the tremendous volume of documentation dictated separate historical and October Revolution archives. In addition, there were six state archives of autonomous oblasti, nine state archives for national okrugi, and sixteen archives and four branches for the sixteen autonomous republics under the RSFSR. Records from republic-level institutions were at that time stored in TsGAOR SSSR in Moscow, as there was no separate central archive for the RSFSR.

State archives which had been developed in the other union republics were also affected by the 1941 reorganization. They all had their own republic-level archival administrations under the general supervision of the Main Archival Administration of the USSR in Moscow. The structure and organization of archives followed the pattern of all-union central state archives in Moscow and Leningrad, with pragmatic modifications according to the volume, nature, and previous organization of the records involved. For each republic there were anywhere from one to five central state archives, depending on local requirements, and state archives for every oblast and autonomous region within the republic.

This basic organization as established in 1941 has remained operative throughout the USSR in subsequent decades, although there have been a series of refinements in the system. On the all-union level this has resulted in the addition of several new central state archives, the dissolution of others, and the consequent relocation of many fonds. There have also been a number of changes in official nomenclature. Such changes at the center have also been reflected in regional archives; a number of structural changes have occurred in the archival organization of almost every republic of the Soviet Union.

With regard to all-union central state archives, developments in the 1950's saw the name of the Central State Literary Archive (TsGLA) officially changed to the Central State Archive of Literature and Art of the USSR [Tsentral'nyi gosudarstvennyi arkhiv literatury i iskusstva SSSR–TsGALI] in 1954. The Leningrad Branch of the Central State Military History Archive was abolished in the mid-50's; between 1955 and 1958 its contents were all transferred to Moscow, where they were consolidated with the Central State Military History Archive (TsGVIA). And in 1958 the name of the Central State Archive of the Red Army changed to the Central State Archive of the Soviet Army [Tsentral'nyi gosudarstvennyi arkhiv Sovetskoi armii–TsGASA].

Particularly significant for the overall archival organization, a separate archival administration was set up for the RSFSR in 1956, distinct from the all-union Main Archival Administration, and in 1957, a Central State Archive of the RSFSR [Tsentral'nyi gosudarstvennyi arkhiv RSFSR] was created in Moscow under this new administration. GAU RSFSR also administered the Central State Archive of the RSFSR Far East [Tsentral'nyi gosudarstvennyi arkhiv RSFSR Dal'nego vostoka] in Tomsk, which had been established in 1943 to bring together both pre- and postrevolutionary records from the territory comprising Khabarovsk krai,

Primor'e krai, and Chita oblast. At the time of the 1960-1961 reorganization, however, the separate archival administration for the RSFSR was abolished, and its archives came under the direct administration of a special division of the Main Archival Administration of the USSR.

Some further significant changes and reorganization of archives followed the 1960 shift of the Main Archival Administration from its subordination to the Ministry of the Interior to its more independent position directly subordinate to the Council of Ministers of the USSR.[35] Most important for the organization of postrevolutionary documents, the economic section of TsGAOR was separated out to form a separate institution, the Central State Archive of the National Economy of the USSR [Tsentral'nyi gosudarstvennyi arkhiv narodnogo khoziaistva SSSR–TsGANKh]. For storage purposes, however, the documents still remained in the same building. The official name of TsGAOR itself was changed to the lengthened form of the Central State Archive of the October Revolution, High Organs of State Government, and Organs of State Administration of the USSR [Tsentral'nyi gosudarstvennyi arkhiv Oktiabr'skoi revoliutsii, vysshikh organov gosudarstvennoi vlasti i organov gosudarstvennogo upravleniia SSSR]; its earlier acronym, however, has remained unaffected.

At the same time, the Central State Historical Archive in Moscow, TsGIAM, was formally liquidated, and the remainder of its holdings–most of which had previously constituted the early Historical-Revolutionary Archive–became the prerevolutionary division of TsGAOR. TsGIAM had already been significantly depleted by the removal of its foreign policy division to the Foreign Ministry Archive (AVPR) in 1946; after that year, when the Foreign Ministry took over the building in which TsGIAM was then housed, the remaining contents of TsGIAM had been moved to a storage area adjacent to TsGAOR so that the 1961 shift appeared to be a logical development. No major movements of documents were involved, although some of the personal family papers from TsGIAM were subsequently transferred to the Central State Historical Archive (TsGIA SSSR) in Leningrad. At the time TsGIAM was abolished, the official name of the Leningrad archive (TsGIAL) was changed to Central State Historical Archive of the USSR [Tsentral'nyi gosudarstvennyi istoricheskii arkhiv SSSR–TsGIA SSSR], thus dropping the city designation.

As a result of these changes in 1960-1961, the total number of central state archives of the USSR stood at nine, seven in Moscow and two in Leningrad. During the 1960's two new central state archives were founded to raise this total to eleven, although both the new archives are still in the process of formation. In 1964 a regulation called for the creation of a new repository for technical documents which hitherto had been a part of TsGAOR and TsGANKh, to be called the Central State Archive of Scientific and Technical Documentation of the USSR [Tsentral'nyi gosudarstvennyi arkhiv nauchno-tekhnicheskoi dokumentatsii SSSR–TsGANTD].

[35] For the archival regulation of 28 July 1961 and the official list of archives at that time, together with further commentary on the reorganization plan, see the references in note 4 above.

In 1967, an official regulation called for the splitting of the Central State Archive of Film, Photo, and Phonographic Documents into two separate archives. The film and photographic sections are to remain in their established location in Krasnogorsk near Moscow with the official name Central State Archive of Film and Photographic Documents of the USSR [Tsentral'nyi gosudarstvennyi arkhiv kinofotodokumentov SSSR–TsGAKFD SSSR], while the sound recording section becomes the basis for an additional archive with the name Central State Archive of Sound Recordings of the USSR [Tsentral'nyi gosudarstvennyi arkhiv zvukozapisei SSSR–TsGAZ SSSR]. Thus the official number of all-union central state archives currently stands at eleven, nine in Moscow and two in Leningrad.

The 1960's also saw considerable changes and reorganization in republic level and other local state archives throughout the Soviet Union. Following the central pattern some additional specialized archives were established in a number of republics, such as those for film and sound recordings and for literary materials. Reshuffling of contents continued among many of the state archives already in existence, but the specifics of these changes outside Moscow and Leningrad cannot concern us here.

In Moscow itself, the Central State Archive of the RSFSR, established in 1957, moved into its newly constructed building in 1964; this meant the transfer of a large volume of records from the TsGAOR complex, thus affecting the internal arrangement of fonds within that archive.[36]

A basic reorganization of archives in the Moscow region in the 1960's brought the establishment of the State Archive of Moscow Oblast [Gosudarstvennyi arkhiv Moskovskoi oblasti–GAMO] on the basis of the earlier State Archive of the October Revolution and Socialist Development of Moscow Oblast [Gosudarstvennyi arkhiv Oktiabr'skoi revoliutsii i sotsialisticheskogo stroitel'stva Moskovskoi oblasti–GAORSS MO], to house post-1922 oblast records. And in 1963 the former State Historical Archive of Moscow Oblast [Gosudarstvennyi istoricheskii arkhiv Moskovskoi oblasti–GIAMO] became part of the newly established Central State Archive of the City of Moscow [Tsentral'nyi gosudarstvennyi arkhiv goroda Moskvy–TsGAgM]; as now constituted this archive combines all the pre-1922 records of Moscow guberniia with records of the city of Moscow dating from both pre- and postrevolutionary periods.

Oblast-level archives in Leningrad retained their previous organization, although there were some comparable changes of nomenclature. The region of the former imperial capital now has three local state repositories: the Leningrad State Archive of the October Revolution and Socialist Development [Leningradskii gosudarstvennyi arkhiv Oktiabr'skoi revoliutsii i sotsialisticheskogo stroitel'stva–LGAORSS], the Leningrad State Historical Archive [Leningradskii gosudarstvennyi istoricheskii arkhiv–LGIA] containing prerevolutionary materials from the Leningrad guberniia, and the Leningrad State Archive of Film, Phonographic, and

---

[36] The guides and descriptions of republic and oblast state archives in Moscow and Leningrad are listed in full in Part G and hence are not repeated here.

Photographic Documents [Leningradskii gosudarstvennyi arkhiv kinofonofoto-dokumentov–LGAKFFD]. A fourth local archive for literature and art established in 1969 is in the process of formation.

These oblast-level archives, like others throughout the country, are directed by oblast-level archival administrations directly subordinate to the Main Archival Administration. They hence constitute an integrated part of the nationwide centralized state archival system. From the beginnings of archival development after the Revolution, the decentralized storage of local records has become a cardinal principle of archival administration. On occasion certain important local records might be removed to Moscow, and the decision of what constitutes local records involves thorny if not highly contested problems in some cases. But given the extreme size and the administrative organization of the Soviet Union, a more centralized storage system for local records would never have been feasible.

Similarly, as we have seen in the development of the all-union central state archives, decentralized storage areas became an established principle early in the twenties. Consolidation of holdings has always been a major consideration, but that consolidation has involved the formation of diverse special archival repositories for different categories of records or collections. Some of these grew out of pre-existing institutions; others developed from pragmatic or rational considerations. Similar subject-matter or chronological divisions are often reflected at the republic or regional level, if not by separate repositories, by administrative divisions within the archives themselves.

Whatever decentralizing tendencies may have accompanied these developments within the state archival system, however, have been kept in check by the strong overall planning and management of the Main Archival Administration. Not only does GAU provide general centralized administration, but it also sets uniform procedures and standards, and coordinates all state archival activities. Thus GAU directly supervises the eleven central state archives of the USSR, even though each retains a certain degree of autonomy, and it likewise administers the central republic-level archives of the RSFSR. Through its related and effectively subordinate republic, oblast, or other local-level archival administrations, GAU supervises and centrally controls the state archival system throughout the USSR.

Archives and Manuscript Repositories not under GAU

The system of state archives under GAU constitutes the most voluminous and extensive part of the Soviet archival scene and the one on which attention is usually focused in any discussion of archival organization and development. Actually, however, it remains only a part of a much more complex and multi-faceted picture which must be considered in an effort to understand the overall organization of repositories and hence to determine the present location of different types of materials. The initial aim of the complete administrative centralization of archival materials in Moscow and Leningrad has been countered by centrifugal forces throughout the development of the Soviet system, so that today, despite the well-organized and relatively centralized system of state archives, major archival repositories remain outside of its management and jurisdiction.

As a prime example, the system of state archives under GAU does not encompass the parallel archival system of the Communist Party; nor does it include the archives of the Foreign Ministry or of the Academy of Sciences and its many subordinate institutes and libraries. And it does not embrace the archival materials and manuscript collections in museums and libraries, many of which fall under the jurisdiction of the Ministry of Culture. On paper and in theory, the Main Archival Administration is of course in charge of the entire State Archival Fond (GAF), which, by definition, includes all the archival and manuscript wealth of the country. In practice, however, many actual repositories, containing a strikingly large and important segment of this wealth, lie outside its direct jurisdiction.

Most important in this regard are the archives of the Communist Party, which since their establishment in the 1920's have remained outside GAU administration. Just as the Communist Party throughout the country has its own organization quite separate from the state governmental bureaucracy, so the Party has developed its own archival system, quite independent of the GAU-administered state system.[37]

At the core of the Party archival system is the Central Party Archive of the Institute of Marxism-Leninism [Tsentral'nyi partiinyi arkhiv Instituta Marksizma-Leninizma pri Tsentral'nom komitete KPSS—TsPA IML]—in Moscow. Founded as the Single Party Archive [Edinyi partiinyi arkhiv] in 1928, it gradually combined the Lenin Archive, established in 1924, and the various Party records under the Institute for Party History (Istpart); some of these had been housed in the Archive of the October Revolution, but most of the Party records had separately been carefully guarded under Party control all along. In 1931 further consolidation of Party records brought them together with the Marx and Engels collections in the newly constructed Central Party Archive of the reorganized Marx-Engels-Lenin Institute. Party archives were also set up on local levels to retain Party files apart from regional state archives. The system of Party archives continued to develop during the 30's and 40's and always remained quite independent from the state archival system. And it goes without saying that these archives hold many of the most important and highly sensitive documents pertaining to the Soviet Union and its political leadership since 1917.

Also completely out of the hands of the Main Archival Administration are the carefully guarded official documents of the Foreign Ministry now controlled by the special Historical-Diplomatic Administration of the Ministry of Foreign Affairs [Istoriko-diplomaticheskoe upravlenie Ministerstva inostrannykh del SSSR],

---

[37] Details on the formation and early development of the Communist Party archive are given in the recent posthumous booklet by V. V. Maksakov, *Organizatsiia arkhivov KPSS (Uchebnoe posobie),* ed. Iu. F. Kononov (Moscow, 1968) (D-1), esp. pp. 56-87, 89-94. See additional bibliography on Party archives in Part D below.

organized in 1958.[38] The Foreign Ministry had already organized its own archive in the 1920's and has been retaining its own postrevolutionary records since 1917. The files from the Soviet period now constitute the Archive of Soviet Foreign Policy [Arkhiv vneshnei politiki SSSR], housed in the Foreign Ministry headquarters at Smolensk Square.

After the Second World War the Foreign Ministry also took over the administration and control of the prerevolutionary official records of Russian foreign relations going back to the reign of Peter the Great, or, more precisely, to 1720. These prerevolutionary documents constitute the separate Archive of Russian Foreign Policy [Arkhiv vneshnei politiki Rossii—AVPR], housed in the building formerly occupied by the Central State Historical Archive in Moscow (TsGIAM). The nineteenth- and early twentieth-century files from the former St. Petersburg Main Archive of the Imperial Foreign Ministry had, in fact, been housed in this building since their transfer to Moscow in the early 20's; in 1946 they were transferred from TsGIAM to Foreign Ministry administration. And at the same time, the eighteenth-century records which had been part of the former Moscow Archive of the Ministry (earlier College) of Foreign Affairs were removed from TsGADA and transferred to AVPR, thus ensuring Foreign Ministry jurisdiction over all official diplomatic records from the eighteenth century to the present. Like the earlier removal of Party archives to separate jurisdiction, this move resulted in the separation of another large and crucially important historical collection of state records from the general administration of the Main Archival Administration.

The Ministry of Defense also maintains its own archive independently of the central state system, but it retains only records dating back to the 1930's, and does not have the elaborate or permanent type of archival system that the Foreign Ministry has developed. Earlier postrevolutionary military records—most particularly those from the Civil War—are stored in the Central State Archive of the Soviet Army (TsGASA), but the sheer bulk of materials pertaining to the Second World War and the research establishment involved with their analysis necessitated a separate institutional arrangement.[39]

Another independent archival system comprises the holdings of the Academy of Sciences of the USSR and the academies of the various union republics containing records of major segments of the scientific and cultural life of the nation.[40] As they do from the Party and Foreign Ministry archives, representatives from the Academy of Sciences sit on the Learned Council of the Main Archival Administration, coordinate many of their archival procedures and policies with those of the state system, and participate in joint publication and catalog efforts. Nevertheless, from an administrative standpoint the Academy archives remain

[38] For more details and descriptive literature about the Foreign Ministry archives, see Part D below.

[39] For more details about the archive of the Ministry of Defense, see Part D below, and especially item D-15.

[40] The various archives and manuscript repositories under the Academy of Sciences of the USSR in Moscow and Leningrad are all described with bibliographies of their descriptive publications in Part C below.

completely independent, and in the course of the fifty years of Soviet power, have developed their own archival network. In 1964 the Academy set up its own archival directorate, the Council on the Organization of Acquisitions and Use of Documentary Materials of the Academy of Sciences of the USSR [Sovet po organizatsii komplektovaniia i ispol'zovaniia arkhivnykh materialov AN SSSR]. In 1967, the Academy held its first archival conference, which brought together representatives of the many archives and manuscript repositories under its jurisdiction. With much less overall administrative centralization than the state archival system, this network now centers on the main Academy archive in Moscow [Arkhiv Akademii nauk SSSR] which, from its formation in 1936 until 1963, had been a branch of the historically more important Leningrad Archive; although much of the research activity of the Academy of Sciences continues in Leningrad, the Leningrad archive now has branch status [Leningradskoe otdelenie Arkhiva Akademii nauk SSSR].

Like the Academy archives themselves, many of the other manuscript repositories under Academy jurisdiction have strong prerevolutionary roots, or are themselves direct descendants of historically important institutions, the distinction of which has often contributed substantially to their own continuing existence and independence. This is particularly true of the Manuscript Division of the Library of the Academy of Sciences in Leningrad, which since its foundation in the eighteenth century has possessed one of the largest and most renowned collections of early books and medieval manuscripts.

The many institutes under the Academy all maintain their own ongoing archives and many contain sizeable earlier archival fonds and manuscript collections usually related to their own research efforts. Prerevolutionary roots are particularly strong for such repositories as the Archive and the Manuscript Division of the Leningrad Branch of the Institute of Oriental Studies, which is the direct descendant of the Asiatic Museum founded under the Academy in 1818, the Archive of the Geographical Society founded toward the end of the nineteenth century, and the Archive of the Leningrad Branch of the Institute of History of the USSR, which took over the collection of the nineteenth-century Imperial Archeographical Commission and several other important prerevolutionary manuscript collections. The Manuscript Division of the Institute of Russian Literature, which still occupies the Pushkin House [Pushkinskii Dom], founded as a memorial museum and center of Pushkin studies in the early twentieth century, has grown to be one of the nation's most renowned repositories not only for its Pushkin collection but also for papers of many other cultural and literary leaders. It now includes the most important folklore archive in the country and a special section for its significant collection of early Slavic manuscripts. The Moscow-based Institute of World Literature, of more recent origin, has organized its own sizeable manuscript division containing a rich group of papers of Soviet authors. It also houses the unique Gor'kii Archive, organized after Gor'kii's death to gather all his papers and those related to his life and literary activities.

The Academies of Sciences of the different union republics, organized at various points during the past fifty years, all maintain their own separate archives.

Repeating the pattern of the all-union Academy of Sciences, archives or sizeable manuscript collections have grown up in many of their subordinate research institutes. And in Georgia and Azerbaijan the Academy of Sciences has organized special republic-level manuscript institutes devoted to the collection, preservation, and study of local historic manuscript treasures. Several major libraries under different republic academies, such as the State Public Library of the Academy of Sciences of the Ukrainian SSR in Kiev and the Central Library of the Academy of Sciences of the Lithuanian SSR in Vilna, also maintain valuable manuscript divisions.

Paralleling and often coordinated with the State Archival Administration, the various archives, libraries, and institutes under the Academy of Sciences have all undertaken extensive publication projects, both of archival documents based on their collections and of guides and inventories to their manuscript riches. Some have compiled bibliographical compendia of their publications and reference materials, and now a comprehensive bibliography of these descriptive publications is under way under the auspices of the Leningrad branch of the Academy archives.[41]

Various institutions under the Academy have also followed the nineteenth-century tradition of archeographical expeditions, uncovering extensive manuscript riches in many parts of the Soviet Union. Such finds have been most significant in the fields of medieval and oriental manuscripts, notably under the auspices of the Library of the Academy (BAN), the Institute of Russian Literature (Pushkinskii Dom), the Leningrad Branch of the Institute of Oriental Studies, and several institutes associated with republic-level academies. As a result of these efforts, an impressive number of early manuscripts has been located, described, and brought into the custody of institutions where they can be properly preserved.[42]

Particularly important in the general progress of location and cataloging of manuscripts has been the work of the Archeographical Commission, now under the Academy's Division of History, with its headquarters in Moscow. Headed for many years by the outstanding medievalist, Academician M. N. Tikhomirov (1893-1965), the Commission has laid out plans and is now actively engaged in the compilation of a comprehensive catalog of early Slavic manuscripts from before the sixteenth century. One of the most ambitious cataloging projects ever undertaken in this field, a preliminary list of such manuscripts to the end of the fourteenth century in Soviet collections was published in 1965.[43] The Commission also sponsors

[41] Under the direction of Iu. A. Vinogradov, the just published first volume covers the publications relating to the central Academy archives of the USSR, and also of other Communist bloc nations—*Arkhivy Akademii nauk sotsialisticheskikh stran. Bibliografia,* vol. 1: *1917-1968,* compiled by L. Kostadinova et al. (Leningrad: Izd-vo "Nauka," 1971, 251 p.).

[42] See the description of this work and suggestions for its further implementation by the director of the medieval section of the Manuscript Division of Pushkinskii Dom, V. I. Malyshev, "Zadachi sobiraniia drevnerusskikh rukopisei," *Trudy Otdela drevnerusskoi literatury Akademii nauk SSSR,* 20(1964):303-32.

[43] A description of the project was published with the first installment, N. B. Shelamanova, "Predvaritel'nyi spisok slaviano-russkikh rukopisei XI-XIV vv.,

conferences related to archeographical projects. As an outlet for learned articles and publications in this field, it has since 1957 published an important yearbook, *Arkheograficheskii ezhegodnik,* which also contains annual bibliographies of archival literature and documentary publications.[44]

Although the Academy of Sciences undoubtedly maintains the most extensive network of documentary repositories and is engaged in archeographical and general archival work more extensively than is any other organization outside the state system (GAU), there are many other collections which must be taken into account in any attempt to comprehend the extent and organization of Soviet documentary holdings. Of particular importance in the general cultural and historical field are the many rich manuscript divisions of libraries and museums under the Ministry of Culture.

Foremost in this category are the extensive archival and manuscript collections of the Manuscript Divisions of the Lenin Library in Moscow and of the Saltykov-Shchedrin State Public Library in Leningrad, both of which were established well before the Revolution. Not only do these institutions possess two of the most extensive library manuscript divisions in the world, but they are also active with their own cataloging and documentary publication projects and have engaged in numerous important archeographical expeditions. Several other small specialized libraries also maintain manuscript holdings of note, such as the Central Music Library and the A. V. Lunacharskii State Theatrical Library in Leningrad.[45]

University libraries, particularly those of prerevolutionary origin, have also tradionally been a gathering-point for manuscript riches. Notable holdings remain in those of Moscow, Leningrad, Kazan, Vilna, Odessa, and several others, and some of the newer universities, such as those in Central Asian republics, have also been building up holdings. In most cases, university archives per se have remained separate from the library collections and have usually been transferred—except for current records—to state oblast archives, but in some instances personal fonds or special documentary collections are retained in the library manuscript divisions.[46]

Among museums, the archival and manuscript holdings of the State Historical Museum in Moscow are probably the largest and best known. In fact, a large number of museums throughout the Soviet Union have their own manuscript divisions, with rich documentary holdings that have not as yet been brought under centralized administration or bibliographic control. During the 1920's and 1930's

khraniashchikhsia v SSSR (Dlia 'Svodnogo kataloga rukopisei khraniashchikhsia v SSSR, do kontsa XIV v. vkliuchitel'no')," *Arkheograficheskii ezhegodnik za 1965 god,* pp. 177-272. See A-17 for a listing of the index and supplement published separately.

[44] See below, A-69, for more details about this publication.

[45] For more detailed descriptions and bibliographies of library and museum manuscript holdings, see Part E for institutions in Moscow and Part F for those in Leningrad.

[46] Brief notes on manuscript divisions in university libraries can be found in the first chapter of *Biblioteki vysshikh uchebnykh zavedenii SSSR. Spravochnik,* compiled by E. Z. Levinson (Moscow, 1964) (see Appendix 1). MGU is covered below in Part E, LGU in Part F.

the State Literary Museum gathered one of the most significant collections of literary materials in the country, which in the 1940's became the basis for the newly founded Central State Literary Archive (now TsGALI); it has since acquired some new archival fonds of considerable interest. Many of the widespread memorial museums have gathered considerable manuscript materials, but the Tolstoi Archive under the Tolstoi Museum is the only example of the complete centralization of papers pertaining to a single author under a commemorative museum, similar as it is in effect to the Pushkin and Gor'kii collections under institutes of the Academy of Sciences; the Vladimir Maiakovskii Museum had started to set up such a centralized fond after its establishment in the 30's, but now the largest group of Maiakovskii papers is located in TsGALI. Other commemorative museums devoted to an individual scientist or cultural figure have retained manuscript materials of varying quantities and significance, from the Mendeleev Museum under Leningrad State University to the Chaikovskii House in Klin.

Several art museums, such as the Russian Museum in Leningrad and the Tret'iakov Gallery in Moscow, have sizeable manuscript divisions especially rich in personal papers. Documentary materials relating to music and the theater are widely dispersed. Some are concentrated in museums or libraries associated with individual theaters such as the Moscow Art Theater or the Leningrad Kirov Ballet Theater, or associated with educational institutions such as the Leningrad Conservatory. Others are concentrated in more centralized repositories such as the Glinka State Museum of Musical Culture, the Bakhrushin State Theatrical Museum in Moscow, and the Leningrad State Theatrical Museum in Leningrad.

Museums also contain such diverse documentary holdings as those relating to architecture and city planning in the Shchusev State Scientific Research Museum of Architecture in Moscow, those of the Leningrad Institute of Railroad Engineers, the map collection of the State Museum of the History and Reconstruction of Moscow, or the military documents in the Artillery History Museum in Leningrad.

As yet there has been no attempt to compile a systematic directory of museum manuscript holdings, although some individual museums have published descriptions or catalogs of their collections. In fact the breadth and diversity of archival and manuscript holdings in museums, libraries, and other smaller repositories in different parts of the country still defies description. Now, through the efforts of the Main Archival Administration and the Museum Research Institute under the Ministry of Culture, many of these holdings are being thoroughly cataloged and knowledge about them is being made more readily available to researchers.

In Russia, as in many other countries, the established church was traditionally the preserve of many of the most important medieval manuscripts. In the Soviet Union today few manuscript collections remain in church hands, the richest and most famous all having been absorbed into other state institutions. Most of these come under either the state archives, the Academy of Sciences repositories, or the Ministry of Culture. But in Armenia the most famous church-related collection has come under entirely independent state jurisdiction as a special institution under the republic's Council of Ministers. The library collection from the monastery of Echmiadzin, founded in the fifth century, is the oldest and certainly one of the most famous manuscript collections in the Soviet Union. Long the center of the Armenian Catholic Church, Echmiadzin became the cultural storehouse of Armenian manuscripts; in 1947 the entire collection was moved to a specially equipped building in Erevan, where it became the basis for the newly established Matenadaran, or State Manuscript Repository of the Armenian SSR.[47]

As is the case with church collections, few other manuscript collections in the Soviet Union still remain in private hands; in the case of oriental and medieval manuscripts, however, there are a few notable exceptions, just as there are a few important groups of personal papers that have not come under state archival control, especially those of contemporary literary figures.

Although the institutions mentioned above stand out as the most important archival systems or manuscript repositories in the Soviet Union, they do not begin to exhaust the list. In turning to different types of archives, mention should also be made of the centralized archive of feature films and shorts, Gosfil'mofond [State Film Archive] administered by the Motion Picture Committee of the Council of Ministers of the USSR.[48] And in the scientific realm, there is the special center for the retention of geological data, the State Geological Fond.

The enumeration of archives and manuscript repositories not under the Main Archival Administration suggests a continuing pattern of decentralization which has persisted during the first half-century of Soviet power. Yet when contrasted with the situation in Russia before 1917 or in most other countries, the present degree of coordination and control appears nothing less than revolutionary. Such progress—and most researchers would consider it progress—has been made largely because of the state's total commitment to complete documentary control, as evidenced in the conception of the State Archival Fond, and through the implementation of total bureaucratic control exercised by a special agency charged with archival administration and records management. Those decentralized elements that still prevail, particularly in the realm of miscellaneous documentary collections, reflect—as archives always reflect—basic bureaucratic patterns and administrative procedures. Although many of the various archival institutions appear to be going their own separate ways, such tendencies are countered by the centralizing forces of overall planning, standardization of procedures, and administrative coordination achieved by the Main Archival Administration in cooperation with the Academy of Sciences and other institutions involved.

Cataloging projects such as the directory of personal papers in archives throughout the country (A-9) and the comprehensive catalog of medieval Slavic

---

[47] An extensive description of the Matenadaran by A. G. Abramian was published in Russian translation, *Rukipisnye sokrovishcha Matenadarana* (Erevan, 1959), and a shorter survey entitled *Matenadaran* (Erevan, 1962) is available in English, Russian and Armenian. See also the short article in English by G. V. Abgarian, "The Matenadaran at Erevan," in *The Book Collector* 9(summer 1960):146-50. A detailed two-volume catalog is also available.

[48] For details about Gosfil'mofond, see Part D below, especially no. D-16.

manuscripts under way (A-17) reflect the benefits of centralized planning and control. Despite such advances the publication of finding aids and other reference materials remains woefully inadequate to the needs of researchers, as will be evident in later parts of this study. But the increased emphasis on the research-facilitating function of archives in recent years portends more progressive developments in this realm. The fact that the archival research institute, VNIIDAD, is studying such topics as general archival planning and computerized information retrieval may not assure an immediate solution to some of the complex organizational and reference problems involved for a large multinational state with a complex and extensive documentary heritage, but it suggests an awareness of and preoccupation with problems of archival management and location of documents that cannot help but promote efficient modernization and facilitate research.

PROCEDURAL INFORMATION

1. ARCHIVAL ARRANGEMENT

The centralization that is the great hallmark of Soviet archival administration has brought with it a high degree of theoretical standardization in internal organization, arrangement, and descriptive schemes. The formulation of strict methodological regulations and guidelines has imposed the new system and methods on virtually all archives and other manuscript repositories throughout the country, and the same formulae are being applied in the largest state archives as well as the smallest museum collections. Even some prerevolutionary materials which had been inadequately arranged under sundry earlier systems are gradually being rearranged to conform to the new standards. The extent of application, however, varies considerably from one repository to another; considerable cataloging backlogs and the legacy of varied or inadequate earlier classification procedures continue to plague most institutions. Indeed, the confusion resulting from past irregularities and changes in guidelines, frequent institutional shifts, and reorganization will probably never be satisfactorily overcome. Yet, despite the variations that still abound, it is helpful for scholars working in the USSR to know something about the general schema, which in many ways varies from systems used in many other countries.[1]

With the introduction of the concept of a comprehensive State Archival Fond (GAF) comprising all official records, as well as the varied manuscript and documentary legacy of the nation, the scope of state archives has been greatly expanded. Hence, the designation "archive" in Soviet usage is not only given to institutions that serve as depositories for non-current government records, but often is also used for repositories that serve as collecting agencies for personal papers, films, medieval manuscript books, and miscellaneous documentary collections. In fact, most officially designated state archives perform both depository and collecting functions simultaneously. The expanded scope of state authority in all realms of society and culture has been accompanied by heightened concerns for documentary preservation and control, in turn reflected in the development of specialized types of archives, such as those for literature and art, sound recordings, photographs, films, and scientific and technical documentation. There is accordingly an increased emphasis on the collecting function of archives and, at the same

---

[1] Details of the classification schemes are given in the basic textbook for the archival training program edited by the former director of MGIAI, L. A. Nikiforov, and the director of GAU, G. A. Belov, *Teoriia i praktika arkhivnogo dela v SSSR* (Moscow, 1966), esp. pp. 137-51, and in the handbook issued by the Main Archival Administration, *Skhema edinoi klassifikatsii dokumental'nykh materialov Gosudarstvennogo arkhivnogo fonda SSSR v katalogakh gosudarstvennykh arkhivov (Sovetskii period),* compiled by A. I. Avtokratova et al., edited by G. A. Belov (Moscow, 1962). An analysis of the cataloging work done before the Revolution is presented in the pamphlet by M. N. Shobukhov, *Opisanie dokumental'nykh materialov v arkhivakh dorevoliutsionnoi Rossii,* edited by K. G. Mitiaeva (Moscow, 1955). For comparison of the system of arrangement used in the USSR with those used elsewhere, see the description of the American and English principles in T. R. Schellenberg, *Modern Archives: Principles and Techniques* (Chicago, 1956), pp. 168-93. For a more precise definition of many of the most common Russian archival terms, see the glossary below.

time, the concentration of a wide variety of different types of documentation in state archival institutions.

But since archival storage in these realms has not been centralized, many specialized repositories not under the state archival system, such as those in libraries, museums, and research institutes, may also simultaneously house various institutional records, personal papers, maps, literary or musical manuscripts, and collections of medieval manuscript books or historical documents. As regards these smaller institutions, there is no standardization in nomenclature or in the division in which manuscript materials might be located. In some institutions early manuscript books or other papers might be found in the library. Elsewhere they might be in a special so-called "manuscript division," or in a "division of manuscripts and rare books," or in the institution's "archive." In some institutions, there might be several specialized divisions housing different types of materials, such as the State Historical Museum (GIM) in Moscow with its separate Division of Written Sources, for modern personal papers, and collections of historical documents, the Manuscript Division proper, for medieval manuscripts, and the Cartographic Division, for manuscript maps. Researchers should be alert to such different possible locations in their efforts to find materials reportedly housed in a specific institution. Also many subject-specialized manuscript repositories or archives may hold different types of materials acquired along with their main holdings that go well beyond the subject-scope of their institution.

Although in many instances both may be housed in the same division or in the same institution, a basic distinction remains between "archives" and "manuscript collections" in terms of the actual materials themselves. As normally used "archive" (often archives in English) refers to the non-current records of any institution, organization, or agency, produced in the course of its normal function or activity; as used in this context, the term "archive" usually implies a record-keeping purpose. In contrast to Western usage, in the Soviet Union the term "archive" is also used for personal and family papers, as well as those from all private institutional sources. And, as mentioned above, the word "archive" may also refer to the division or institution in which such records and collections of papers are kept.

In origin and nature, manuscript collections differ from archives in that their common feature is usually their collector or the broad subject matter that they represent. A collection (in Russian *sobranie,* or *kollektsiia*) often comprises a group of medieval Slavic, oriental, or other distinctive manuscripts. Or it might consist of a group of historical or literary documents, musical manuscripts, or famous autographs. Collections are not systematic records of any organization, but rather miscellaneous manuscripts or documents artificially assembled apart from their creating agencies or originating sources, and usually have some historical or literary value. They are traditionally named after the individuals who brought the manuscripts together or the institutions—such as libraries, monasteries, museums, or academies—where they were housed. A number of important prerevolutionary collections have been broken up and dispersed since the Revolution, but more recent Soviet archival practice has made increased efforts to retain earlier collections intact. In most present-day repositories, particularly those that specialize in traditional manuscripts rather than archival records, the collection has been guarded as a basic organizational unit. Where possible, original classification numbers have been retained to correspond with earlier catalogs, or corresponding cross-reference tables have been worked out. Usually repositories are supposed to assign fond numbers to collections as units and to modify their earlier arrangement schemes to meet current standards.

Following the generally accepted archival principle of provenance, Soviet archivists usually maintain records and manuscripts within a classification scheme that reflects as closely as possible their natural order in their originating source. They avoid, so far as possible, the imposition of rationalized filing schemes. However, because of the complicated history of archives, documentary migrations, and frequent reorganization of archival holdings, the reality of archival pressures has forced compromise with the ideal. In many cases respect for the original organization of the materials in their creating agency has given way to respect for their previous organization in an earlier repository where they had been arranged and described in a workable form.

The imposition of rationalized chronological or subject-matter divisions in the course of postrevolutionary archival development has resulted in the creation of some artificial groupings, which might technically be considered archival collections. Such has been the case with many of the groupings in the Communist Party archives. The prerevolutionary division of TsGAOR containing police records that had originally been brought together to form the Historical-Revolutionary Archive in the 1920's is a prime example of an entire archive artificially created around the revolutionary movement as a special subject without regard for the integrity of the records of the creating agency of the documents. The Lenin, Tolstoi, and Gor'kii archives are further examples of artificially assembled groupings, where attempts have been made to centralize all the papers pertaining to a single individual. Such efforts at consolidation have had certain research advantages, particularly in cases in which over the years documents from a single institution or relating to a single individual have been dispersed into a number of different repositories. However, in recent years archivists have been reacting against such centralizing tendencies, and they are now only rarely being put into practice.

The basic organizational unit within all Soviet repositories is the *fond,* a type of archival grouping which, in name and concept, derives from the practice in some European archives.[2] All documents or manuscripts in archives and other re-

---

[2] The closest technical equivalent in American archival terminology would be the concept of a "record group," or, in British usage, "archive group." These terms, however, should not be used as exact translations. In the Soviet Union, unlike other countries, the term "fond" is used in all archives and manuscript repositories and for all types of materials, whether personal papers, institutional records, or manuscript or other documentary collections. And in Soviet archival arrangement, a "fond" might also be the equivalent of a "series" or "subgroup," as such subdivisions might be designated in the U. S. National Archives. To avoid

positories are now divided into fonds (or in the Russian plural *fondy*) and assigned permanent fond numbers. Individual archival fonds bear a direct and logical relationship to their provenance, i.e., the source or originating agency of the materials. The papers of large governmental units such as ministries, for example, are normally divided into many different fonds, each containing documents from a specific office or well-defined section of the organization. These different fonds are usually assigned contiguous fond numbers; collectively, however, they might be spoken of as the "fond" of their particular ministry.

By the same scheme, all the personal papers coming from a particular family or individual would be considered a single fond and assigned a single fond number, although for a large group of family papers stretching over several generations, different fond numbers might be assigned to the papers of different individuals within the family. The fond is commonly referred to by the name of the family whose papers it contains, but the Soviet use of this concept is much more rigid than the equivalent English "papers," particularly since it always bears the basic archival classification or fond number.

The practice of dividing all archival documents into fonds has not always been in use in the Soviet Union; hence earlier classification systems carry over in many repositories, especially for manuscripts that have been transferred from extinct institutions. Gradually, as recataloging proceeds, they are brought under the present principles of classification and assigned fond numbers, although the internal arrangement established by the original archive, if adequate, is apt to be retained to avoid scholarly confusion. For example, in the former State Archive of the Russian Empire, documents from which are now located in the Central State Archive of Ancient Acts (TsGADA), the classification division was known as a *razriad*; within TsGADA, each *razriad* has simply been assigned a separate fond number without revamping the original organization. Again, in the Archive of Russian Foreign Policy (AVPR), many of the prerevolutionary filing schemes have also been retained. Documents remain grouped according to the institutional organization of the ministry and retain the divisional names rather than fond numbers; thus the entire chancellery division is still classified as a single fond and has not been broken down or reclassified into fonds covering smaller sections.

Within individual fonds, materials are normally not arranged in intermediate rationalized subgroups or series divisions as is the practice in many Western archives. The division into separate fonds is usually made in a logical and meaningful way reflecting the origin of the records or manuscripts so that intermediate rational subdivisions are deemed unnecessary. Fonds are divided or

---

any confusion it is preferable to retain the exact term "fond" rather than to use any other English word in translation. A helpful compendium of Soviet archival terminology was published recently by GAU: *Kratkii slovar' arkhivnoi terminologii*, ed. I. S. Nazin et al. (Moscow/Leningrad, 1968). Some of the most important terms are explained in G. M. Gorfein and L. E. Shepelev, *Arkhivovedenie. Uchebnoe posobie* (Leningrad, 1971), pp. 9-11. For further explanation see the glossary below.

arranged directly into basic filing units; each *edinitsa khraneniia* (literally, "storage unit") is assigned a number within the fond. In the course of arrangement, the individual storage units are listed in a master inventory, or *opis'*. However, in the case of larger fonds, or according to some classification procedures, a fond may have more than one *opis'*, and in some instances different *opisi* may serve as a type of series division. When there is more than one *opis'*, an *opis'* number is also assigned, and the full identification or citation of an item would also necessarily include the *opis'* number. When the fond has only one *opis'*, however, usually no number is cited.

As well as providing the administrative control or shelf list, the *opis'* also serves as the preliminary descriptive inventory, and hence the basic finding aid for the fond. The amount and nature of descriptive information recorded in the *opis'* varies considerably from fond to fond or from institution to institution. Some may be prepared hurriedly in exceedingly abbreviated preliminary form; others may be highly refined with an exacting amount of technical and substantive detail. Basically, the *opis'* lists the physical or structural nature of the contents of each storage unit and the number of items or folios contained therein. Ideally it will also list substantive elements such as the date or dates covered, the persons addressed in the case of correspondence, the organizational and functional origin of the items, and other pertinent identifying or analytic information; if the fond had been previously inventoried or had once been part of a different fond, the previous classification number is also recorded.

Each storage unit, or *edinitsa khraneniia*, as the smallest grouping within the fond, bears a separate number. The unit may be an individual manuscript or group of documents, as the term is now used both for manuscript collections and for archives. In many state archives with official records, such a unit consists of an individual *delo* (plural, *dela*), or classification item, and is referred to as such; it may be a large dossier with several folders, or a file folder containing a group of letters, memoranda, or reports. An individual storage unit might consist of a single charter or manuscript book, a film, or a bound album of documents, or a *sbornik* [convolute or collection], consisting of several manuscripts or copies of manuscripts bound together.

Storage units are set up to comprise logical and easily identifiable categories. For example, in the case of personal papers, a unit might include all the correspondence of a specific individual with another individual, or the manuscript draft of a complete literary work, or it might consist of a single letter. Often letters received during a specific period or other groups of papers have been bound together or pasted in bound volumes, as it was customary in many families and institutions to bind papers together; in such cases, a storage unit would consist of a single volume. Usually archival folders rather than bound volumes are used today, but papers already bound in volumes have usually been retained in their original form, unless the materials were bound without any semblance of workable organization.

Although strict guidelines are now in operation for the arrangement of materials into storage units, in cases of fonds previously inventoried with a workable *opis'*, archivists tend to retain the original arrangement scheme to avoid the confusion of change and to give cataloging priority to their backlog of unclassified or inadequately described fonds.

Within each unit that consists of more than one folio or page, the folios [*listy*; singular, *list*] are numbered consecutively, normally only on the recto; the verso is normally cited as the *oborotnaia storona* (abbreviated *ob.*). When ordering documents in an archive, the reader does not usually need to give the folio numbers, because documents are brought out as complete storage units.

Full citation from archival sources should thus usually contain, following the standard abbreviated name (or acronym) of the archival repository: 1) the number and preferably also the name of the fond, 2) the inventory or shelf list [*opis'*] number, if applicable, 3) the storage unit [*edinitsa khraneniia* or *delo*] number, and 4) the folio [*list*] numbers. In the case of shorter documents or letters, when the names of the correspondents and the date of the letter are furnished, it is often not necessary to cite the folio number in addition.[3]

2. PUBLISHED FINDING AIDS

Published finding aids and other descriptive literature for archives and manuscript repositories also follow more or less standard formats in the Soviet Union, although there have been a number of variations in the past.[4]

The most basic type of published finding aid for Soviet archives is the *putevoditel'* [guide]. It is the most common form of published description for state archives, and its format has also been adapted for a number of other types of manuscript repositories. Normally a single volume covers a separate archive, providing a short history and general description of the holdings. It is usually arranged in accordance with the major archival subdivisions, such as documents

---

[3] The following abbreviations are usually used in Soviet citations: *fond=f.; edinitsa khraneniia=ed.kh.; delo=d.; list, listy=1.,11.* Particularly since folio numbers have usually been added later, and in some cases changed in the course of archival rearrangement, dates where available are important in citations. In note-taking, however, it is often advisable to record the folio numbers for future reference if needed, or for ordering copies.

[4] Detailed formulae for preparing these publications, along with the shelf-lists from which they are taken, are outlined in the text by Belov and Nikiforov, *Teoriia i praktika arkhivnogo dela v SSSR,* pp. 162-300. A description of the different types of finding aids with examples and illustrations from the perspective of researchers is given by G. M. Gorfein and L. E. Shepelev, *Arkhivovedenie. Uchebnoe posobie* (Leningrad, 1971), pp. 33-53. For more precise definitions of the Russian terms for different finding aids, see the glossary below.

from particular periods or types of institutions, or special collections of manuscripts; most often the division is between prerevolutionary and postrevolutionary materials (in cases where both are housed in the same repository) and between official documents and manuscript collections or personal papers. Further subdivisions follow standardized formats for different types of archives.

The *putevoditel'* systematically covers the major—and often lists the minor—fonds in the archive, giving their fond numbers and a precise description of their contents. It does not, however, furnish the storage unit numbers, beyond indicating how many units there are in a given fond and what dates they cover. It usually lists the most important names of individuals or government offices whose correspondence and other papers are to be found in the fond. Considerable variance will be found in the amount of detail actually furnished, and a scholar cannot necessarily assume that all important contents will be mentioned. The most scholarly type of *putevoditel'* will usually give a brief history of the fond or group of fonds involved and will give precise bibliographic references to more detailed catalogs or publications that have been made from the repository.

Unfortunately, however, most Soviet repositories lack adequate published guides; in the case of many state archives, guides published earlier have never been brought up to date despite considerable archival reorganization, new acquisitions, and transfers of holdings. Some repositories that have not prepared a complete *putevoditel'* publish more generalized surveys of their holdings. Such a publication might be entitled a *spravochnik* [handbook] or *kratkii spravochnik* [short handbook], an *obzor fondov* [survey of holdings] or *kratkii obzor* [short survey]. Depending on the extent of coverage, it might be issued in book, pamphlet, or article form, and might describe the contents of the entire institution or only selected highlights. Normally a survey of this type does not provide fond numbers; rarely does it provide sufficient detail about the size or contents of the holdings to serve as an actual finding aid. Nonetheless, in the absence of more detailed information, it may provide the only indication of the general nature of the holdings of a given repository or the location of certain bodies of materials. And in some cases, a book-length *obzor* covering a particular section of an archive or devoted to a specialized subject might provide as much scholarly detail as a more traditional *putevoditel'*.

Soviet scholarly journals in recent decades have published a prodigious number of article-length surveys of archival materials relating to specialized subjects. These range from highly scholarly descriptions of specific fonds or manuscript collections in a single repository to more generalized coverage of materials on a given subject in a number of different institutions. Their value as finding aids varies as considerably as do their length and orientation, but because of the characteristic dearth of alternative finding aids they can be of crucial importance in revealing the nature of documentation available. Although *obzor* is the most frequent term used as part of the title, such surveys may appear in a wide variety of formats and of different types of publications; hence they often remain defiant of comprehensive bibliographical control. The large majority, however, can be located through specialized subject bibliographies and usually appear in general bibliographies of archival literature.

The most detailed and therefore valuable type of archival finding aid is the actual inventory or manuscript catalog. The titles *opis'* [inventory], *opisanie* [description, or descriptive catalog], or *katalog* [catalog], may indicate different degrees of detail, but are often used interchangeably (see glossary). Taking as its basis the preliminary *opis'* or shelf list of the fond or collection, the inventory enumerates, item by item or unit by unit, the contents of the specified fond or part thereof, usually on the basis of the actual manuscript, storage unit, or *delo* numbers. The amount of detail provided varies widely; the most scholarly versions provide considerable technical data about the structural and substantive nature of the manuscripts or records involved.

Comprehensive inventories of the calendar type are rare for modern archival fonds because of the bulk of records involved; but detailed inventories that were prepared before the Revolution for a few important groups of early records still serve as basic finding aids. A few inventories of this type have been published since the Revolution, the most detailed of which cover some holdings in repositories under the Academy of Sciences. Regrettably few examples of the inventory type of finding aids have been issued by state archives, the notable exception being the series of sketchy pamphlets covering some major literary figures and a few other scattered volumes mostly covering personal fonds.

Detailed catalogs are more usual in the case of special manuscript collections. Institutions under the Academy of Sciences have been most productive in this area, but still relatively few collections have benefited from the tremendous scholarly effort involved. Unfortunately, many manuscript collections in Soviet repositories still have to rely on early prerevolutionary catalogs, despite their often outmoded technical and substantive descriptions. Renewed efforts undertaken in recent years have resulted both in some measure of bibliographic control of earlier catalogs and in some new comprehensive catalogs. Nevertheless, many decades of increased staff and scholarly output will be necessary to overcome the substantial cataloging backlog in most manuscript repositories.

In addition to the specific types of finding aids described above, a number of specialized reference publications have been prepared to help scholars locate specific types of materials in a number of different archives, to provide bibliographic information about published finding aids, or to serve as a directory for specific types of repositories. These general reference aids, which cover more than one archive, will be described in the general bibliographical introduction below.

Archival finding aids and related publications—especially the *putevoditeli* issued by state archives—are normally not offered for commercial sale in bookstores in the Soviet Union. When still available, they are usually sold only by the issuing repository, but since they are issued in extremely small editions they invariably become immediate bibliographical rarities. Visiting scholars should also be warned that in some instances reference copies of older guides and published catalogs are not always readily available for use in Soviet libraries. Some institutions maintain the practice of keeping a reference copy of their basic finding aids up-to-date with pencilled corrections and additions, but unfortunately this is the exception rather than the general rule.

3. ACCESS TO RECORDS

The question of access to archives or manuscript collections is apt to be the first consideration of a foreign scholar contemplating research in the Soviet Union. It would be easier to explain if the Soviet authorities had a clear rule on the subject. But even to the extent that there is a policy on paper, practice varies considerably, so that exceptions rather than general rules often seem to guide individual cases at different times.

The situation is further complicated because many basic factors which may adversely affect permission to work in archives are not really archival matters at all. The most fundamental difficulty is, of course, that of traveling to the Soviet Union; a foreigner cannot simply arrive—as he can in most countries of the world—without complicated prior arrangements and approvals. The act of withholding or delaying the necessary visa can prevent a legitimate scholar from even applying for archival access. Even the increasing ease of obtaining a tourist visa really does not help the potential researcher, because arrangements for archival access are so complicated for foreigners (see section 4 below) that it is usually out of the question for anyone not going as an official cultural exchange participant.

As an official exchange visitor, the scholar has a sponsoring Soviet institution, with established procedures for archival applications, and an official Soviet host scholar or advisor whose personal interest and assistance may often prove the crucial element in archival arrangements. However, many people who might have legitimate reasons for archival research may not qualify for the student or senior scholar exchanges from their home countries. Moreover, by rejecting exchange nominees for a variety of political, scholarly, or personal reasons, the Soviet Union may effectively prevent archival access before an application even reaches the archival administration.

Since 1956 Soviet archives have been gradually opening their doors to interested researchers from all parts of the world. This tendency corresponds with the increasing emphasis on archival research within the Soviet scholarly community and with the general expansion of the Soviet research establishment. Policies enunciated by the archival administration in the late 50's reflect the increased emphasis on the research-facilitating function of archives.[5] To be sure, there remain certain archives

---

[5] The move toward opening Soviet archives in the mid-1950s is revealed, for example, in the article by L. I. Iakovlev, "Zadachi sovetskikh arkhivnykh

where foreigners have not worked, and there remain many files which have been difficult, if not impossible, to consult. Yet published lists of scholars who have worked in state archives in recent years and their topics attest to the wide range of materials that have been open and the many individuals who have taken advantage of Soviet archival riches.[6]

This increasing openness of Soviet archives is a rather new development, and earlier attitudes have not been completely obliterated. The Soviet Union has traditionally viewed archival research, especially by foreigners, as a special privilege, not as an unrestricted public right. This attitude further reflects a tendency—by no means limited to the Soviet Union—to consider the prime archival function to be that of protecting and preserving documents. As a corollary of this view, and as a second important function of archives, documents should be made available to the public only through highly selective documentary publications, often with recognizable political objectives. Making documents readily and openly available to researchers has been seen as a definitely subordinate function. Such attitudes definitely preclude the type of widespread or comprehensive microfilm publication projects that have been undertaken in the United States. Since 1956, the research-facilitating function of archives has been significantly increased, but the carry-over from earlier policies may often still be encountered, particularly in the persisting procedure by which archival officials choose which documents an individual foreign reader should be shown.

With the gradual opening of archives to foreign scholars in the late 1950's and early 60's, the Soviet Union started enunciating an ostensibly liberal policy of access. Typical of such announcements is the statement of the director of the Main Archival Administration, published in a British archival journal, that "the use of documents preserved in the state archives is completely democratic" and that "any citizen, irrespective of his social position or his place of work or education, can study in the state archives." In practice, even Soviet researchers would have reason to question this claim were it not carefully modified by the accompanying

---

uchrezhdenii v svete reshenii XX s"ezda KPSS," *Istoricheskii arkhiv,* 1956, no. 3, pp. 171-78. It is also demonstrated through the increased use of party archival sources in Soviet dissertations since 1953, as noted by John Armstrong, "Clues to the Soviet Political Archives," *Russian Review* 16 (April 1957): 47-52.

[6] *Tematika issledovanii po dokumental'nym materialam v Tsentral'nykh gosudarstvennykh arkhivakh SSSR. Spravochnik,* Part 1: *za 1962 g.* (Moscow, 1964; 303 p.); Part 2: *za 1963 g.* (Moscow, 1965; 259 p.); Part 3: *za 1964 g.* (Moscow, 1965; 252 p.); Part 4: *za 1965 g.* (Moscow, 1966; 242 p.); Part 5: *za 1966 g.* (Moscow, 1968). These volumes list the names and research topics of people who have worked in the central state archives. The first volume for 1962 has a supplementary list of 95 foreigners who that year used central archives, most of whom were from Eastern Europe. See also the general remarks on access, especially with reference to contemporary military history, by John Erickson, "A Marginal Note on Soviet Archives," in *Contemporary History in Europe: Problems and Perspectives,* ed. D.C. Watt (London, 1969; New York, 1969), pp. 345-51. See also the remarks of a recent visiting British scholar, Geoffrey A. Hosking, printed in *History* (London) 55 (1970):211-13.

statement that "although naturally, as in every country, there is limited access to particular documents affecting the interests of the state or of individual citizens."[7] Foreign scholars have generally found the phrase "limited access" to be more appropriate to the overall policy; this appraisal is particularly apparent to American scholars, who might compare Soviet practice with the relatively open-door and open-catalog policies of the National Archives, and to British scholars familiar with their government's new policy of a thirty-year as opposed to the former fifty-year time lag after which state records may openly be consulted.[8]

In most countries the date of a particular document or record group is usually the most important factor in determining access for scholarly research. Soviet archives, however, are remarkably liberal in this regard, their officially announced policy being that "there are no limits of date restricting the issue of documents to searchers in the Soviet Union."[9] But though official policy avoids any strict time-bound regulation, dates do have a general bearing on the ease of access to certain records.

Generally, documents dating from the post-1917 period are likely to be closed, particularly to foreign scholars; such a policy would coincide with the fifty-year rule, long in force in many countries. However, many exceptions can be cited where relatively apolitical materials, such as literary manuscripts from postrevolutionary years have been made available to foreign researchers. A negative policy is more likely to apply to foreigners in the case of political, economic, and definitely military and diplomatic documents, although a few chosen scholars from neighboring Communist nations have been shown highly selected documents from later years. At the other end of the time spectrum, medieval manuscripts and archival materials up to and usually including the eighteenth century are almost invariably open. Although the older the documents the more likely they are to be accessible to research, the date of a given set of documents is usually not likely to be the controlling factor governing access.

The criterion of "interest of state" is rarely openly admitted to a scholar applying for a particular set of documents, but political sensitivity is usually the

---

[7] G. A. Belov, "The Organization of the Archive System in the USSR," *Archives* 6 (October 1964): 219-20.

[8] For a comparative perspective on the problem of liberalization of access to archives, see the discussion and recommendations in the report presented to the Sixth International Congress on Archives in Madrid in September 1968, on behalf Of the Working Group of Liberalization, by Charles Kecskeméti, "La libéral-isation en matière d'accès aux archives et de politique de microfilmage," *Actes du VIe Congrès international des archives (Madrid, 3-7 septembre 1968), Archivum* 19 (1968):25-48; the report was earlier available in English translation in mimeographed form for congress participants. See also the earlier discussion of the problem of access in the earlier congress and committee reports cited by Kecskeméti. To cite two conservative examples, the Vatican has only recently advanced to 1878 the date up to which its records may be consulted, and Belgium has, not long since, adopted a "fifty-year rule" in place of a "hundred-year rule" for its official documents.

[9] G. A. Belov, "The Organization of the Archive System in the USSR, "*Archives* 6 (October 1964):219-20.

reason suspected when documents are not readily available. The Soviet Union is certainly not alone in its restriction on archival use for reasons of state or political interest, but it often tends to apply such restriction to much broader categories and time-spans than is the case in most other nations. Political factors are understandably the major causes of the continued closing of the Communist Party archives to foreign, and generally non-Communist, scholars, and is certainly also considered the reason for the closing of all postrevolutionary military and diplomatic archives and many other political and economic documents dating from the Soviet period. But in the Soviet Union, reason of state can—with much less apparent reason—also affect the availability of certain prerevolutionary materials such as those pertaining to Jewish or non-Russian nationality affairs, and most particularly those pertaining to military or foreign policy. Foreigners often have difficulty understanding why documents regarding Russo-Turkish relations in the 1860's or 1880's, or those regarding Russo-Polish relations in the late eighteenth and early nineteenth centuries, could affect current foreign relations, but these types of restrictions are often applied even to many Soviet citizens and to scholars from neighboring nations in Eastern Europe.

Equally frustrating to foreign scholars is the Soviet practice of restricting archival access on the basis of research topic. There have been a number of instances in the past in which a graduate student has been refused as an exchange participant because "his topic is not studied at Soviet universities." In other words, it is often not just an archival matter of keeping certain files closed, but rather a broader attempt to control subjects on which exhaustive research is permitted. In some cases the very nature of the topic might be cause for refusal, as might the scholar's approach to his subject as revealed in his initial statement of purpose. Many diplomatic or contemporary political topics are as likely to be ruled out as are studies of certain sensitive literary figures, revolutionaries, or reactionary intellectuals. And yet archival files that are not available for one topic might with some modification be open for a closely related one. In many cases such a decision would not come from the archive itself, but rather from the Soviet institution with which the foreigner is affiliated during his stay in the country. Soviet scholars must normally have the approval of their institutions for research projects, and the right of similar control is usually extended to foreigners.

Another perturbing type of control over archival access is the policy, practiced in the state archives under GAU, of reserving for archival officials the right and obligation to choose which documents individual foreign researchers should be shown for a specific research topic. In other words, even after he has been admitted to a state archive a scholar is not free to choose and order those documents he might want to consult. Nor is he free to examine the comprehensive inventories or shelf lists (*opisi*) that have been prepared for almost all fonds and that might enable him to make his own choice. Thus relevance to the stated research topic—or the archival staff's determination of such "relevance"—has a direct bearing on the availability of specific documents. In many cases the services of a knowledgeable archivist are essential in the selection process, especially for a beginning researcher, but more mature scholars are likely to be frustrated by the procedure, aggravated as it is by the restricted nature and limited quality of finding aids. These types of restrictions vary considerably from one institution to another, and generally inventories and fuller card catalogs are available in the manuscript divisions of libraries and museums and in many of the institutions under the Academy of Sciences.

As is apparent from this variance in procedures, the decentralized tendency in the organization of Soviet archival institutions has notably strong repercussions on the matter of access. Not only does the Soviet Union lack a precise standard for access to records in state archives, but separate archival institutions not under GAU authority exercise relatively complete control of their own individual admission and access policies. The most rigidly restrictive is, as one might expect, the main archive of the Communist Party and its various branches; only under very unusual and special circumstances has a foreign scholar been shown any documents there. Almost equally well-guarded are the Foreign Ministry, military, and naval archives; the postrevolutionary diplomatic and military files are generally completely off limits to foreign readers, and the prerevolutionary records have been opened only for a few carefully selected projects.[10] Generally, archives and manuscript collections administered by the Academy of Sciences have been much more readily available to foreigners than have state archives, but preference is sometimes given to senior scholars who are visiting the country under Academy auspices.

Policies in regard to state archives administered by GAU vary considerably; TsGADA, the repository housing the most ancient historical records, has generally been the most open; the various military and naval archives have been the most tightly closed, as have postrevolutionary state records in TsGAOR. Local records in regional state archives have usually been less available to foreigners than those in the all-union central state archives. In some cases, the physical location of the materials can have a bearing on their accessibility, as it is often difficult to arrange extensive research visits to outlying institutions; travel restrictions and local institutional arrangements for visiting foreigners sometimes complicate this problem. However, recent improvements and opportunities for work in a variety of areas suggest that enterprising foreign scholars may find a welcome in many more outlying repositories, and in some cases the archival administration is willing to have documents brought in from regional archives for use in Moscow or Leningrad.

The manuscript divisions of state libraries have generally been the most easy of access, partly, of course, because their contents are likely to be the least official and hence least politically sensitive; the same usually applies to museums, although the State Historical Museum, partly because the extremely limited size of its reader facilities, has been relatively restrictive. Because of the specific variations in entry

[10] Foreign Ministry archives in most every country are subject to more stringent restraints and regulation; Soviet practice is not uncommon in this respect as is made evident in a mimeographed report on comparative access prepared by the Historical Office of the U. S. Department of State, "Public Availability of Diplomatic Archives" (Washington, Department of State, May 1968).

policies, further details about procedures for individual archives will be given in the later sections pertaining to their holdings.

Aside from the reasons of political sensitivity, several other general factors often affect archival access policies. As mentioned earlier, the official publication function of archives has traditionally had precedence over individual research projects, and this can often result in serious access restrictions. When an editing project is under way for the publication of a documentary series or officially sanctioned related research studies, documents involved are likely to be unavailable to the general public until the project is completed. And, more frustrating, it is not unusual for a scholar to be told that all the important or relevant documents to his project have already been published, even if he has information to the contrary, or if his own sense of "relevance" differs from that of the editors.

Similar in effect is the time-honored practice of reserving certain manuscripts or documentary collections for the use of a particular scholar. Well-established Soviet scholars or those working on special projects are able to tie up documents for long periods. Archival directors are hesitant to make manuscripts available to foreigners if there is an important Soviet scholar known to be working in the field, or if the documents relate to a special subject or person planned for study in the near future. Occasionally, a restriction of this type is negotiable, by consultation with the archival director or a leading Soviet scholar in the field, but more often than not such negotiations involve more effort than they merit.

Archives normally are not allowed to make documents available to foreigners if the contents are not familiar to the archive director or member of his staff, or if they have not been previously studied. Accordingly, documents that have not been fully cataloged or inventoried are not readily available for use; if they are made available in special cases, delays and restrictions upon their use may well be imposed. Many repositories still have large cataloging backlogs, resulting both from the tremendous volume of materials that have come under the jurisdiction of the state since 1917 and from the shortage of adequately trained staff. Thus documents listed in public card catalogs available in certain repositories, in published catalogs or inventories, or described in some detail in published guides to the archives or cited in earlier publications, are more likely to be more available than are those that have not been so well identified. Delays are not unusual when less well-known materials are requested, because someone on the staff may have to search at length for the document in question and check out its substance. If the documents have been arranged for cataloging, or if the inventory procedure is under way, similar delays are understandable.

Further restrictions can be expected if the documents requested are found to be in poor condition, or if it is thought that further use could damage or impair them. Some archives have started microfilming documents in such condition, and researchers are restricted to use of the microfilm. But the general shortage of microfilm and the inadequate development of microfilm laboratories may mean that documents in questionable condition have been put aside for filming, and archival staffs are hesitant to pull them out before the filming can be accomplished.

PROCEDURAL INFORMATION

Aside from these procedural restrictions, there are several more personal aspects to the problem of control of access that often affect foreign scholars. Who a scholar is and why he wants access may be much more important factors than what he wants to see. In other words, personal or political factors may have a considerable effect on both a scholar's initial acceptance on the cultural exchange and the availability of materials once he is admitted to an archive. "Irresponsible" writings or interpretations that might be considered polemical can adversely affect such a decision as much as may émigré political activities or previous government intelligence research. At a particular time, documents denied an American of anti-Soviet orientation may be shown to a left-wing Italian historian, and what is closed to one scholar one year might be open to another a year later. Extensive literary contacts or journalistic forays on the subject of the contemporary intelligentsia might make it impossible to obtain a visa at certain times, and diplomats associated with foreign embassies in the Soviet Union have usually not been granted archival access even though their personal research project might be entirely unrelated to their diplomatic function. In several cases, exchange participants whose non-academic interests in the Soviet Union have left officials in doubt as to their scholarly concerns have found relations with archival institutions difficult. Conversely, because of the Soviet respect for scholarship, a distinguished foreign scholar well versed in language and paleography and respected by his Soviet colleagues might well be shown materials or catered to by the archival staff to a greater extent than would a young graduate student, with no publications to his credit, doing preliminary research on his dissertation.

Although authority for control of access theoretically rests with the archives, in practice the matter may already be decided before the question even reaches archival authorities. A variety of personal, political, and even bureaucratic factors may be involved, and the institution with which the visiting foreigner is affiliated in the Soviet Union may exert a large influence. And it is often not only the impersonal institutional sponsorship itself that is crucial so much as personal sponsorship of the particular individual scholars with whom the visitor is associated. If a graduate student's Soviet advisor has decided he does not need archival materials to complete his dissertation—whatever the rationale—it is unlikely that the student will be admitted to the archives. On the other hand, when a Soviet advisor is impressed with a particular student or visiting professor and interested in his project he may be willing to go out of his way both to facilitate archival access and to arrange for the consultation of particular documents. Indeed, visiting foreigners are very much dependent on their Soviet hosts, not only for their official recommendations but also for their personal knowledge of the intricacies of archival arrangements and of the location of relevant materials.

Thus personal factors, along with political and bureaucratic ones, can play a crucial role in scholarly research in Soviet archives. And it is the resulting complexities and interaction of all these factors in specific cases that make generalization about the problems of access to manuscripts and archival records in Soviet repositories so impossibly difficult. In many cases, one never knows without actually going through the mechanics of trying whether a Soviet visa or institutional sponsorship may be forthcoming at a particular time, or whether a certain archival file might be available or not. And one never knows until one gets into the archive itself how much of a given file one may be allowed to consult.

But despite the various difficulties that remain—and most likely many will continue to remain—prospects for fruitful archival work in the Soviet Union appear brighter than they have in many years. Fundamental changes are not going to come overnight, but foreign scholars will continue to find the wealth of documentary materials well worth many of the frustrations of gaining access to them.

4. APPLICATION FOR ARCHIVAL WORK

The scholar cannot, as he can in most countries, simply apply for admission directly to the archive concerned; application must be made on his behalf through the appropriate bureaucratic procedures.

Normally, archival research is limited to scholars who are taking part in one of the USSR's educational exchange programs, and formal arrangements for such research are made by the appropriate office of the scholar's host institution in consultation with his Soviet advisor. Thus, applications for scholars who are connected with Moscow or Leningrad State Universities or other institutions of higher learning or research are handled by the *inotdel* [foreign division] of the appropriate university. In the case of scholars under the aegis of the Academy of Sciences, archival access is arranged with the assistance of the foreign secretary of the specific institute with which the scholar is affiliated, or in some cases through the *inotdel* of the Academy presidium.

In most cases, precise requests for work in given archives should be included in the scholar's original exchange application and study program, and are hence acted upon in advance of his arrival. The fact that his topic is not adjudged suitable for the archival research requested might be reason for the rejection of a candidate. Normally, if a candidate has been accepted by the Soviet authorities within the scholarly exchange program, his topic and archival research program would have been approved ipso facto, or he would have been notified of any contingencies. In many cases, however, it has been possible for scholars to arrange through the foreign divisions of their Soviet institutions for archival work in repositories which might not have been originally requested, as such needs arise in the course of research.

For American citizens, arrangements for participation in scholarly exchange programs are handled by, and information is available from, the International Research and Exchanges Board (IREX), 110 East 59th Street, New York, New York 10022. This organization, which was established in 1968, has taken over the administration of all the academic exchanges in the fields of social sciences and humanities—the graduate-student, younger- and senior-scholar programs with the Soviet Ministry of Higher and Specialized Secondary Education (formerly administered by the Inter-University Committee on Travel Grants), and the senior-scholar exchange between the American Council of Learned Societies and the Academy of Sciences of the USSR.

For British subjects, the postgraduate student exchange with the Soviet Ministry of Higher and Specialized Secondary Education is handled by, and information is available from, Universities Department, British Council, State House, High Holborn, London, W.C. 1. The exchange programs for university teachers in the United Kingdom both with the Soviet Ministry of Higher and Specialized Secondary Education and with the Academy of Sciences of the USSR are administered by, and inquiries should be addressed to, the Committee of Vice-Chancellors, 29 Tavistock Square, London, W.C. 1.

Both the American National Academy of Sciences and the British Royal Society have exchanges with the Soviet Academy of Sciences, but as these are only in the fields of science and mathematics they are not likely to involve participants with archival interests.

Archival research possibilities are extremely limited for scholars not associated with one of the exchange programs and hence not having an official affiliation with a Soviet research institution. In some cases it has been possible for scholars who had started archival research projects during an exchange visit, and who had maintained ties with their Soviet hosts, to return later for a shorter period of time in order to continue; it is to be hoped that this type of arrangement will be more possible in the future. Otherwise only in a few isolated, exceptional cases has archival work been possible for non-exchange participants, as a result of special connections or arranged with the assistance of some interested Soviet scholar or research institution under unusual circumstances. But generally the high cost of independent tourist travel to the Soviet Union, the complicated bureaucratic arrangements, and the length of time required for research—which can rarely be fitted into a limited tourist itinerary—have generally discouraged the would-be researcher and have made archival work virtually impossible to all but those who can arrange for a longer-term official stay. A scholar with a very limited project, particularly one that might involve only a few documents or one that might take him to the manuscript division of a library or museum rather than to state archives, might stand a better chance of success. But in any event, a scholar should not embark for the Soviet Union on a tourist visa, especially in the summer tourist season, counting on archival work or hoping for on-the-spot arrangements, unless some advance assurances have been secured.

For those who remain anxious to try, there is no standardized procedure for independent applications for foreigners. Some archives or manuscript repositories may be willing to reply to a letter of inquiry from abroad (a registered letter is recommended) directly, or through the office that handles their foreign contacts; such a reply, if forthcoming at all, may require several months. Admission of foreigners to all state archives is handled through the foreign division of the Main

Archival Administration (Moscow G-435, Bol'shaia Pirogovskaia ulitsa, 17); they may be addressed by letter far in advance, but normally will not receive scholars on a tourist visa.

In some cases the foreign division of the Academy of Sciences of the USSR (Moscow V-71, Leninskii prospekt, 14) has been willing to assist visiting scholars to make contact with their Soviet colleagues in Academy institutions; they may also on occasion be willing to assist scholars who wish to consult libraries or manuscript collections under their jurisdiction. This procedure is most likely to involve referral to the specialized institution under the Academy with which the scholar's work is associated. Although it is usually advisable to go through the main foreign office of the Academy, it is sometimes possible to approach the institutes of the Academy directly by mail, or through the office which handles their foreign contacts.

In a few cases, diplomatic channels have been helpful, and Soviet officials suggest this as an appropriate route. If the cultural section of his embassy is willing, it can make formal application on behalf of a visiting scholar by a letter (or a covering letter enclosing the scholar's own letter of explanation and request) to the cultural section of the USSR Foreign Ministry, or to the foreign division of the Soviet institution involved. This procedure may be used as a supplemental or follow-up channel for the more direct approaches. Occasionally it has also been worthwhile for a prospective visitor to get in touch with the cultural section of the Soviet Embassy in his home country.

In a few cases, cultural relations organizations or "friendship societies" have also been willing to help foreign scholars make contact with their Soviet colleagues or with the Academy of Sciences. Intourist, the state agency that handles all foreigners' travel arrangements, is usually unwilling to get involved with archival or other research arrangements, although occasionally it may be willing to help a scholar visiting under its auspices to make contact with the Academy of Sciences, the universities, or some other organization which might help.

Any of these procedures is likely to entail lengthy delays and cannot be counted on to yield results. The situation is always subject to change, and lack of reply does not always constitute a refusal.

Scholars contemplating archival work of any kind should bear in mind that formal requests for admission, through whatever channel they might be presented, are necessarily going to require as precise a reference as possible to the documents to be consulted. Usually such a reference should include the name, and where possible the number, of the fond; although published catalog information may not always make it possible for the applicant to provide the exact item numbers within the fond, a reasonably precise description of the materials should be furnished. It is often advisable to present an exact citation from the archival guide or other reference work where the desired materials are described. The aim and purpose of the research (dissertation, monograph, article, etc.) should also be indicated, together with a general description of the research topic. Some mention of previous publications and academic credentials should be included, and it is advisable to retain copies of all correspondence and official letters of recommendation, etc., because they may be needed again on arrival.

5. RESEARCH CONDITIONS

Once a scholar has been officially accepted for archival admission, the director of the archive or one of his assistants from the archival foreign office will normally set up an appointment to discuss the detailed research arrangements and documentary materials to be used. At this point, the scholar normally obtains a pass or reader's ticket that will admit him to the building, and he is introduced to the archival worker [*sotrudnik* or *sotrudnitsa*] to whom he will make specific requests for materials. (Normally in central state archives selected archival workers connected to the archival foreign office are assigned to deal with foreign readers.) Depending on the institution and the materials involved, it may be several days after this initial visit that the scholar may actually start work, since often there will be some time required for paging and checking the materials requested, if this has not already been done.

In most of the central state archives, foreign scholars are normally segregated in a special reading room separate from the main reading room used by Soviet researchers. In Moscow, foreign readers using documents from TsGADA, TsGAOR, and TsGANKh all use a common foreigners' reading room in the building housing the GAU foreign division office (Bol'shaia Pirogovskaia ulitsa, 17) at the center of the complex of archival buildings where these archives are located. Materials from TsGVIA and state oblast or other regional archives are usually also transported to this reading room for foreign readers. Readers in TsGALI, however, work directly in the main archival reading room or the microfilm room adjacent to it. In Leningrad a special foreigners' reading room is located in TsGIA, where documents from TsGAVMF and other local state archives are also usually consulted.

There is considerable variety in the type and extent of finding aids available in different Soviet manuscript repositories, and the visiting scholar must be prepared to face some frustrations in the form of catalogs that are inadequate and insufficiently up-to-date for his purpose. And in central state archives the foreign scholar must be prepared for the further frustration that shelf lists of the inventory type are normally not available for his use. Although the nature of catalogs available in individual repositories and problems regarding their use will be explained in the section on "working conditions" under different institutions, some general remarks here might help orient the researcher.

The most important catalog device in Soviet archives is the master inventory or shelf-list [*opis'*] which is prepared for each fond as it is acquired and organized. (See above, section 1). The *opis'* lists each storage unit item by item, usually with a description of the dates of the documents included, the titles, correspondents, or other descriptive details of the subjects covered, the number of folios, and any other pertinent information. Usually the *opisi* of each fond are prepared in manuscript notebooks and retained in a special place in the storage area or in a special office of the archive. For certain fonds in some repositories, the *opisi* have been typed and copies shelved in the reading room or catalog room.

State archives in the Soviet Union have the unfortunate and indeed frustrating policy of not allowing foreign readers to consult the *opisi*. There have been complaints about the withholding of *opisi* from all readers, but in most repositories now, the practice is limited to foreigners.[11] Modern reproductive processes have ruled out the explanation that many of the *opisi* are not in good condition, or that only one copy exists. To be sure, many of them were prepared long ago so that subsequent corrections and rearrangements might make them difficult to use, and it is understandable that an archivist might be hesitant to make them readily available. But often a scholar has no way of knowing that he has covered all the relevant materials until he has checked through such inventories, and often much research time and effort could be saved by knowing the extent or coverage of a given fond. It is thus no wonder that this practice incurs the most frequent and vociferous criticism from foreign scholars working in Soviet state archives. Normally the practice is not followed in manuscript divisions of libraries and museums under the Ministry of Culture or in institutions under the Academy of Sciences, where *opisi* or other similar catalogs are usually more readily available.

The shelf lists or *opisi* serve as the basis for card catalogs or other types of finding aids compiled in most repositories. Unfortunately for the researcher, most state archives in the Soviet Union do not maintain public card catalogs. Almost all archives have extensive card files covering their holdings and some are in the process of preparing elaborate systematic card catalogs; but with few exceptions these are available for staff use only and may not be consulted by readers. Certain collections or groups of fonds have their own card catalogs, some of which were prepared before the Revolution in their earlier locations; in most cases, these too are kept in the storage area near the documents themselves and are open only for staff use.

Thus, for the actual location of documents in state archives, as for the prior preparation of archival applications, the researcher must rely on what guides and surveys have been published, on the occasional inventory or catalog which may cover the manuscripts for his particular subject, or on previous writings of Soviet scholars who have used the same fond or related documents. Once in the archive, he must rely on the archivists' knowledge and willingness to ferret out materials for his subject.

In library manuscript divisions, and in many older museums and repositories under the Academy of Sciences, much more extensive finding aids are usually available to readers. Some of the card catalogs are exceedingly thorough and revealing in their cross-references to the names of addressees of letters or even people who figure significantly in the manuscripts involved; some catalogs have been prepared for subject analysis of holdings. However, such catalogs, particularly

---

[11] The lack of adequate catalogs and the practice of withholding inventories in one historical archive was criticized publicly by a group of Soviet historians in an open letter to a major Soviet historical journal, "Pis'mo v redaktsiiu zhurnala 'Istoriia SSSR,' " *Istoriia SSSR,* 1964, no. 2, pp. 242-43. It is interesting to note that the editors upheld the signers of the letter in their criticism of the reference facilities and bureaucratic impediments to scholarly work in TsGADA. From more recent reports, the practice of withholding inventories is now usually limited only to foreigners.

because of the continuing large volume of acquisitions, are apt to be far from comprehensive or complete in their coverage and are often limited to the older, better-known parts of the holdings. In addition to the public card catalogs, most of these repositories have a more open policy with respect to the use of *opisi,* many of which have been typed up and filed in the catalog areas of the reading room or brought out to readers on request.

Archives and manuscript divisions of other institutions in the Soviet Union all maintain their own collections of reference books and printed materials related to their documents. Most particularly, these collections may be expected to contain published catalogs or other descriptive literature about their own and other, related holdings, published versions of the manuscripts or related documents, books or articles resulting from manuscript-related research, and other reference materials relating to the collections. Scholars are supposed to present repositories with copies of their publications based on research there, and such gift copies have increased their published collections accordingly. Although these libraries are maintained primarily for the use of the archival staff, readers are generally permitted to request publications or to use the library when such use is directly related to their manuscript research. Exact information about the location and holdings of these libraries is included in the library guides listed in Appendix 1. In the case of manuscript divisions in libraries, manuscript readers are normally permitted to order books or journals from the main library collections.

6. DUPLICATION AND MICROFILM

Various forms of duplication and microfilm have been developing rapidly in the Soviet Union in recent years, but the quality of equipment and film available—as well as the ease of ordering—still lags considerably behind that of the United States and some other Western countries.[12] The Xerox machine has still not found its adequate Russian equivalent, but some types of photographic processes are in use in some libraries and archives.

Microfilm has remained the most economical means of copying large numbers of documents and has been accepted by Soviet archives themselves as the most satisfactory means of preserving deteriorating manuscripts and overly voluminous records. The possibility of ordering microfilm of manuscript materials in Soviet archives and manuscript collections fluctuates considerably and varies with different repositories and types of requests. Restrictions are most likely to be

---

[12] Soviet work with microfilm is well illustrated by the instructional book published for archival workers by K. B. Gel'man-Vinogradov, *Mikrofotokopiro-vanie dokumental'nykh materialov i organizatsiia raboty s mikrofotokopiiami v arkhivakh SSSR* (Moscow, 1961).

placed on sensitive documents, unpublished literary manuscripts, and long consecutive runs from a single fond or storage unit. Local arrangements tend to be unpredictable for both orders and deliveries. Payment policies have varied widely from specific microfilm exchange agreements or other "barter" to payment in hard currency through the Soviet book outlets [Mezhknig] in the scholar's home country. Microfilm orders continue to be a problem, but it is to be hoped that a more efficient system of order and delivery can be worked out.

In a few cases, microfilms of limited specific archival holdings have been ordered from abroad, but here again local variations abound; most success has come with exchange microfilm arrangements, often through institutions with established library exchange programs.

Facilities for and local practice regarding microfilming will be noted in subsequent chapters in the course of discussion of working conditions in individual repositories.

PART A

GENERAL ARCHIVAL BIBLIOGRAPHY AND RESEARCH AIDS

PART A

GENERAL ARCHIVAL BIBLIOGRAPHY AND RESEARCH AIDS

Many available reference tools aid the researcher in finding information about Soviet archival holdings, in locating specific inventories or catalogs, or in establishing the whereabouts of specific documents. The most important and/or most current will be listed here with appropriate annotations. Only works providing general bibliography or describing documents in more than one repository will be included in this section. Coverage is highly selective and only the most general materials have been included; it has especially not been feasible to include all articles on narrow subjects or limited time spans.

In addition to the literature listed below, supplemental bibliographical compilations appear regularly in serial publications for specialized fields. See especially the archival serials listed at the end of this section. For literature published since 1955, one of the most extensive international bibliographies of archival literature appears in the Czech serial *Sborník archivních prácí*; the entire second issue of volume 14 (1964) covers the years 1955-1962; volume 17, no. 1 (1967), pp. 61-296, covers 1963-1965, and volume 20, no. 1 (1970), covers 1966-1968.

1. GENERAL BIBLIOGRAPHIES

A-1. [Russia (1923-USSR).   Glavnoe arkhivnoe upravlenie.]
Katalog arkhivovedcheskoi literatury, 1917-1959 gg. Compiled by Z. A. Silaeva, I. F. Kovalev, and S. V. Nefedova. Edited by A. I. Loginova and I. N. Firsov. Moscow: GAU, 1961. 191 p.
[DLC-Z6208.A7R8; MH-Slav601.167]

> The most comprehensive bibliographical coverage of archival literature published in the Soviet Union between 1917 and 1959. The first part of the volume, entitled "Composition and Contents of State Archival Fonds in the USSR," provides an exceedingly comprehensive list of descriptive publications; it is further subdivided into five lists covering guides and handbooks, catalogs, inventories, descriptions, and surveys. Its organization, however, makes it extremely difficult to use. For example, the placement of items in one or another subdivision is usually determined by the appropriate key word in the title, with the result that one has little recourse but to check the entire 38-page list, unless one knows that the appropriate archive or fond has a published *opis'* as opposed to an *opisanie* or a *katalog*, or a *putevoditel'* as opposed to an *obzor fondov*. Furthermore, a particular item might be listed by title, editor, issuing institution, or archival name, with neither cross-referencing nor indexing, thus making the recovery task even more difficult.

The latter three parts of the book, devoted to the history and organization of archives in the Soviet Union, the theory and practice of archival affairs, and archival developments abroad, will be of less value to scholars using the archives; except for the foreign section, these lists provide the most comphehensive, if not the only, cumulative bibliography of the subject. Despite its drawbacks, this volume together with its supplements (see below) is one of the most important items for scholars concerned with archives and should be on the reference shelf of every major library.

A-2. [Russia (1923-USSR). Glavnoe arkhivnoe upravlenie.]
Katalog arkhivovedcheskoi literatury i sbornikov dokumentov (1960-1963 gg.).
Compiled by S. V. Nefedova, A. A. Khodak, and L. I. Shekhanova. Edited by I. N. Firsov. Moscow: GAU, 1964. 138 p.
[DLC-Z6208.A7R82; MH-Slav601.167.5]
> This supplement to A-1 covering archival literature published through 1963 also contains a supplement to the earlier bibliography of published documents (A-65). The first three sections of the volume devoted to archival literature follow the format of the earlier volume, and accordingly present similar retrieval problems. The supplement does have an index, covering only the names of compilers or editors; but this is inadequate for the scholar seeking information on a specific subject or archive.

A-3. [Russia (1923-USSR). Glavnoe arkhivnoe upravlenie.]
Katalog arkhivovedcheskoi literatury i sbornikov dokumentov (1964-1967 gg.).
Compiled by A. A. Khodak, S. M. Voenushkina, L. N. Il'inskaia, and V. V. Liubimova. Edited by G. P. Lebedev. Moscow: GAU & VNIIDAD, 1970. 183 p.
[MH-Slav601.167.10]
> Similar in format to A-2 above, this supplement to A-1 continues coverage of publications through 1967. Again the first section (pp. 5-40) will be of most interest to scholars using archival materials. The fourth section is a further supplement to A-65, covering official documentary publications. Annual supplemental bibliographical compilations of literature on archives appear in serial publications on specific subjects or in the periodicals discussed in the list below (see especially A-69).

A-4. Kolmakov, P. K.
"Arkhivovedenie v entsiklopediiakh." *Sovetskie arkhivy,* 1966, no. 2, pp. 110-14.
> Lists articles—many of which merit considerable scholarly attention—relating to archives in prerevolutionary, Soviet, and foreign encyclopedias, and provides a brief general bibliography of its own.

A-5. Maichel, Karol.
Guide to Russian Reference Books.
Vol. 1: *General Bibliographies and Reference Books.* Edited by J. S. G. Simmons. Hoover Institution Bibliographical Series, vol. 10. Stanford, 1962. 92 p.
Vol. 2: *History, Auxiliary Historical Sciences, Ethnography, and Geography.*

Edited by J. S. G. Simmons. Hoover Institution Bibliographical Series, vol. 18. Stanford, 1964. 297 p.

Vol. 5: *Science, Technology, and Medicine.* Hoover Institution Bibliographical Series, vol. 32. Stanford, 1967. 384 p.

[DLC-Z2491.M25; MH-Slav600.176.RR1.10]

> These volumes present a wide range of bibliographical material with helpful annotations; their coverage of archival literature, however, is disappointingly thin. Since they are unfortunately coming out on a very slow publication schedule, the general archival items listed in the first volume are already outdated. The specific sections on archives in the second volume are highly selective and there is no archival coverage in the fifth volume. It is to be hoped that subsequent volumes scheduled for publication soon—volume 3, "Social Sciences, Religion, and Philosophy," and volume 4, "Humanities"—will include additional reference to archival materials in their fields. The series does include many important entries which can guide the reader to more precise information.

2. GENERAL RESEARCH AIDS

A-6. Shepelev, Leonid Efimovich.

Arkhivnye razyskaniia i issledovaniia. Moscow: Izd-vo "Vysshaia shkola," 1971. 144 p. [MH]

> An elementary guide for students doing archival research, this short text describes Soviet archival organization, classification methods, and reference publications from the standpoint of the researcher. Of particular help to historians working with eighteenth- and nineteenth-century materials, it describes Russian administrative organization with reference to prerevolutionary state documentation, its current archival locations and classification schemes. A selected bibliography lists major archival guides and reference publications up to 1970. This volume is an updated and slightly revised version of Shepelev's earlier *Rabota issledovatelia s arkhivnymi dokumentami* (Leningrad: Izd-vo "Nauka," 1966; 128 p.; [DLC-CD1711.S5; MH-Slav612.156]). The volume is further supplemented by the pamphlet by G. M. Gorfein and Shepelev, *Arkhivovedenie. Uchebnoe posobie* (Leningrad: Izd-vo LGU, 1971; 85 p.).

3. DIRECTORY OF STATE ARCHIVES

A-7. [Russia (1923-USSR). Glavnoe arkhivnoe upravlenie.]

Gosudarstvennye arkhivy Soiuza SSR. Kratkii spravochnik. Edited by G. A. Belov, A. I. Loginova, S. V. Nefedova, and I. N. Firsov. Moscow: GAU, 1956. 507 p.

[DLC-CD1711.A54; MH-Slav612.95]

> The only general descriptive handbook to Soviet archives ever published covers the nine all-union central state archives as they were organized in

1956, as well as the state archives on the krai, oblast, and republic levels.
Descriptions ranging in length from a paragraph for lesser repositories to
several pages for the larger ones give a general idea of the history, size,
and dates covered by the holdings of the various state archives. A brief
bibliography at the end presents a list of some of the guides, inventories,
and surveys published between 1941 and 1956. Reorganization and changes
in archival names and holdings in the late 1950's and 1960's make its
description of several of the central state archives of the USSR outdated, and
some changes have also occurred in regional archives. It nevertheless remains
indispensable, providing in many cases the only descriptions available.

4. DIRECTORY OF MANUSCRIPT REPOSITORIES IN LENINGRAD

A-8. *Rukopisnye fondy leningradskikh khranilishch. Kratkii spravochnik po fondam
bibliotek, muzeev, nauchno-issledovatel'skikh i drugikh uchrezhdenii.* Compiled by
A. S. Myl'nikov. Leningrad: GPB, 1970. 92 p. Mimeographed.
[MH-B3687.52]

This very brief directory of manuscript holdings in a variety of Leningrad
institutions is a valuable addition to the basic archival reference materials
published in the Soviet Union in recent years but its publication in a small
rotaprint format, with a tirage of only 200 copies, drastically curtails its
availability. It covers a total of 35 institutions, from the large Manuscript
Division of the Leningrad Public Library (**GPB**) to the very limited holdings
of the Lenin Museum. It includes the main library and most of the institutes
of the Academy of Sciences that are covered more fully in Part C, below.
Coverage is exceedingly brief and incomplete. The bibliographical data are
very scant, especially for the larger and better-established repositories.
Except for a few small institutions with manuscript holdings of under 300
storage units, all the institutions listed in this directory are included in Part F
below. For a supplement to this coverage see also the short article by
V. G. Putsko, "Maloizvestnye rukopisnye sobraniia Leningrada," in *Trudy
Otdela drevnerusskoi literatury Akademii nauk SSSR* 25(1970):345-48,
which includes notes on 4 different repositories covered in Part F.

5. PERSONAL PAPERS

a. General Directory

A-9. [Russia (1923-USSR). Glavnoe arkhivnoe upravlenie.]
Lichnye arkhivnye fondy v gosudarstvennykh khranilishchakh SSSR. Ukazatel'.
Compiled by E. V. Kolosova, A. A. Khodak, V. V. Tsaplin, et al. Edited by Iu. I.
Gerasimova, S. S. Dmitriev, S. V. Zhitomirskaia, et al.
Vol. 1: *A-M.* Moscow, 1962. 470 p.
Vol. 2: *N-Ia.* Moscow, 1963. 502 p.
Both volumes are published jointly by GAU, GBL, and Arkhiv AN SSSR.

[DLC-CD1739.5.A1A5; MH-Slav612.140]

One of the most significant Soviet archival reference publications, this two-volume directory of personal or family papers in state repositories resulted from the joint efforts of the Main Archival Administration, the Lenin Library, and the Archive of the Academy of Sciences, with the participation of a host of regional and relatively minor repositories. Providing a comprehensive list of the papers of important families and individuals from a wide variety of fields, it is particularly valuable for its coverage of fonds to be found in minor archives as well as lesser known manuscript holdings in regional repositories, libraries, and museums. Its coverage is more extensive than would be the case in most countries because in the Soviet Union family archives have with few exceptions been all transferred to state repositories. In many cases it provides a location for papers not otherwise covered by a guide or descriptive literature.

Fonds are listed alphabetically according to the family names of the former owners; individuals whose papers are included are briefly identified. The years covered, number of items, and archival location are given for each fond. Professions and subjects, personal names, geographical localities, institutions, and periodical publications are all covered by extensive separate indexes. It is naturally not exhaustive for personal papers because often correspondence and other papers of a given individual may be included in the papers of a friend or associate and hence would not be listed; nor would personal papers be covered if they are located within institutional fonds. Since the directory neither describes the fond in any detail nor gives bibliographical data regarding available descriptions or inventories, it must be used in conjunction with other sources of information, once a particular set of papers or fond has been located. But what is most important is that it provides a ready location for such papers, which often have been dispersed in several different archives. It does not, however, include references to any holdings most likely to be found in the Communist Party archives, nor to the fonds of many politically sensitive individuals. The greatest value is, accordingly, for the coverage of prerevolutionary figures. Although the papers of some revolutionary or postrevolutionary figures are covered, they are predominantly in cultural realms. A supplementary volume updating and extending the coverage is currently in preparation.

b. Individual Family Papers

For additional coverage of literary figures, see the appropriate sections in the general literary bibliographies listed below, A-48, A-49, and A-50.

P. I. Chaikovskii (Tchaikovsky) (1840-1893)

A-10. *Muzykal'noe nasledie Chaikovskogo. Iz istorii ego proizvedenii.* Edited by K. Iu. Davydova, V. V. Protopopov, and N. V. Tumanina. Moscow: Izd-vo AN SSSR, 1958. 542 p.

[DLC-ML134.C42M9; MH-Music Library]

Although this is not technically a catalog of manuscripts, after the description of each composition there is a detailed list of manuscript locations. A more abbreviated coverage is available in the shorter handbook by Grigorii Savel'evich Dombaev, *Muzykal'noe nasledie P. I. Chaikovskogo. Spravochnik.* (Moscow: "Sovetskii kompozitor," 1958; 77 p. [DLC-ML134.C42D6]).

F. M. Dostoevskii (1821-1881)

A-11. Nechaeva, Vera Stepanovna, ed.

Opisanie rukopisei F. M. Dostoevskogo. Moscow, 1957. 587 p.

[DLC-Z6616.D67N4]

Published jointly by the Lenin Library, TsGALI, and the Institute of Russian Literature (PD), this extensive, systematic catalog covers Dostoevskii's literary manuscripts, correspondence, etc., in about 15 different repositories; the great bulk is to be found in GBL, PD, and TsGALI. It gives detailed technical descriptions of manuscripts, correlates manuscripts with published editions, and provides extensive annotations and other bibliographical references.

M. V. Lomonosov (1711-1765)

A-12. "Obozrenie rukopisei Lomonosova i materialov o nem, khraniashchikhsia v moskovskikh i leningradskikh arkhivakh, muzeiakh i bibliotekakh," compiled by A. I. Andreev et al. In *Lomonosov. Sbornik statei i materialov,* edited by A. I. Andreev et al., 3:373-470. Moscow/Leningrad: Izd-vo AN SSSR, 1951.

[DLC-Q143.L8A6; MH-S136.4]

Separate articles cover materials in TsGADA, TsGIA SSSR, and TsGAVMF, and a composite article covers TsGALI, GIM, and GBL. For coverage of the principal Lomonosov fond in the Leningrad Branch of the Archive of the Academy of Sciences, see the separate catalog, C-14.

V. V. Maiakovskii (1893-1930)

A-13. [Russia (1923-USSR). Tsentral'nyi gosudarstvennyi arkhiv literatury i iskusstva.]

V. V. Maiakovskii. Opisanie dokumental'nykh materialov.

Vol. 1: *"Okna" Rosta i glavpolitprosveta 1919-1922 gg.* Compiled by K. N. Suvorova. Edited by V. D. Duvakina. Moscow: GAU & TsGALI, 1964. 287 p.

Vol. 2: *Rukopisi. Zapisnye knizhki. Zhivopis'. Risunki. Afishi. Programmy. Zapisi golosa.* Compiled by V. A. Arutcheva et al. Edited by N. V. Reformatskaia. Moscow: GAU, TsGALI, and BMM, 1965. 303 p.

[DLC-Z8542.9.R87(vol. 1); MH-Slav 4565.41.1]

These volumes cover Maiakovskii materials in a variety of repositories with detailed technical descriptions and correlations with published editions; the great bulk of materials are in TsGALI and BMM. See B-67 and E-58.

6. MEDIEVAL SLAVIC MANUSCRIPTS AND EARLY RUSSIAN HISTORY

Since a full bibliography of earlier bibliographies and reference publications in the field of Russian medieval studies is included in the introductory sections of numbers A-14 and A-15 below, they will not be repeated here. Many of these earlier publications will still be of crucial importance for those using prerevolutionary manuscript collections. See especially the extensive descriptions and published lists of catalogs in the relevant chapters of V. S. Ikonnikov's *Opyt russkoi istoriografii* (A-83). Students of early Russian history will find much assistance in the introductory study of historical sources by M. N. Tikhomirov, *Istochnikovedenie istorii SSSR*, vol. 1: *S drevneishego vremeni do kontsa XVIII veka. Uchebnoe posobie.* (Moscow: Izd-vo sotsial'no-ekonomicheskoi literatury, 1962; 495 p.), which is a considerable expansion of the first edition published in 1941. For a list of studies of Russian paleography and other ancillary disciplines, see Appendix 2.

A-14. [Bel'chikov, Nikolai Fedorovich.]
Spravochnik-ukazatel' pechatnykh opisanii slaviano-russkikh rukopisei. Compiled by Iu. K. Begunov, N. F. Bel'chikov, and N. P. Rozhdestvenskii. Edited by N. F. Bel'chikov. Moscow/Leningrad: Izd-vo AN SSSR, 1963. 360 p.
[DLC-Z6601.A1B4; MH-Slav251.3]

The most comprehensive bibliographical directory of catalogs of medieval Slavic manuscripts, published under the sponsorship of the Commission for the History of Philology of the Academy of Sciences, is divided into three parts. The first, with 79 entries, lists general bibliographies, previous directories, and other reference works including studies of paleography and diplomatics, organized according to the date of publication. The second and by far largest part of the book, with over 2,000 items, is organized first by republics, starting with the Russian RSFSR, second by administrative units within the republic, and third by manuscript repositories; for larger repositories, the list is further subdivided according to specific collections. In each case the list includes specialized inventories, catalogs, and general surveys for individual collections or groups of holdings, and general guides or other descriptive literature covering the archive library, or museum. The third and final part—with 675 entries—covers descriptive literature for collections of medieval Slavic manuscripts outside the Soviet Union. Personal and geographical name indexes are furnished, but more thorough indexing would be desirable. The directory is of value for scholars in archival work other than medieval, because the general guides or descriptive literature about the repositories listed often cover other parts of their archival holdings. Although it is certainly the most comprehensive list available, its research value is impaired by its often inadequate annotations, particularly since some items are of only marginal relevance and since many prerevolutionary catalogs included are outdated by loss, recataloging, and institutional changes.

93

Some institutional changes since 1962 and increased publication in this field already make the need for a new edition apparent; it is to be hoped that such an updated edition will be forthcoming with more extensive annotation and more thorough indexing.

A-15. Djaparidzé, David.
Mediaeval Slavic Manuscripts: A Bibliography of Printed Catalogues. Cambridge, Mass., 1957. 134 p. Mediaeval Academy of America, Publication no. 64. [DLC-Z6601.A1D52; MH-Slav251.18]

Less comprehensive and up-to-date than the previous entry (A-14), with only 338 entries to Begunov's 2086, and with many errors about locations and other details, this volume is still helpful since it is generally more fully annotated and indexed and more conveniently presented. Of particular value is the introductory chapter annotating 113 "General Bibliographies and Reference Works," with subsections devoted to paleography, diplomatics, and works covering specific categories of documents cutting across archival or institutional divisions.

The main chapter (pp. 22-96), listing manuscript catalogs for the USSR, should be verified against the Begunov list (A-14). Because Djaparidzé was unable to visit the Soviet Union or have his text checked locally prior to publication, there are many inaccuracies, especially in regard to present locations. For example, the author distinguishes inadequately among different repositories of the Academy of Sciences in Leningrad: there is no mention of the Archive of the Leningrad Branch of the Institute of History where some of the collections listed as being elsewhere are now housed; some of the materials listed under "Komi ASSR," should be under Pushkinskii Dom; and the collection of the former Imperial Geographical Society listed as being in Moscow should be listed under the Archive of the Geographical Society of the Academy of Sciences in Leningrad.

The chapter covering catalogs of collections outside the USSR is also less comprehensive than the Begunov compilation; Latvia and Lithuania are here included as separate countries, with limited coverage of their archival arrangements.

Although the volume was the only comprehensive repertory of its kind from 1917 until the Begunov volume (A-14) in 1963, for present use it has some of the same deficiencies of the last prerevolutionary compilation by I. M. Smirnov, *Ukazatel' opisanii slavianskikh i russkikh rukopisei, otechestvennykh i zagranichnykh,* published as a supplement to *Bogoslovskii vestnik* in 1916. These deficiencies, together with a review of the Rogov volume (A-16), were pointed out by Iu. K. Begunov, "Osnovnye zadachi sostavleniia opisaniia opisanii sobranii slaviano-russkikh rukopisei," in *Trudy Otdela drevnerusskoi literatury AN SSSR* 20 (1964):188-302. It is regrettable that Djaparidzé did not live to complete the projected revised edition.

A-16. Rogov, Aleksandr Ivanovich.
Svedeniia o nebol'shikh sobraniiakh slaviano-russkikh rukopisei v SSSR. Edited
by M. N. Tikhomirov. Moscow: Izd-vo AN SSSR, 1962. 298 p.
[DLC-Z6620.R9R6; MH-Slav 251.400]
> This invaluable volume describes 569 small collections (under 600 units) of
> Slavic manuscripts in the Soviet Union, the largest number of which were
> gathered before the Revolution; it is subdivided into chapters covering
> collections made by archives, libraries, museums, educational institutions,
> societies or institutes, monasteries, and churches, and by private collectors.
> Listed under the name of the collector, short paragraphs describe the present
> location, and list published catalogs or descriptions of the collection. The
> only index is geographical. A review by the principal compiler of A-14,
> Iu. K. Begunov ("Spravochnik slaviano-russkikh rukopisei," *Voprosy
> arkhivovedeniia,* 1964, no. 2, pp. 122-24), gives additional indications.

A-17. Shelamanova, N. B.
"Predvaritel'nyi spisok slaviano-russkikh rukopisei XI-XIV vv., khraniashchikhsia
v SSSR (dlia 'Svodnogo kataloga rukopisei, khraniashchikhsia v SSSR, do kontsa
XIV v. vkliuchitel'no')." *Arkheograficheskii ezhegodnik za 1965 god,* pp. 177-272.
> Started by the late Academician M. N. Tikhomirov, this comprehensive
> general catalog of medieval Russian and Slavic manuscripts in the USSR being
> prepared under the auspices of the Archeographical Commission of the
> Academy of Sciences of the USSR is one of the most ambitious cataloging
> ventures attempted. This first section gives an idea of the extent and nature of
> the project as well as providing an invaluable reference aid. An index, without
> which it is most difficult to use, has now been published by L. P.
> Zhukovskaia, "Pamiatniki russkoi i slavianskoi pis'mennosti XI-XIV vv. v
> knigokhranilishchakh SSSR," in *Sovetskoe slavianovedenie*, 1969, no. 1,
> pp. 57-71. See also the supplementary list by L. P. Zhukovskaia, "Drevnie
> slavianskie perevody vizantiiskikh i siriiskikh pamiatnikov v
> knigokhranilishchakh SSSR," *Palestinskii sbornik* 19 (82) (1969): 171-76.

A-18. Vodoff, Wladimir.
"La publication des catalogues de manuscrits slaves et des inventaires d'archives
en U.R.S.S." *Journal des savants,* 1970, no. 1 (Jan.-Mar.), pp. 29-52.
> This general bibliographical review article covers a number of recent Soviet
> publications regarding medieval manuscripts, including general bibliographies,
> directories, catalogs, archive guides, and paleographical handbooks. Although
> it has the disadvantage of the author's lack of first-hand experience with
> institutions in the Soviet Union, it provides a helpful critical survey and
> thus serves as a starting point for foreign scholars working in this field.

A-19. Kashtanov, S. M., V. D. Nazarov, and B. N. Floria.
"Khronologicheskii perechen' immunitetnykh gramot XVI v."
> Part 1: *Arkheograficheskii ezhegodnik za 1957 god*, pp. 302-76.
> Part 2: *Arkheograficheskii ezhegodnik za 1960 god*, pp. 129-200.

PART A – GENERAL BIBLIOGRAPHY

Part 3: *Arkheograficheskii ezhegodnik za 1966 god*, pp. 197-253.

> This is a detailed catalog of sixteenth-century charters of immunity with precise archival references and correlations with publications and other published catalogs.

A-20. Bychkova, M. E.

"Obzor rodoslovnykh knig XVI-XVII vv." *Arkheograficheskii ezhegodnik za 1966 god*, pp. 254-75.

> Covers genealogical registration books in GBL, GIM, TsGADA, GPB, BAN, LOII, TsGIA SSSR, and several oblast collections.

A-21. Tikhomirov, Mikhail Nikolaevich.

Kratkie zametki o letopisnykh proizvedeniiakh v rukopisnykh sobraniiakh Moskvy. Moscow: Izd-vo AN SSSR, 1962. 181 p.

[DLC-Z6620.R9T5; MH-Slav251.277.255]

> This volume provides detailed coverage with annotations and bibliographical references for medieval chronicle materials in Moscow repositories.

7. ORIENTAL MANUSCRIPTS

a. General

A-22. [Akademiia nauk SSSR. Institut narodov Azii.]

Vostokovednye fondy krupneishikh bibliotek Sovetskogo Soiuza. Stat'i i soobshcheniia. Compiled by A. S. Tveritinova. Edited by A. I. Bendik, A. S. Tveritinova, and N. P. Shastina. Moscow: Izd-vo vostochnoi literatury, 1963. 238 p.

[DLC-Z688.O55A6; MH-OL69.63]

> Sections of this volume prepared by many different specialists describe the principal oriental manuscript and book collections in the Soviet Union. General descriptions of manuscript holdings are given for the Leningrad Branch of the Institute of Oriental Studies (at the time of publication the present Institut vostokovedeniia was called Institut narodov Azii), the Library of the Uzbek Academy of Sciences in Tashkent, the Buriat complex of the Siberian Branch of the USSR Academy of Sciences in Ulan-Ude, the Matenadaran in Erevan, the Saltykov-Shchedrin State Public Library, and the libraries of Moscow, Leningrad, and Kazan State Universities. In each case selected bibliographical notes are given covering catalogs and other descriptive publications available.

A-23. Pearson, J. D.

Oriental Manuscripts in Europe and North America: A Survey. Zug, Switzerland: Inter Documentation Company AG, 1971. 515 p. Bibliotheca Asiatica, 7.

> This extensive and general directory of repositories of oriental manuscripts prepared under UNESCO sponsorship is organized by language group, and then by country and institution where the manuscripts are found. Different sections briefly describe the size and nature of Soviet holdings in the

following categories: Hebraic, Ethiopic, Egyptian and Coptic, Armenian, Georgian, Arabic, Persian, Turkish, Indian, Central Asian, Southeast Asian, and Chinese and East Asian. Each section provides bibliographic listings of catalogs and other descriptive publications regarding the manuscripts. Although the coverage of both holdings and catalog bibliography is selective and somewhat uneven, since the author did not have a chance to visit all the outlying areas in the Soviet Union, the extensive volume should serve as an invaluable starting point for foreign scholars trying to locate different manuscripts and descriptive literature.

b. Special Language Groups

Arabic Manuscripts

A-24. Huisman, A.J.W.
Les manuscrits arabes dans le monde. Une bibliographie des catalogues. Leiden: E. J. Brill, 1967. 100 p.
[DLC-Z6605.A6H8; MH-OL19000.16.5]
> The coverage of the USSR on pages 79-84 lists published catalogs or descriptive articles for manuscripts in Baku, Bukhara, Pushkin, Dushanbe, Kazan, Kharkhov, Kiev, Leningrad, Moscow, and Tashkent. This largely updates the coverage of the USSR in the earlier publication by Georges Vajda, *Répertoire des catalogues et inventaires de manuscrits arabes* (Paris: Centre national de la recherche scientifique, 1949; 47 p. [DLC-Z6605.A6A28; MH-OL190016]).

A-25. Rozenfel'd, B. A.
"Arabskie i persidskie fiziko-matematicheskie rukopisi v bibliotekakh Sovetskogo Soiuza." In *Fiziko-matematicheskie nauki v stranakh vostoka. Sbornik statei i publikatsii* 1:256-89. Moscow: Izd-vo "Nauka," 1966 [MH-5950.5.5]

Ethiopic Manuscripts

A-26. Zanutto, Silvio.
Manoscritti Etiopici. Bibliografia Etiopica, vol. 2. Rome: Sindacato italiano arti grafiche [1929]. 168 p.
[DLC-Z3521.F97Z3; MH-Afr 4226.1.10]
> The coverage of the Soviet Union (pp. 121-36) is still of value, although the names of many of the institutions involved have been changed. See also the prerevolutionary inventory covering St. Petersburg holdings by B. Turaev, *Efiopskie rukopisi v S.-Peterburge* (St. Petersburg: Tipografiia AN, 1906; 136 p.; Pamiatniki efiopskoi pis'mennosti, 3).

Hebraic Manuscripts

A-27 Katsh, Abraham I.
"Hebrew and Judeo-Arabic MSS. in the Collections of the USSR." In *Trudy dvadtsat'piatogo Mezhdunarodnogo kongressa vostokovedov, Moskva 9- 16 avgusta 1960,* 1:421-29. Moscow: Izd-vc vostochnoi literatury, 1962.

[MH-OL58.9.91]
Briefly surveys major Hebraic holdings in the USSR.

Indian Manuscripts

A-28. Janert, Klaus Ludwig.
An Annotated Bibliography of the Catalogues of Indian Manuscripts. Part 1.
Wiesbaden: Franz Steiner Verlag GMBH, 1965. 175 p.
[DLC-Z6605.O7V42Bd.1; MH-B3515.30.2]
Includes seven published catalogs of Indian manuscripts in the USSR.

Mongol, Kalmuk, and Buriat Manuscripts

A-29. Iorish, I. I.
*Materialy o mongolakh, kalmykakh i buriatakh v arkhivakh Leningrada. Istoriia,
pravo, ekonomika.* Moscow: Izd-vo "Nauka," 1966. 206 p.
[DLC-Z3107.M7I65; MH-Ch270.17]
Inventories Mongol, Kalmuk, and Buriat manuscripts in nine Leningrad
collections.

Persian Manuscripts
See also item A-25.

A-30. Storey, C. A.
Persidskaia literatura. Biobibliograficheskii obzor. Vol. 1: *Koranicheskaia
literatura, vseobshchaia istoriia.* Translated, revised, and augmented by Iu. E.
Bretel'. Edited by Iu. E. Borshchevskii. Moscow: Izd-vo "Nauka," forthcoming.
A translation with bibliographical updating of Storey's *Persian Literature:
A Bio-bibliographical Survey*, vol. 1: Section 1: *Qur'anic Literature*
(London, 1927) and the first part of Section 2, *General History* (London,
1938). The Russian edition gives particularly extensive coverage for
manuscripts in the Soviet Union which were barely covered in the
original.

A-31. Akimushkin, O. F. and Iu. E. Borshchevskii.
"Materialy dlia bibliografii rabot o persidskikh rukopisiakh." In *Narody Azii
i Afriki*, 1963, no. 3, pp. 165-74; 1963, no. 6, pp. 228-41.
Gives a comprehensive list of catalogs and descriptions of Persian
manuscripts. The first part emphasizes manuscripts in the Leningrad Branch
of the Institute of Oriental Studies (see C-70 below), and the second part
covers holdings in other Soviet cities and abroad.

A-32. Shafa, Shuja-edin, ed.
Jahan-i iranshinasi. Vol. 1: Tehran, 1968. 1500 p. In Persian.
[DLC-Z3366.S5]
This first volume of a projected ten-volume directory of Persian studies
throughout the world sponsored by the Pahlavi Library in Tehran has an
extensive section (pp. 857-1500) on the Soviet Union. It describes Persian

manuscript holdings in all parts of the country with a bibliography of book-length catalogs and other descriptions (articles are not included) under each institution.

-33. Tiuzal'ian, L. T. and M. M. D'iakonov.
Rukopisi Shakh-name v leningradskikh sobraniiakh. Leningrad: Izd-vo AN SSSR, 1934. 124 p.
[MH]
> Covers manuscripts in GPB, LGU, and the Leningrad Branch of the Institute of Oriental Studies, along with several from private holdings now in the Archive of the Academy of Sciences.

Syriac Manuscripts
-34. Pigulevskaia, N. V.
Katalog siriiskikh rukopisei Leningrada. Published as *Palestinskii sbornik* 6(69). Moscow/Leningrad: Izd-vo AN SSSR, 1960. 230 p.
[DLC-DS32.5.P3; MH-Asia9202.13(6)]
> Manuscripts included are located in the Leningrad Branch of the Institute of Oriental Studies and in GPB.

8. GREEK, LATIN, AND OTHER WESTERN MANUSCRIPTS

-35. Liublinskaia, A. D.
"Zapadnoevropeiskie rukopisi, khraniashchiesia v SSSR." *Vestnik Matendarana*, 1962, no. 6, pp. 533-46.
> This is a short summary covering TsGADA, GPB, and LOII, among others. .

-36. [Akademiia nauk SSSR. Institut russkoi literatury.]
Neizdannye pis'ma inostrannykh pisatelei XVIII-XIX vekov iz Leningradskikh rukopisnykh sobranii. Edited by M. P. Alekseev. Moscow/Leningrad: Izd-vo AN SSSR, 1960. 380 p.
[DLC-Z6620.R9A63]
> Although most of the volume is devoted to publications of letters of Western authors, the long introduction by the editor, M. P. Alekseev, "Iz istorii russkikh rukopisnykh sobranii," pp. 7-122, contains a great deal of information about Western manuscripts, especially literary autographs, in different Soviet collections; see also the references to specific Leningrad repositories, pp. 357-60.

Greek Manuscripts

-37. Richard, Marcel.
Répertoire des bibliothèques et des catalogues de manuscrits grecs. 2nd ed. Paris: Centre national de la recherche scientifique, 1958. 277 p. Publications de l'Institut de recherche et d'historie des textes, no. 1.

Supplement 1 (1958-1963). Paris: Centre national de la recherche scientifique, 1964. 77 p. Documents, études et répertoires publiés par l'Institut de recherche et d'histoire des textes, no. 9.
[DLC-Z6601.A1R39.1958; MH-3506.50]

> Contains sections listing published catalogs in major repositories in the Soviet Union. Additional notes on these holdings are contained in the author's report on his research there, "Rapport sur une mission d'étude en U.R.S.S. (5 octobre-3 novembre 1960)", in *Bulletin d'information de l'Institut de recherche et d'histoire des textes,* no. 10 (1961), pp. 43-56. Amendments to this catalog with more extensive bibliographical data have been brought together in a reference chapter in the *Kandidat* dissertation by B. L. Fonkich, "Grecheskaia kodikologiia (na materiale rukopisei X-XVII vv. sobranii Moskvy i Leningrada)"; these data are published in the relevant dissertation abstract (Moscow: Izd-vo Moskovskogo universiteta, 1969), pp. 6-9. The article by E. E. Granstrem, "Grecheskaia paleografiia v Rossii," in *Vspomogatel'nye istoricheskie distsipliny* 2(1969):121-34, also includes a number of references to catalogs of Greek manuscripts along with historical data about the history of Greek manuscript collections in Russia; an English translation of this article prepared by J.S.G. Simmons, is published in the *Bulletin* of the Institute of Classical Studies of the University of London (17[1970]:124-35).

A-38. Granstrem, E. E.
"Katalog grecheskikh rukopisei leningradskikh khranilischch."
> "I. Rukopisi IV-IX vv." *Vizantiiskii vremennik* 16(1959):216-43.
> "II. Rukopisi X v." *Ibid.* 18(1961):254-74.
> "III. Rukopisi XI v." *Ibid.* 19(1961):194-239.
> "IV. Rukopisi XII v." *Ibid.* 23(1963):166-204.
> "V. Rukopisi XIII v." *Ibid.* 24(1964):166-97, and *ibid.* 25(1964):184-211.
> "VI. Rukopisi XIV v." *Ibid.* 27(1967):273-94, and *ibid.* 28(1968):238-55.
[DLC-DF501.V48]

> Inventories manuscripts in different Leningrad repositories. The seventh and eighth parts are on press; the eighth consists of supplements and a complete index. See also the same author's survey article, "Grecheskie srednevekovye rukopisi v Leningrade," *Vizantiiskii vremenik* 8(1956): 192-207, describing some of the highlights of the Leningrad holdings.

A-39. Treu, Kurt.
Die griechischen Handschriften des Neuen Testaments in der UdSSR. Eine systematische Auswertung der Texthandschriften in Leningrad, Moskau, Kiev, Odessa, Tbilisi und Erevan. Berlin: Akademie-Verlag, 1966. 392 p. Texte und Untersuchungen zur Geschichte der altchristlichen Literatur, vol. 91.
[DLC-BR45.T4(91); MH-C532.46(91)]

> A detailed inventory of Greek New Testament manuscripts in the USSR.

Latin Manuscripts

-40. Kristeller, Paul Oskar.
Latin Manuscript Books before 1600: A List of the Printed Catalogues and Unpublished Inventories of Extant Collections. 3d ed. New York: Fordham University Press, 1965. 284 p.
[DLC-Z6601.A1K7.1965; MH-B3360.7.3]
> Includes extensive coverage based on the author's research in Moscow and Leningrad. The study was first published in *Traditio: Studies in Ancient and Medieval History, Thought and Religion* 6(1948):227-317 and 9(1953):393-418. The third edition is a reprint of the second edition (Fordham University Press, 1960) through page 232, with a 50-page supplement which includes one additional listing for Leningrad and one for Moscow.

9. MODERN RUSSIAN HISTORY

Only a few specialized bibilographies pertaining directly to archival holdings are listed below. Many detailed historical bibliographies will provide further assistance. Of special note, the recent volume by A. L. Shapiro, *Bibliografiia istorii SSSR* (Moscow: Izd-vo "Vysshaia shkola," 1968; 287 p.) includes an introductory bibliographical discussion of historical bibliographies and specialized literature. An annotated comprehensive list of earlier historical bibliography is provided in the second volume of the Hoover Institution reference series by Karol Maichel, *Historical Sciences* (see A-5 above). The recent study of historical sources for the nineteenth and early twentieth centuries, edited by I. A. Fedosov, I. I. Astaf'ev, and I. D. Koval'chenko, *Istochnikovedenie istorii SSSR XIX-nachala XX v.* (Moscow: Izd-vo MGU, 1970; 469 p.), will be of particular help to students of that period, although its archival coverage is limited. The general research aid by L. E. Shepelev, *Arkhivnye razyskaniia i issledovaniia* (see A-6) is of special importance for modern history; for economic and peasant history, see also items A-66 and A-67 below. For continuing historical bibliographical coverage, including new archival reference aids, see the serial bulletin issued monthly by the Fundamental Library of Social Sciences of the Academy of Sciences (Fundamental'naia biblioteka obshchestven-nykh nauk AN SSSR), *Novaia sovetskaia literatura po istorii, arkheologii i etnografii.*

-41. *A. M. Gor'kii i sozdanie istorii fabrik i zavodov. Sbornik dokumentov i materialov v pomoshch' rabotaiushchim nad istoriei fabrik i zavodov SSSR.* Compiled by L. M. Zak and S. S. Zimina. Moscow: Izd-vo Sotsial'no-ekonomicheskoi literatury, 1959. 364 p.
[DLC-HD2356.R9.A6; MH-Slav4350.12.1180]
> The appendices of this volume (pp. 255-344) survey the documentary records of many factories organized according to their current archival location in

Moscow and Leningrad repositories, with separate coverage for TsGAOR (and the former TsGIAM), TsGIA SSSR, and local state archives in Moscow and Leningrad.

A-42. [Akademiia nauk SSSR. Institut istorii. Leningradskoe otdelenie.]
Oktiabr'skoe vooruzhennoe vosstanie v Petrograde. Sbornik statei.
Moscow/Leningrad: Izd-vo AN SSSR, 1957. 444 p.
[DLC-DK265.8.L4A6; MH-FilmW1604]

> The final section, "Obzor dokumentov o podgotovke i provedenii oktiabr'skogo vooruzhennogo vosstaniia v Petrograde v 1917 g., khraniashchikhsia v arkhivakh Moskvy i Leningrada," pp. 359-434, gives a detailed survey of holdings relating to the October Revolution in state archives in Moscow and Leningrad. See also the coverage by I. A. Bulygin, F. E. Reikhberg, and Iu. S. Tokarev, "Obzor dokumental'nykh istochnikov o podgotovke i provedenii vooruzhennogo vosstaniia v Petrograde v 1917 g.," *Arkheograficheskii ezhegodnik za 1957 god*, pp. 243-64, covering materials in TsGAOR, TsGVIA, GAORLO, and TsGAVMF.

A-43. Shepelev, L. E.
"Izuchenie deloproizvodstvennykh dokumentov XIX–nachala XX v."
Vspomogatel'nye istoricheskie distsipliny 1(1968):119-38.

> Gives bibliographical data for a number of reference aids relating to documents for business history in the late nineteenth and early twentieth centuries, along with a discussion of the types of documents available.

A-44. [Akademiia nauk SSSR. Institut slavianovedeniia.]
K stoletiiu geroicheskoi bor'by "Za nashu i vashu svobodu." Sbornik statei i materialov o vostanii 1863 g. Edited by V. A. D'iakov, I. S. Miller, and S. M. Fal'kovich. Moscow: Izd-vo "Nauka," 1964. 448 p.
[DLC-DK437.A682; MH-Slav5760.16]

> Contains surveys of materials relating to the 1863 Polish uprising in a number of repositories in Moscow and Leningrad. See especially the general article by L. A. Obushenkova, "Arkhivnye materialy sudebno-sledstvennykh uchrezhdenii 1863-1866 gg. po delam uchastnikov vosstaniia," pp. 211-79, with a detailed chart covering archival holdings in TsGVIA, TsGIA SSSR, and historical archives in the Ukraine, Belorussia, and Lithuania. More substantive articles relate particularly to Zygmunt Sierakowskii. The articles covering the files in the Artillery History Museum (F-117) and in Pushkinskii Dom (C-45) are described in more detail below.

10. MILITARY HISTORY

A-45. Beskrovnyi, Liubomir Grigor'evich.
Ocherki po istochnikovedeniiu voennoi istorii Rossii. Moscow: Izd-vo AN SSSR, 1957. 453 p.
[DLC-DK51.7.B49; MH-Slav630.38.5]

Gives extensive coverage of archival sources for prerevolutionary Russian military history, listing relevant fond numbers in many different repositories. It does not, however, give bibliographic references to printed catalogs, relevant archival guides, or other descriptive literature.

11. AMERICAN HISTORY

-46. Golder, Frank A.
Guide to Materials for American History in Russian Archives.
   Vol. 1: Washington, D.C., 1917. 177 p.
   Vol. 2: Washington, D.C., 1937. 55 p. Publication no. 239 of the Carnegie Institution of Washington.
[DLC-CD1718.U6G6; MH-US63.23RR3621.58]

> Compiled before the Revolution, this guide is partly outdated by changes in archival arrangements and organization; its inventory type of descriptions of documents, however, are still useful, because they have not been superseded by more recent publications. It is most helpful for the extensive coverage of the Foreign Ministry archive (AVPR) but also covers other repositories. Volume 1 describes materials through 1853; volume 2 covers the years 1854-1870, but only for the Foreign Ministry records. Listed also as D-13 below.

12. RUSSIAN LITERATURE

See also the items covering personal archival fonds listed in Section 4 above.

-47. Bel'chikov, N. F.
Puti i navyki literaturovedcheskogo truda. Moscow: Izd-vo "Nauka," 1965. 333 p.
[DLC-PG2942.B4; MH-Slav4120.717]

> This basic reference aid for literary studies contains a number of sections helpful to the literary scholar with an abundance of basic bibliographical data. Of particular value as a starting point for scholars planning literary research in archives is the section "Nauchnye opisaniia rukopisnykh materialov," pp. 184-95, which covers finding aids for GBL, PD, TsGALI, GPB, and special sections on Pushkin and Gor'kii manuscripts.

-48. [Stepanov, V. P.]
Istoriia russkoi literatury XVIII veka. Bibliograficheskii ukazatel'. Compiled by V. P. Stepanov and Iu. V. Stennik. Edited by P. N. Berkov. Leningrad: Izd-vo "Nauka," 1968. 500 p.
[DLC-Z2502.S76; MH]

> The bibliographical listings are classified under individual authors with some introductory general coverage. The final section devoted to each author includes references to surveys or catalogs of archival materials, as does a special section in the introductory general part.

PART A – GENERAL BIBLIOGRAPHY

A-49. [Akademiia nauk SSSR. Institut russkoi literatury.]
Istoriia russkoi literatury XIX veka. Bibliograficheskii ukazatel'. Edited by K. D.
Muratova. Moscow/Leningrad: Izd-vo AN SSSR, 1962. 966 p.
[DLC-Z2503.A47; MH-Slav4055.505(RR3402.9)]
　　　Similar in format and coverage to the above, A-48.

A-50. [Akademiia nauk SSSR. Institut russkoi literatury.]
Istoriia russkoi literatury kontsa XIX-nachala XX veka. Bibliograficheskii ukazatel'.
Edited by K. D. Muratova. Moscow/Leningrad: Izd-vo AN SSSR, 1963. 519 p.
[DLC-Z2503.A474; MH-Slav4055.506]
　　　Similar in format and coverage to A-48 and A-49 above.

13. THEATER AND MUSIC MATERIALS

A-51. [Akademiia nauk SSSR. Institut istorii iskusstv.]
Teatr i muzyka. Dokumenty i materialy. Edited by A. D. Alekseev and I. F.
Petrovskaia. Moscow/Leningrad: Izd-vo AN SSSR, 1963. 194 p.
[DLC-PN2721.A65; MH-Slav4135.200.40]
　　　This collection of articles surveying theatrical and musical manuscript
materials in a variety of Soviet repositories includes two general ones by I. F.
Petrovskaia on manuscripts in different institutions in Leningrad. The
coverage is more extensive for theatrical than for musical manuscripts.
Specific articles cover materials in GPB, GBL, GIM, and LGIA.
Supersedes the pamphlet by A. M. Brianskii, *Teatral'nye biblioteki,
muzei i arkhivy Leningrada* (Moscow/Leningrad: Gosudarstvennoe
izd-vo iskusstva, 1940; 36 p.)

A-52. Petrovskaia, I. F., ed. and comp.
*Materialy k istorii russkogo teatra v gosudarstvennykh arkhivakh SSSR. Obzory
dokumentov. XVII vek - 1917 g.* Moscow: GAU and Leningradskii gosudarstvennyi
institut teatra, muzyki i kinematografii, 1966. 285 p.
[DLC-PN2721.P4; MH-Slav4135.200.45]
　　　A companion volume with the previous entry, it extends the coverage of
theatrical manuscripts to a variety of Soviet state archives; a general article by
I. F. Petrovskaia surveys documents for theater history and provides a
bibliography of catalogs and other descriptive literature. Specific articles
cover materials in TsGADA, TsGIA SSSR, and in republic and oblast archives.

A-53. Golubovskii, Ivan Vasil'evich, ed.
Muzykal'nyi Leningrad, 1917-1957. Compiled and edited by I. V. Golubovskii.
Leningrad: Gosudarstvennoe muzykal'noe izd-vo, 1958. 527 p.
[DLC-ML300.8.L4G6; MH-Slav3203.1.260]
　　　The chapter covering libraries and museums, "Biblioteki i muzei,"
pp. 351-428, gives a short description of both manuscript and printed musical
materials in both large and small repositories in Leningrad. The most
comprehensive survey available, now supplemented by A-8.

-54. Petrovskaia, I. F.
Istochnikovedenie istorii russkogo dorevoliutsionnogo dramaticheskogo teatra.
Leningrad: Izd-vo "Iskusstvo," 1971. 199 p.
[DLC-PN2721.P37;MH]

> Comprehensive coverage of materials for Russian theater history. See
> especially the section "Materialy gosudarstvennykh arkhivov," pp. 33-63.

-55. "Perechni dokumentov i materialov po istorii russkogo sovetskogo teatra
1917-1921 gg., khraniashchikhsia v TsGAOR SSSR, TsGASA, TsGALI SSSR
LGAORSS." In *Sovetskii teatr. Russkii sovetskii teatr, 1917-1921. Dokumenty i
materialy,* pp. 403-81. Edited by A. Z. Iufit et al. Leningrad: Izd-vo "Iskusstva,"
1968. 548 p.
[DLC-PN2724.R87; MH-Slav4137.568.15(1)]
"Perechen' dokumentov i materialov po istorii russkogo sovetskogo teatra
1917-1921 gg., khraniashchikhsia v mestnykh arkhivakh RSFSR." In *ibid.,*
pp. 482-96.

> A detailed inventory of items relating to theater history during the years
> 1917-1921 in the 4 state archives indicated is followed by a similar inventory
> of items in regional state archives of the RSFSR.

-56. *Teatral'nye muzei v SSSR.* Edited by N. V. Mints and B. Kh. Georgiev. Published as
*Trudy Nauchno-issledovatel'skogo instituta muzeevedeniia i okhrany pamiatnikov
istorii i kul'tury,* part 23. Moscow, 1969. 173 p.
[MH-Slav610.90(23)]

> Includes articles on manuscript holdings in different Moscow theatrical
> museums that will be listed in more detail in appropriate sections in Part E
> (see nos. E-65 and E-66). But it does not provide the systematic or
> comprehensive coverage its title suggests.

14. MOTION PICTURE ARCHIVES

A-57. Voiculescu, Ervin.
*Repertoriu mondial al filmografilor naţionale/Répertoire mondial des
filmographies nationales,* pp. 71-75. Bucharest: Arhiva naţională de filme, 1970.
[American Film Institute]

> The section covering the Soviet Union of this international bibliography
> provides a list of published film catalogs, studies of the history of the Soviet
> cinema, and other descriptive and critical writings of value to those using film
> archives. Some of the materials covered pertain to Gosfil'mofond, some to
> TsGAKFD, and some to collections of films produced by different union
> republics. No annotations are provided. The list is not complete for all
> publications relating to film archives, and most particularly does not include
> articles, but it is the only extensive bibliography available.

PART A – GENERAL BIBLIOGRAPHY

15. FOLKLORE MATERIALS

A-58. *Russkii fol'klor. Bibliograficheskii ukazatel'.* Compiled by M. Ia. Melts. Edited by
A. M. Astakhova and S. P. Luppov.
  Vol. 1: *1945-1959.* Leningrad, 1961. 402 p.
  Vol. 2: *1917-1944.* Leningrad: BAN, 1966. 683 p.
  Vol. 3: *1960-1965.* Leningrad: BAN, 1967. 539 p.
  [DLC-Z5984.R9R8; MH-27232.361.3]
    These general bibliographical directories of folklore literature include
    references to descriptions of archival materials. The first volume (1945-1959),
    does not have a separate section on archives, as do the second and third
    volumes (vol. 2, pp. 435-38; vol. 3, pp. 291-95).

16. CARTOGRAPHIC MATERIALS

A-59. Gibson, James R.
  "Archival Research on the Historical Geography of Russia." *Professional
  Geographer* 18 (May 1966): 164-67.
    A general and exceedingly helpful introduction by a Canadian scholar
    covering the main repositories in Moscow and Leningrad.

A-60. Fel', S. E.
  Kartografiia Rossii XVIII veka. Moscow: Izd-vo geodezicheskoi literatury, 1960.
  226 p.
  [DLC-GA933.6.A1F4; MH-Geog3070.145]
    This general study of eighteenth-century Russian cartography contains much
    information about the location of manuscript materials. See also the
    pamphlet by O. M. Medushevskaia, *Kartograficheskie istochniki XVII-XVIII vv.*
    (Moscow: MGIAI, 1957; 28 p. [DLC-GA933.6.A1M4]), which provides a
    good orientation but scant information about specific repositories.

A-61. Gel'man, E. G.
  "Ispol'zovanie kartograficheskikh materialov XVIII veka." *Sovetskie arkhivy*, 1967,
  no. 6, pp. 44-49.
    Mostly regarding materials on Novgorod, this article also gives some general
    bibliographical indications and discusses general problems. See also the same
    author's article, "Kartograficheskie materialy kak istochnik po istoricheskoi
    geografii Novgorodskoi gubernii XVIII v.," in *Trudy MGIAI*
    24(1966):114-33.

A-62. Gol'denberg, L. A.
  "Kartograficheskie materialy kak istoricheskii istochnik i ikh klassifikatsiia
  (XVII-XVIII vv.)." *Problemy istochnikovedeniia* 7(1959):296-347.
    Includes many references to archival holdings of maps. See also the same
    author's article, "O printsipakh klassifikatsii kartograficheskikh materialov v
    gosudarstvennykh istoricheskikh arkhivakh," *Istoricheskii arkhiv,* 1958, no. 1,

pp. 202-11, which includes a chart of classification schemes for TsGVIA, TsGADA, and TsGIAL (now TsGIA SSSR).

A-63. Kabuzan, V. M.
"Nekotorye materialy dlia izucheniia istoricheskoi geografii Rossii XVIII-nachala XIX vv. (Po fondam tsentral'nykh arkhivov i bibliotek Moskvy i Leningrada)." *Problemy istochnikovedeniia* 11(1963):153-95.

> Surveys cartographic materials in Moscow and Leningrad. Extensive tables provide archival locations for maps of the late eighteenth and early nineteenth centuries, covering holdings in TsGADA, TsGIA SSSR, TsGVIA, LOII, GPB, GBL, and a few in the Archive AN SSSR.

A-64. Tsvetkov, M. A.
"Kartograficheskie materialy general'nogo mezhevaniia." *Voprosy geografii* 31(1953):90-105. English translation by James R. Gibson, "Cartographic Results of the General Survey of Russia, 1766-1861," *Canadian Cartographer* 6 (June 1969):1-14.

> This article, listed also as B-90 below, surveys the manuscript maps and plans of the Russian Empire prepared in connection with the General Survey. Most of these are located in TsGADA, but some of the materials described are to be found in TsGVIA and TsGIA SSSR.

17. BIBLIOGRAPHY OF PUBLISHED DOCUMENTS

The publications listed below can serve only as a starting point for information about major official Soviet publications. The location of smaller and especially unofficial publications is more difficult, particularly for the prerevolutionary period, for which they tend to be extremely diffuse. For this purpose, the best starting place is in standard historical or literary bibliographies, the most important of which are listed in the Hoover Institution's *Guide to Russian Reference Books* (A-5). The annual bibliographical compilations since 1956 in *Arkheograficheskii ezhegodnik* (A-6), include sections listing published documents.

A-65. [Russia (1923-USSR). Glavnoe arkhivnoe upravlenie.]
Katalog sbornikov dokumentov, izdannykh arkhivnymi uchrezhdeniiami SSSR 1917-1960 gg. Compiled by E. V. Markina, L. I. Shekhanova, et al. Edited by A. I. Loginova and L. I. Iakovlev. Moscow: GAU, 1961. 110 p.
[DLC-Z2506.A25; MH-Slav601.166]

> The major Soviet documentary publications in book form from 1917 through 1960 are listed in this comprehensive catalog with a total of 631 entries divided according to historical periods. Chapters are further subdivided by topic, and within topics, by year of publication, with multi-volume series broken down into separate entries. A list of major critical reviews is included under most entries. Indices are unfortunately lacking. Although the catalog is helpful for the location of major official publications (i.e., documents

published with official archival sponsorship), few individual articles are included, since publications by outside scholars or small projects in article form are explicitly excluded. Two supplements to this list covering official publications for the years 1960 through 1963 and the years 1964 through 1967 have been published as the fourth section of the supplements to the GAU catalog of archival literature for those years (A-2 and A-3 above). The arrangement by periods parallels the original volume. An alphabetical index of titles of the documentary series included is a helpful addition.

A-66. Paina, E. S.
Ekonomicheskaia istoriia Rossii, 1861-1917 gg. Obzor publikatsii gosudarstvennykh arkhivov SSSR (1918-1963). Moscow: GAU, 1967. 90 p.
[DLC-Z7165.R9P29; MH-Slav3085.660]

In the course of coverage of documentary publications, this essay also gives much information about archival holdings in a variety of repositories.

A-67. Paina, E. S.
Krest'ianskoe dvizhenie v Rossii v XIX-nachale XX vv. Obzor publikatsii gosudarstvennykh arkhivov SSSR. Moscow: GAU, 1963. 81 p.
[DLC-Z7165.R9P3; MH-Slav3096.2.5]

Gives limited information about additional archival holdings in the course of surveying publications in this field.

18. SERIALS RELATING TO ARCHIVES

In addition to those journals listed below, traditional historical and literary journals often publish some articles on archival problems, but these usually can be found in the cumulative bibliographical lists referred to above or in other more general bibliographical sources. Periodical bibliographies in specialized fields often list recent books and articles relating to archives. See especially the regular monthly coverage of archival bibliography in *Novaia sovetskaia literatura po istorii, arkheologii i etnografii,* issued by the Fundamental Library of Social Sciences of the Academy of Sciences of the USSR. Archival journals or serial publications issued by different Soviet republics are not included in the list below; among current titles, *Arkhivy Ukrainy* is the most important.

A-68. [Akademiia nauk SSSR. Institut istorii.]
Problemy istochnikovedeniia. Sbornik. Moscow. 1933-1963. Irregular. 11 vols. published in all.
[DLC-DK38.A55; MH-Slav601.65]

This discontinued series has been a major outlet for scholarly articles about manuscripts and related problems of paleography, diplomatics, etc. Of particular importance to scholars using archives, it includes many specialized surveys of the contents of specific archival fonds or of documents available on limited subjects in different fonds. An index of the first ten volumes is included in volume 10, pages 438-47. It is now largely superseded by A-77.

A-69. *Arkheograficheskii ezhegodnik*. Moscow. 1957+ Annual. Issued by
Arkheograficheskaia komissiia AN SSSR.
[DLC-DK3.A2773; MH-Arc275.30]

> This yearbook of the Archeographical Commission of the Academy of
> Sciences of the USSR publishes inventories, descriptions, or scholarly catalogs
> of archival or manuscript collections, as well as documents and other articles
> related to archeographical affairs. Of particular value to scholars using
> manuscript sources, it publishes a most comprehensive bibliography of
> archival literature with sections on documentary publications, general archival
> affairs, archival guides, and catalogs or other descriptions of individual fonds
> and archival holdings. From 1957 until his death in 1965 it was edited by
> M. N. Tikhomirov. There is now usually a time-lag of a year or two in its
> publication.

A-70. *Arkhivnoe delo*. Moscow. 1923-1941. Irregular, nos. 1-58. Issued by GAU (with
variations of name).
[DLC-microfilm (incomplete); MH-B8825.223]

> This early professional archival journal, at times issued quarterly, contains
> some descriptions of individual archives and their history, but mostly reports
> on archival techniques and administrative developments, of particular interest
> for the history of the Soviet state archival system. A bibliographical
> description of its contents during the first six years was published by Fritz T.
> Epstein in *Archivalische Zeitschrift* 39(1930):282-308. A short description
> was published in French by Inna Lubimenko, "Une nouvelle revue d'archives
> russe," in *Nederlandsch Archievenblad* 35(1927-28):119-23.

A-71. *Bibliograficheskii ukazatel' po otechestvennym materialam. Dokumentovedenie i
arkhivnoe delo*. Moscow. 1968+. Monthly. Issued by VNIIDAD.

> Issued monthly by the archival research institute under GAU, this new series
> is published in limited edition (foreign subscriptions not available) in an
> offset format that can be cut up for card catalogs. It provides comprehensive
> bibliographical indications, usually with abstracts or annotations, about
> books and articles published in the Soviet Union on all phases of archival
> affairs and documentation problems. The 1968 issues were put out in an even
> more limited edition, but starting with 1969 the issues have been available in
> bibliographical reference collections in major libraries and archives in the
> Soviet Union.

A-72. *Bibliograficheskii ukazatel' po zarubezhnym materialam. Dokumentovedenie i
arkhivnoe delo*. Moscow. 1969+. Monthly. Issued by VNIIDAD.

> Similar in format to the above (A-71), this series presents monthly abstracts
> of important books and articles on archival affairs and documentation
> problems published abroad from a wide range of foreign sources.

A-73. *Istoricheskii arkhiv.* Moscow. 1955-1962. Bimonthly. Issued by Institut istorii AN SSSR.
[DLC-DK1.A3274; MH-Slav610.8.16]

> Published by the Institute of History of the Academy of Sciences with the cooperation of the Main Archival Administration and the Institute of Marxism-Leninism, it includes documentary publications, scholarly articles, bibliographical and archival descriptions, inventories, and news of archival developments. Its excellent annual bibliographies of archival literature largely duplicate those in *Arkheograficheskii ezhegodnik* (A-69). The archival coverage has now been largely taken over by *Sovetskie arkhivy* (A-74) with which journal several of its former editors are now associated. The journal had a predecessor in a series of volumes under the same title, issued by the Institute of History of the Academy of Sciences and edited by B. D. Grekov, of which ten volumes were published between the years 1936 and 1954 (vols. 1-3, 1936-1940; vols. 4-10, 1949-1954).

A-74. *Sovetskie arkhivy.* Moscow. 1966+. Bimonthly. Supersedes *Voprosy arkhivovedeniia* (A-76). Issued by GAU.
[DLC-CD1710.S6; MH-Slav612.116]

> Published by the Main Archival Administration with the cooperation of the Institute of Marxism-Leninism and the Institute of History of the USSR of the Academy of Sciences and now available on an open subscription basis, it publishes articles on archival development, methods, and organization, as well as occasional short historical articles and documentary publications. It reviews selected recent publications in the field and presents news from the Main Archival Administration, information about foreign archival developments, and reports of conferences and meetings related to archival affairs. Principally of interest to archivists, it occasionally contains descriptions of groups of documents or of specific archives, usually describing organizational changes.

A-75. [Moscow. Gosudarstvennyi istoriko-arkhivnyi institut.]
Trudy Moskovskogo gosudarstvennogo istoriko-arkhivnogo instituta. 1939+. Irregular. (Abbreviated-*Trudy MGIAI*)
[DLC-DK1.M625(incomplete); MH-PSlav467.60]

> The first four volumes (1939-1948) were entitled *Trudy Istoriko-arkhivnogo instituta.* This series, 26 volumes of which have been issued through 1968, publishes predominantly articles or monographs on archival subjects written by faculty and advanced students of the Moscow State Historico-Archival Institute (MGIAI). Many of the publications are procedural or methodological in nature, but there are others of historical or descriptive nature which are of value to researchers using the archives.

A-76. *Voprosy arkhivovedeniia. Nauchno-informatsionnyi biulleten'.* Moscow. 1959-65. Quarterly. Superseded by *Sovetskie arkhivy.* Issued by GAU.
[DLC-CD15.R9V6; MH-Slav612.115]

The official professional archival journal between 1959 and 1965, like its successor, *Sovetskie arkhivy* (A-74) but with more limited circulation and less popular format, contains articles on archival administration, methods, and developments. It was actually a continuation of an earlier *Informatsionnyi biulleten'* [MH-Film SC142], 10 numbers of which were issued irregularly between 1956 and 1959 in a mimeographed format and contain articles of relatively narrow interest to archivists. A descriptive summary of the history of *Voprosy arkhivovedeniia* and the earlier *Informatsionnyi biulleten'*, together with a complete index of their contents since 1956, is published in the first issue of *Sovetskie arkhivy* (1966, no. 1, pp. 101-14): "Po stranitsam 'Voprosov arkhivovedeniia' za 10 let."

A-77. *Vspomogatel'nye istoricheskie distsipliny.* Leningrad. 1968+. Irregular.
[DLC-D1.V8; MH-Slav602.91.10]

This new serial planned for annual publication is edited by S. N. Valk under the auspices of the Leningrad Branch of the Archeographical Commission of the Academy of Sciences. The first volumes available contain a number of articles on the auxiliary historical sciences of crucial importance to scholars working with medieval manuscripts (See Appendix 2), and the series promises to be of continuing importance for archival affairs.

19. REPORTS OF RECENT SYMPOSIA AND CONFERENCES

A-78. [Akademiia nauk SSSR. Institut istorii. Leningradskoe otdelenie.]
Issledovaniia po otechestvennomu istochnikovedeniiu. Sbornik statei, posviashchennykh 75-letiiu professora S. N. Valka. Leningrad: Izd-vo "Nauka," 1964. *Trudy Leningradskogo otdeleniia Instituta istorii AN SSSR*, vol. 7.
[DLC-DK38.A595; MH-Slav602.375]

Contains short articles on historical sources for different subjects, many involving surveys of groups of archival materials. The period covered ranges from the earliest centuries of Russian history to the Soviet regime. There are also a few articles relating to archival development or early repositories.

A-79. [Russia (1923-USSR). Glavnoe arkhivnoe upravlenie.]
Trudy nauchnoi konferentsii po voprosam arkhivnogo dela v SSSR. Edited by L. N. Krivoshein et al. 2 vols. Moscow: GAU, 1965. 594 p. 420 p.
[MH-Slav612.152]

Contains a variety of reports on different phases of archival history and technical developments, a few of which include information regarding contents of different repositories.

A-80. [Nauchnaia konferentsiia arkhivistov Leningrada, Leningrad, 1964.]
Problemy arkhivovedeniia i istochnikovedeniia. Materialy nauchnoi konferentsii arkhivistov Leningrada, 4-6 fevralia 1964 g. Edited by V. V. Bedin, G. M. Gorfein et al. Leningrad: Izd-vo "Nauka," 1964. 283 p.

[DLC-CD28.1964.N35]

> Contains a number of articles originally presented as reports to the congress regarding repositories in Leningrad. A few are helpful in the coverage of sources—see, for example, B-124 and B-125 below—but most relate to technical problems of archival management and reference work.

A-81. [Russia (1923-USSR). Glavnoe arkhivnoe upravlenie. Tsentral'nyi gosudarstvennyi istoricheskii arkhiv SSSR]
Nekotorye voprosy izucheniia istoricheskikh dokumentov XIX-nachala XX v. Sbornik statei. Edited by I. N. Firsov, G. M. Gorfein, and L. E. Shepelev. Leningrad: Izd-vo LGU, 1967. 264 p.
[MH-Slav602.59.5]

> Although most of the articles in this volume relate to materials in TsGIA SSSR in Leningrad, a few are of general interest, covering as they do various problems in the development of Soviet archives. See more specific references listed under B-104, and the surveys covering TsGIA holdings.

A-82. [Iubileinaia nauchnaia konferentsiia arkhivistov Leningrada, Leningrad, 1968.]
Problemy arkhivovedeniia i istorii arkhivnykh uchrezhdenii. Materialy iubileinoi nauchnoi konferentsii arkhivistov Leningrada 13-14 iiunia 1968 g. Edited by I. N. Solov'ev et al. Leningrad: Izd-vo LGU, 1970. 256 p.
[MH-Slav612.163]

> Although many of the articles in this volume pertain to problems of archival techniques and reference practices, a number include surveys of materials in particular repositories or on particular subjects. Several important articles pertain to archival history, particularly the contribution by S. O. Shmidt, "K istorii arkhivnogo stroitel'stva v pervye gody Sovetskoi vlasti," pp. 19-35.

20. ARCHIVAL HISTORY

a. Prerevolutionary Period

For additional bibliography of publications roughly to the end of 1963, see the appropriate sections of *Istoriia istoricheskoi nauki v SSSR. Dooktiabr'skii period. Bibliografiia* (Moscow: Izd-vo "Nauka," 1965), pp. 112-13, 123-33, 153-59, 171-73, 180-83, 186.

A-83. Ikonnikov, Vladimir Stepanovich.
Opyt russkoi istoriografii. 2 vols. in 4. Kiev: Tipografiia Imperatorskogo universiteta Sv. Vladimira V. Zavadskogo, 1891-1908. Reprint edition Osnabrück: Otto Zeller, 1966.
[DLC-Z2506.T4; MH-Slav600.2]

> The first volume (in two parts) of this classic but unfinished work on early Russian historiography provides the most extensive and fully documented survey of prerevolutionary archives and manuscript collections. Chapters 4 through 7 of the first section (included in vol. 1, part 1) cover the growth of

archival and library collections of historical sources. The second section (spanning the two parts of vol. 1) presents a directory of Russian archives and manuscript collections as they existed at the time of publication; nine chapters cover different categories such as state archives, public and religious libraries, institutional and private manuscript collections, and foreign libraries and archives with material regarding Russian history. Extensive bibliographical footnotes, end-of-chapter bibliographies and bibliographical supplements give the most comprehensive coverage of the archival-related literature ever assembled. The value of the work as a current research tool has naturally been reduced by postrevolutionary reorganizations, but it remains most helpful for its descriptions and bibliographies of the prerevolutionary archives and collections, many of which remain intact.

A-84. Korneva, I. I., E. M. Tal'man, and D. M. Epshtein.
Istoriia arkheografii v dorevoliutsionnoi Rossii. Uchebnoe posobie. Edited by M. S. Seleznev. Moscow: MGIAI, 1969. 227 p.
[DLC]

> This volume presents a comprehensive coverage of manuscript-recovery and documentary-publication projects before 1917. Early chapters cover the medieval chronicles and the eighteenth century, but the bulk of the volume relates to the activities of the nineteenth and early twentieth centuries. Although more extensive, it does not completely replace the earlier volume by P. G. Sofinov (see A-90).

A-85. Maiakovskii, Il'ia Lukich.
Ocherki po istorii arkhivnogo dela v SSSR. 2d rev. ed. Moscow, 1960. 338 p. A publication of GAU and MGIAI.
[DLC-CD1711.M355; MH-Slav612.110]

> Covering the period up to 1917, this is the most comprehensive and up-to-date survey of the history of the prerevolutionary development of archives in the area now constituting the Soviet Union. Written from the contemporary Soviet perspective on archives administration, it is most extensive in its coverage of state institutional developments, and shows less appreciation for details about private, religious, and other non-state collections. Its depth of scholarship fails to measure up to Ikonnikov's earlier study (A-83). Footnotes are kept to a minimum and the volume is particularly marred by complete absence of indices and by the lack of bibliography, beyond the brief introductory survey of previous general works. Many parts of the 1960 edition are revised and expanded from the 1941 edition. Undoubtedly based on the author's lectures at MGIAI, both of these editions can be compared to the author's earlier lecture series at the Petrograd Archeological Institute in 1918, published as *Istoricheskii ocherk arkhivnogo dela v Rossii* (Petrograd, 1920; 175 p.). Both Maiakovskii's 1941 and 1960 editions are more comprehensive in coverage than the corresponding

prerevolutionary section in the 1940 volume by A. V. Chernov, *Istoriia i organizatsiia arkhivnogo dela v SSSR (Kratkii ocherk)* (Moscow: GAU, 1940; 267 p.).

A-86. Maksakov, V. V.
"Archives in the Soviet Union: 1. Archives in Prerevolutionary Russia,"
Indian Archives 12 (Jan.-Dec. 1958): 63-75.

>   The only published summary in English, this article is based largely on Maiakovskii's more extensive treatment (A-85). It lacks notes and bibliography. Its basically factual, but somewhat unappreciative, approach is explicitly intended to set the stage for the subsequent laudatory coverage of Soviet achievements in the second part of the article (see A-97).

A-87. [Russia. Laws, statutes, etc.]
Sbornik materialov, otnosiashchikhsia do arkhivnoi chasti v Rossii. 2 vols.
Petrograd: Tipografiia Glavnogo upravleniia udelov, 1916-1917.
[DLC-LawKR670.A1 and CD1711.R8; MH-Slav620.98]

>   Issued by the Imperial Russian Historical Society, these volumes present a comprehensive digest of prerevolutionary laws and regulations relating to state archives. Drawn from the complete collection of Russian laws, they provide the legal framework for a study of the development of state repositories by detailing the official statutory actions taken by the state with regard to documentary records.

A-88. Samokvasov, D. Ia.
Arkhivnoe delo v Rossii. 2 vols. Moscow: Tipografiia A. I. Mamontova, 1902.
>   Vol. 1: *Sovremennoe russkoe arkhivnoe nestroenie.* 131 + 37 p.
>   Vol. 2: *Proshedshaia, nastoiashchaia i budushchaia postanovka arkhivnogo dela v Rossii.* 125 + 180 p.
[DLC-YudinCD1711.S19; MH-Slav612.20]

>   This important work by the director of the Moscow archive of the Ministry of Justice was published in conjunction with his program for archival reform, *Proekt arkhivnoi reformy i sovremennoe sostoianie okonchatel'nykh arkhivov v Rossii* (Moscow: Tovarishchestvo tipografii A. I. Mamontova, 1902; 48 p.). The first volume surveys the administration of archives in the country, describes the archival work of the St. Petersburg Archeological Institute, the work of regional archival commissions, and other local archival efforts, and gives some coverage to the central historical archives in Moscow and archival publications. The second volume presents a brief history of archives, a survey of their present organization, and argues the case for reform. The appendix to the second volume presents important statistical data about archival holdings at that time, providing the most complete available list of prerevolutionary repositories and data about them.

A-89. Slukhovskii, Mikhail Ivanovich.
Bibliotechnoe delo v Rossii do XVIII veka. Iz istorii knizhnogo prosveshcheniia.
Moscow: Izd-vo "Kniga," 1968. 231 p.
[DLC-Z819.A1.S57; MH-B8825.77]

> This brief survey of the development of libraries in Russia, with extensive
> notes and some bibliography, brings up to date but does not completely
> replace the earlier volume by V. E. Vasil'chenko, *Ocherk istorii
> bibliotechnogo dela v Rossii XI-XVIII vv.* (Moscow: Gosudarstvennoe izd-vo
> kul'turno-prosvetitel'noi literatury, 1948; 157 p.)

A-90. Sofinov, Pavel Georgievich
Iz istorii russkoi dorevoliutsionnoi arkheografii (Kratkii ocherk). Moscow, 1957.
157 p.
[DLC-Z286.H5S6; MH-Slav602.82.5]

> Presents brief but fairly comprehensive coverage of manuscript recovery and
> publication projects during the eighteenth and nineteenth centuries with
> details about archeographical expeditions, the Archeographical Commission,
> and the archeographical work of the Academy of Sciences and other
> institutions.

b. Soviet Period

The following bibliography lists only the most general and comprehensive books
and articles, and does not include the many short articles published in the Soviet
Union and abroad. For a more extensive bibliography of Soviet publications to
1959, see *Katalog arkhivovedcheskoi literatury, 1917-1959 gg.* (A-1), pp. 47-132;
see also the supplements covering publications through 1963 (A-2), pp. 43-92, and
from 1964 through 1967 (A-3), pp. 41-114. Additional bibliographical compilations can be found in the annual *Arkheograficheskii ezhegodnik* (A-69).

A-91. Belov, G. A.
"The Organization of the Archive System in the USSR." *Archives* 7 (October
1964):211-22.

> This laudatory but factual survey of Soviet archival developments and the
> organization of central state archives prior to the 1961 reform by the director
> of the Main Archival Administration is the best summary available in English.
> It contains much more information than does the more popularized article
> published by Belov in the American archival journal: "History that Lives
> Again: Archives in the USSR," *American Archivist* 26 (October
> 1963):439-42. See also the similar article "L'organizzazione degli archivi
> nell'unione delle Repubbliche sovietiche socialiste," *Rassegna degli Archivi di
> Stato* 24, no. 1 (1964):23-42.

A-92. Belov, G. A.
*Zur Geschichte, Theorie and Praxis des Archivwesens in der UdSSR/Voprosy istorii,
teorii i praktiki arkhivnogo dela v SSSR.* Marburg, 1971. 208 p.
Veröffentlichungen der Archivschule Marburg–Institut für Archivwissenschaft, no. 6.

PART A — GENERAL BIBLIOGRAPHY

This bilingual text on the development of the Soviet archival system is an adaptation of a series of popularized lectures given by the Director General of the Soviet Main Archival Administration at the Marburg Archive School in 1969. The new version updates and somewhat expands the coverage presented in the other articles, but offers little more substantive information than was already available in other sources, and is completely undocumented.

A-93. Belov, G. A., and V. V. Maksakov.
"Arkhivy." In *Sovetskaia istoricheskaia entsiklopediia* 1 (1961):846-67.
An extensive description of the archival organization before the 1961 reform, with some historical notes and bibliography.

A-94.Epstein, Fritz T.
"Archives Administration in the Soviet Union." *American Archivist* 20 (April 1957):131-45.
A sketchy, critical summary of developments in Soviet state archives through the early 1950's based on information available in the West.

A-95. *Istoriia sovetskoi arkheografii. Uchebnoe posobie.* Edited by M. S. Seleznev.
Moscow: MGIAI, 1966-1967.
[DLC-Z286.H5I85; MH-Slav602.80.25]
Vol. 1: *Pobeda Velikoi Oktiabr'skoi sotsialisticheskoi revoliutsii i pervye shagi sovetskoi arkheografii (1917-1920 gg.).* By M. S. Seleznev. Moscow: MGIAI, 1966. 45 p.
Vol. 2: *Arkheografiia v 1920-e do serediny 30kh godov.* By I. I. Korneva and E. M. Tal'man. Moscow: MGIAI, 1966. 85 p.
Vol. 3: *Arkheografiia v predvoennye gody (Serdina 1930-kh gg.–iiun' 1941 g.).* By T. V. Bataeva. Moscow: MGIAI, 1967. 56 p.
Vol. 4: *Arkheografiia v gody Velikoi otechestvennoi voiny (1941-1945).* By D. M. Epshtein and L. I. Arapova. Moscow: MGIAI, 1966. 43 p.
Vol. 5: *Arkheografiia v poslevoennye gody (1945-1955).* By T. V. Bataeva, E. M. Tal'man, and D. M. Epshtein. Moscow: MGIAI, 1967. 83 p.
Vol. 6: *Arkheografiia v period razvernutogo stroitel'stva kommunizma.* By I. I. Korneva, E. M. Tal'man, and D. M. Epshtein. Moscow: MGIAI, 1967. 110 p.
The short pamphlets which make up this series give the most extensive coverage available of documentary publication and other archeographical activities of all types of Soviet archival or manuscript repositories. See also the earlier treatise by S. N. Valk, *Sovetskaia arkheografiia.* Leningrad: Izd-vo AN SSSR, 1948; 289 p.

A-96. Kozlitin, I. P.
Arkhivy uchrezhdenii, organizatsii, i predpriiatii SSSR. Zakonodatel'stvo i sovremennaia organizatsiia. Edited by V. V. Maksakov. Moscow, 1957. 88 p.
[DLC-CD1736.A3K6; MH]
This short survey lecture on the development of archival organization is less complete than others but useful for its inclusion of a section on manuscript

divisions of libraries and museums and the Academy of Sciences collections.
Largely superseded by other publications.

A-97. Maksakov, V. V.
"Archives in the Soviet Union: II. Archives since the Victory of the Great October
Socialist Revolution." *Indian Archives* 13 (1959-1960):74-99.

> After a very sketchy historical introduction, this article—translated from the
> text of the noted Soviet archivist—gives a brief description of the nine central
> state archives as they were organized just before the 1961 reform, and
> includes brief notes about the Communist Party, Foreign Ministry, and other
> archival repositories in the USSR. For Part I of the article see A-86.

A-98. Maksakov, V. V.
Istoriia i organizatsiia arkhivnogo dela v SSSR (1917-1945 gg.). Edited by Iu. F.
Kononov. Moscow: Izd-vo "Nauka," 1969. 431 p.
[DLC-CD1711.M38; MH-Slav612.159.5]

> This recent posthumous volume gives the most thorough and extensive
> coverage of Soviet archival development up to 1945, with emphasis on the
> state archival system including both central and regional aspects. It includes
> the bulk of the author's earlier volume, *Arkhivnoe delo v pervye gody
> sovetskoi vlasti* (Moscow: GAU, 1959; 161 p.), re-edited and slightly
> expanded in some sections. A very factual presentation, in places it lacks
> adequate analysis of the rationale behind new developments, and of the
> relationship between the regulations summarized and prior institutional
> arrangements, thus leaving the reader at times confused about the transitions
> between successive organizational patterns. The final section covering the
> archival reorganization of 1941 is regrettably sketchy. Footnote references
> which have been updated give a key to the most important literature on the
> subject, but there is no bibliography, except for the short introductory essay
> by the editor. The lack of adequate indexing (only personal names are
> covered) is a further drawback for reference use.

A-99. [Russia (1923-USSR). Laws, statutes, etc.]
Sbornik rukovodiashchikh materialov po arkhivnomu delu (1917–iiun' 1941 gg.).
Moscow: GAU, MGIAI, 1961. 266 p.
[DLC-Law KR2295.A7.1961]

> This collection of reprints of a selection of laws and regulations on archival
> matters up to 1941 is very helpful for the establishment of the official
> decrees, name changes, and other details. The volume gives more extensive
> coverage to the 20's than the 30's, and does not cover the extensive
> reorganization of 1941. A few of the most important archival regulations,
> including the more recent ones from 1958 and 1961, are reprinted in the
> small booklet, *K 50-letiiu sovetskogo arkhivnogo dela. Osnovnye
> postanovleniia Sovetskogo pravitel'stva* (Moscow: GAU, 1968; 62 p.), put out
> on the occasion of the fiftieth anniversary celebration.

MU ARCHIVES

PART B
CENTRAL STATE ARCHIVES OF THE USSR

PART B

CENTRAL STATE ARCHIVES OF THE USSR

At the heart of the system of Soviet archives, the all-union central state archives serve as the repository for the bulk of official state records from the earliest documents of the appanage principalities and the Moscow state to the contemporary files of the Soviet government. They also include a wide range of other types of documentation, from rich collections of medieval religious manuscripts to the personal papers of leading cultural figures and extensive files of documentary films and sound recordings.

Currently eleven separate repositories make up the central state archives of the USSR, nine in Moscow and two in Leningrad. Although to a certain extent the divisions among the archives have been rationalized according to date, subject, or nature of the documentation, much overlapping remains. The consequent difficulties of knowing which materials will be located in which institution arise from the complex history and past organization of archives and from the fact that in archival arrangements precedence has usually been given to the origin or previous location of documents rather than to strictly rationalized chronological or subject-matter categories. Each of these eleven archives has its own director and staff, but all are directly controlled by the Main Archival Administration under the Council of Ministers of the USSR (GAU). They are listed below in the order in which they appear in official Soviet publications; the abbreviations in parentheses following the official archive names form the acronyms by which the archives are usually known in the Soviet Union and referred to in the documentation of Soviet publications:

1) Tsentral'nyi gosudarstvennyi arkhiv Oktiabr'skoi revoliutsii, vysshikh organov gosudarstvennoi vlasti i organov gosudarstvennogo upravleniia SSSR (TsGAOR SSSR) [Central State Archive of the October Revolution, High Organs of State Government, and Organs of State Administration of the USSR];
2) Tsentral'nyi gosudarstvennyi arkhiv narodnogo khoziaistva SSSR (TsGANKh SSSR) [Central State Archive of the National Economy of the USSR];
3) Tsentral'nyi gosudarstvennyi arkhiv Sovetskoi Armii (TsGASA) [Central State Archive of the Soviet Army];
4) Tsentral'nyi gosudarstvennyi arkhiv Voenno-Morskogo Flota SSSR (TsGAVMF SSSR) [Central State Archive of the Navy of the USSR], in Leningrad;
5) Tsentral'nyi gosudarstvennyi arkhiv literatury i iskusstva SSSR (TsGALI SSSR) [Central State Archive of Literature and Art of the USSR];
6) Tsentral'nyi gosudarstvennyi arkhiv drevnikh aktov (TsGADA) [Central State Archive of Ancient Acts];
7) Tsentral'nyi gosudarstvennyi istoricheskii arkhiv SSSR (TsGIA SSSR) [Central State Historical Archive of the USSR], in Leningrad;
8) Tsentral'nyi gosudarstvennyi voenno-istoricheskii arkhiv SSSR (TsGVIA SSSR) [Central State Military History Archive of the USSR];
9) Tsentral'nyi gosudarstvennyi arkhiv kinofotodokumentov SSSR

PART B — CENTRAL STATE ARCHIVES

(TsGAKFD SSSR) [Central State Archive of Film and Photographic Documents of the USSR];

10) Tsentral'nyi gosudarstvennyi arkhiv zvukozapisei SSSR (TsGAZ SSSR) [Central State Archive of Sound-Recordings of the USSR];

11) Tsentral'nyi gosudarstvennyi arkhiv nauchno-tekhnicheskoi dokumentatsii SSSR (TsGANTD SSSR) [Central State Archive of Scientific and Technical Documentation of the USSR].

The list of central state archives in this category has varied considerably in the course of the fifty-year development of Soviet archives through frequent changes in nomenclature and reorganization of the breakdown and administration of repositories as explained in the historical introduction above. The most recent major reorganization of the state archival system took place in 1961 following the shift of the Main Archival Administration from the Ministry of Internal Affairs to its more independent status directly under the Council of Ministers of the USSR. This reorganization involved chiefly TsGAOR, whose economic sections were split off to form an independent Central State Archive of the National Economy (TsGANKh). At the same time, the Central State Historical Archive in Moscow (Tsentral'nyi gosudarstvennyi istoricheskii arkhiv v Moskve—TsGIAM) was liquidated and its fonds were transferred to the administration of TsGAOR, where they now constitute a prerevolutionary division of the archive; some of the personal fonds from TsGIAM were subsequently transferred to TsGIA SSSR in Leningrad. With the abolishment of TsGIAM, the Central State Historical Archive in Leningrad (TsGIAL) became officially the Central State Historical Archive of the USSR (TsGIA SSSR). Thus in 1961 there were nine central state archives. The additional two all-union central archives added during the 1960's—TsGANTD in 1964 and TsGAZ in 1967—are still in the process of formation and have not yet opened as working repositories for research.

The Central State Archive of the Russian SFSR in Moscow will be covered in Part G below together with the other regional or city-level state archives located in Moscow and Leningrad.

The following pages describe briefly the history, scope, and contents of the eleven current all-union central state archives, and, to the extent possible, present information about working conditions for foreign scholars. A separate section under each archive will provide an annotated bibliography of the available published guides, and their general descriptions. A final section will present a list of the most important published catalogs or inventories of different fonds or collections. Again, to the extent possible, coverage will also extend to selected articles surveying different fonds or materials on specialized subjects; this addition has been deemed important for these archives because of the general lack of adequate published finding aids, and because card catalogs and unpublished shelf lists or inventories (*opisi*) are usually not available to foreign readers. The lists of reference literature, however, are far from exhaustive and can be used only as a starting point for researchers interested in the holdings.

1. TsENTRAL'NYI GOSUDARSTVENNYI ARKHIV OKTIABR'SKOI REVO-LIUTSII, VYSSHIKH ORGANOV GOSUDARSTVENNOI VLASTI I ORGANOV GOSUDARSTVENNOGO UPRAVLENIIA SSSR (TsGAOR SSSR)

[Central State Archive of the October Revolution, High Organs of State Government, and Organs of State Administration of the USSR]

Address: Moscow, G-435, Bol'shaia Pirogovskaia ulitsa, 17

HISTORY AND CONTENTS

The Central State Archive of the October Revolution of the USSR, or TsGAOR, since its beginnings in 1920 has developed into one of the most extensive and significant archives in the Soviet Union encompassing over 3,000 separate fonds with more than 3,000,000 storage units (as of 1969 figures). Most significantly, TsGAOR houses the majority of records of Soviet central government and various organs of state administration since 1917. Its prerevolutionary division contains many records from the late nineteenth and early twentieth centuries, including the majority of prerevolutionary police records and many files relating to the Russian revolutionary movement and the revolutions of 1917.

TsGAOR SSSR owes its origin to the fourth section of the State Archive of the Russian Federation [Gosudarstvennyi arkhiv RSFSR–Gosarkhiv], which in the fall of 1920 became the gathering point for materials directly relating to the October Revolution; this section became known as the Archive of the October Revolution [Arkhiv Oktiabr'skoi revoliutsii–AOR] and subsequently acquired the status of a separate repository within the state system. It was officially established as the Central Archive of the October Revolution [Tsentral'nyi arkhiv Oktiabr'skoi revoliutsii–TsAOR] in 1925, by which time it had become the principal repository for records of many phases of the new Soviet government as well. In the early 20's, TsAOR was also the storage point for documents gathered for the history of the Bolshevik Party (Istpart), but when the Communist Party Archive was established in 1927-1928 under the Lenin Institute, Party materials were transferred there, and all subsequent records of the Party and its leaders remained in this separate repository (see Part D).

In 1938 TsAOR was renamed the Central State Archive of the October Revolution [Tsentral'nyi gosudarstvennyi arkhiv Oktiabr'skoi revoliutsii], which gave it the acronym TsGAOR that it has retained ever since. In 1941 its official name was changed to the Central State Archive of the October Revolution and Socialist Development [Tsentral'nyi gosudarstvennyi arkhiv Oktiabr'skoi revoliutsii i sotsialisticheskogo stroitel'stva], which name it kept until it acquired its present official name in 1961. At that time, as mentioned above, the predominantly economic sections of TsGAOR were separated from it to form the distinctive Central State Archive of the National Economy (TsGANKh), newly established and adjacent to TsGAOR in the central complex of archival buildings housing the headquarters of the Main Archival Administration. Also in the early 1960's, many groups of fonds relating primarily to the Russian SFSR were transferred to the newly established Central State Archive of the RSFSR (see Part G below). A further division of TsGAOR records is now taking place with the formation of the new Central State Archive of Scientific and Technical Documentation (TsGANTD), but this new archive will predominantly be drawing materials from TsGANKh rather than from TsGAOR itself. Before 1961, TsGAOR contained materials only from the postrevolutionary period and from 1917 itself, but after 1961, with the dissolution of the Central State Historical Archive in Moscow (TsGIAM), TsGAOR took over most of its fonds to form a separate prerevolutionary division.

By far the largest volume of materials in TsGAOR make up the "Division of Fonds of the High Organs of State Government of the USSR." These include the records of the ministries and other Soviet administrative organs, with the notable exception of the Foreign Ministry records retained separately under the administration of the Foreign Ministry, military records retained in TsGASA and the Defense Ministry archive, naval records in TsGAVMF, and files relating to economic affairs now in TsGANKh. Communist Party records, of course, are also all retained separately. In the case of defunct agencies, the records are transferred to TsGAOR after the office is dissolved. For ongoing governmental organs, there is usually a fifteen-year time lag before the files are transferred to the archive, so by the end of 1969, documents extended up to 1955. However, there is some variance in this time lag for certain special types of materials. For details of some of the early governmental fonds in TsGAOR, mostly from the pre-1924 period, see the published guide (B-1), pp. 36-209.

In earlier years, records relating specifically to the Russian federation were also retained in TsGAOR and its predecessors, but since the creation of a separate Central State Archive of the RSFSR in 1957 most files relating to the RSFSR since its formation in 1923 have been transferred there; the notable exception is the case of files of the Ministry of Internal Affairs (MVD) and its predecessor, the People's Commissariat of Internal Affairs (NKVD) which have all been retained in TsGAOR because there was no separate internal ministry for the Russian republic. TsGAOR also contains materials relating to the courts and other prosecuting and legal organs of the RSFSR as well as for the USSR (for the period 1918-1924, see B-1, pp. 204-09).

The second division of TsGAOR is referred to as the "Division of Fonds of Trade Unions and Other Social Organizations." This division includes the holdings transferred from the former Central Archive of the Trade-Union Movement and Labor Organizations [Tsentral'nyi arkhiv profdvizheniia i organizatsii truda] which had existed independently from 1930 to 1941, and the records still stored in the central archive of the All-Union Central Council of Trade Unions [Vsesoiuznyi Tsentral'nyi sovet professional'nykh soiuzov] but now administered by TsGAOR (see B-3 and B-1, pp. 227-68). A section of these materials is comprised of the records of different cooperative organizations, including some from the early 1920's (B-1, pp. 269-88). Another section includes fonds of institutions, organizations, and publications involved in various scientific, educational, and cultural activities, particularly those related to social and labor organizations (see B-1, pp. 211-26).

Also from the postrevolutionary period, TsGAOR now has approximately 50 fonds of the private papers of governmental leaders, although none of these would pertain to high Party officials whose papers would be deposited in the Party archives.

The "Division of Prerevolutionary Fonds," constituting the third division of TsGAOR, was established after the 1961 reorganization liquidated the former Central State Historical Archive in Moscow (TsGIAM). In reality this involved more a change of name than a major transfer of documents, because since 1946 both TsGAOR and TsGIAM had been housed in the same complex of buildings; even many of the same fond numbers formerly used in TsGIAM are actually still used for the location of documents in the prerevolutionary division of TsGAOR, and the original TsGIAM guide remains, with certain notable exceptions, the only available description of these holdings (see B-2).

As originally constituted, TsGIAM evolved from the seventh (historical-revolutionary) division of the Single State Archival Fond organized in 1918 to contain documents relating to the revolutionary movement before the October Revolution. The largest section was established as the Petrograd Historical-Revolutionary Archive [Petrogradskii istoriko-revoliutsionnyi arkhiv]. The section which was gathered in Moscow in 1920 became the third division of the State Archive of the RSFSR (Gosarkhiv) and was usually referred to as the Moscow Historical-Revolutionary Archive [Moskovskii istoriko-revoliutsionnyi arkhiv]. From the outset, this archive—in contrast to others organized at the time—consisted of an artificially contrived collection, gathering documents by virtue of their pertinence to the revolutionary movement rather than according to their archival or institutional origin. Most particularly, it gathered all the files of prerevolutionary police and various sections of the gendarme corps from several different sources. The documentary materials that had been gathered in the Petrograd section were moved to Moscow in 1924, at which time the Moscow Historical-Revolutionary Archive was combined with the former St. Petersburg Main Archive of the Ministry of Foreign Affairs to become the Archive of the Revolution and Foreign Policy [Arkhiv revoliutsii i vneshnei politiki]. From 1925 through 1932 this archive officially remained as one of the principal storage divisions of the Moscow Central Historical Archive [Moskovskii tsentral'nyi istoricheskii arkhiv].

In 1933 the Archive of the Revolution and Foreign Policy was split to form the State Archive of the Revolution [Gosudarstvennyi arkhiv revoliutsii] and the separate Archive of Foreign Policy [Arkhiv vneshnei politiki]. However, both archives continued to be housed in the same building, and were administratively recombined again in 1941 to form the Central State Historical Archive in Moscow (TsGIAM). At that time TsGIAM had three divisions—internal policy, foreign policy, and personal papers; the third division, which included the Romanov family papers from the earlier Novoromanovskii arkhiv of the 1920's, consisted of private fonds, mostly from the nineteenth and early twentieth centuries, that had earlier been part of the former Moscow Central Historical Archive. In 1946 the foreign policy division became the separate Archive of Russian Foreign Policy [Arkhiv vneshnei politiki Rossii—AVPR] under the archival administration of the Ministry of Foreign Affairs. Since AVPR took over the building formerly occupied by TsGIAM, the remaining divisions of TsGIAM were moved to the building adjacent to TsGAOR, and then became the prerevolutionary division of TsGAOR in 1961. In recent years there has been some discussion of reuniting the entire prerevolutionary divison of TsGAOR with TsGIA SSSR in Leningrad, which actually houses the rest of the prerevolutionary archives of the Ministries of Justice and Internal Affairs from which the TsGIAM fonds were originally separated, but the project has not reached the actual planning stage.

By far the largest part of the prerevolutionary division of TsGAOR contains the records of police and censorship activities, originating from several different sources. A large section contains the records of the Third Department of His Majesty's Own Chancellery from its establishment by Nicholas I in 1826 to 1880; these are filed according to their original organization, including the records of the different "expeditions" of the department charged with various types of police functions and censorship.

The later police records in TsGAOR are principally those from the Department of Police under the Ministry of Internal Affairs dating from 1881 to 1917. The bulk of this ministry archive is now housed in TsGIA SSSR in Leningrad (see B-102, pp. 99-135); aside from the main files of the Department of Police, only a few other chancellery files (roughly 1802-1917), and some other materials directly relating to the revolutionary movement—including the large collection of illegal publications— were removed to the Historical Revolutionary Archive which has now ended up in TsGAOR.

Several files from the nineteenth-century Ministry of Justice records, the bulk of which are also located in TsGIA SSSR, are also now found in TsGAOR; these are mostly materials relating to prison administration in the late nineteenth century, although the records from the Shlissel'burg Fortress go back to the end of the eighteenth century.

Another group of fonds are the records of special investigating commissions charged with looking into subversion or revolutionary affairs, such as the commission charged with investigating the Decembrists in 1826. There are also groups of police files that have been drawn from guberniia records, such as those from the Moscow and St. Petersburg gendarme administration and other similar internal security organs; these fonds date from the 1860's to 1917. Finally, there are a group of fonds relating to political parties in Russia during the 1905-1917 period, including the files of the Constitutional Democratic Party (Cadets), the "Union of the Russian People," and the "Union of the 17th of October."

A separate section of TsGIAM contained some three hundred different fonds of the private papers of many important Russian families, mostly of the nineteenth and early twentieth centuries, but some going back as far as the fifteenth century. About 30 of these fonds have been transferred to TsGIA SSSR in Leningrad since 1961, and plans are underway for further shifts. One especially important collection that still remains in TsGAOR are the personal papers of members of the Romanov family.

Another important section of papers in TsGAOR is made up of the remains of the original Archive of the October Revolution that had gathered materials specifically relating to 1917. Although now the most significant materials relating to the Bolshevik Party activities during 1917 in preparation for and in pursuance of the October Revolution have been transferred to the Central Party Archive, TsGAOR retains an important group of fonds pertaining to developments between February and October, including many of the records of the Fourth State Duma, of the Provisional Government, of the Petrograd Soviet, and of military-revolutionary committees during 1917 (B-1, pp. 14-33). Another group of materials relate to "counter-revolutionary groups" during the period of civil war and foreign intervention (B-1, pp. 289-97).

The large group of fonds and documentary collections that constituted the former Russian Archive in Prague, which were transferred to Moscow in 1945, is of particular interest to scholars concerned with the late nineteenth and early twentieth centuries and with the Russian emigration. This archive, which had been under the control of the Czechoslovak Foreign Ministry, had been founded in Prague by a group of Russian émigrés as the repository of their papers; in the course of the late 1920's and 1930's it had grown to be the most significant collection of documents on the Russian revolutionary period outside the Soviet Union; in addition to documents, it also contained significant runs of serials and collections of pamphlets, etc. All of the manuscript materials were brought to Moscow. Most of them are now housed in TsGAOR, where they have generally remained closed to research. They include some materials on anarchist revolutionaries who had been in exile in the West before the Revolution, on Russian participation in the First World War, and on the February Revolution and Civil War. The largest section represents materials contributed by post-1917 Russian émigrés (see B-10).

A special division of TsGAOR is devoted to the storage of microfilms; these contain a wide range of documentary materials relating to the Soviet Union and Russian history which have been acquired from various archives throughout the world through extensive international efforts and exchange programs. Although many foreign microfilm acquisitions go to other archives, libraries, or institutes under the Academy of Sciences in connection with specific projects, the microfilm division of TsGAOR is officially the centralized microfilm repository for the USSR and is supposed to keep records of all foreign documentary materials available on microfilm (see B-13).

A final storage division of TsGAOR consists of printed materials of various types. Included here is one of the most extensive collections of pre-1917 illegal revolutionary publications. There is also a rich collection of revolutionary handbills, posters, and pamphlets, and other types of printed documentation dating from 1917 and postrevolutionary years (see B-14).

WORKING CONDITIONS

Access to different fonds in TsGAOR for foreign scholars varies considerably depending on the research topic and specific materials involved. As a general rule,

PART B – CENTRAL STATE ARCHIVES

Western scholars have not had access to postrevolutionary documents in this archive, although in a few instances documents from less sensitive fonds from the 1920's have been made available. On the other hand, many prerevolutionary materials have remained closed or available only on a highly selective basis, particularly those dating close to 1917. Access has not been permitted to the entire group of fonds that constituted the former Russian Archive in Prague.

The lack of adequate guides and catalogs often makes the working conditions for foreign scholars in TsGAOR exceedingly difficult. The early guides, although sorely dated, are still helpful, but reorganization of some parts of the holdings, added to the sketchy nature of those guides, makes the unavailability of a more extensive catalog most frustrating. As with most of the central state archives, unpublished inventories (*opisi*) of individual fonds are usually not made available, so that the researcher is dependent on the archival staff to choose his materials.

There is an extensive card catalog, the compilation of which is still in progress, but it is available only for staff use, and hence completely closed to foreign scholars. Foreign scholars normally work in the special reading room for foreigners, shared with other archives in the same complex of buildings housing the headquarters of the Main Archival Administration.

TsGAOR has its own large library with many general reference materials and other published sources relating to the materials in the archive. Foreign scholars do not have direct access to the library stacks or its catalogs, but volumes may be requested and will be brought to the foreigners' reading room, when these pertain to the manuscript research in progress.

PUBLISHED GUIDES AND GENERAL DESCRIPTIONS

There is no up-to-date guide or general description of TsGAOR SSSR as it is currently organized, although a general handbook is reportedly in preparation. The most recent description of the development of the archive by its current director, N. P. Prokopenko, "TsGAOR SSSR–50 let," in *Sovetskie arkhivy*, 1970, no. 5, pp. 3-13, describes only the general categories of documents to be found there and some of the major publication projects. The same is true of Prokopenko's earlier article, "Ob osnovnykh napravleniiakh raboty TsGAOR SSSR," in *Voprosy arkhivovedeniia*, 1965, no. 2, pp. 3-12. The only fuller description consists of the two short sections covering TsGAOR and the now defunct TsGIAM before their merger, prepared some 15 years ago and published in 1956 in the general directory of state archives, *Gosudarstvennye arkhivy Soiuza SSR. Kratkii spravochnik* (A-7), pp. 9-16, and 37-43. See also the article by N. P. Prokopenko, "Tsentral'nyi gosudarstvennyi arkhiv Oktiabr'skoi revoliutsii i sotsialisticheskogo stroitel'stva SSSR," in *Istoricheskii arkhiv*, 1957, no. 5, pp. 247-58. The two general guides to these archives listed below, although now 25 years old, remain the only comprehensive coverage of major segments of the holdings.

A brief historical sketch of the development of TsGAOR can also be found in the article by A. F. Butenko, "Iz istorii TsGAOR SSSR," in the early publication of Glavnoe arkhivnoe upravlenie, *Informatsionnyi biulleten'*, no. 7 (1958), pp. 37-49.

On the earlier period, see also the short article by B. Dalago, "Arkhiv revoliutsii za 20 let," *Arkhivnoe delo* 47 (1938, no. 3):79-87, and by G. Kostomarov, "Tsentral'-nyi arkhiv Velikoi Oktiabr'skoi sotsialisticheskoi revoliutsii," *Arkhivnoe delo* 47 (1938, no. 3):30-52.

Division of State Fonds of the USSR

B-1. [Russia (1923-USSR). Tsentral'nyi gosudarstvennyi arkhiv Oktiabr'skoi revoliutsii i sotsialisticheskogo stroitel'stva.]
Tsentral'nyi gosudarstvennyi arkhiv Oktiabr'skoi revoliutsii i sotsialisticheskogo stroitel'stva. Putevoditel'. Edited by V. V. Maksakov. Moscow: GAU, 1946. 367 p.
[DLC-CD1716.A5.1946]

> This 1946 guide to TsGAOR is now hopelessly out of date as a full description of the archive but, being the only guide published, it still serves the valuable purpose of describing the earlier postrevolutionary fonds in many of the original TsGAOR sections. The holdings covered date from the years 1917 to the early 30's with the bulk of the material described relating to the 20's. The guide gives fond number, dates covered, and number of storage units, followed by a brief description of the contents of each fond; it also indicates the type of inventory prepared (not available to foreign readers) but contains no further bibliography. A good subject index helps locate the materials covered, as does a summary of contents. Attention should be called to the fact that many of the fonds specifically relating to economic and commercial affairs described in this guide have been transferred to the newly established TsGANKh, although there is no list available giving the fond numbers involved in the transfer. A similar situation exists with reference to the fonds specifically relating to the RSFSR that are listed in this guide, some of which have been transferred to the Central State Archive of the RSFSR.

Prerevolutionary Division

B-2. [Russia (1923-USSR). Tsentral'nyi gosudarstvennyi istoricheskii arkhiv.]
Tsentral'nyi gosudarstvennyi istoricheskii arkhiv v Moskve. Putevoditel'.
Edited by I. Nikitinskii, P. Sofinov, and V. Maksakov. Moscow: GAU, 1946. 234 p.
[DLC-CD1713.A5.1946; MH-Film W973]

> This guide surveys the contents of the now defunct TsGIAM which, for the most part, now forms the prerevolutionary division of TsGAOR. Some of the private fonds listed (pp. 113-96) have been transferred to TsGIA SSSR in Leningrad, although no exact list of these changes is available. Despite the datedness of the volume due to this reorganization, and despite its sketchy coverage and lack of item numbers, it remains the only available description of the prerevolutionary division of TsGAOR and hence is crucial to anyone working with these materials. The guide indicates the size and dates covered by the different fonds, describes the agencies from which they were drawn, and gives a brief outline of their contents. There is no indication about the existence of catalogs or inventories, although hand- or typewritten ones have

been made for most of the fonds. Neither does it give any bibliographical indications about published descriptions or about publications from different fonds. Some fonds not actually described in the guide are listed with their fond numbers at the end. Personal-name and subject indexes are included.

Fonds of Soviet Trade Unions

B-3. [Vsesoiuznyi tsentral'nyi sovet professional'nykh soiuzov. Tsentral'nyi arkhiv.] *Putevoditel'*. Edited by P. I. Kabanov et al. Volume 1. Moscow: Profizdat, 1958. 368 p.
[DLC-HD8522.V8743; MH-Slav1711.700.6]

> Describes the archival fonds of the central council of trade unions and the various sections devoted to the fonds of the different unions that form part of the council, all of which are now under the administration of TsGAOR SSSR. An appendix chronologically lists plenum meetings of the council. Additional appendices list fonds transferred earlier from the organization's archive to TsGAOR (pp. 349-54), and other fonds in TsGAOR relating to the unions (pp. 355-60). A descriptive table of contents, but neither index nor bibliography, is included. On the development of the earlier, more independent Central Archive of the Trade Union Movement and Labor Organizations, see T. Illeritskaia, "Sozdanie i deiatel'nost' Tsentral'nogo arkhiva profdvizheniia i organizatsii truda," *Arkhivnoe delo* 47(1938, no. 3):69-78, and the more recent article by N. A. Orlova, "Tsentral'nyi arkhiv profdvizheniia i organizatsii truda (1930-1941 gg.)," *Trudy MGIAI* 15(1962):199-228. The most recent general survey of the holdings of this division is the article by I. I. Belonosov, "Obzor dokumental'nykh materialov Tsentral'nogo arkhiva VTsSPS," in [Akademiia nauk SSSR. Institut istorii.], *Izmeneniia v chislennosti i sostave sovetskogo rabochego klassa. Sbornik statei* (Moscow, 1961), pp. 234-316.

SPECIALIZED PUBLISHED DESCRIPTIONS

Documents for the History of Soviet Society

B-4. Kovalenko, N. B.
"Istochniki po istorii sovetskogo obshchestva v TsGAOR SSSR." *Voprosy istorii*, 1966, no. 3, pp. 154-60.

B-5. Butenko, A. F.
"Materialy po istorii rabochego klassa SSSR v fondakh Tsentral'nogo gosudarstvennogo arkhiva Oktiabr'skoi revoliutsii i sotsialisticheskogo stroitel'stva SSSR (Obzor)." In [Leningrad. Universitet.] *Voprosy istoriografii i istochnikovedeniia istorii rabochego klassa SSSR. Sbornik statei*, pp. 75-88. Leningrad, 1962.

Prerevolutionary History

For additional coverage of documents pertaining to labor and factory history see the files described in items A-41, pp. 255-89, A-42, pp. 361-66, A-43 and those listed in A-66.

B-6. Snytko, T.
"Neopublikovannye materialy po istorii dekabristskogo dvizheniia po fondam Tsentral'nogo istoricheskogo arkhiva v Moskve." *Voprosy istorii*, 1950, no. 12, pp. 122-33.

B-7. Ivanova, N. A., and I. M. Pushkareva.
"Memuary po istorii Rossii perioda imperializma v lichnykh fondakh TsGAOR SSSR." *Voprosy arkhivovedeniia*, 1964, no. 1, pp. 105-10.

B-8. Kheifets, M. I.
"Arkhivnye materialy M. T. Loris-Melikova (K istorii vtoroi revoliutsionnoi situatsii v Rossii)." *Istoricheskii arkhiv,* 1959, no. 1, pp. 193-203.
Also covers some materials in TsGIA SSSR and other archives.

B-9. Aleksandrov, F. L., and L. M. Shalaginova.
"Den' 9 ianvaria v Rossii v 1908-1917 gg. (obzor dokumentov TsGIAM)." *Istoricheskii arkhiv*, 1958, no. 1, pp. 212-21.

Émigré Collection—Russian Archive in Prague

B-10. Fischer, George.
"The Russian Archive in Prague." *American Slavic and East European Review* 8 (Dec. 1949):289-95.
Traces the history of the Russian Archive in Prague founded by an émigré group after 1917. It mentions the especially rich materials on the early twentieth century, particularly the revolution, civil war, and later emigration, which were moved to Moscow in 1945. Bibliographical footnotes give references to publications from and about the archive, including catalogs of some parts of the holdings.

Theater History

B-11. Buss, R. Ia.
"Otdel dorevoliutsionnykh fondov TsGAOR SSSR." In Petrovskaia, I. F., *Materialy k istorii russkogo teatra v gosudarstvennykh arkhivakh SSSR. Obzory dokumentov. XVII vek–1917 g.*, pp. 171-85. Moscow: GAU, 1966. (See A-52.)

B-12. Terent'eva, L. I., and M. F. Frosina.
Section on TsGAOR in "Perechni dokumentov i materialov po istorii russkogo sovetskogo teatra 1917-1921 gg., khraniashchikhsia v TsGAOR SSSR, TsGASA, TsGALI SSSR, LGAORSS." In *Sovetskii teatr. Dokumenty i materialy. Russkii sovetskii teatr 1917-1921 gg.* (A-55), pp. 403-21.

PART B – CENTRAL STATE ARCHIVES

Microfilm Division

B-13. Belov, G. A.

"Rasshirenie istochnikovedcheskoi bazy istorii narodov SSSR za schet dokumentov, khraniashchikhsia v zarubezhnykh arkhivakh." *Arkheograficheskii ezhegodnik za 1963 god,* pp. 223-40.

> For further comments on materials acquired on microfilm from archives abroad, see the later article by Belov, "Popolnenie Gosudarstvennogo arkhivnogo fonda SSSR dokumentami zarubezhnykh arkhivov," *Voprosy istorii,* 1967, no. 6, pp. 171-78.

Printed Materials

B-14. Paramonova, N. A., and T. N. Pobezhimova.

"Fondy otdela pechatnykh izdanii TsGAOR." *Istoricheskii arkhiv,* 1960, no. 2, pp. 239-43.

2. TsENTRAL'NYI GOSUDARSTVENNYI ARKHIV NARODNOGO KhOZIAISTVA SSSR (TsGANKh SSSR)

[Central State Archive of the National Economy of the USSR]
Address: Moscow, G-435, Bol'shaia Pirogovskaia ulitsa, 17

CONTENTS

The Central State Archive of the National Economy or TsGANKh, which was established at the end of 1961, is, as its name indicates, the repository for records relating essentially to economic affairs; most have been transferred from TsGAOR or received directly from the institutions or agencies involved. As of January 1969, it contained some 1804 fonds with close to 2,900,000 storage units, mostly dating from 1918 to 1954. Thus documents in TsGANKh, with the exception of some personal fonds, all date from the Soviet period; records customarily remain in their institutional sources for fifteen years, hence the 1954 cut-off date. The six main storage divisions of TsGANKh contain fonds relating to 1) heavy industry, 2) food and light industries, 3) construction and metallurgy, 4) plans of financial organs, 5) agriculture, and 6) transportation and communications. Sections cover the records and results of the five-year industrialization plans, and of the process of agrarian collectivization; others contain the archives of ministries and organizations involved in economic matters. Already over 150 fonds containing the papers of private individuals related to economic, financial, or commercial affairs are also deposited here. The archive until recently contained extensive files of technical materials but these fonds are now being transferred to the newly established special archive for scientific and technical documentation (TsGANTD).

WORKING CONDITIONS

Although the archive is not categorically closed, there have been no records of any Western scholars who have worked there. Most of the foreign readers have been from Eastern European countries.

The archive is located in the central complex of buildings that houses the headquarters of the Main Archival Administration. It shares the main reading room with TsGAOR, but, as in the case of other archives in this complex, foreign scholars normally work in the special foreigners' reading room.

Shelf lists or inventories have been prepared for almost all the fonds in the archive and a general card catalog is in process of being compiled, but these reference aids are normally available only for the internal use of the archival staff. The archive maintains its own extensive reference library.

PUBLISHED DESCRIPTIONS

There is no published guide or general description of this archive, although a general handbook currently being prepared should be published within the next few years.

PART B – CENTRAL STATE ARCHIVES

The following short articles, the only published information available, give some general indications of the nature and organization of the holdings, but should not be considered actual finding aids:

Fedorov, A. G.

"Nekotorye itogi raboty Tsentral'nogo gosudarstvennogo arkhiva narodnogo khoziaistva SSSR." *Voprosy arkhivovedeniia*, 1964, no. 4, pp. 17-24.

Nikolaeva, M. E., and A. G. Fedorov.

"Nauchno-spravochnyi apparat v TsGANKh SSSR." *Voprosy arkhivovedeniia*, 1965, no. 4, pp. 30-37.

Beklemisheva, M. A., and F. I. Sharonov.

"Ratsional'noe razmeshchenie dokumental'nykh materialov v khranilishchakh TsGANKh SSSR." *Sovetskie arkhivy*, 1967, no. 4, pp. 78-81.

Fedorov, A.

"Dokumenty o podvigakh sovetskogo naroda." *Ekonomicheskaia gazeta* August, 1969, no. 32, p. 3.

PUBLISHED INVENTORIES AND SPECIALIZED DESCRIPTIONS

B-15. [Russia (1923-USSR). Tsentral'nyi gosudarstvennyi arkhiv Oktiabr'skoi revoliutsii i sotsialisticheskogo stroitel'stva.]
Michurin, Ivan Vladimirovich (1855-1935). Opis' dokumental'nykh materialov
lichnogo fonda No. 6556. Edited by A. N. Bakharev. Moscow: GAU, 1952. 142 p.
[DLC-Z8572.7.R8]

A complete inventory of the fond of the noted Soviet biologist is now located in TsGANKh (the inventory was prepared while the fond was still in TsGAOR). It includes a bibliography of Michurin's works, but this is not coordinated with the manuscript materials, nor are there cross-references to materials in other archives. This is the only published inventory covering a fond in TsGANKh.

B-16. Tarle, G. Ia.
"Sobranie dokumentov po istorii narodnogo khoziaistva SSSR (1917-1931 gg.)."
Istoricheskii arkhiv, 1960, no. 1, pp. 175-86.

Covers the records of the All-Union Councils of the Economy of the Russian Federation and the USSR (VSNKh RSFSR, and VSNKh SSSR).

3. TsENTRAL'NYI GOSUDARSTVENNYI ARKHIV SOVETSKOI ARMII (TsGASA)

[Central State Archive of the Soviet Army]
    Address: Moscow, G-435, Bol'shaia Pirogovskaia ulitsa, 17

CONTENTS

The archive of the Soviet Army, or TsGASA, the official repository for postrevolutionary military records, grew out of the original military section of the Single State Archival Fond, which took the name Archive of the Red Army [Arkhiv Krasnoi Armii] in 1920. It was reorganized in 1933 as the Central Archive of the Red Army [Tsentral'nyi arkhiv Krasnoi Armii] and in 1941 was renamed the Central State Archive of the Red Army [Tsentral'nyi gosudarstvennyi arkhiv Krasnoi Armii]; it took its present name in 1958. Currently the archive contains over 36,000 fonds, the earliest of which date back to the end of 1917.

The only holdings which have been outlined in published descriptions are those which date from the period of the Civil War. Seven main sections, as described in some detail in the 1945 guide (B-17), include documents relating to: 1) high command activities, 2) army unit commands and operations on different fronts, 3) commands of army corps and divisions, 4) military district commands, 5) Far East area activities, 6) independent military authorities and special services, and 7) military training schools, etc. In addition, important sections contain records of partisan and Red Guard activities. These materials all date from 1918 to 1925.

This archive also contains a division of private papers of prominent military leaders.

The voluminous military records of the Second World War remain in a special archive under the Ministry of Defense in Podol'sk, not far from Moscow, along with other records of the Soviet armed forces. (See the description below under Part D, section 3.)

WORKING CONDITIONS

The archive is officially closed to foreign scholars. Presumably, working conditions would be similar to those in other archives within this complex, as the archive is in the central buildings housing the headquarters of the Main Archival Administration.

PUBLISHED GUIDES AND GENERAL DESCRIPTIONS

There is no up-to-date guide to this archive. The most recent general description of the holdings appears in the directory of state archives, *Gosudarstvennye arkhivy Soiuza SSR. Kratkii spravochnik* (A-7), pp. 43-45. The recent article by V. V. Dushen'kin, "K 50-letiiu Tsentral'nogo gosudarstvennogo arkhiva Sovetskoi armii," in *Sovetskie arkhivy*, 1970, no. 3, pp. 44-49, summarizes the development and activities of the archive since 1920. The earlier article by F. E. Kuznetsov, "Fondy tsentral'nykh gosudarstvennykh voennykh arkhivov SSSR i ikh nauchnoe ispol'zovanie," in *Trudy MGIAI* 4 (1948):73-112, discusses its development in relation to other military archives. For details about the early development of the archive in the 1920's and 1930's see the article by M. Sokolov, "Tsentral'nyi arkhiv Krasnoi Armii za 20 let," *Arkhivnoe delo* 47 (1938, no. 3):53-68. The article by A. F. Gorlenko and A. M. Ivanov, "Osnovnye printsipy fondirovaniia dokumental'nykh materialov v Tsentral'nom gosudarstvennom arkhive Krasnoi Armii," in *Istoricheskii arkhiv,* 1956, no. 1, pp. 203-07, describes some rearrangements made since the 1945 guide (B-17); the later article by A. M. Ivanov, "Obrazovanie ob" edinennykh arkhivnykh fondov v Tsentral'nom gosudarstvennom arkhive Sovetskoi Armii," in *Voprosy arkhivovedeniia,* 1963, no. 4, pp. 46-50, adds little information about the contents or use of the materials for the researcher.

B-17. [Russia (1923-USSR). Tsentral'nyi gosudarstvennyi arkhiv Sovetskoi armii.]
Tsentral'nyi gosudarstvennyi arkhiv Krasnoi armii. Putevoditel'. Edited by
P. Sofinov. Moscow: GAU, 1945. 470 p.
[DLC-CD1732.A5.1945; MH-Slav1705.350.310]

> Covers the materials from the Red Army Archive relating to the period of the Civil War, with a few fonds going up to 1926; organized into the seven sections mentioned above, it lists many of the fond numbers and briefly describes the contents. It gives references neither to available catalogs nor to publications from the fonds. A helpful series of tables at the back explains the organization of some of the archival materials with reference to the military activities of the period. A short subject index is also provided. This guide is much more comprehensive than the 1933 edition, B-18.

B-18. [Russia (1923-USSR). Tsentral'nyi gosudarstvennyi arkhiv Sovetskoi armii.]
Arkhiv Krasnoi Armii. Compiled by A. K. Bochkov et al. Moscow: Izdanie Shtaba
RKKA, 1933. 135 p.
[no U.S. location reported]

> Briefly describes the materials dating from 1917 to 1925 located in the Archive of the Red Army as TsGASA was then called. It gives no fond numbers or other details, and is thus largely outdated by the more comprehensive 1945 guide listed above, B-17.

SPECIALIZED PUBLISHED DESCRIPTIONS

Civil War Materials

B-19. Portnov, V. P., and L. M. Chizhova.
"Partiino-politicheskaia rabota v Krasnoi Armii v gody inostrannoi voennoi interventsii i grazhdanskoi voiny v SSSR (Obzor dokumental'nykh materialov Tsentral'nogo gosudarstvennogo arkhiva Sovetskoi Armii za 1918-1920 gg.)."
Voprosy arkhivovedeniia, 1961, no. 1, pp. 85-91.

Theater History

20. Ivanov, A. M., and L. M. Chizhova.

Section on TsGASA in "Perechni dokumentov i materialov po istorii russkogo sovetskogo teatra 1917-1921 gg., khraniashchikhsia v TsGAOR SSSR, TsGASA, TsGALI SSSR, LGAORSS." In *Sovetskii teatr. Dokumenty i materialy. Russkii sovetskii teatr 1917-1921 gg.* (A-55), pp. 421-32.

World War II Materials

These documents remain in a special archive under the Ministry of Defense in Podol'sk (Moscow oblast). For the work being done with them there, see below under D-15.

PART B – CENTRAL STATE ARCHIVES

4. TsENTRAL'NYI GOSUDARSTVENNYI ARKHIV VOENNO-MORSKOGO FLOTA SSSR (TsGAVMF)

[Central State Archive of the Navy of the USSR]
Address: Leningrad, D-65, ulitsa Khalturina, 36

HISTORY AND CONTENTS

The Central State Archive of the Navy, located in Leningrad in the building constructed for its nineteenth-century predecessor, contains over 3,000 fonds relating to naval affairs, dating from the end of the seventeenth century through the Second World War. Its continuous history goes back to the early eighteenth century when the archive of the Admiralty College was established in 1718; the eighteenth-century records were taken over in the nineteenth century by the archive of the Ministry of the Navy and usually called the Main Naval Archive [Glavnyi morskoi arkhiv], one of the oldest and best-organized ministerial archives of the prerevolutionary period.

After the Revolution these records first became part of the military-naval section of the Single State Archival Fond, and were subsequently administered under the Leningrad Branch of the Central Archive of the RSFSR [Leningradskoe otdelenie Tsentral'nogo arkhiva RSFSR] and later under the Leningrad Branch of the Central Historical Archive [Leningradskoe otdelenie Tsentral'nogo istoricheskogo arkhiva]. Despite these many administrative changes, the naval records always remained housed in their own building that was constructed in the 1880's and was usually referred to by its prerevolutionary name. In 1934 the Naval History Archive [Morskoi-istoricheskii arkhiv] was established as a separately administered repository, combining the prerevolutionary holdings with more contemporary records. It adopted its present name at the time of the 1941 archival reorganization.

The earliest sections of the archive date from the beginnings of the Russian navy under Peter the Great; they contain materials relating to the founding of St. Petersburg and Kronstadt, early training schools, the early development of the Baltic and Black Sea fleets, and the chancelleries of early admirals and naval administration.

The fonds of the College of the Admiralty date from 1718 to 1827 and contain materials regarding the activities of the fleet during this period, especially the Turkish and Swedish wars; they also contain the chancellery papers of many important leaders who served in the administration of the navy.

Another section of materials relate to geographical expeditions of the eighteenth and the beginning of the nineteenth century. Materials relating to the early nineteenth century through the period of the Russo-Turkish wars of the late 1870's constitute another section of the archive. These come mostly from the different departments of the Ministry of the Navy, the chancelleries of the naval chiefs of staff, the ministerial chancellery, the fleet inspection departments, and the high commands of the different fleets.

Other parts of the archive contain the same types of records from the late nineteenth century through the First World War and the period of the Civil War, including fonds relating to naval schools and geographic expeditions.

Many fonds containing the private papers of distinguished naval figures are also housed in TsGAVMF, in many cases broadening the scope of the archival holdings since these families were often important in other fields.

Varied materials pertaining to the Soviet navy from 1917 to the mid-1950's are contained in the more contemporary sections of TsGVMF. These include documents relating to the central administration of the navy and many related affairs.

The rich map depository of the naval ministry has traditionally been maintained separately from the main naval archive; officially called the Archive of the Central Cartographic Production of the Navy (Arkhiv Tsentral'nogo kartograficheskogo proizvodstva VMF), it is housed in the same archive building. Gathered here are a wide variety of manuscript maps and navigational charts dating from the seventeenth, eighteenth, and early nineteenth centuries as well as printed ones (see B-35).

WORKING CONDITIONS

This archive is officially closed to foreign readers, but documents from some of the earlier historical fonds are on occasion made available to foreign readers in the reading room of TsGIA SSSR.

TsGAVMF maintains its own library of some 15,000 volumes relating to its holdings and to all aspects of naval history and administration. The valuable prerevolutionary library from which the present one was developed was described in the comprehensive 1916 catalog, [Russia. Morskoe ministerstvo. Biblioteka], *Sistematicheskii katalog biblioteki Morskogo ministerstva* (Petrograd: Tipografiia Morskogo ministerstva, 1916 [DLC-Z6836.R95.1916]).

PUBLISHED DESCRIPTIONS

There is no published guide to this archive. The most recent description of the holdings appears in the general directory of state archives, *Gosudarstvennye arkhivy SSSR. Kratkii spravochnik* (A-7), pp. 29-37, but the section covering the holdings in the 1933 guide listed below (B-21), gives much more detail. Several articles regarding institutional developments and publication activities in TsGAVMF are included in the recent report, *Problemy arkhivovedeniia i istorii arkhivnykh uchrezhdenii* (A-82), pp. 57-84, 114-23, and 193-203.

B-21. "Voenno-morskaia sektsiia: II-Morskoi otdel."
In [Russia (1923-USSR). Tsentral'nyi gosudarstvennyi istoricheskii arkhiv v Leningrade], *Arkhivy SSSR. Leningradskoe otdelenie Tsentral'nogo istoricheskogo arkhiva. Putevoditel' po fondam Leningradskogo otdeleniia Tsentral'nogo istoricheskogo arkhiva*, edited by A. K. Drezen, pp. 197-248. Leningrad: Lenoblizdat, 1933. (See B-103)

PART B – CENTRAL STATE ARCHIVES

A summary description of the major parts of the prerevolutionary holdings of TsGAVMF which at that time were still a division of the Military-naval section of the Leningrad Branch of the Central Historical Archive (predecessor of TsGIA SSSR); they remain housed in the same building, and the same organization of fonds has been maintained, although parts of the numbering system have been modified with the administrative reorganization. The materials covered (dating from the seventeenth century to 1926) are listed with fond numbers, very brief descriptions, and bibliographical references; published inventories are listed when available, so it is possible to tell from this guide which fonds (or parts thereof) are covered by the inventories listed below.

PUBLISHED INVENTORIES

B-22. [Russia. Morskoe ministerstvo.]
Opisanie del arkhiva Morskogo ministerstva za vremia s poloviny XVII do nachala XIX stoletiia. 10 vols. St. Petersburg, 1877-1906.
[DLC-Yudin-CD1729.0; MH-Slav644.8]
> Individual volumes, which vary between 650 and 1100 pages in length, are indexed separately with a table of dates covered by the documents; they are divided more by source of documents than by date, although the predominantly older materials fall in the earlier volumes and vice-versa. Most of the materials inventoried are from the eighteenth century, although some of the volumes extend as late as the 1820's. References to specific coverage are given under individual fonds in the 1933 descriptive guide listed above (B-21).

B-23. [Russia. Morskoe ministerstvo.]
Opis' delam Artilleriiskogo departamenta Morskogo ministerstva, 1827-1852 g. St. Petersburg: Tipografiia Morskogo kadetskogo korpusa, 1857. 117 p.
[GPB]

B-24. [Russia. Morskoe ministerstvo.]
Opis' delam departamenta korabel'nykh lesov Morskogo ministerstva, khraniashchimsia v Glavnom morskom arkhive, 1799-1853 g. St. Petersburg: Tipografiia Morskogo kadetskogo korpusa, 1858. 96 p.
[GPB]

B-25. [Russia. Morskoe ministerstvo.]
Opis' delam Glavnogo meditsinskogo upravleniia Morskogo ministerstva, khraniashchimsia v arkhive ministerstva. Part 1: *1827-1852.* [St. Petersburg, 1853-1856] . 36 p.
[GPB]

B-26. [Russia. Morskoe ministerstvo.]
Opis' delam Inspektorskogo departamenta Morskogo ministerstva, khraniashchimsia

v Glavnom morskom arkhive. Part 1: *1827-1836*; Part 2: *1837-1850.* 2 parts in 1.
[St. Petersburg, 1853-1856] . 229 p.; 267 p.
[DLC-Yudin-CD1729]

·27. [Russia. Morskoe ministerstvo.]
Opis' delam i zhurnalam bumag voenno-pokhodnoi E.I.V. kantseliarii po morskoi
chasti i delam kantseliarii Morskogo ministerstva. Part 1: *1836-1855.*
St. Petersburg: Tipografiia Morskogo kadetskogo korpusa, 1856. 197 p.
[GPB]

▪-28. [Russia. Morskoe ministerstvo.]
Opis' delam Kantseliarii flota general-intendanta, khraniashchimsia v obshchem
arkhive Morskogo ministerstva, 1827-1855. St. Petersburg: Tipografiia Morskogo
kadetskogo korpusa, 1859. 90 p.
[GPB]

▪-29. [Russia. Morskoe ministerstvo.]
Opis' delam Korablestroitel'nogo departamenta Morskogo ministerstva
khraniashchimsia v Glavnom morskom arkhive. Part 1: *1827-1850, No. del 1-2449.*
[St. Petersburg, 185?] . 299 p.
[GPB]

▪-30. [Russia. Morskoe ministerstvo.]
Opis' delam Upravleniia general-gidrografa i Gidrograficheskogo departamenta
Morskogo ministerstva, 1827-1852 gg. St. Petersburg: Tipografiia Morskogo
kadetskogo korpusa, 1857. 137 p.
[GPB]

▪-31. [Russia. Morskoe ministerstvo.]
Opis' shkanechnykh zhurnalov s 1719 po 1853 god i reestr klerkskim protokolam i
zhurnalam kantseliarii flagmanov, s 1723 g. po 1826 g. St. Petersburg, 1856.
Dopolnenie k opisi shkanechnym zhurnalam 1736-1832 gg. [n.d.]
[GPB]

3-32. [Russia. Morskoe ministerstvo.]
Opisi delam uprazdnennykh v 1836 g. Kantseliarii Morskogo ministra,
Admiralteistv-soveta i kantseliarii Nachal'nika Glavnogo morskogo shtaba Ego
Imperatorskogo Velichestva, 1827-1836 gg. [St. Petersburg, 1853-1856] . 168 p.
[DLC-Yudin-JN6550.M8.1836]

▪-33. [Russia. Morskoe ministerstvo.]
Opisi delam i dokumentam Komissii dlia sostavleniia smetnykh ischislenii na
postroennie korablei i drugikh sudov, 1824-1827 gg. i delam i zhurnalam
Korablestroitel'nogo i uchetnogo komiteta, 1827-1852 gg. St. Petersburg:
Tipografiia Morskogo kadetskogo korpusa, 1857. 234 p.
[GPB]

PART B — CENTRAL STATE ARCHIVES

Materials Regarding Lomonosov

B-34. Svirskaia, V. R.
"Tsentral'nyi gosudarstvennyi arkhiv Voenno-morskogo flota v Leningrade."
In *Lomonosov. Sbornik statei i materialov,* 3:457-70. (See A-12).

Archive of the Cartographic Division

B-35. [Russia (1923-USSR). Voenno-morskoi Flot. Upravlenie nachal'nika
gidrograficheskoi sluzhby.]
*Opisanie starinnykh atlasov, kart i planov XVI, XVII, XVIII, i poloviny XIX vv.,
khraniashchikhsia v arkhive Tsentral'nogo kartograficheskogo proizvodstva VMF.*
Compiled by V. V. Kolgushkin. [Leningrad] , 1958. 270 p.
[GBL]

> This comprehensive catalog updates the earlier prerevolutionary catalogs, the
> first one published in two volumes in 1849 and 1852, and the later ones
> published in several different editions between 1868 and 1900.

5. TsENTRAL'NYI GOSUDARSTVENNYI ARKHIV LITERATURY I ISKUSSTVA SSSR (TsGALI SSSR)

[Central State Archive of Literature and Art]
  Address: Moscow, A-212, Leningradskoe shosse, 50

CONTENTS

The Central State Archive of Literature and Art, or TsGALI, now located in its own specially constructed building a thirty-minute metro ride from the center of Moscow, was founded in 1941 as the Central State Literary Archive (Tsentral'nyi gosudarstvennyi literaturnyi arkhiv—TsGLA); its present name dates from 1954. Plans for a literary and cultural archive had been considered in the 1920's, but it was the 1940's before the large and rich groups of archival fonds of the State Literary Museum (Gosudarstvennyi literaturnyi muzei-Goslitmuzei, or GLM), were transferred to the newly established literary archive, and the former institution, although still in existence today, ceased to be a major manuscript repository (for its current holdings, see below, Part E, section 4). Since 1941 TsGALI has grown through the addition of manuscripts from other specialized literary museums, most of which had centered on important individuals, and through the incorporation of literary or artistic fonds from other state archives and historical or cultural museums. TsGALI now contains around 2,500 fonds with about 650,000 storage units, spanning the period from the sixteenth century to the present. Its two major divisions cover literature and the arts, the latter including theater, ballet, music, and cinema, in addition to such aspects of the visual arts as sculpture, architecture, and painting. Although TsGALI retains some materials related to the institutional history of the Soviet cinema, films themselves and many materials relating to motion-picture history are to be found in the State Film Archive, Gosfil'mofond (see below, Part D, section 4); documentary films, however, are stored in TsGAKFD (see below, Part B, section 9).

The largest sections of each of these divisions contain personal fonds, each organized around a single important literary or artistic figure. Most of these fonds are listed alphabetically and described briefly under the family name in the guides to the literary and artistic divisions respectively (literary, B-37, pp. 17-540 and 627-75, and arts, B-36, pp. 13-242, and 239-358, and in the supplemental volume B-38, pp. 13-268).

A relatively small section in each division is devoted to special collections, sometimes centering on an important individual whose main archives are elsewhere, such as the Pushkin or Tolstoi collections, but often preserving together materials from a particular source or relating to a particular theme, such as folklore.

The third section of each division contains the archives of different governmental agencies, cultural organizations, or institutions. In the literary division, a subsection covers literary unions, circles, or other literary-social organizations such as the fonds from *Proletkul't* (1917-1932), the All-Union Society of Proletarian Writers—*Kuznitsa*—(1920-1959). Other subsections cover educational institutes, museums, publishing houses, and publications such as encyclopedias and almanacs. The subsections covering journals and newspapers include the archives of some prerevolutionary publications such as *Russkii vestnik, Delo, Russkie vedomosti, Kur'er,* and *Rech'*, along with more recent Soviet literary publications.

The corresponding third section of the artistic division contains subsections covering government artistic committees or organizations, unions or societies such as those of actors, composers, or painters, and academies or educational institutions in the arts. Other subsections contain the archives of theaters and concert ensembles, museums, and artistic publications.

In the three decades since its foundation, TsGALI has made monumental strides in building up its holdings and reference services. However, as scholars working in this area will readily understand, it has not become the truly centralized archive for literature and art its name might imply. In fact, a large percentage of personal papers and documentary materials in the cultural realm remain highly dispersed in a wide range of libraries and museums under the Ministry of Culture and in various institutes under the Academy of Sciences, as will be apparent in the descriptions of holdings below in Parts C, E, and F.

WORKING CONDITIONS

Accessibility of manuscripts in TsGALI varies widely according to the subject or individual concerned. Many contemporary authors understandably come into the "restricted" category; fonds of recent cultural figures whose family or associates are still living often require special permission of the family. The use of unpublished literary manuscripts is sometimes restricted.

The most difficult problem for foreign scholars is the lack of adequate finding aids. More complete and up-to-date than those of any other state archive, the comprehensive published guides, although excellent reference aids of their type, are no substitute for the detailed type of catalogs needed for scholarly research, but brief inventories have been published for only a few better-known, less politically sensitive individuals (see below). As in other central state archives under the Main Archival Administration, typed or handwritten inventories—which have been prepared for almost all the fonds in the archive—are not normally available to foreign scholars, since materials relevant to their topics are usually chosen for them by the archival staff.

The archive maintains a small card catalog in the reading room with an alphabetical list of individuals whose fonds are to be found in TsGALI; it appears to be fairly complete, but it does not contain any details about the fond, except the dates of materials included and number of storage units. More extensive card catalogs of the archival holdings are available only for staff use.

Foreign scholars normally work in the main archival reading room or microfilm room, but there is usually a special assistant or page assigned to handle their requests for manuscripts. Paging is frequently slow, and in some cases, particularly involving sensitive fonds, takes two to five days or longer for foreigners, since documents must be cleared.

In the case of manuscripts in poor condition, the archive has a comprehensive program of microfilming, with the result that scholars in many cases are required to use the microfilm rather than the original.

TsGALI maintains a library related to its holdings containing in excess of 70,000 volumes and close to 500 journals. Scholars using the archive normally are permitted to use these published materials, but the stacks are closed, as are the card catalogs in most cases.

PUBLISHED GUIDES

Of all the central state archives, the TsGALI holdings are best covered by comprehensive published guides. The most current volumes for literature (1963) and art (1959) were supplemented in 1968 by a third, bringing the coverage up to date for both divisions. The short article by the current director, N. B. Volkova, "Sokrovishchnitsa sovetskoi kul'tury," *Sovetskie arkhivy,* 1966, no. 2, pp. 34-40, on the occasion of the twenty-fifth anniversary of the establishment of the archive, gives a brief description of the contents and publication activities. See also the earlier short description in the general directory of state archives, *Gosudarstvennyi arkhivy Soiuza SSR. Kratkii spravochnik* (A-7), pp. 46-50, and the historical survey by V. I. Popov and N. D. Chernikov, "Tsentral'nyi gosudarstvennyi arkhiv literatury i iskusstva SSSR (1941-1956 gg.)," *Istoricheskii arkhiv,* 1956, no. 4, pp. 229-34.

B-36. [Russia (1923-USSR). Tsentral'nyi gosudarstvennyi arkhiv literatury i iskusstva.]
Tsentral'nyi gosudarstvennyi arkhiv literatury i iskusstva SSSR. Putevoditel'.
Iskusstvo. Compiled by K. N. Kirilenko, E. R. Kogan, V. N. Kolechenkova et al.
Edited by N. F. Bel'chikov and Iu. A. Dmitriev. Moscow: GAU, 1959. 445 p.
[DLC-Z5961.R9A5; MH-Slav251.277.45]

> This guide to the artistic division of TsGALI is divided into sections covering personal fonds, special collections, and the archives of organizations and artistic institutions. Smaller fonds of individuals and some late acquisitions are listed toward the end. By far the largest section of the guide is devoted to the personal fonds of individual artists. These are listed alphabetically with a note of identification of the individuals and of the size and dates covered by the fond. Indications are given in the case of the few fonds for which a published catalog is available, but no other bibliographical information about inventories or descriptions is provided. Separate indexes cover the proper names of individuals and list organizations or subject matter. For additional holdings in the artistic division of TsGALI, see the list included at the end of the literary guide (B-37) and the supplemental (1968) guide (B-38) described below.

B-37. [Russia (1923-USSR). Tsentral'nyi gosudarstvennyi arkhiv literatury i iskusstva.]
Tsentral'nyi gosudarstvennyi arkhiv literatury i iskusstva SSSR. Putevoditel'.
Literatura. Compiled by N. B. Volkova, R. D. Voliak, E. N. Vorob'eva, et al. Edited by N. F. Bel'chikov and A. A. Volkov. Moscow: GAU, 1963. 810 p.

[DLC-Z2501.R95; MH-Slav251.277.46]

This voluminous guide to the literary section of TsGALI presents brief descriptions of the different fonds. Its organization follows that of the archive, with by far the largest space devoted to fonds of individual literary figures. In the case of these personal fonds, it gives a brief identification of the individual and the dates covered by his papers; it lists many of the manuscripts included, and for correspondence names the correspondents and the dates covered. Item numbers, however, are not provided. A similar type of brief description is provided for the institutional fonds or other collections contained in the second and third sections of the archive. There are no bibliographical data about published descriptions, etc., although mention is made (without bibliographical particulars) of the few fonds for which inventories have been published. The extensive personal-name index is particularly helpful in locating correspondence or other materials about a given author in other than his own fonds (his own is indicated in bold-face type). Subject indexes include names of organizations and societies, etc. The volume also provides a list (without details) of newly received fonds in the artistic division of the archive which were not included in the earlier guide to that division (B-36).

B-38. [Russia (1923-USSR). Tsentral'nyi gosudarstvennyi arkhiv literatury i iskusstva.] *Tsentral'nyi gosudarstvennyi arkhiv literatury i iskusstva SSSR. Putevoditel'.* Vol. 3: *Fondy, postupivshie v TsGALI SSSR v 1962-1966 gg.* Compiled by I. I. Abroskina et al. Edited by Iu. A. Krasovskii. Moscow: GAU, 1968. 484 p. [MH-Slav1684.520]

This volume supplements the two previous guides to TsGALI by describing materials received between the years 1962 and 1966. The first and largest part contains brief descriptions of 216 fonds (or additional parts of fonds), and, like the preceding volumes, includes the number of storage units, dates covered, and a brief biographical identification of the individual. A second short section describes four collections of letters, autographs, and other documents. The third section covers fonds of state institutions or cultural organizations, theaters, film studios, artistic educational establishments, publishing houses, and periodicals, etc. A fourth section lists the most recent acquisitions which are not more fully described elsewhere. Two short final sections describe other miscellaneous recent acquisitions. An extensive family-name index covers individuals mentioned in the various descriptions, and another short index covers organizations and institutions.

B-39. [Russia (1923-USSR). Tsentral'nyi gosudarstvennyi arkhiv literatury i iskusstva.] *Tsentral'nyi gosudarstvennyi arkhiv literatury i iskusstva. Putevoditel'.* Edited by N. F. Bel'chikov. Moscow: GAU, 1951. 626 p. [MH-Slav251.277.35]

This early guide to TsGALI summarizes the contents of the archive as they were up to about 1947, but since the archive had only been in existence for about five years at that time and has been subsequently greatly expanded, it is now largely superseded by the three volumes listed above (B-36, B-37, and B-38). Nevertheless, in the case of a few fonds, the descriptions of the contents differ sufficiently between the two editions to make it advisable for scholars to compare them, in the event that some correspondents or other materials might be listed in the early guide which might not appear in the more recent edition.

PUBLISHED INVENTORIES AND SPECIALIZED DESCRIPTIONS

Since there is no conveniently published list of the available published inventories (the only ones scholars are normally permitted to consult in the archives), they will be listed here, first the series published by TsGALI and then the series published earlier by the State Literary Museum.

TsGALI Series

The TsGALI series, unless otherwise indicated, are all in a similar format, published as short pamphlets that list the contents of a fond containing materials of or about a specific artistic figure. Except when so noted, they have neither bibliographies nor references to published writings; nor are the manuscripts correlated with published texts. Usually a short list at the end indicates other relevant materials in TsGALI (with fond, but not with item numbers). Complete references to materials of or about the individual in other archives are not provided, although passing references to other parts of his archive are often made in the preface. They are here listed alphabetically according to the name of the individual covered; the Library of Congress heading is the same in all cases unless otherwise indicated:

"[Russia (1923-USSR). Tsentral'nyi gosudarstvennyi arkhiv literatury i iskusstva.]"

B-40. *Briusov, Valerii Iakovlevich (1873-1924). Opis' dokumental'nykh materialov lichnogo fonda No. 56.* Edited by N. A. Serbova. Moscow: GAU, 1950. 16 p. [DLC-Z8120.3.R8; MH-Slav4139.78.5]

B-41. *Chaikovskii, Petr Il'ich (1840-1893 gg.). Opis' dokumental'nykh materialov lichnogo fonda No. 905.* Compiled by G. D. Andreeva. Edited by V. A. Kiselev. Moscow: GAU, 1955. 19 p.
[MH]
> See also the handbook to Chaikovskii manuscripts, A-10, and the additional Chaikovskii materials in E-63 and E-64.

B-42. *A. P. Chekhov. Rukopisi, pis'ma, biograficheskie dokumenty, vospominaniia, teatral'nye postanovki, risunki, fotografii. Opisanie materialov Tsentral'nogo gosudarstvennogo arkhiva literatury i iskusstva SSSR.* Compiled by V. P. Nechaev and Iu. M. Mirkina. Edited by Iu. A. Krasovskii. Moscow: Izd-vo "Sovetskaia Rossiia," 1960. 272 p. A publication of GAU.

[DLC-PG3458.Z7R8; MH-Slav4337.2.1085]

This extensive annotated inventory with full description of TsGALI holdings by and about Chekhov is carefully correlated with published editions. Fond, *opis'*, and *delo* numbers are provided for his personal manuscripts, correspondence, and other papers, as well as for correspondence and materials relating to him in other TsGALI fonds.

B-43. *Chernyshevskii, Nikolai Gavrilovich (1828-1889). Opis' dokumental'nykh materialov fonda lichnogo proiskhozhdeniia No. 1.* Edited by B. P. Koz'min. Moscow: GAU, 1955. 118 p.
[DLC-Z6616.C5.R8; MH-Slav4337.8.935]

An extensive annotated inventory with bibliographical references to published versions of manuscripts in the fond, this volume also summarizes materials of or relating to Chernyshevskii located in other archives in the USSR with their appropriate fond numbers. A few manuscript materials are retained in the Chernyshevskii memorial museum in Saratov; on this see the article by N. M. Chernyshevskaia and B. I. Lazerson, "Obzor deiatel'nosti doma muzeia N. G. Chernyshevskogo v Saratove," in *Voprosy raboty muzeev literaturnogo profilia*, published as [Moscow. Nauchno-issledovatel'skii institut muzeevedeniia.], *Trudy* 6(1961): 94-105.

B-44. *Furmanov, Dmitrii Andreevich (1891-1926). Opis' dokumental'nykh materialov lichnogo fonda No. 522.* Edited by E. M. Bolotin. Moscow: GAU, 1949. 8 p.
[DLC-Z8318.53.R8; MH-Slav4139.78.5]

B-45. *Gertsen, Aleksandr Ivanovich (1812-1870). Opis' dokumental'nykh materialov fonda No. 129.* Edited by B. P. Koz'min. Moscow: GAU, 1951. 31 p.
[DLC-Z8400.7.R8; MH-Slav4139.78.5]
For an earlier coverage of Herzen (Gertsen) papers, see B-61.

B-46. *Gogol', Nikolai Vasil'evich (1809-1852). Opis' dokumental'nykh materialov lichnogo fonda No. 139.* Edited by N. I. Prokof'ev. Moscow: GAU, 1951. 20 p.
[DLC-Z8351.7.R8; MH-Slav4139.78.5]

B-47. *Grekov, Mitrofan Borisovich (1882-1934). Opis' dokumental'nykh materialov lichnogo fonda No. 1996.* Compiled by E. R. Kogan. Edited by M. N. Tikhomirov. Moscow: GAU, 1955. 50 p.
[no US location reported]

B-48. *Korolenko, Vladimir Galaktionovich (1853-1921). Opis' dokumental'nykh materialov lichnogo fonda No. 284.* Edited by N. L. Brodskii. Moscow: GAU, 1949. 24 p.
[DLC-Z8467.44.R8; MH-Slav4139.78.5]

B-49. *Krymov, Iurii (Beklemishev, Iurii Solomonovich) (1908-1941). Opis' dokumental'nykh materialov lichnogo fonda No. 593.* Edited by E. M. Bolotin. Moscow: GAU, 1949. 14 p.
[DLC-Z8467.92.R8; MH-Slav4139.78.5]

B-50. *Makarenko, Anton Semenovich (1888-1939). Opis' dokumental'nykh materialov fonda No. 332.* Edited by G. S. Makarenko. Moscow: GAU, 1950. 28 p.
[DLC-Z8544.R87; MH-Slav4139.78.5]

B-51. *Nekrasov, Nikolai Alekseevich (1821-1878). Opis' dokumental'nykh materialov lichnogo fonda No. 338.* Edited by I. N. Rozanov. Moscow: GAU, 1949. 34 p.
[DLC-Z8617.45.R8; MH-Slav4139.78.5]

B-52. *Ogarev, Nikolai Platonovich (1813-1877). Opis' dokumental'nykh materialov lichnogo fonda No. 359.* Edited by B. P. Koz'min. Moscow: GAU, 1950. 24 p.
[DLC-Z8641.8.R8; MH-Slav 4139.78.5]
For earlier coverage of Ogarev papers, see B-54.

B-53. *Ostrovskii, Nikolai Alekseevich (1904-1936). Opis' dokumental'nykh materialov lichnogo fonda No. 363.* Edited by R. P. Ostrovskii. Moscow: GAU, 1954. 29 p.
[no US location reported]

B-54. *Serafimovich, Aleksandr Serafimovich (1863-1949). Opis' dokumental'nykh materialov lichnogo fonda No. 457.* Edited by V. I. Popova. Moscow: GAU, 1955. 130 p.
[MH-Slav4638.74.850]

B-55. *Shishkin, Ivan Ivanovich (1832-1898). Opis' dokumental'nykh materialov lichnogo fonda No. 917.* Edited by A. N. Shchekotov. Moscow: GAU, 1949. 14 p.
[DLC-Z8817.4.R8; MH-Slav4139.78.5]

B-56. *Turgenev, Ivan Sergeevich (1818-1883). Opis' dokumental'nykh materialov lichnogo fonda No. 509.* Edited by N. L. Brodskii. Moscow: GAU, 1951. 27 p.
[DLC-Z8893.7.R8; MH-Slav4139.78.5]
For Turgenev papers, see also the earlier more extensive coverage in the 1935 volume (B-58).

B-57. *Vasnetsov, Viktor Mikhailovich (1848-1926). Opis' dokumental'nykh materialov lichnogo fonda No. 716.* Edited by A. Shchekotova. Moscow: GAU, 1949. 16 p.
[DLC-ND699.V3R8; MH-Slav4139.78.5]

State Literary Museum Series

A series of eight inventories covering literary manuscripts were published when the fonds were still housed in the State Literary Museum, in the series *Biulleteni Gosudarstvennogo literaturnogo muzeia,* nos. 1-5 (1935-1940), continued as *Katalog fondov Gosudarstvennogo literaturnogo muzeia,* nos. 6-8 (1941-1949). Those available are cataloged as monographs by the Library of Congress, under the heading "Moscow. Gosudarstvennyi literaturnyi muzei." The second volume covers Tolstoi papers which are now housed in the Tolstoi archive and is accordingly listed below under that institution (see E-62).

B-58. *I. S. Turgenev. Rukopisi, perepiska i dokumenty.* Compiled by K. P. Bogaevskii. Edited by N. P. Chulkov. *Biulleteni Gosudarstvennogo literaturnogo muzeia,* no. 1.

Moscow: Zhurnal'no-gazetnoe ob''edinenie, 1935. 182 p.
[DLC-Z6616.T9M6;MH-Slav4354.3.870]
Compare with the later, much shorter inventory, B-56

B-59. *A. N. Ostrovskii, N. S. Leskov. Rukopisi, perepiska, dokumenty.* Compiled by
N. P. Kashin et al. Edited by N. P. Kashin. *Biulleteni Gosudarstvennogo
literaturnogo muzeia*, no. 3. Moscow: Izdanie GLM, 1938. 230 p.
[no US location reported]

B-60. *Lubok.* Part 1: *Russkaia pesnia.* Compiled by S. A. Klepikov. *Biulleteni
Gosudarstvennogo literaturnogo muzeia,* no. 4. Moscow: Izdanie GLM, 1939.
273 p.
[MH-FA5785.435]
Includes two sections, 1) songs of the eighteenth and nineteenth centuries
and 2) songs of the twentieth century.

B-61. *Gertsen, Ogarev i ikh okruzhenie. Rukopisi, perepiska i dokumenty.* Compiled by
L. E. Barsukov et al. Edited by B. P. Koz'min. *Biulleteni Gosudarstvennogo
literaturnogo muzeia*, no. 5. Moscow: Izdanie GLM, 1940. 440 p.
[DLC-Slavic unclassified: Cyr.4-Z145; MH-Slav1457.451.63]
In addition to A. I. Herzen (Gertsen) and N. P. and M. L. Ogarev, the volume
inventories manuscripts of P. V. Annenkov, M. A. Bakunin, V. P. Botkin, T. N.
Granovskii, K. D. Kavelin, N. A. Ogareva-Tuchkova, E. A. Herzen, V. S.
Pecherin, N. I. Sazonov, E. V. Salias de Turnemir, N. M. and E. A. Satin, A. A.
and N. A. Serno-Solov'evich, A. A. Tuchkov, N. I. Utkin, and M. Ia. and P. Ia.
Chaadaev.

B-62. *Latyshskie skazki.* Edited by V. M. Sidel'nikov. *Katalog fondov Gosudarstvennogo
literaturnogo muzeia*, no. 6. Moscow: Izdanie GLM, 1941. 72 p.
[DLC-PG9145.R8.S5]

B-63. *A. S. Pushkin. Rukopisi, dokumenty, illiustratsii.* Compiled by K. P. Bogaevskaia
et al. Edited by V. Bonch-Bruevich. *Katalog fondov Gosudarstvennogo
literaturnogo muzeia*, no. 7. Moscow: Izdanie Goslitmuzeia, 1948. 324 p.
[DLC-Z8718.M68]
Some of the Pushkin papers have been transferred to Pushkinskii Dom in
Leningrad; hence compare this inventory with the catalogs listed under that
institution (see C-40).

B-64. *D. N. Mamin-Sibiriak. Rukopisi i perepiska.* Compiled by B. Udintsev et al.
Edited by V. Bonch-Bruevich. *Katalog fondov Gosudarstvennogo literaturnogo
muzeia*, no. 8. Moscow, 1949.
[no US location reported]

Other Personal Fonds

F. M. Dostoevskii (1821-1881)

B-65. Nechaeva, Vera Stepanovna, ed.
Opisanie rukopisei F. M. Dostoevskogo. Moscow, 1957. 587 p.
[DLC-Z6616.D67.N4; MH-Slav4338.2.1195]

> Covers Dostoevskii manuscripts in about 15 repositories, but one of the largest
> fonds is in TsGALI. Includes detailed correlations with published editions and
> other bibliographical references. See A-11.

M. Iu. Lermontov (1814-1841)

B-66. [Moscow. Gosudarstvennyi literaturnyi muzei.]
Vystavka Lermontovskikh fondov moskovskikh muzeev. Compiled by N. P.
Pakhomov and M. D. Beliaev. *Katalogi Gosudarstvennogo literaturnogo muzeia,*
no. 1. Moscow: Izdanie Goslitmuzeia, 1940. 184 p.
[MH-XP3599]

> Not to be confused with the series of catalogs from GLM listed above, this
> volume surveys Lermontov documents in different Moscow repositories, many
> of which have now been consolidated in TsGALI.

V. V. Maiakovskii (1893-1930)

B-67. [Russia (1923-USSR). Tsentral'nyi gosudarstvennyi arkhiv literatury i iskusstva.]
V. V. Maiakovskii. Opisanie dokumental'nykh materialov.
> Vol. 1: *"Okna" Rosta i glavpolitprosveta 1919-1922 gg.* Compiled by K. N.
> Suvorova. Edited by V. D. Duvakina. Moscow: GAU & TsGALI, 1964. 287 p.
> Vol. 2: *Rukopisi. Zapisnye knizhki. Zhivopis'. Risunki. Afishi. Programmy.*
> *Zapisi golosa.* Compiled by V. A. Arutcheva et al. Edited by N. V.
> Reformatskaia. Moscow: GAU, TsGALI, and BMM, 1965. 303 p.
[DLC-Z8542.9.R87; MH-Slav4565.4.1.v.l-2]

> Also listed as A-13 and E-58.

Theater History

Although there is no single chapter devoted to TsGALI, there are many
references to materials in the archive in *Materialy k istorii russkogo teatra v gosu-*
darstvennykh arkhivakh SSSR. Obzory dokumentov. XVII vek-1917 g., edited by
I. F. Petrovskaia (A-52), especially pp. 19-35.

B-68. Kirilenko, K. N.
Section on TsGALI in "Perechni dokumentov i materialov po istorii russkogo
sovetskogo teatra 1917-1921 gg., khraniashchikhsia v TsGAOR SSSR, TsGASA,
TsGALI SSSR, LGAORSS." In *Sovetskii teatr. Dokumenty i materialy. Russkii*
sovetskii teatr 1917-1921 gg., edited by A. Z. Iufit et al., pp. 432-63. Leningrad:
Izd-vo "Iskusstvo," 1968. (See A-55.)

PART B – CENTRAL STATE ARCHIVES

Cinema History

B-69. Krasovskii, Iu. "Materialy po istorii sovetskoi kinematografii v Tsentral'nom gosudarstvennom arkhive literatury i iskusstva SSSR." In *Iz istorii kino. Materialy i dokumenty*, no. 1, pp. 134-45. Moscow: Izd-vo AN SSSR, 1958.

Provides a general description of types of materials, institutions, and people covered, but gives no fond numbers.

6. TsENTRAL'NYI GOSUDARSTVENNYI ARKHIV DREVNIKH AKTOV (TsGADA)

[Central State Archive of Ancient Acts]
Address: Moscow, G-435, Bol'shaia Pirogovskaia ulitsa, 17

HISTORY AND CONTENTS

The Central State Archive of Ancient Acts, or TsGADA, as it is usually called, is the main repository for historical records dating from the earliest periods of Russian history through the early nineteenth century. It now contains approximately 1,600 fonds with close to 3,000,000 storage units, from the eleventh to the nineteenth centuries. Although prerevolutionary documents post-dating 1801 are theoretically located in the Central State Historical Archive (TsGIA SSSR) in Leningrad, many fonds in TsGADA extend well into the nineteenth century, just as some fonds in TsGIA include earlier materials. Its main offices and reading room share with the Main Archival Administration headquarters the building constructed in 1886 to house the Moscow Archive of the Ministry of Justice [Moskovskii arkhiv Ministerstva iustitsii—MAMIu]. TsGADA in fact is the direct heir of this major pre-revolutionary historical archive, which in its late nineteenth-century organization was conceived as the major repository for the pre-nineteenth-century records of the Russian state. Immediately after the Revolution, MAMIu was incorporated into the Moscow division of the second (juridical) section of the Single State Archival Fond.

Meanwhile, other prerevolutionary archives with early historical materials became part of different sections of the State Archival Fond. The former Moscow Main Archive of the Ministry (formerly College) of Foreign Affairs [Moskovskii glavnyi arkhiv MID] became the basis of the first (political) section in Moscow, and in 1920 became one of the major divisions of the then established State Archive of the RSFSR, or Gosarkhiv (Gosudarstvennyi arkhiv RSFSR). The former State Archive of the Russian Empire [Gosudarstvennyi arkhiv Rossiiskoi imperii], also known as Gosarkhiv, was put under the same administrative framework of the new Gosarkhiv and its contents transferred to Moscow in 1923. Gosarkhiv RSFSR as an administrative entity was abandoned in 1925, at which time the Moscow Central Historical Archive was created [Moskovskii tsentral'nyi istoricheskii arkhiv] with several different divisions that gradually became separate archives.

The Repository of Early Records, or Drevlekhranilishche, was organized to consolidate earlier groups of archival material predominantly predating the nineteenth century. This new archive took the former MAMIu building as its headquarters, and administratively consolidated the MAMIu holdings with those of two other pre-revolutionary archives—the former State Archive of the Russian Empire and the former Moscow Main Archive of the Ministry of Foreign Affairs which, as mentioned above, had recently been under the administration of Gosarkhiv RSFSR. At this time the Drevlekhranilishche also absorbed the former Moscow Branch of the Archive of the Ministry of the Imperial Court [Moskovskoe otdelenie Obshchego arkhiva Ministerstva imperatorskogo dvora]. The archival and manuscript collections of many famous monasteries, as well as the personal and estate papers of many important old Russian families, were also deposited in this same archive. Although officially still a section of the Moscow Central Historical Archive, it virtually became a distinctive repository at this time.

In 1931 the Repository of Early Records [Drevlekhranilishche] was officially recognized as the separate State Archive of the Feudal-Serfdom Epoch [Gosudarstvennyi arkhiv feodal'no-krepostnicheskoi epokhi–GAFKE]. In 1938 it incorporated the holdings of the Central Land Survey Archive [Tsentral'nyi mezhevoi arkhiv], which had been a separate archive since the eighteenth century. At the time of the 1941 archival reorganization, GAFKE was renamed the Central State Archive of Ancient Acts, or TsGADA, but retained its former location and internal organization.

Thus TsGADA is really the amalgamation of five major prerevolutionary historical archives, augmented by private papers and manuscripts of important monasteries and religious institutions and individual families and estates. The different divisions of the archive now largely follow the original prerevolutionary archival organization of the documents involved, so that most of the prerevolutionary cataloging has continued to be used with the addition of archival fond numbers along with new *opis'* and *delo* numbers where necessary. Because of this, many of the prerevolutionary published or handwritten inventories and card catalogs are still in use by the archival staff.

Moscow Main Archive of the Ministry of Foreign Affairs

The holdings from the prerevolutionary Moscow Main Archive of the Ministry of Foreign Affairs [Moskovskii glavnyi arkhiv Ministerstva inostrannykh del] are divided into ten main sections, and, for the most part, TsGADA has retained their original organization. The archive itself dates back to 1720 when it was founded as the Moscow Archive of the College of Foreign Affairs [Moskovskii arkhiv Kollegii inostrannykh del], at which time it took over the holdings of the earlier archive of the Posol'skii Prikaz [Prikaz of Ambassadors], as well as the records of several other defunct prikazy (see B-75b).

The first and relatively small section contains medieval Russian charters and other miscellaneous manuscripts dating from 1265 to 1767 (see B-70a, pp. 16-22, and B-75a).

The large second section contains materials relating to Russian foreign relations under the early Posol'skii Prikaz up to 1720. The documentary records of the College of Foreign Affairs (from 1720 to the early nineteenth century) originally constituted a large and important part of the fonds in this section, but with few exceptions these have now been transferred to the archival administration of the Foreign Ministry, where they constitute the eighteenth-century division of the Archive of Russian Foreign Policy [Arkhiv vneshnei politiki Rossii–AVPR]. Since the transfer took place after the publication of the TsGADA guide, however, they are listed there as being located in TsGADA (see B-70a and D-11, pp. 22-80; see Part D, section 2b below, for details of those documents now housed in AVPR).

A third section (all of which has been retained by TsGADA) contains documents from the Posol'skii Prikaz and later College of Foreign Affairs pertaining to relations with border peoples in the Baltic area, Central Asia, the Crimea, the Caucasus, and Siberia (see B-70a, pp. 80-98).

The small fourth section formerly located in TsGADA with miscellaneous materials relating to foreign affairs from 1725 to 1801—mostly secret memoranda or reports from collegiate directors to the emperor—has now been transferred to AVPR (see B-70a, pp. 98-99), as has the fifth section containing similar types of high-level diplomatic and trade materials, some going back to the seventeenth century (see B-70a, pp. 99-101).

The large sixth section from the Prikaz of Ambassadors and later College of Foreign Affairs, pertaining to internal affairs and relations among different parts of the empire from the thirteenth to the early nineteenth century, remains in TsGADA, where it forms one of the most voluminous historical collections in the country covering the medieval period (see B-70a, pp. 101-31). A small seventh section covers internal imperial administration from 1726 to 1762 (see B-70a, pp. 132-34).

The eighth section contains several rich collections of medieval Russian, Slavic, and foreign manuscripts and maps, dating back as far as the tenth century, which originally had been part of the manuscript division of the library of the former Moscow Archive of the Ministry of Foreign Affairs; these include the manuscript collections of F. F. Mazurin and M. A. Obolenskii and the collection from the manuscript holdings of the former Moscow Synod Press. This section of TsGADA also houses the extensive map collections from the cartographic divisions of the prerevolutionary Moscow archives of the Ministries of Justice and Foreign Affairs (see B-70a, pp. 134-40).

A ninth section of the Moscow Foreign Ministry Archive holdings is devoted to personal fonds of private family papers, mostly prior to 1800, but a few extending into the early nineteenth century (see B-70a, pp. 141-55). The final section covers fonds from the chancellery of the archive, extending into the twentieth century to cover its locations after the Revolution (see B-70a, pp. 155-56).

State Archive of the Russian Empire

Another major archival division in TsGADA came from the former State Archive of the Russian Empire (Gosudarstvennyi arkhiv Rossiiskoi imperii—Gosarkhiv) founded in St. Petersburg in 1834. It subsequently became the repository for important high governmental papers, especially personal documents of the imperial family and miscellaneous papers from the imperial chancellery, including many from the St. Petersburg archives of the Senate and the Ministry of Foreign Affairs, and the St. Petersburg State Archive of Ancient Records [S.-Peterburgskii gosudarstvennyi arkhiv starykh del]. In 1865 its administration was consolidated with the St. Petersburg Archive of the Ministry of Foreign Affairs, with which it shared the same building although it retained its separate identity.

The documents from Gosarkhiv, as this division is usually called, cover a wide variety of subjects and date from the seventeenth to the early twentieth century, although the bulk of the materials is from the eighteenth and early nineteenth centuries. They are grouped into 30 sections (*razriady*), each of which now bears the corresponding fond numbers from 1 to 30. The organization and contents, however, are exceedingly circumstantial, since the documents were originally drawn from so many disparate sources; hence in most cases it is difficult to determine what documents are to be found there and in what section. Mention of some of the sections will give an idea of the extent and variety of the holdings. Several contain various correspondence of members of the imperial family and of other very high-ranking individuals; separate sections contain materials from the imperial cabinets of Peter I and Catherine II. Several sections contain miscellaneous documents relating to foreign policy (mostly eighteenth and early nineteenth centuries); special sections relate to Siberia in the eighteenth century, the Caucasus (1762-1804), Poland and Lithuania (1510-1854), and the Ukraine (1606-1790). There are some miscellaneous sections on internal administration and court affairs (mostly eighteenth and early nineteenth centuries). Separate sections contain materials relating to finance (1700-1857), the fleet (1700-1854), the army (1700-1852), educational and cultural affairs (1718-1856), and spiritual affairs (1701-1833). Here too are the records of the early Prikaz of Secret Affairs [Prikaz tainykh del] (1422-1715) and of the later Secret Chancellery and secret expeditions of the Senate (1638-1816). (See B-73 and B-70a, pp. 157-201.)

Moscow Archive of the Ministry of Justice

The prerevolutionary Moscow Archive of the Ministry of Justice [Moskovskii arkhiv Ministerstva iustitsii—MAMIu] constitutes a third major division of TsGADA. This exceedingly large and important archive, founded in 1852, actually brought together three earlier archives, the documents from which still form major parts of this division: 1) the Razriad-Senate Archive [Razriadno-Senatskii arkhiv], founded in 1763 to incorporate the Moscow records of the Senate since its establishment in 1711, and the earlier records from the original archive of the Razriadnyi Prikaz; 2) the Moscow Archive of Ancient Records [Moskovskii arkhiv starykh del], founded in 1782; and 3) the archive of the Department of Lands and Estates [Arkhiv pomestno-votchinnogo departamenta], founded in 1786. (See B-79.)

The major part of this Ministry of Justice division relates to the central and regional government of the Russian Empire from the seventeenth to the nineteenth century. Here are to be found records relating to the early administration of the country under the governmental departments, or *prikazy*, during the period from 1545 to the mid-eighteenth century (see B-70a, pp. 206-37.) Particularly large groups have been preserved from the Razriadnyi Prikaz (1545-1713), the Siberian Prikaz (1564-1768), the Prikaz of Printing [Pechatnyi Prikaz] (1613-1722), the Prikaz of the Patriarchial Palace [Patriarshii kazennyi Prikaz] (1624-1789), the Apothecary Prikaz [Aptekarskii Prikaz] (1629-1704), Prikaz of Little Russia [Malorossiiskii Prikaz] (1649-1722), and the Prikaz of Monasteries [Monastyrskii

Prikaz] (1701-1725). This section also includes the rich Economic College collection of charters dating from 1300-1795 [Gramoty Kollegii-ekonomii].

Later documents relating to the central administration of the country during the eighteenth century are to be found in the files of the Senate starting with its establishment in 1711 (see B-70a, pp. 237-90). Included here are the records of the Senate chancellery (1711-1796), the various commissions and offices under the Senate, the First, Second, Third, and Fourth Departments of the Senate, as well as the papers relating to many of its expeditions. Those sections of the Senate records containing materials postdating 1796, i.e., the papers relating to the Sixth, Seventh, and Eighth Departments of the Senate, as well as the records of its inspectors (1800-1828) and of the Moscow Senate Press—which were originally part of TsGADA fonds—have now been transferred to the Central State Historical Archive (TsGIA SSSR) in Leningrad (these fonds nos. 270, 269, 264, 265, 266, 255, and 395 are described in the TsGADA guide, B-70a, pp. 261-63). Many of the eighteenth-century administrative fonds had formerly come from the early Moscow Archive of Ancient Records (see especially those fonds described in B-70a, pp. 264-82).

Another major section of the former Moscow Ministry of Justice Archive contains the medieval records from the earlier Archive of the Department of Lands and Estates [Arkhiv Pomestno-votchinnogo departamenta]. Here, for example, are to be found the records of the Pomestnyi Prikaz (1540-1720), the Votchinnaia Kollegiia (1721-1786), the eighteenth-century records of the Moscow votchina office and the St. Petersburg votchina office, and the Votchina Department (1786-1864) (see B-70b, pp. 11-16).

Also included are many documentary fonds regarding local administration in the seventeenth and eighteenth centuries (see B-70b, pp. 16-58). The oldest records are those of local affairs of towns and military districts under the Prikaznye izby. Following post-Petrine administrative reforms there are guberniia chancellery records and local records of town and guberniia magistrates, court registration bureaus, and military and economic records, including records pertaining to peasant affairs and local reform later in the eighteenth century under Catherine II. In general, however, these regional records in TsGADA now extend only to 1775. Many guberniia files, city court, and other local records after this date were transferred to local RSFSR oblast archives after the Second World War. More recently, a number of valuable eighteenth-century administrative records have been transferred to TsGADA from state oblast archives in the RSFSR.

Moscow Archive of the Ministry of the Imperial Court

A fourth major division in TsGADA came from the former Moscow Court Archive [Moskovskoe otdelenie Obshchego arkhiva Ministerstva imperatorskogo dvora], which was itself founded between 1869 and 1872 (see B-70b, pp. 65-80). The oldest documents are those from the earlier Archive of the Moscow Armory [Oruzheinaia palata], most of which consist of imperial court records from the seventeenth and eighteenth centuries, although a few documents date to the fifteenth century (see B-90). The later records start with the fonds from the Cabinet of His Imperial Highness [Kabinet Ego Imperatorskogo Velichestva] (1716-1847). Here, too, are to be found the papers of various court chancelleries, the chancelleries of several high court officials, and other court-related offices or institutions.

Central Land Survey Archive

The prerevolutionary Central Land Survey Archive [Tsentral'nyi mezhevoi arkhiv] dates from the mid-eighteenth century and became part of TsGADA in 1938. The group of fonds in this division contains boundary and survey records from the eighteenth century to 1917 (see B-70b, pp. 129-37). Included here are the records of the central chancellery of the survey, survey records on the guberniia and oblast levels, and the papers of related bureaus and the Moscow Survey Institute. There are also extensive cartographic materials in these records, mostly dating from the eighteenth century to roughly 1840 (see B-90).

Fonds from Monasteries and Religious Institutions

Since the Revolution, TsGADA has become a repository for fonds and manuscript collections from many religious institutions (see B-70b, pp. 80-95). Most important and extensive is the fond from the Moscow office of the Holy Synod, and the related fond of the Moscow Synod Press. Fonds received from monasteries include not only many from the Moscow region, but also some from as far away as Suzdal.

Personal Family Papers

In addition to the personal papers which came to TsGADA from the former Moscow Archive of the Ministry of Foreign Affairs, TsGADA has become the repository for about 40 important fonds of family and estate papers, some of which go as far back as the sixteenth century (see B-70b, pp. 95-123). The largest fonds include those from the Abamelek-Lazarev, Bariatinskii, Bakhmetev, Chicherin, Demidov, Gagarin, Goncharov, Iusupov, Naryshkin, Orlov-Davydov, Panin, Polianskii, Stroganov, Sheremetev, Shuvalov, and Vorontsov families.

Rare Books

Aside from manuscripts, TsGADA also has some very important collections of early books, most notably the collection of some 5,000 books dating from 1475 to 1835 which made up the library of the Moscow Archive of the Ministry of Foreign Affairs. This collection, with its handwritten catalog, now forms part of the extensive library of TsGADA, although it is classified as one of the archival fonds. Other important collections of early books found in this library include the 4,000 volumes (1485-1825) from the library of the Moscow Synod Press, and the 3,000 volumes (1493-1825) from the F. F. Mazurin collection.

WORKING CONDITIONS

Documents in this archive are likely to be more readily available than in most other state archives because of their earlier dates, but the problem of the precise location of documents often remains difficult for foreign scholars, due to the lack of adequate finding aids. The often frustrating policy whereby the archival staff chooses for the scholar those documents relevant to his topic remains in effect here.

As in other central state archives, unpublished inventories (*opisi*) are normally not available to foreign scholars, although they have been prepared for nearly all of the fonds. A few parts of the holdings have been analyzed in card catalogs, but these are also available only for staff use.

In some cases, particularly in regard to earlier fonds, there are more detailed guides or prerevolutionary published inventories which aid exact location; many of these are shelved in the main TsGADA reading room and can be brought to the nearby foreigners' reading room on request. Usually, however, readers have to be content with the brief descriptions in the published guides and with the extensive knowledge of the archival staff. Foreign scholars normally work in the special small reading room for foreigners shared with the other archives in the same complex of buildings, and have to transmit requests through the special assistant assigned to deal with them.

The archive maintains a large library, which, as mentioned above, contains many rare early books from prerevolutionary collections, along with the publications and reference materials related to the archival holdings. The library totals about 200,000 entries, including the rare books and some two hundred journals.

GUIDES AND PUBLISHED DESCRIPTIONS

The now dated archival guides published in 1946 and 1947, supplemented by the special survey of pre-seventeenth-century materials published in 1954, provide minimal coverage, but a more detailed up-to-date guide is now badly needed. See also the short description of TsGADA in the directory of state archives, *Gosudarstvennye arkhivy Soiuza SSR. Kratkii spravochnik* (A-7), pp. 5-9.

An historical description of the formation of the archive and its various predecessors is presented in the article by G. A. Dremina, "Tsentral'nyi gosudarstvennyi arkhiv drevnikh aktov SSSR (K istorii obrazovaniia arkhiva)," *Trudy MGIAI* 11 (1958):297-363. A somewhat different version of this survey with an outline of the current organization was published by G. A. Dremina in conjunction with E. V. Kraiskaia and Iu. F. Kononov as "Tsentral'nyi gosudarstvennyi arkhiv drevnikh aktov SSSR," edited by V. V. Maksakov, in the pamphlet series *Gosudarstvennye arkhivy SSSR. Uchebnoe posobie* (Moscow: MGIAI, 1960– [MH-Slav612.120]), pp. 37-109; although a good treatment of the development of the archive, it gives few details that would help the prospective researcher, except for its mention of some of the more recent transfers of documents to other archives. The earlier article by N. Lapin, "Drevlekhranilishche Moskovskogo Tsentral'nogo istoricheskogo arkhiva," *Arkhivnoe delo* 24-25 (1930, no. 3-4):40-68, gives a detailed description of the holdings as they were organized at the time; the article includes some historical notations about the various component divisions and an extensive bibliography. See also the later summary by A. Birze, "Gosudarstvennyi arkhiv feodal'no-krepostnicheskoi epokhi. K dvadtsatiletiiu leninskogo dekreta," *Arkhivnoe delo* 47 (1938, no. 3):110-15.

B-70. [Russia (1923-USSR). Tsentral'nyi gosudarstvennyi arkhiv drevnikh aktov.]
    Tsentral'nyi gosudarstvennyi arkhiv drevnikh aktov. Putevoditel'.
  B-70a. Part 1: Compiled by V. N. Shumilov et al. Edited by S. K. Bogoiavlenskii. Moscow: GAU, 1946. 363 p.
  B-70b. Part 2: Compiled by V. N. Shumilov et al. Edited by A. I. Iakovlev. Moscow: GAU, 1947. 184 p.
    [DLC-CD1713.A53 (part 1 only); MH-Slav610.40 (1 and 2)]

These original guides to TsGADA, although sketchy and now out of date because of reorganization, remain the basic finding aids for this archive. In addition to providing a short description of the contents and dates of the fonds, they give a brief history of the different divisions and some bibliographical indications of documentary publications from individual fonds as well as inventories or other descriptive literature, some of which go back to prerevolutionary years. Indexes of subject, personal, and geographical names aid in the location of materials.

The first volume covers two major divisions of the archive: 1) the fonds relating to early government and foreign relations, comprising holdings from the former Main Moscow Archive of the Ministry of Foreign Affairs (see lists furnished under D-11 of those fonds relating to foreign policy that have been transferred to AVPR) and from the former State Archive of the Russian Empire and, 2) the records of seventeenth- and eighteenth-century administration from the archives of the early prikazy and the chancellery and departments under the Senate, all of which were housed before the Revolution in the Moscow Archive of the Ministry of Justice.

The second volume covers the records of the Department of Lands and Estates, also from the Moscow Archive of the Ministry of Justice. It also covers the materials coming from the Moscow Archive of the Ministry of the Imperial Court, and the holdings originating in the Land Survey Archive. The papers of private families held in TsGADA are briefly described, as are the many collections coming from monasteries and religious institutions.

B-71. [Russia (1923-USSR). Tsentral'nyi gosudarstvennyi arkhiv drevnikh aktov.]
    Obzor dokumental'nykh materialov Tsentral'nogo gosudarstvennogo arkhiva drevnikh aktov po istorii SSSR perioda feodalizma XI-XVI vv. Edited by V. N. Shumilov and M. N. Tikhomirov. Moscow: GAU, 1954. 304 p.
    [IU]

Materials relating to the period from the eleventh to the sixteenth centuries are here listed and described more extensively and in a format which is often more helpful for their identification than that in the more comprehensive TsGADA guides above.

INVENTORIES AND SPECIALIZED DESCRIPTIONS

For a comprehensive bibliography of many of the published catalogs and descriptions for documents as well as for medieval manuscripts in TsGADA, including many of the prerevolutionary publications still in use for the location or identification of materials in these collections, see the general directory of catalogs to medieval Slavic manuscripts, *Spravochnik-ukazatel' pechatnykh opisanii slaviano-russkikh rukopisei*, compiled by Iu. K. Begunov et al. (A-14), pp. 162-78. Some additional bibliographical indications are given in the TsGADA guides (B-70 and B-71). Only the most extensive earlier catalogs, especially those not covered by Begunov, and more recent publications will be listed below.

History of Moscow

B-72. [Russia (1923-USSR). Tsentral'nyi gosudarstvennyi arkhiv drevnikh aktov.]
Obzor dokumental'nykh materialov po istorii g. Moskvy s drevneishikh vremen do XIX v. Compiled by V. N. Shumilov and S. V. Bakhrushin. Moscow: GAU, 1949. 187 p.
[DLC-Z6621.M83R8; MH-Slav3197.1.250]
This useful and well-indexed volume is one of the most extensive and thorough descriptions of its kind. It follows four of the major divisions of the archive as described above and indicates specific item numbers which relate to the history of Moscow. For the materials covered, it is thus a more detailed directory than the other TsGADA guides. It does not, however, provide details of the individual items beyond indicating their general category and listing the item numbers and usually their dates.

State Archive of the Russian Empire (Gosarkhiv)

B-73. Kononov, Iu. F.
"Iz istorii organizatsii i komplektovaniia b. Gosudarstvennogo arkhiva Rossiiskoi imperii." *Trudy MGIAI* 8 (1957):279-354.
In the course of discussing the formation of this rich but badly organized section of TsGADA, this article provides many detailed references to the documents to be found there, although unfortunately it does not list current *delo* numbers.

B-74. Goriainov, S.
Gosudarstvennyi arkhiv. Razriad II. "Dela sobstvenno do imperatorskoi familii otnosiashchiiasia." St. Petersburg: Tipografiia M. A. Aleksandrova, 1913. 66 p.
[MH-L]
Published by the Ministry of Foreign Affairs, this inventory covers the second division (*razriad*) of the former Gosarkhiv with materials from 1682 to 1912.

Holdings from the Moscow Archive of the Ministry
(College) of Foreign Affairs

B-75. Dremina, G. A.
Iz istorii Tsentral'nogo gosudarstvennogo arkhiva drevnikh aktov SSSR. Edited by
V. V. Maksakov. Moscow: MGIAI, 1959. 69 p.
[DLC-CD1713.D7; MH-Slav612.121]

> The pamphlet contains two separate articles: the first (B-75a), by G. A.
> Dremina and A. V. Chernov, "Gosudarstvennoe-drevlekhranilishche khartii i
> rukopisei" (pp. 3-22), briefly describes the history and contents of the
> important collections of early Russian charters and manuscripts which came
> from the Moscow Main Archive of the Ministry of Foreign Affairs (cf. B-70a,
> pp. 16-22). The second (B-75b), by G. A. Dremina, "Moskovskii arkhiv
> Kollegii inostrannykh del" (pp. 23-69), gives a general survey of the holdings
> of the pre-nineteenth-century archive of the College of Foreign Affairs;
> post-1720 sections of the records relating directly to foreign relations have
> now been transferred to AVPR.

B-76. Bantysh-Kamenskii, N. N.
Obzor vneshnikh snoshenii Rossii (po 1800 god).
> Vol. 1: *(Avstriia, Angliia, Vengriia, Gollandiia, Daniia, Ispaniia).* Moscow:
> Tipografiia E. Lissnera i Iu. Romana, 1894. 303 p.
> Vol. 2: *(Germaniia i Italiia).* Moscow: Tipografiia E. Lissnera i Iu. Romana,
> 1896. 271 p.
> Vol. 3: *(Kurliandiia, Lifliandiia, Estliandiia, Finliandiia, Pol'sha i Portugaliia).*
> Moscow: Tipografiia E. Lissnera i Iu. Romana, 1897. 319 p.
> Vol. 4: *(Prussiia, Frantsiia i Shvetsiia).* Moscow: Tipografiia G. Lissnera i
> A. Geshelia, 1902. 463 p.

[MH-Slav778.1; MH-L]

> These volumes, although technically not archival catalogs, provide detailed
> descriptions of the diplomatic records which up to the year 1720 are
> preserved in TsGADA. They were originally prepared (but never published) at
> the beginning of the nineteenth century by the then director of the Moscow
> archive, under the title "Sokrashchennoe izvestie o vzaimnykh mezhdu
> Rossiiskimi monarkhami i evropeiskimi dvorami posol'stvakh, perepiskakh i
> dogovorakh, khraniashchikhsia v Gosudarstvennoi kollegii inostrannykh del v
> Moskovskom arkhive s 1481 po 1801 god." See also item D-12 under AVPR
> in Part D.

B-77. Putsillo, Mikhail Pavlovich.
*Ukazatel' delam i rukopisiam, otnosiashchimsia do Sibiri i prinadlezhashchim
Moskovskomu Glavnomu arkhivu Ministerstva inostrannykh del.* Moscow:
Tipografiia A. Gattsuka, 1879. 123 p.
[DLC-Z3401.P8 and Yudin-Z3407.P9; MH-Slav3610.8]

**Holdings from the Moscow Archive of the
Ministry of Justice (MAMIu)**

B-78. [Russia. Ministerstvo iustitsii. Moskovskii arkhiv.]
Pamiatnaia knizhka Moskovskogo arkhiva Ministerstva iustitsii. Moscow:
Tipo-litografiia I. I. Kushnerev, 1890. 235 p.
[DLC-Yudin CD1719.M7P2; MH-Slav612.60; MH-L]

> This general handbook of the former Moscow Archive of the Ministry of
> Justice (MAMIu) describes the then current archival organization, history,
> and composition of the various fonds from older archival institutions and
> gives a bibliography of other published descriptions.

B-79. [Russia. Ministerstvo iustitsii. Moskovskii arkhiv.]
*Opisanie dokumentov i bumag, khraniashchikhsia v Moskovskom arkhive
Ministerstva iustitsii.* 21 vols. Vols. 1-2: St. Petersburg: Tipografiia
Pravitel'stvuiushchego senata, 1869; vols. 3-21: Moscow, 1876-[1921].
[DLC-Yudin CD1719.M7 (vols. 1-19); MH-Slav610.20 (vols.1-21)]

> This large and important series put out by the former Moscow Archive of the
> Ministry of Justice (MAMIu) includes descriptions and inventories of various
> sections of the archive along with historical monographs about the archive
> and based on some of its component sections. The first volume surveys the
> archive holdings. Records of the Razriadnyi Prikaz are given the most
> extensive coverage, with inventories comprising parts of volumes 4 and 6-9,
> and volumes 10-20. Extended coverage is given to the records of the
> Pomestnyi Prikaz in volumes 1, 2, and 5, and to those of the Sysknoi Prikaz
> in volumes 2 and 4. The current fond numbers were added after the
> Revolution, but the old system of enumeration has been retained so that this
> publication is still used extensively by the archival staff for the identification
> of the records covered. Bibliographic references to parts of this series and
> some correlation with the current fonds involved are provided in the guides to
> TsGADA (B-70).

B-80. Ivanov, Petr Ivanovich.
*Opisanie Gosudarstvennogo razriadnogo arkhiva, s prisovokupleniem snimkov so
mnogikh khraniashchikhsia v onom liubopytnykh dokumentov.* Moscow:
Tipografiia S. Selivanovskogo, 1842. 452 p.
[DLC-Yudin DK3.I92; MH-Slav815.35]

> Compare this earlier more summary description with the coverage of the
> *Razriadnyi prikaz* records from the sixteenth and seventeenth centuries in the
> series above (B-79).

B-81. Ivanov, Petr Ivanovich.
Opisanie Gosudarstvennogo arkhiva starykh del. Moscow: Tipografiia
S. Selivanovskogo, 1850. 390 p.
[DLC-Yudin CD1719.I93; MH-Slav612.70]

> Provides early extensive description of the records included in this former

archive, which was later amalgamated into the Moscow Archive of the Ministry of Justice.

B-82. [Russia. Sibirskii prikaz.]
Obozrenie stolbtsov i knig Sibirskogo prikaza (1592-1768 gg.). Compiled by N. N. Ogloblin. 4 vols. Moscow: Universitetskaia tipografiia, 1895-1901.
    Vol. 1: *Dokumenty voevodskogo upravleniia.* 429 p.
    Vol. 2: *Dokumenty tamozhennogo upravleniia.* 162 p.
    Vol. 3: *Dokumenty po snosheniiam mestnogo upravleniia s tsentral'nym.* 394 p.
    Vol. 4: *Dokumenty tsentral'nogo upravleniia.* 287 p.
[MH-L]

B-83. [Russia. Tsentral'nyi gosudarstvennyi arkhiv drevnikh aktov.]
Razriadnyi prikaz (nachalo XVI v.–1711 g.). Opis' stolbtsov dopolnitel'nogo otdela arkhivnogo fonda No. 210. Edited by A. A. Novosel'skii. Moscow: GAU, 1950. 144 p.
[MH-Slav610.40.5]

B-84. Grubzinskaia, A. P.
"Dokumenty Sysknykh komissii vtoroi poloviny XVII v. kak istoricheskii istochnik." *Arkheograficheskii ezhegodnik za 1967 god*, pp. 107-118.
    General survey discussion.

B-85. Nikolaev, I. N.
Ukazatel' chertezhei moskovskim tserkvam i sostoiavshim v ikh prikhodakh dvoram i lavkam za 1775-1782 gg.
    Part 1: Moscow: Tipografiia L. F. Snegireva, 1884. 177 p.
[no US location reported]
    Covers the fond of the Kamennyi Prikaz with a survey and inventory that is still used for identification of the materials.

B-86. [Russia. Pravitel'stvuiushchii senat. Arkhiv.]
Arkhiv pravitel'stvuiushchego senata.
    Vol. 1: *Opis' imennym vysochaishim ukazam i poveleniiam tsarstvovaniia imperatora Petra Velikogo, 1704-1725.* Compiled by P. Baranov. St. Petersburg, 1872. 167 p.
    Opis' vysochaishim ukazam i poveleniiam, khraniashchimsia v S.-Peterburgskom senatskom arkhive za XVIII vek. Compiled by P. Baranov.
    Vol. 2: *1725-1740.* St. Petersburg, 1875. 1002 p.
    Vol. 3: *1740-1762.* St. Petersburg, 1878. 513 p. With separate index volume, 305 p.
[DLC-Yudin DK129.B22]
    Volume 2 includes indexes for volumes 1 and 2. Copies of many of these eighteenth-century documents are found in both TsGADA and TsGIA SSSR. (Listed also as B-110.) The inventories coordinate the entries with the published ukazy in *Polnoe sobranie zakonov Rossiiskoi Imperii* and include many which have not been published.

Documents from the Former Archive of the Imperial Court

B-87. Viktorov, Aleksei Egorovich.
Opisanie zapisnykh knig i bumag starinnykh dvortsovykh prikazov, 1584-1725.
2 vols. Moscow, 1877-1883. 660 p. (pagination continuous).
[MH-Slav815.10]
> An alphabetical index to these volumes was published as a supplement,
> *Alfavitnye ukazateli* (Moscow, 1906; 154 p.), to the subsequent volume,
> compiled by A. I. Uspenskii, listed below (B-88).

B-88. Uspenskii, Aleksandr Ivanovich.
[Russia. Ministerstvo Imperatorskogo dvora. Obshchii arkhiv. Moskovskoe otdelenie.]
Zapisnye knigi i bumagi starinnykh dvortsovykh prikazov. Dokumenty XVIII-XIX vv. byvshego Arkhiva Oruzheinoi palaty. Moscow: Pechatnia A. I. Snegirevoi, 1906.
247 p. Izdanie Obshchego arkhiva Ministerstva Imperatorskogo dvora.
[DLC-Z2507.A54; MH-Slav815.11]
> Includes an index supplement covering the volumes compiled by A. E.
> Viktorov listed above (B-87).

B-89. Boguslavskii, G. A.
"Iz istorii arkhiva Oruzheinoi palaty." *Istoricheskii arkhiv*, 1959, no. 2, pp. 215-23.
> Historical in approach, this gives further bibliographical references.

Documents from the Land Survey Archive

See also the general historical account of the Land Survey Archive by
V. Gerasimiuk, "Kratkii istoricheskii ocherk Tsentral'nogo mezhevogo arkhiva (byv.
Arkhiva Mezhevoi Kantseliarii) 1768-1938 gg.," *Arkhivnoe delo* 51 (1939, no.
3):127-35.

B-90. Tsvetkov, M. A.
"Kartograficheskiie materialy general'nogo mezhevaniia." *Voprosy geografii* 31
(1953):90-105. English translation by James R. Gibson, "Cartographic Results of
the General Survey of Russia, 1766-1861," *Canadian Cartographer* 6 (June
1969):1-14.
> This article, listed also as A-64 above, surveys the manuscript maps and plans
> of the Russian Empire prepared in connection with the General Survey, most
> of which are now located in TsGADA.

Eighteenth-century Commerce

B-91. Kaidanov, Nikolai Ivanovich.
[Russia. Gosudarstvennaia kommerts-kollegiia.]
Sistematicheskii katalog delam Gosudarstvennoi kommerts-kollegii. St. Petersburg:
Tiopografiia V. Kirshbauma, 1884. 408 p.
[DLC-Yudin HF3625.G68; MH-Econ6665.2.5]

Covers the records from the Commerce College from roughly 1718 to 1810, all of which are now located in TsGADA.

B-92. Kaidanov, Nikolai Ivanovich.
[Russia. Departament tamozhennykh sborov.]
Sistematicheskii katalog delam kommissii o kommertsii i o poshlinakh,
khraniashchimsia v arkhive Departamenta tamozhennykh sborov. St. Petersburg:
Tipografiia V. Kirshbauma, 1887. 91 p.
[DLC-HF3625.K34]

B-93. Kaidanov, Nikolai Ivanovich.
[Russia. Departament tamozhennykh sborov.]
Sistematicheskii katalog delam Sibirskogo prikaza, Moskovskogo kommissarstva i
drugikh byvshikh uchrezhdenii po chasti promyshlennosti i torgovli,
khraniashchimsia v Arkhive Departamenta tamozhennykh sborov. Also includes:
Dopolneniia k katalogu delam Departamenta vneshnei torgovli, izdannomu v 1877
godu. Compiled by N. Kaidanov. St. Petersburg, 1888. 204 p.
[DLC-HF3625.K35; MH-Econ6665.2.10]
Part of the materials covered dating from the nineteenth century are now
located in TsGIA SSSR.

Medical History

B-94. *Istoriia razvitiia meditsiny i zdravookhraneniia v Rossii. Obzor dokumental'nykh*
materialov. Compiled by R. Iu. Matskina. Edited by B. D. Petrov.
Moscow/Leningrad: GAU, 1958. 99 p.
[no US location reported]
Many of these materials, and all those dating from the eighteenth century, are
located in TsGADA, although the survey was published by TsGIA SSSR.

Military History

See the many references to materials in TsGADA in the general directory of
military sources by L. G. Beskrovnyi, *Ocherki po istochnikovedeniiu voennoi istorii*
Rossii (Moscow: Izd-vo AN SSSR, 1957) (A-45).

B-95. Chernov, A. V.
"Tsentral'nyi gosudarstvennyi arkhiv drevnikh aktov kak istochnik po voennoi
istorii russkogo gosudarstva do XVIII v." *Trudy MGIAI* 4 (1948):113-57.

Theater History

B-96. Koroleva, I. G.
"Tsentral'nyi gosudarstvennyi arkhiv drevnikh aktov." In *Materialy k istorii*
russkogo teatra v gosudarstvennykh arkhivakh SSSR. Obsory dokumentov. XVII
vek-1917 g., edited by I. F. Petrovskaia, pp. 54-66. Moscow: GAU, 1966. (A-52).

Personal or Family Fonds

Iusupov Family Papers

B-97. Minarik, L. P.
"Obzor materialov po istorii pomeshchich'ego khoziaistva v epokhu imperializma (1900-1917 gg.). O fonde Iusupovykh v Tsentral'nom gosudarstvennom arkhive drevnikh aktov." *Problemy istochnikovedeniia* 10 (1962):71-84.

M. V. Lomonosov (1711-1765)

B-98. Aleksandrova, E. V.
"Tsentral'nyi gosudarstvennyi arkhiv drevnikh aktov v Moskve." In *Lomonosov. Sbornik statei i materialov*, edited by A. I. Andreev et al., 3:376-422. Moscow/Leningrad: Izd-vo AN SSSR, 1951. (See A-12.)

G. F. Müller (1705-1783)

B-99. Golitsyn, N. V.
Portfeli G. F. Millera. Moscow: Tipografiia G. Lissnera and A. Geshelia, 1899. 150 p.
[no US location reported]
> Covers the Müller manuscript collection, fond 199, which originally came from the library of the Moscow Archive of the Ministry (College) of Foreign Affairs.

Vorontsov Family Papers

-100. Dzhincharadze, V. Z.
"Obzor fonda Vorontsovykh, khraniashchegosia v TsGADA." *Istoricheskie zapiski* 32 (1950):242-68.

-101. Dzhincharadze, V. Z., and F. A. Ostankovich.
"Obzor khoziaistvenno-imushchestvennykh materialov fonda Vorontsovykh, khraniashchegosia v TsGADA." *Istoricheskie zapiski* 37 (1951):252-79.

7. TsENTRAL'NYI GOSUDARSTVENNYI ISTORICHESKII ARKHIV SSSR (TsGIA SSSR)

[Central State Historical Archive of the USSR]
    Address: Leningrad, naberezhnaia Krasnogo flota, 4

HISTORY AND CONTENTS

Housed in an impressive group of buildings on the Neva embankment which include the former palace of the Senate and the Holy Synod facing the Senate Square, the Central State Historical Archive of the USSR is the principal repository for the prerevolutionary papers of the central governmental organs of imperial Russia during the nineteenth and early twentieth centuries. Although 1801 is the theoretical cut-off date which determines whether documents are to be found in TsGADA or TsGIA SSSR, the latter also retains some eighteenth-century materials, just as TsGADA in Moscow contains some fonds which extend well into the nineteenth century. About twice the size of TsGADA in terms of documentary volume, TsGIA SSSR currently contains about 1,360 fonds with approximately 7,000,000 storage units.

The archives of the Senate and Holy Synod had been housed in these same buildings before the Revolution, as had the archive of the State Council, but most of the other fonds now in TsGIA had remained dispersed in the archives of their respective ministries or other institutions, or in private hands. When all archival records were nationalized after the Revolution, Petrograd divisions were established for the eight (and later nine) sections of the Single State Archival Fond. These buildings became one of the main storage centers for several different sections comprising state documents of the nineteenth and early twentieth centuries gathered from various Leningrad archival sources and from the files of ministries and other prerevolutionary state institutions whose records had never before been centralized. These state records were subsequently augmented by papers from a variety of private institutions, commercial enterprises, and important Russian families.

Between 1922 and 1925 these holdings came under the administration of the Leningrad Branch of the Central Archive of the RSFSR [Leningradskoe otdelenie Tsentral'nogo arkhiva RSFSR], whose holdings encompassed virtually all the state documentary records in Leningrad, housed as they were in several different storage centers. In 1925 all the historical records in Leningrad state archives were administratively consolidated under the Leningrad Central Historical Archive [Leningradskii tsentral'nyi istoricheskii arkhiv]; between 1929 and 1934 it had the official name of the Leningrad Branch of the Central Historical Archive [Leningradskoe otdelenie Tsentral'nogo istoricheskogo arkhiva—LOTsIA]. This historical archive comprised several different storage areas and was much more extensive than the current TsGIA, encompassing as it did the military, naval, and cultural divisions, as well as the present-day TsGIA holdings (see the extent of these holdings in the 1933 guide, B-103).

In 1934, LOTsIA was split into four independent state archives. The military and naval divisions were split off permanently, but the other two—the Archive of National Economy [Arkhiv narodnogo khoziaistva] and the Archive of Internal Policy, Culture, and Life [Arkhiv vnutrennei politiki, kul'tury i byta] – remained housed in the present TsGIA buildings. In the 1941 archival reorganization, these latter two archives were administratively reunited as the Central State Historical Archive in Leningrad [Tsentral'nyi gosudarstvennyi arkhiv v g. Leningrade—TsGIAL], the immediate predecessor of TsGIA SSSR. At the same time a Moscow counterpart, the Central State Historical Archive in Moscow, TsGIAM, was established and lasted until 1961. When TsGIAM was dissolved in the reorganization of 1961, TsGIAL became simply the Central State Historical Archive of the USSR (TsGIA SSSR). Since this date, some of the private papers from TsGIAM have been transferred to TsGIA in Leningrad, but the bulk of TsGIAM, containing materials from the nineteenth- and early twentieth-century police and Ministry of Justice archives, became the prerevolutionary division of TsGAOR in Moscow. There has been some discussion of centralizing all these prerevolutionary state documents in TsGIA, which houses the rest of the archives from which the TsGIAM materials were taken, but such a consolidation has not reached the formal planning stage.

The organization of fonds in TsGIA SSSR reflects the various institutions in which they originated. Among the archives of the highest governmental bodies, TsGIA contains the records of the State Council from 1810 to 1917, along with its various chancelleries and departments, and the papers of different committees or commissions which were formerly retained in the Archive of the State Council [Arkhiv Gosudarstvennogo soveta] (see B-102, pp. 11-36). Many of these documents are covered in the prerevolutionary published inventories of this archive (B-106).

Also included in this division for the records of highest governmental bodies are the chancellery files of the State Duma (1905-1917) (see B-102, pp. 36-39, and B-107), the records of the Committee of Ministers (1802-1905) with their various sub-committee papers and the Council of Ministers (1857-1905; 1905-1917) (B-102, pp. 39-48, and B-108), and the files of various codification commissions (B-102, pp. 48-51).

The division of TsGIA containing the former St. Petersburg Archive of the Senate [Arkhiv Pravitel'stvuiushchego Senata] (E-102, pp. 55-85, and B-109—B-112) dates back to the time of Peter the Great. Some of the eighteenth-century Senate records which had originally been housed in Leningrad were transferred to TsGADA in Moscow, but many of the eighteenth-century files have been retained in TsGIA; some of these duplicate materials already in TsGADA, and further consolidation of these documents is being contemplated. Many of the nineteenth-century Senate files, i.e., those post-dating 1796, formerly housed in TsGADA have now been transferred to TsGIA; these include materials from fonds numbered 270, 269, 264-66, 255, and 395, as described in the 1946 guide to TsGADA (B-70a, pp. 261-63).

Another section of the same archival division houses the former Archive of the Holy Synod [Arkhiv Sviateishego pravitel'stvuiushchego Sinoda] (B-102, pp. 87-95, and B-112–B-116); all the eighteenth-century materials from this archive have been retained in TsGIA. In addition to documentary materials, the Synod archive also contains an extensive collection of medieval and later religious manuscripts, dating from the fourteenth to the early twentieth century (see B-116).

By far the largest division of TsGIA contains the records of the various ministries of the imperial government during the nineteenth and early twentieth centuries, including their various commissions and departments (see B-102, pp. 98-304). Ministries whose records are preserved in this repository include those of the Interior, Justice (those parts not located in Moscow), Commerce, Finance, Trade and Transportation, Lands, Communications, Education, and the Court. Among the records of the Ministry of the Imperial Court are to be found various files of the Imperial Chancellery and other court enterprises. In general, ministerial fonds have been organized around the specific departments, commissions, or sections of the ministry in which they originated. Ministerial materials not found in TsGIA include those of the Ministry of the Navy (in TsGAVMF), of Foreign Affairs (in AVPR), of War (in TsGVIA), and most police files from the Ministry of Justice (in TsGAOR SSSR).

In addition to the fonds of the Ministry of the Imperial Court, another group of fonds in TsGIA contains the records of various court functions, including sections of His Majesty's Own Chancellery (except for the Third Department records, which are all in TsGAOR), and other court-related files (B-102, pp. 305-24).

Another rich and varied section of TsGIA contains the archives of a variety of commercial and financial enterprises, including banks, factories, and other economic, scientific, and cultural societies (B-102, pp. 325-60). These materials had all been in private hands before the Revolution and only subsequently brought under state jurisdiction.

Private family papers make up a final important division of the TsGIA documentary holdings. Here are to be found close to two hundred personal archives, including many of Russia's leading prerevolutionary families; some of the fonds date back to the eighteenth century or earlier, but most are from the nineteenth and early twentieth centuries (B-102, pp. 361-425).

WORKING CONDITIONS

In TsGIA SSSR, as in other central state archives, the shortage of available inventories or catalogs is the greatest impediment to research for foreign scholars. Published inventories which had been prepared for some of the major archival repositories before the Revolution are still of great importance for those fonds covered. As a rule, however, the handwritten or typed inventories which have been prepared for other fonds are unfortunately not made available to foreign researchers. The visitor is thus largely dependent on the diligence of the archival staff.

Foreign scholars normally work in a special reading room instead of the large public one. They are assigned special archival assistants to transmit their orders and deliver documents, which normally involves the choice of materials for them. Paging tends to take two or more days in most cases, but usually there are few complaints that scholars are not provided enough materials to work with. Where more extensive delays occur, they usually involve materials in the process of reorganization or those which have not been thoroughly inventoried. Often, materials have been prepared in advance so that they are ready by the time that a scholar is granted admission. Thus advance arrangements and careful definition of the project are particularly important here.

The archival staff is in the process of preparing a comprehensive card catalog of many sections of the archive, but this catalog is limited to internal staff use. The archive has its own extensive library which grew out of the library of the prerevolutionary State Council. It now has over 300,000 volumes and some two thousand periodical publications. It is particularly rich in nineteenth-century materials, including newspapers, official publications, memoirs, and other documentary records. There are also several valuable collections of early manuscript books. Books bearing on current research will be brought to the archival reading room on request.

PUBLISHED GUIDES, GENERAL DESCRIPTION, AND BIBLIOGRAPHY

The extensive 1956 guide for TsGIA SSSR (then called TsGIAL) remains the starting point for researchers, but some may also want to consult the short description of the holdings in the general directory of state archives, *Gosudarstvennye arkhivy Soiuza SSR. Kratkii spravochnik* (A-7), pp. 16-22. The short survey of the history and contents of the archive by G. A. Dremina and T. V. Kuznetsova, *Tsentral'nyi gosudarstvennyi istoricheskii arkhiv SSSR v g. Leningrade. Uchebnoe posobie,* edited by N. A. Ivnitskii and V. V. Maksakov (Moscow: MGIAI, 1959; 64 p. [MH-Slav 610.100], does not go beyond the published guide in aiding the researcher in the identification of materials; nor does the historical article by V. V. Bedin, "TsGIA SSSR v Leningrade za 40 let," *Informatsionnyi biulleten' GAU MVD SSSR,* 1958, no. 10, pp. 5-21. The short report by the director, I. N. Firsov, and L. E. Shepelev, "Napravlenie i osnovnye itogi raboty TsGIA SSSR v 1960-1965 gg.," *Voprosy arkhivovedeniia,* 1965, no. 3, pp. 26-34, updates the historical survey and mentions some of the organizational changes. The most recent published reports of TsGIA developments and publication activities are available in the volume, published by GAU, edited by I. N. Solov'ev et al., *Problemy arkhivovedeniia i istorii arkhivnykh uchrezhdenii* (A-82), pp. 95-104, 124-36, 152-59, 170-78, and 204-16.

102. [Russia (1923-USSR). Tsentral'nyi gosudarstvennyi istoricheskii arkhiv v Leningrade.]
Tsentral'nyi gosudarstvennyi istoricheskii arkhiv SSSR v Leningrade. Putevoditel'. Edited by S. N. Valk and V. V. Bedin. Leningrad: GAU, 1956. 607 p.
[DLC-CD1716.A5.1956; MH-Slav 612.100.15]
    This extensive guide is organized along the pattern of the archive as described above. It provides brief descriptions of many of the fonds with dates of the

documents covered and some bibliographical indications of published catalogs, histories, and major documentary publications. At the end of the volume (pp. 433-81) is a list of many of the fonds in the archive not described in more detail, and a list of the many fonds transferred from TsGIA to other archives in the USSR in recent years (pp. 566-91). However, since further reorganization and transfers have occurred since the volume's publication, the guide is not up-to-date in this respect. A supplementary volume is currently in preparation. This guide has extensive subject, personal, and geographic name indexes.

B-103. [Russia (1923-USSR). Tsentral'nyi gosudarstvennyi istoricheskii arkhiv v Leningrade.]
Arkhivy SSSR. Leningradskoe otdelenie Tsentral'nogo istoricheskogo arkhiva. Putevoditel' po fondam. Compiled by M. Akhun, V. Lukomskii, S. Rozanov, and A. Shilov. Edited by A. K. Drezen. Leningrad: Lenoblizdat, 1933. 280 p.
[DLC-CD1713.A5.1933; MH-Slav 612.25]

An early guide which covered the Leningrad Branch of the Central Historical Archive as it was then organized, including the sections of political, economic, cultural, and military-naval documentation, before their division in 1934 into several independent state archives.

For the TsGIA holdings—the political and economic sections—the guide has been entirely superseded by the more up-to-date and comprehensive guide mentioned above (B-102). Some of the cultural materials are now housed in TsGALI and are described more extensively in those guides. Virtually all of those listed in the military section have been transferred to TsGVIA in Moscow, but are not described in any other guide or published description; similarly, the naval section, now independently administered as TsGAVMF, has not been adequately described elsewhere, so that this remains the only published list of its contents, although hardly a satisfactorily comprehensive or up-to-date one.

B-104. [Russia (1923-USSR). Glavnoe arkhivnoe upravlenie. Tsentral'nyi istoricheskii arkhiv SSSR.]
Nekotorye voprosy izucheniia istoricheskikh dokumentov XIX-nachala XX v. Sbornik statei. Edited by I. N. Firsov, G. M. Gorfein, and L. E. Shepelev. Leningrad: Izd-vo LGU, 1967. 264 p.
[MH-Slav 602.59.5]

This collection of articles by TsGIA archivists covers different sections of the archive. Some of the articles survey materials on specific subjects (see references below). Of more general interest are those by R. Iu. Matskina, "K voprosu ob opredelenii sostava arkhivnykh fondov vysshikh i tsentral'nykh uchrezhdenii XIX-nachala XX v." (pp. 24-43), and G. M. Gorfein, "Osnovnye istochniki po istorii vysshikh i tsentral'nykh uchrezhdenii XIX-nachala XX v." (pp. 73-110). See also listing under A-81.

105. [Russia (1923-USSR). Tsentral'nyi gosudarstvennyi istoricheskii arkhiv SSSR v Leningrade.]

Dokumenty TsGIA SSSR v Leningrade v rabotakh sovetskikh issledovatelei. Bibliograficheskii ukazatel'. Part 1: *Stat'i i publikatsii na russkom iazyke v periodicheskikh i prodolzhaiushchikhsia izdaniiakh 1917-1957 gg.* Compiled by A. L. Vainshtein, G. M. Gorfein, N. G. Markova, and M. D. Filippova. Edited by V. V. Bedin. Leningrad: GAU, 1960. 282 p.

Dokumenty TsGIA SSSR v rabotakh sovetskikh issledovatelei. Bibliograficheskii ukazatel'. Part 2: *Knigi, stat'i i publikatsii na russkom iazyke 1958-1966 gg.* Compiled by A. L. Vainshtein, N. G. Markova, and M. D. Filippova. Edited by V. V. Bedin and L. E. Shepelev. Leningrad: GAU, 1966. 327 p.

[MH-Slav 612.100.10]

Although these two volumes do not themselves survey the TsGIA holdings, they are extremely important to any scholar working there. They provide a comprehensive list of Soviet documentary publications and published studies based on TsGIA materials which have appeared since 1917. Lists are purely alphabetical by name of author. Annotations give the fond number of the documents involved and, frequently, brief comments about the materials. Indexes aid in the identification of subject matter, etc.

PUBLISHED CATALOGS AND SPECIAL DESCRIPTIONS

Archive of the State Council

106. [Russia. Gosudarstvennyi sovet. Arkhiv.]

Opis' del arkhiva Gosudarstvennogo soveta. 17 vols. St. Petersburg: Gosudarstvennaia tipografiia, 1908-1914.

[MH-L]

The publication of this series was never completed. The seventeen volumes are numbered 1-12, 15-16, and 19-21. The current fond numbers of this collection of documents are marked on the master copy in the TsGIA library. The table below gives the coverage or subtitles of the individual volumes together with their year of publication in St. Petersburg and pagination:

Vol. 1:	*1810-1829.*	1908. 916 p.
Vol. 2:	*1830-1839.*	1908. 471 p.
Vol. 3:	*1840-1849.*	1908. 557 p.
Vol. 4:	*1850-1856.*	1910. 445 p.
Vol. 5:	*1857-1862.*	1910. 434 p.
Vol. 6:	*1863-1866.*	1911. 447 p.
Vol. 7:	*1867-1870.*	1911. 464 p.
Vol. 8:	*1871-1876.*	1913. 483 p.
Vol. 9:	*1877-1882.*	1912. 424 p.
Vol. 10:	*1883-1888.*	1913. 445 p.
Vol. 11:	*1889-1894.*	1914. 467 p.
Vol. 12:	*1895-1899.*	1914. 510 p.

Vol. 15: *Dela Sekretnogo komiteta i Glavnykh komitetov po krest'ianskomu delu i ob ustroistve sel'skogo sostoianiia, 1857-1882*. 1911. 525 p.

Vol. 16: *Dela Gosudarstvennogo soveta i Gosudarstvennoi kantseliarii, 1807-1910*. 1912. 923 p.

Vol. 19: *Dela Stats-sekretariata Gertsogstva varshavskogo i Tsarstva pol'skogo, 1807-1825*. 1910. 321 p.

Vol. 20: *Dela Sobstvennoi ego Imperatorskogo Velichestva Kantseliarii po delam Tsarstva pol'skogo, 1826-1835*. 1911. 450 p.

Vol. 21: *Dela Sobstvennoi ego Imperatorskogo Velichestva Kantseliarii po delam Tsarstva pol'skogo, 1836-1845*. 1913. 569 p.

Archive of the State Duma

B-107. [Russia. Gosudarstvennaia duma. Kantseliariia.]
Opis' del arkhiva kantseliarii Gosudarstvennoi dumy. 2 vols. Petrograd: Gosudarstvennaia tipografiia, 1914-1915. 126 p.; 143 p.
[NN; CSt-H]

The first volume covers the first session (April 27-July 8, 1906); the second covers the second session (February 20-June 2, 1907).

Fond of the Council of Ministers

B-108. Diatlova, N. P., and R. Iu. Matskina.
"Obzor fonda 'Soveta ministrov' (Tsentral'nyi gosudarstvennyi istoricheskii arkhiv SSSR v Leningrade)." *Arkheograficheskii ezhegodnik za 1958 god*, pp. 233-56.

Archive of the Senate

In addition to the prerevolutionary inventories described below, see the three survey articles relating to the Senate fonds in the TsGIA publication, *Nekotorye voprosy izucheniia istoricheskikh dokumentov XIX-nachala XX v. Sbornik statei* (B-104 [also listed as A-81]): L. V. Vinogradova, "Osnovnye vidy dokumentov Senata i organizatsiia ego deloproizvodstva," *ibid.*, pp. 111-32; A. V. Tapanova, "Dokumenty appelliatsionnykh departamentov Senata kak istochnik dlia izucheniia pomestnogo khoziaistva doreformennoi Rossii," *ibid.*, pp. 133-46; and E. S. Paina, "Senatorskie revizii i ikh arkhivnye materialy (XIX-nachala XX v.)," *ibid.*, pp. 147-75.

B-109. Klochkov, Mikhail Vasil'evich.
Pamiatnaia knizhka Senatskogo arkhiva. Edited under the direction of I. A. Blinov. St. Petersburg: Senatskaia tipografiia, 1913. 257 p.
[DLC-CD1731.S4.K4; MH-L]

B-110. [Russia. Pravitel'stvuiushchii Senat. Arkhiv.]
Arkhiv Pravitel'stvuiushchego Senata.
Vol. 1: *Opis' imennym vysochaishim ukazam i poveleniiam tsarstvovaniia*

imperatora Petra Velikogo, 1704-1725. Compiled by P. Baranov. St. Petersburg, 1872. 167 p.

Opis' vysochaishim ukazam i poveleniiam, khraniashchimsia v S.-Peterburgskom Senatskom arkhive za XVIII vek. Compiled by P. Baranov.

Vol. 2: *1725-1740.* St. Petersburg, 1875. 1002 p. Includes indexes for volumes 1 and 2.

Vol. 3: *1740-1762.* St. Petersburg, 1878. 513 p. With separate index volume. 305 p.

[DLC-Yudin DK129.B22; CSt-H]

> Copies of many of the eighteenth-century documents covered by these volumes exist in both TsGIA and TsGADA. The inventories coordinate the entries with the published ukazy in *Polnoe sobranie zakonov Rossiiskoi Imperii* and include many which have not been published. See B-86.

111. [Russia. Pravitel'stvuiushchii Senat.]

Opis' dokumentov i del, khraniashchikhsia v Senatskom arkhive. 9 vols. St. Petersburg/Petrograd: Senatskaia tipografiia, 1909-1917.

Series I:

Vol. 1: *1703-1725 gg.* 1909. 282 p.

Vol. 2: *1725-1733 gg.* 1910. 612 p.

Vol. 3: *1734-1737 gg.* 1915. 984 p.

Vol. 3, part 2: *Ukazateli i prilozheniia.* 1915. 412 p.

Series II:

Vol. 1: 1797 g.-mart 1801 g. 1909. 98 p.

Vol. 2: *Aprel' 1801 g.-1803 g.* 1910. 142 p.

Vol. 3: *Mart 1803 g.-aprel' 1806 g.* 1915. 78 p.

Series III:

Vol. 1: *Dela kantseliarii General-Prokurora 1797 g.* 1910. 359 p.

Vol. 2: *Dela kantseliarii General-Prokurora 1798-1799 gg.* 1911. 446 p.

Vol. 3: *Del kantseliarii General-Prokurora 1797-1800 gg.* 1917. 235 p.

[MH-Slav 251.330.10; MH-L]

112. [Russia. Pravitel'stvuiushchii Senat.]

Opis' dokumentov i del, khraniashchikhsia v Senatskom arkhive. Otechestvennaia voina i kampanii 1813-1815 gg. St. Petersburg: Senatskaia tipografiia, 1912. 339 p.

[DLC-Yudin CD 1731.S4S4; MH-Slav 251.330.12]

Archive of the Holy Synod

113. Nasper, G. M.

"Kratkii obzor dokumental'nykh materialov XVII-XVIII vv. v fonde Sinoda."

Arkheograficheskii ezhegodnik za 1959 g., pp. 303-10.

> For a prerevolutionary short survey of the archival and library holdings of the Synod, see the pamphlet by K. Ia. Zdravomyslov, *Arkhiv i biblioteka Sv. Sinoda i konsistorskie arkhivy.* St. Petersburg: Sinodal'naia tipografiia, 1906. 61 p.

B-114. [Russia. Sviateishii pravitel'stvuiushchii Sinod.]
Opisanie dokumentov i del, khraniashchikhsia v arkhive Sviateishego pravitel'stvuiushchego Sinoda. 30 vols. in 31. St. Petersburg: Sinodal'naia tipografiia, 1868-1917.
[DLC-CD1726.A3 (incomplete); CSt-H (incomplete); NN]

This extensive series with its many large volumes—often over a 1,000 pages each—was never completed, but got only as far as the mid-eighteenth century. Except for the first volume, which covers documents from the years 1542-1721, each volume covers a single year. They were not published consecutively, and there remain gaps in the series. Volumes 2-12 cover the years 1723-1732; volumes 14-24, 1734-1743; volume 26, 1746; volumes 28-29, 1748-1749; volumes 31-32, 1751-1752; volume 34, 1754; volume 39, 1959; and volume 50 covers 1770. Additional volumes exist in manuscript form in the archive. The publication up to 1915 is described in more detail in *Piatidesiatiletie vysochaishe utverzhdennoi Kommissii po razboru i opisaniiu arkhiva Sviateishego Sinoda, 1865-1915. Istoricheskaia zapiska* (Petrograd, 1915, 454 p.), pp. 172-77.

B-115. [Russia. Sviateishii pravitel'stvuiushchii Sinod.]
Opisanie dokumentov arkhiva zapadno-russkikh uniatskikh mitropolitov. 2 vols. St. Petersburg, 1897-1907.
[MH-C5160.13]

The first volume covers 1470-1700, the second 1701-1839.

B-116. [Orthodox Eastern Church, Russian. Sinod. Arkhiv.]
[Russia. Sviateishii pravitel'stvuiushchii Sinod.]
Opisanie rukopisei, khraniashchikhsia v arkhive Sviateishego pravitel'stvuiushchego Sinoda. 2 vols. in 3. St. Petersburg: Sinodal'naia tipografiia, 1904-1910.

Vol. 1: *Rukopisi bogosluzhebnye.* 1904. 631 p. 66 p.

Vol. 2: part 1, 1906; part 2, 1910.

[DLC-CD1726.A54 (Vol. 1); MH-Slav 251.330]

Documents from the Imperial Chancellery and Court Estates

B-117. [Russia.]
Arkhiv Ministerstva gosudarstvennykh imushchestv. Sistematicheskaia opis' delam byvshego V-go otdeleniia Sobstvennoi Ego Imperatorskogo Velichestva kantseliarii, 1824-1856. St. Petersburg, 1887. 236 p.
[no US location reported]

Covers documents from the fifth department of the Imperial Chancellery for the years of Nicholas I, particularly materials relating to state domains.

B-118. [Russia. Ministerstvo zemledeliia i gosudarstvennykh imushchestv.]
Arkhiv Ministerstva zemledeliia i gosudarstvennykh imushchestv. (Istoricheskii ocherk, ustroistvo i sostav del). Compiled by P. A. Shafranov. St. Petersburg: Tipografiia V. F. Kirshbauma, 1904. 247 p.

[DLC Yudin JN6550.Z5S5]
Describes materials relating to state domains from the former ministry archives.

Interior Ministry Documents

119. Deich, G. M., and Melamedova, V. M.
"Obzor fonda Zemskogo otdela." *Istoricheskii arkhiv*, 1960, no. 1, pp. 191-99.

120. Polianskaia, L.
"Arkhivnyi fond Glanogo upravleniia po delam pechati. Obzor." *Literaturnoe nasledstvo* 22-24 (1935): 603-34.
Surveys censorship files of fond no. 776.

121. Polianskaia, L.
"Obzor fonda Tsentral'nogo komiteta tsenzury inostrannoi."*Arkhivnoe delo* 45 (1938, no. 1): 62-116.
Surveys censorship files for foreign publications now classified as fond no. 799.

Archive of the Ministry of Education

122. [Russia. Ministerstvo narodnogo prosveshcheniia. Arkhiv.]
Opisanie del arkhiva Ministerstva narodnogo prosveshcheniia.
Vol. 1: Edited by S. F. Platonov and A. S. Nikolaev. Petrograd, 1917. 447 p.
Covers various papers of the ministry from 1782-1803 with some additional documentary materials.
Vol. 2: Edited by A. S. Nikolaev and S. A. Pereselenkov. Petrograd, 1921. 416 p.
Covers censorship materials for the years 1802-1817.
[MH-Educ 1193.35 (vol. 1); NN; CSt-H]

123. Polianskaia, L. I.
"Dokumenty po istorii vysshego obrazovaniia v Rossii." *Istoricheskii arkhiv*, 1958, no. 1, pp. 222-27.
Briefly surveys materials on higher education.

Documents on Administrative History

124. Diatlova, N. P.
"Otchety gubernatorov kak istoricheskii istochnik." *Problemy arkhivovedeniia i istochnikovedeniia. Materialy nauchnoi konferentsii arkhivistov Leningrada, 4-6 fevralia 1964 g.* (Leningrad: Izd-vo "Nauka," 1964), pp. 227-46. (See A-80.)

125. Matskina, R. Iu.
"Ministerskie otchety i ikh osobennosti kak istoricheskogo istochnika." *Problemy arkhivovedeniia i istochnikovedeniia. Materialy nauchnoi konferentsii arkhivistov Leningrada, 4-6 fevralia 1964 g.* (Leningrad: Izd-vo "Nauka," 1964), pp. 209-26. (See A-80.)

Documents on Economic Development, Manufacturing, and Trade

B-126. Paina, E. S.
Ekonomicheskaia istoriia Rossii, 1861-1917 gg. Obzor publikatsii gosudarstvennykh arkhivov SSSR (1918-1963). Moscow: GAU, 1967. 90 p.
[DLC-Z7165.R9P29; MH-Slav 3085.660]
In connection with the coverage of documentary publications from TsGIA, this essay gives much information about the archival holdings. See A-66.

B-127. Mal'tseva, N. A.
"Obzor dokumental'nykh materialov fonda Ministerstva torgovli i promyshlennosti." *Istoricheskii arkhiv*, 1958, no. 2, pp. 202-09.

B-128. Pliukhina, M. A., and L. E. Shepelev.
"Ob ekonomicheskom polozhenii Rossii nakanune Velikoi Oktiabr'skoi sotsialisticheskoi revoliutsii. Obzor dokumental'nykh materialov Tsentral'nogo gosudarstvennogo istoricheskogo arkhiva SSSR v Leningrade." *Istoricheskii arkhiv*, 1957, no. 2, pp. 167-77.

B-129. Kaidanov, Nikolai Ivanovich.
[Russia. Departament tamozhennykh sborov.]
Sistematicheskii katalog delam Departamenta vneshnei torgovli, khraniashchimsia v Arkhive Departamenta tamozhennykh sborov. Compiled by N. Kaidanov. St. Petersburg, 1877. 643 p.
[DLC-Yudin-HF3625.K4; MH-Econ6665.2]
Covers foreign trade materials between 1811 and roughly 1865. See also the supplementary materials listed in item B-93, *Dopolneniia k katalogu delam Departamenta vneshnei torgovli, izdannomu v 1877 godu*, compiled by N. Kaidanov (St. Petersburg, 1888).

B-130. Kaidanov, Nikolai Ivanovich.
[Russia. Departament tamozhennykh sborov.]
Sistematicheskii katalog delam Departamenta tamozhennykh sborov. Compiled by N. Kaidanov. St. Petersburg, 1886. 227 p. [DLC-HF3625.K34]
Covers documents dealing with customs and trade from roughly 1825 to 1883, but the bulk of the materials date from the 1850's, 60's, and early 70's. See also the additional coverage in the volume published in 1888 by Kaidanov, most of the documents from which are now located in TsGADA (see B-93).

B-131. [Russia (1923-USSR). Tsentral'nyi gosudarstvennyi istoricheskii arkhiv v Leningrade.]
Obzor dokumental'nykh materialov Tsentral'nogo gosudarstvennogo istoricheskogo arkhiva SSSR po istorii obrabatyvaiushchei promyshlennosti Rossii v pervoi polovine XIX veka. Compiled by M. S. Semenova, G. S. Khomiakova, and L. E. Shepelev. Edited by V. V. Bedin.
Part 1: Moscow/Leningrad: GAU, 1957. 60 p.

[DLC-HD9735.R92A55; MH-Slav 3085.500.01]
   Part 2: *Obzor dokumental'nykh materialov Tsentral'nogo gosudarstvennogo istoricheskogo arkhiva SSSR po istorii obrabatyvaiushchei promyshlennosti Rossii v 1864-1914 gg.* Leningrad: GAU, 1962. 151 p.
   [MH-Slav 3085.500.01]
   See also A-43 for further discussion of materials relating to business history.

-**132.** Pavlov, V. P., M. S. Shusterova, and V. I. Kardashev.
   "Obzor dokumental'nykh materialov po istorii promyshlennykh predpriiatii Rossii Tsentral'nogo gosudarstvennogo istoricheskogo arkhiva SSSR v Leningrade." In *A. M. Gor'kii i sozdanie istorii fabrik i zavodov. Sbornik dokumentov i materialov v pomoshch' rabotaiushchim nad istoriei fabrik i zavodov SSSR,* compiled by L. M. Zak and S. S. Zimina, pp. 290-310. Moscow: Izd-vo sotsial'no-ekonomicheskoi literatury, 1959. (A-41.)

Labor History and Revolutionary Movements
   See also documents covered by A-42 on the October Revolution

-**133.** Rutman, R. E.
   "Materialy TsGIAL po istorii rabochego dvizheniia v Rossii nakanune otmeny krepostnogo prava." *Istoricheskii arkhiv*, 1961, no. 4, pp. 209-14.

-**134.** Melamedova, V. M., and M. A. Pliukhina.
   "Obzor dokumental'nykh materialov TsGIAL SSSR o rabochem dvizhenii v revoliutsii 1905-1907 gg." *Istoricheskii arkhiv*, 1956, no. 3, pp. 194-210.
      Includes detailed list of fonds, in addition to a general survey of materials on working class movements, 1905-1907.

-**135.** Dorzhiev, N. N., and M. A. Pliukhina.
   "Obzor dokumental'nykh materialov Tsentral'nogo gosudarstvennogo istoricheskogo arkhiva SSSR v Leningrade o revoliutsionnom dvizhenii rabochikh, krest'ian, soldat i matrosov v 1917 g." *Istoriia SSSR*, 1957, no. 5, pp. 211-19.

Documents on the Peasant Question
   See also listing under A-67

-**136.** Kudriavtseva, E. I.
   "Dokumenty vysshikh i tsentral'nykh uchrezhdenii po istorii udel'nykh krest'ian (1797-1863 gg.)." In *Nekotorye voprosy izucheniia istoricheskikh dokumentov XIX-nachala XX v. Sbornik statei.* (B-104), pp. 176-203.

Communications History

-**137.** *Materialy po istorii sviazi v Rossii XVIII–nachala XX vv. Obzor dokumental'nykh materialov.* Compiled by F. I. Bunina et al. Edited by N. A. Mal'tseva. Leningrad: GAU, 1966. 335 p.
   [DLC-HE8214.M3; MH-Slav 3085.500.60]

See also under F-112 and G-18, since this volume also surveys materials in LGIA and in the Central Museum of Communications in Leningrad.

History of Medicine

B-138. *Istoriia razvitiia meditsiny i zdravookhraneniia v Rossii. Obzor dokumental'nykh materialov.* Compiled by R. Iu. Matskina. Edited by B. D. Petrov.
Moscow/Leningrad: GAU, 1958. 99 p.
[no US location reported]
> Some of these materials relating to the development of medicine and public health, especially those dating from the eighteenth century, are housed in TsGADA. See B-94.

Materials on Non-Russian Nationalities
See also the materials on the Mongols, Kalmuks, and Buriats covered by item A-29.

B-139. Kovalev, I. F.
"Dokumenty po istorii kalmykskogo naroda." *Istoriia SSSR,* 1960, no. 1, pp. 181-82.
> Brief survey of materials relating to the Kalmuks.

B-140. Genkina, K. P.
"Obzor dokumental'nykh materialov po istorii Kirgizii." *Istoriia SSSR*, 1963, no. 5, pp. 217-21.
> Brief survey of materials relating to the Kirghiz peoples.

Documents on Foreign Relations

B-141. Vinogradov, S. A.
"Iz istorii russko-cheshskikh sviazei v XIX—nachale XX v. (Obzor dokumental'nykh materialov)." *Novaia i noveishaia istoriia,* 1960, no. 4, pp. 183-86.
> Brief survey of materials pertaining to Russian-Czech relations in the nineteenth and early twentieth centuries.

B-142. Bedin, V. V., and V. M. Melamedova.
"Dokumental'nye materialy TsGIAL po istorii Finliandii." *Istoricheskii arkhiv,* 1959, no. 4, pp. 198-204.
> Brief survey of documents pertaining to Finnish history.

B-143. Trivysh, L. L.
"Dokumenty o sodruzhestve Rossii i Frantsii v oblasti nauki i kul'tury." *Novaia i noveishaia istoriia,* 1960, no. 4, pp. 186-87.
> Brief survey of documents pertaining to cultural relations between Russia and France from the eighteenth to the early twentieth centuries.

3-144. Kovalev, I. F.

"O druzhestvennykh sviaziakh Rossii s Indiei." *Istoricheskii arkhiv*, 1959, no. 6, p. 194.

Brief survey of documents pertaining to Russian relations with India.

3-145. Paina, E. S.

"Russko-ital'ianskie kul'turnye sviazi v XIX–nachale XX v." *Istoricheskii arkhiv,* 1960, no. 3, pp. 234-37.

Brief survey of documents pertaining to Russian cultural relations with Italy in the nineteenth and early twentieth centuries.

Documents on Theater History

3-146. Petrovskaia, I. F., ed. and comp.

Materialy k istorii russkogo teatra v gosudarstvennykh arkhivakh SSSR. Obzory dokumentov. XVII vek–1917 g. Moscow: GAU and Leningradskii gosudarstvennyi institut teatra, muzyki i kinematografii, 1966. 285 p. (See A-52.) [DLC-PN2721.P4; MH-Slav4135.200.45]

This volume includes five different articles specifically surveying theatrical materials in TsGIA SSSR:

Markova, N. G., and V. A. Tsinkovich-Nikolaeva. "Fond Direktsii imperatorskikh teatrov" (pp. 67-102).

Artem'eva, A. N. "Fond raznykh uchrezhdenii Ministerstva dvora, khraniashchiesia v TsGIA SSSR" (pp. 103-18).

Nasper, G. M. "Fondy tsenzurnykh uchrezhdenii (pp. 119-42).

Petrovskaia, I. F. "Fondy vysshikh organov vlasti, ustanovlenii Ministerstva vnutrennikh del i nekotorykh drugikh gosudarstvennykh uchrezhdenii v TsGIA SSSR. Dokumenty o dramaticheskom teatre v lichnykh fondakh etogo arkhiva" (pp. 143-66).

Artem'eva, A. N. "Materialy o muzykal'nom teatre v lichnykh fondakh TsGIA SSSR" (pp. 167-70).

3-147. [Russia. Direktsiia imperatorskikh teatrov. Arkhiv.]

Arkhiv direktsii Imperatorskikh teatrov. Part 1 (1746-1801 gg.) Otdel I–Opis' dokumentam. Compiled by V. P. Pogozhev, A. E. Molchanov, and K. A. Petrov. St. Petersburg: Tipografiia Imperatorskikh Teatrov, 1892. 344 p. [MH-Slav 4135.492.5F]

Although the fond has been somewhat reorganized, this inventory is still useful for the location of materials.

Personal Fonds

M. V. Lomonosov (1711-1765)

3-148. Suslova, E. N., and V. R. Svirskaia.

"Tsentral'nyi gosudarstvennyi istoricheskii arkhiv v Leningrade." In *Lomonosov. Sbornik statei i materialov*, edited by A. I. Andreev et al., 3: 426-56. Moscow/Leningrad: Izd-vo AN SSSR, 1951. (See A-12.)

Medieval Slavic Manuscripts

For a comprehensive bibliography of published catalogs and descriptions of the medieval manuscripts in TsGIA, see the general directory compiled by Iu. K. Begunov et al, *Spravochnik-ukazatel' pechatnykh opisanii slaviano-russkikh rukopisei* (A-14), pp. 119-22. See also item B-116 covering manuscripts from the Synod Library.

B-149. Polianskaia, L. I.

"Pamiatniki drevnerusskoi pis'mennosti v sobranii Tsentral'nogo gosudarstvennogo istoricheskogo arkhiva SSSR v Leningrade." *Trudy otdela drevenerusskoi literatury Instituta russkoi literatury AN SSSR* 13(1957):559-73.

Printed Materials

B-150. Shepeleva, O. N.

"Listovki RSDRP v fondakh Tsentral'nogo gosudarstvennogo istoricheskogo arkhiva SSSR i organizatsiia ikh ispol'zovaniia." In *Problemy arkhivovedeniia i istorii arkhivnykh uchrezhdenii. Materialy iubileinoi nauchnoi konferentsii arkhivistov Leningrada, 13-14 iiunia 1968 g.*, edited by I. N. Solov'ev et al., pp. 152-59. Leningrad: Izd-vo LGU, 1970. (See A-82.)

8. TsENTRAL'NYI GOSUDARSTVENNYI VOENNO-ISTORICHESKII ARKHIV SSR (TsGVIA SSSR)

[Central State Military History Archive of the USSR]
   Address: Moscow, B-5, 2-ia Baumanskaia, 3

HISTORY AND CONTENTS

The Central State Military History Archive, or TsGVIA as it is usually called, has brought together in a single repository almost all of the prerevolutionary military records of the Russian Empire with documents dating from the seventeenth century through World War I. Now located in the historic Lefort Palace in the old "German Suburb" section of Moscow, the archive houses over 15,000 fonds with over 3,250,000 storage units.

The present archive, which recently celebrated its 150th anniversary, is the direct descendant of the Moscow division of the Archive of the Inspectors' Department of the General Staff [Moskovskoe otdelenie Arkhiva Inspektorskogo departamenta Glavnogo shtaba] established in 1819; in 1865 the archive was moved from the Kremlin to its present location where it became traditionally known as the Lefort Archive, but officially called the Moscow Division of the General Archive of the General Staff [Moskovskoe otdelenie Obshchego arkhiva Glavnogo shtaba; after 1906, Moskovskoe otdelenie Obshchego arkhiva Glavnogo upravleniia General'nogo shtaba]. Other military archives were later also deposited in the same location so that the Lefort Archive gained the tradition of a centralized repository for military records in the Moscow region, but also housed documents from many parts of the Russian Empire.

After the Revolution, this storage area remained a principal repository for the Moscow section of the military-naval division of the Single State Archival Fond and was immediately enriched by the voluminous military records of the First World War. At this time it was combined with the important prerevolutionary Military Science Archive, the holdings of which were moved from Petrograd to Moscow in 1918. This archive had grown out of the Imperial Map Depot founded in 1797 under Paul I, which later had come under the Ministry of War as the Military Topographical Depot [Voenno-topograficheskoe depo]; in 1863 it was reorganized as the Military History Archive [Voenno-istoricheskii arkhiv] and in 1867 became the Military Science Archive of the General Staff [Voenno-uchenyi arkhiv Glavnogo shtaba-VUA; after 1906, Voenno-uchenyi arkhiv Glavnogo upravleniia General'nogo shtaba].

Combining as it did these two major prerevolutionary archives and acquiring at the same time various other prerevolutionary military records from the Moscow area, the Lefort Archive became the main repository for the Moscow Division of the Third, or Military-Naval, Section of the Single State Archival Fond. It then came under the administration of the Central Archive of the RSFSR (Tsentral'nyi arkhiv RSFSR—Tsentrarkhiv), when this latter organ was set up in 1922.

PART B – CENTRAL STATE ARCHIVES

With the 1925 archival reorganization the Lefort Archive in effect became a separate repository named the Military History Archive [Voenno-istoricheskii arkhiv], although administratively under the Moscow Central Historical Archive. In 1933, as a more separate administrative unit, it was renamed the Central Military History Archive [Tsentral'nyi voenno-istoricheskii arkhiv]. TsGVIA took its present name in 1941, at which time additional materials relating to military history were transferred to it from other regional repositories.

A further large-scale move towards the centralization of military history records in TsGVIA took place in 1956-1958, when the entire contents of the former Leningrad Branch of the Military History Archive [Filial Tsentral'nogo gosudarstvennogo voenno-istoricheskogo arkhiva] were transferred to Moscow. This important consolidation brought to TsGVIA the high-level military records, especially from the nineteenth and early twentieth centuries, that had been traditionally preserved in Leningrad, brought together there after the Revolution from a variety of separate repositories in which they had been previously stored. In fact, the Petrograd Division of the Military-Naval (Third) Section of the Single State Archival Fond grew directly out of the General Archive of the General Staff [Obshchii arkhiv Glavnogo shtaba] which had been founded originally in St. Petersburg in 1819 as the army's Archive of the Inspectors' Department of the General Staff [Arkhiv Inspektorskogo departamenta Glavnogo shtaba], until the liquidation of the Inspectors' Department in 1865. Its name was further modified in 1906 although it continued to function as the main archive of the General Staff [Obshchii arkhiv Glavnogo upravleniia General'nogo shtaba] and never became a centralized military archive, since many records remained with their issuing agencies. After the Revolution its holdings were amalgamated with the various archival deposits of the Ministry of War, the Petersburg and Finnish Military Districts, military academies and training schools, and other scattered army records from the Petrograd region.

In 1925 these military fonds that had been brought together in Leningrad became part of the newly established Leningrad Branch of the Central Historical Archive [Leningradskoe otdelenie Tsentral'nogo istoricheskogo arkhiva–LOTsIA]. The military section, while officially part of the Military-Naval Division of LOTsIA, remained housed in a separate repository (for its holdings as of 1932, see B-151). When LOTsIA split into four separate archives in 1934, the military section was established independently as the Leningrad Military History Archive [Leningradskii voenno-istoricheskii arkhiv]. In the 1941 archival reform, although effectively retaining its autonomy, this archive became officially a branch of TsGVIA [Filial Tsentral'nogo gosudarstvennogo voenno-istoricheskogo arkhiva]. Later in the 1950's, however, the Leningrad branch was completely dissolved and its holdings transferred to TsGVIA in Moscow by 1958.

TsGVIA is continuing to gather materials from regional repositories in other parts of the Soviet Union in an effort to centralize all documents relating to prerevolutionary Russian military affairs; one of the recent acquisitions is a large group of fonds transferred from the Georgian SSR.

One of the major categories of documents in TsGVIA covers the central and regional administration of the Russian army and military affairs from the eighteenth century to 1918. A small fond from the military chancellery includes documents of the period from 1705 to 1719. More extensive are the papers from the College of War, from its establishment by Peter the Great in 1719 to roughly 1812 (although the college was formally abolished in 1802, its function and hence its records continued later). Most of the administrative fonds of the subsequent Ministry of War postdate 1812; the chancellery and different departments of the ministry are represented by separate fonds. Extensive documentation is preserved here from regional military districts, most of which dates from the late nineteenth and early twentieth centuries. Also included are fonds containing the records of the General Staff and various other high organs of military command (see B-151, pp. 9-60).

The group of fonds that came to TsGVIA from the former Military Science Archive date back as early as the late fifteenth century and contain a variety of cartographic and statistical documents (see B-151, pp. 61-64). There is a particularly rich collection of over 20,000 Russian military maps, plans, and early atlases along with other graphic materials mostly from the seventeenth and eighteenth centuries. Published catalogs are available for many of these fonds (see B-154). There are also a number of fonds of military intelligence documents containing maps and topographical and statistical documents relating to Western Europe and the Orient dating from the sixteenth century to 1914.

A large group of fonds in TsGVIA are organized historically around materials relating to specific wars and expeditions (for a general description, see B-151, pp. 90-180). A few scattered documents date from the sixteenth and seventeenth centuries, but all the wars of the eighteenth and nineteenth centuries are well represented. By far the largest bulk of materials in this category are the military records of World War I, which are extensive not only in quantity but also in variety of documentation included.

The private papers of approximately two hundred forty important prerevolutionary figures who distinguished themselves in the military realm are also to be found in TsGVIA. Particularly large or significant fonds are those of A. A. Arakcheev, M. B. Barclay de Tolly, A. B. Buturlin, G. A. Potemkin-Tavricheskii, K. G. Razumovskii, N. I. Saltykov, P. I. Shuvalov, P. K. Sukhtelen, and A. V. Suvorov (see B-151, pp. 65-89).

Close to 700 fonds, most of which had come from different prerevolutionary military files in the St. Petersburg area, were transferred to Moscow during the 1956-1958 period from the now dissolved Leningrad branch of TsGVIA. These include many of the central records of the imperial war ministry, the records of the St. Petersburg and Finnish military districts, the papers of several different military educational and research establishments, and a variety of other military records, almost all of which date from the nineteenth and early twentieth centuries (see the list of some of these fonds in B-151, pp. 193-94, and the more complete coverage in B-152).

Most of the documents to be found in TsGVIA naturally come from a specifically military source or bear a strong military orientation; however, the archive contains materials relating to many different aspects of Russian history. Particularly because military affairs were involved in or related to so many phases of Russian life, the archive should be considered an important source for a wide variety of topics from education to peasant uprisings, and from bureaucratic administration and diplomacy to the Decembrists and other phases of the revolutionary movement. And because so many of the individuals whose family papers are preserved here were prominent in so many realms, documents here have a much wider importance than might at first be recognized.

Also of special note is the TsGVIA library which has a collection of about 70,000 books and periodicals, including many rare books and military publications.

WORKING CONDITIONS

Although most sections of TsGVIA are officially open to scholars, relatively few foreign scholars have used the archive. Access to the archival fonds appears to be more restricted than that to other central state archives covering the same period. Those who have worked with TsGVIA documents normally have not been admitted to the archive itself, but instead have worked in the special foreigners' reading room at GAU headquarters, where materials have been transported across the city for them to consult. This system has been satisfactory enough for the scholar who wants only a few specifically identifiable documents, but it is exceedingly difficult when the reader needs to consult the very knowledgeable archival staff or to consult the library or reference literature belonging to the archive.

A new directory for the archive is now in preparation to replace the badly outdated 1941 edition of the guide. A large number of prerevolutionary printed catalogs cover some portions of the archive, which has largely maintained the original organization of fonds; a typewritten summary table of contents of these inventories has been prepared for use by the archival staff. Handwritten or typed inventories have been prepared for other parts of the archive, and extensive card catalogs cover some sections (many of these had been prepared before the Revolution), but these are normally for internal staff use only and are not available to foreign researchers.

PUBLISHED GUIDES AND GENERAL DESCRIPTIONS

There is no comprehensive up-to-date guide to TsGVIA. Many of the most important fonds are covered in the earlier guides listed below. The brief description of the holdings by Major G. Bogdanov, "Tsentral'nyi gosudarstvennyi voenno-istoricheskii arkhiv—sokrovishchnitsa voenno-istoricheskikh dokumentov," in *Voenno-istoricheskii zhurnal*, 1959, no. 2, pp. 107-11, takes into account the materials moved to Moscow from the now defunct Leningrad branch of the archive; see also the somewhat older brief description in the general handbook to state archives, *Gosudarstvennye arkhivy Soiuza SSR. Kratkii spravochnik*, (A-7), pp. 22-29.

The article by V. I. Vialikov, "Tsentral'nyi gosudarstvennyi voenno-istoricheskii arkhiv SSSR," printed as the first and title section of the pamphlet in the series

Gosudarstvennye arkhivy SSSR. Uchebnoe posobie (Moscow: MGIAI, 1960 [MH-Slav 612.120]), pp. 3-36, gives the best account of the historical development of the archive. For earlier historical coverage, see the articles by I. Khripach, "Moskovskii Tsentral'nyi istoricheskii arkhiv: Voenno-istoricheskii arkhiv," *Arkhivnoe delo* 8-9 (1926): 3-25, and I. Nazin and M. Semin, "Tsentral'nyi voenno-istoricheskii arkhiv," *Arkhivnoe delo* 47 (1938, no. 3):85-99.

Two short articles published in honor of the 150th anniversary of the archive are too brief to be of much value for the potential researcher although they are the most recent descriptions of the archive: I. G. Tishin, "Khranilishche dokumentov po voennoi istorii Rossii (K 150-letiiu Tsentral'nogo gosudarstvennogo voenno-istoricheskogo arkhiva SSSR)," *Voenno-istoricheskii zhurnal*, 1969, no. 2, pp. 122-25; and E. P. Voronin and I. G. Tishin, "K 150-letiiu Tsentral'nogo gosudar-stvennogo voenno-istoricheskogo arkhiva," *Sovetskie arkhivy*, 1969, no. 1, pp. 45-49. The earlier but more extensive article by F. E. Kuznetsov, "Fondy Tsentral'nykh gosudarstvennykh voennykh arkhivov SSSR i ikh nauchnoe ispol'zovanie," in *Trudy MGIAI* 4 (1948):73-112, gives further historical background on the development of military archives.

151. [Russia (1923-USSR). Tsentral'nyi gosudarstvennyi voenno-istoricheskii arkhiv.]
Putevoditel' po Tsentral'nomu gosudarstvennomu voenno-istoricheskomu arkhivu.
Moscow: Upravlenie gosudarstvennymi arkhivami NKVD SSSR, 1941. 199 p.
[DLC-CD1732.A5.1941]

> Now completely out-of-date as a comprehensive guide to TsGVIA, this early 1941 volume nevertheless remains the starting point for anyone interested in the holdings; it is the only guide available, since a second edition which had been prepared after World War II was subsequently withdrawn. It describes many of the most important materials in the archive and lists the fonds which were originally located in the Leningrad branch; a separate appendix details the organization of World War I documents. Fond numbers are provided and the existence of an inventory or card catalog indicated, following the descriptions of the materials. As frustrating as the lack of more extensive descriptions is the lack of bibliographical data and indexes covering the fonds; even when the existence of a printed inventory is mentioned, the exact correlation or publication data are not provided.

152. "Voenno-morskaia sektsiis–I-Voennyi otdel."
In *Arkhivy SSSR. Leningradskoe otdelenie Tsentral'nogo istoricheskogo arkhiva. Putevoditel' po fondam.* Edited by A. K. Drezen. Compiled by M. Akhun, V. Lukomskii, S. Rozanov, and A. Shilov, pp. 167-96. Leningrad: Lenoblizdat, 1933. (See B-103.)
[DLC-CD1713.A5.1933; MH-Slav612.25]

> This section gives more descriptive detail for the fonds from the former Leningrad branch of TsGVIA than the later TsGVIA guide (B-151, pp. 193-94); these fonds were transferred to Moscow (1956-58) and, except for some minor changes, have generally retained their earlier organization.

Although descriptions are regrettably brief, some bibliographical data are given. A short article describing these documents, published while they were still in Leningrad, may be of further interest to researchers: L. A. Mandrykina, "Filial Tsentral'nogo gosudarstvennogo voenno-istoricheskogo arkhiva v Leningrade," *Voprosy istorii,* 1946, no. 11-12, pp. 170-73.

B-153. Beskrovnyi, Liubomir Grigor'evich.
Ocherki po istochnikovedeniiu voennoi istorii Rossii. Moscow: Izd-vo AN SSSR, 1957. 435 p.
[DLC-DK51.7.B49; MH-Slav630.38.5]
Listed earlier because it provides references to materials for military history in several different archives (A-45), this volume merits special mention here because of its brief coverage of many documents in TsGVIA. It lists many fond numbers, but makes no references to published guides or inventories. Its chronological organization is particularly helpful to the historian who might be working on materials from a specific period. See also the author's recent article "Znachenie dokumentov TsGVIA SSSR dlia razvitiia voennoi istoriografii (K-150-letiiu arkhiva)," *Sovetskie arkhivy*, 1969, no. 4, pp. 22-23.

PUBLISHED INVENTORIES AND SPECIALIZED DESCRIPTIONS

See also the coverage of materials relating to the 1863 Polish uprising in A-44.

B-154. [Russia. Armiia. Glavnyi shtab. Voenno-uchenyi arkhiv.]
Katalog Voenno-uchenogo arkhiva Glavnogo shtaba. Edited by M. O. Bender. 2nd edition. 4 vols. St. Petersburg, 1905-1914.
[IU (vols. 1-3)]
The inventories in these volumes, expanded from the first edition (7 parts. St. Petersburg, 1886-1895 [NN]), cover some of the fonds from the former Military Science Archive, described in the TsGVIA guide (B-151), pp. 61-64.

B-155. [Russia (1923-USSR). Tsentral'nyi gosudarstvennyi voenno-istoricheskii arkhiv.]
Suvorov, Aleksandr Vasil'evich (1730-1800). Opis' dokumental'nykh materialov arkhivnogo fonda no. 43. Edited by N. P. Shliapnikov. Moscow: GAU, 1952. 76 p.
[MH-Slav 1043.2.55]
Covers materials dating from 1760 to 1820. The only inventory of a separate fond which the archive has published since the Revolution.

B-156. [Russia. Armiia. Glavnyi shtab. Obshchii arkhiv. Moskovskoe otdelenie.]
Opisi del (alternate title *Katalog*) *Moskovskogo otdeleniia Obshchego arkhiva Glavnogo shtaba.* 4 vols. Edited by D. F. Maslovskii. Vol. 1: Moscow: Tipografiia shtaba M. voennogo okruga, 1890; vols. 2-4: St. Petersburg: Tipografiia I. N. Skorokhodova, 1891-1893.
[DLC-Yudin Z2515.M6G5(vol. 3 only); NN]
Vol. 1: *Opis' del sekretnogo pobyt'ia Moskovskogo otdeleniia Obshchego arkhiva Glavnogo shtaba. (47-ia opis').*
Vol. 2: *Opis' del voinskoi komissii i kabineta (121 i 119 opisi).*
Vol. 3: *Opis' del fel'dmarshalov grafa Rumiantseva-Zadunaiskogo i kniazia*

Potemkina-Tavricheskogo (193 i 194 opisi).
Vol. 4: *Opis' del: a)Prezidenta voennoi kollegii, general-fel'dmarshala grafa Nikolaia Ivanovicha Saltykova, b)Vitse-prezidenta Lamba i v)Korpusa byvshego v Gollandii (199, 200 i 153 opisi).*

The first four volumes of this series covering some eighteenth-century documents are still used in the archive and also available in the Lenin Library. It is impossible to determine the exact number of later volumes published in this series as they were issued in very small editions and bound in various formats; the archive itself has prepared a table coordinating them with present archival organization. The later printed inventories in the same series are extremely rare, but copies of eight additional volumes published in 1912 and 1913, edited by Polikarpov, are to be found in the Saltykov-Shchedrin State Public Library in Leningrad. They bear the same series title in most cases, but sometimes only bear the number of the *opis'*; they are here listed by this identifying *opis'* number of their title and their publication date with an indication of their coverage:

Op. 152. (1912). Imperial chancellery, 1796-1812.
Op. 160. (1912). Grand Duke Constantine Pavlovich, 1800-1819.
Op. 161a. (1912). Grand Duke Constantine Pavlovich, 1812-1832.
Op. 291 (11a). (1912). Danubian army, 1809-1835.
Op. 292 (9a). (1912). Danubian army, 1812-1835.
Op. 293 (7a). (1913). Barclay de Tolly, etc. 1813-1847.
Op. 133-136, 138-147. (1913). Inspectors' Department 1812-1816.
Op. 208a, 208b, 208v i 208 g. (1913). Armies of Wittgenstein, Wintzingerode, and other armies of the period 1812-1817.

157. [Russia. Armiia. Glavnyi shtab. Obshchii arkhiv. Moskovskoe otdelenie.]
Opis' kazach'ikh del Moskovskogo otdeleniia Obshchego arkhiva Glavnogo shtaba.
Compiled by I. I. Dmitrenko. St. Petersburg, 1899.
[NN]

A separate publication in the same general series as the above (B-156), this large volume covers the Cossack section of the archive for the documents dating from 1723-1812.

158. "Spisok topograficheskikh opisanii i atlasov namestnichestv, khraniashchikhsia v TsGVIA v Moskve." *Voprosy geografii* 31(1953):106-110.
Lists some of the prerevolutionary cartographic materials—topographical descriptions and atlases held by the archive.

159. Zhukovskaia, N. P.
"Katalog rukopisnykh istoricheskikh kart v fondakh Tsentral'nogo gosudarstvennogo voenno-istoricheskogo arkhiva SSSR." In [Geograficheskoe obshchestvo SSSR. Moskovskii filial.] *Istoriia geograficheskikh znanii i istoricheskaia geografiia. Etnografiia,* vol. 3 (1969):49-51.
[MH-Geog 115.5]
Describes work on the project of cataloging the map holdings.

9. TsENTRAL'NYI GOSUDARSTVENNYI ARKHIV KINOFOTODOKUMENTOV SSSR (TsGAKFD SSSR)

[Central State Archive of Film and Photographic Documents of the USSR]
Address: Moskovskaia oblast', g. Krasnogorsk, Rechnaia ulitsa, 1

HISTORY AND CONTENTS

The Central State Archive of Film and Photographic Documents, located in the Moscow suburb of Krasnogorsk, is undoubtedly one of the largest and best organized archives of its kind in the world, housing some 80,000 documentary films and over 500,000 photographs, complete with extensive catalogs, laboratories, and viewing facilities.

The collection as it exists today was started soon after the Revolution as part of the eighth division (for printed documentation) of the Single State Archival Fond; in 1921 the Archive of the October Revolution [Arkhiv Oktiabr'skoi revoliutsii] set up a division for illustrative materials which gathered a valuable film and photograph collection of great historical importance. This was subsequently transferred to the separate repository for documentary films and photographs which was established in Moscow in 1926. In 1932 a separate Central Archive of Sound Recordings [Tsentral'nyi arkhiv zvukozapisei] was set up, and in 1935 these two archives were combined to form the all-union Central Photo, Phonographic, and Film Archive of the USSR [Tsentral'nyi foto-fono-kinoarkhiv SSSR]. The official name was changed in 1941 to the Central State Archive of Film, Photo, and Phonographic Documents of the USSR [Tsentral'nyi gosudarstvennyi arkhiv kino-foto-fonodokumentov SSSR–TsGAKFFD], which lasted until 1967. At that time, it was decided to remove sound recordings to an independent Central State Archive of Sound Recordings [Tsentral'nyi gosudarstvennyi arkhiv zvukozapisei–TsGAZ], which is still in the process of formation.

The central film and photo archive as it is organized today receives copies of selected films and film strips from state documentary film studios and original negatives and one copy of selected photographs from news agencies such as Tass, Novosti, and Sovfoto, and from the major central newspapers and magazines. But even in the documentary realm, it should be noted, it is not set up as a centralized comprehensive all-union archive. News agencies and newspapers still maintain their own photographic archives, from which selected copies are transferred to TsGAKFD. Television studios—now one of the major sources and users of documentary films—maintain their own separate archives and do not deposit video tapes in TsGAKFD. Artistic and popular films also are not included in the TsGAKFD complex, but are rather deposited in the independent film archive officially called Gosfil'mofond [State Film Archive], administered by the Motion Picture Committee under the Council of Ministers of the USSR (formerly under the Ministry of Culture); see further coverage in Part D, section 4, below. In addition, major film studios such as Mosfilm and Lenfilm maintain their own film archives. Many other state archives, manuscript repositories, libraries, museums, and other institutes also maintain files of films and especially photographs, particularly when these form part of individual fonds or special collections. Such diversity of film and photographic storage points within the total Soviet archival arrangements, however, should not detract from the uniqueness and importance of the TsGAKFD documentary holdings.

In the case of photographs, the earliest materials date back to the Crimean War with an album of photographs entitled "Sevastopol in 1855-1856." There are many other early photographs including some interesting albums from the 1877-1878 Russo-Turkish war, the Russo-Japanese war of 1904-1905, and the 1905 revolution. Many films or film strips from the early twentieth century are also preserved. The earliest documentary film in the archive, the first made in Russia, is the sequence filmed at the coronation of Nicholas II in 1896. Other early motion pictures include sequences of Tolstoi, Chekhov, Gor'kii and other literary figures filmed in 1903 and 1904. (On the prerevolutionary section see B-160, pp. 12-23.)

A particularly rich collection of pictorial materials from 1917 and from the Civil War, a large part of which had originally been gathered in the 1920's for the Archive of the October Revolution, are now preserved in TsGAKFD; these have now been described in detail in a special catalog (B-163; see also B-160, pp. 24-57).

With the modern developments in photographic techniques, postrevolutionary documentary materials naturally predominate in TsGAKFD. On the whole, these are organized according to date, type, and region of origin, and cover a wide range of subjects from the industrialization drive of the 1930's to scenes of the Second World War and postwar developments.

WORKING CONDITIONS

The archive occasionally receives foreign visitors for special needs or reference work, but usually specific requests from foreign journalists or other sources are handled through the participating news agencies such as Novosti or Tass.

The archive maintains elaborate thematic catalogs for films and photographs, along with catalogs of personal names covered and various other types of geographic or chronological coverage. The catalog cards in the photographic division usually include small reproductions of the pictures to aid in choice or identification. Film catalogs have detailed descriptions of sequences, and modern individual viewing facilities are available in the film reading rooms.

Unlike other Soviet archives, the TsGAKFD holdings are not organized into fonds, but rather are given individual catalog numbers.

PUBLISHED GUIDES AND GENERAL DESCRIPTIONS

In addition to the publications listed below, the archive is briefly described in the general handbook to state archives, *Gosudarstvennye arkhivy Soiuza SSR. Kratkii spravochnik* (A-7), pp. 41-56.

60. [Russia (1917-USSR). Tsentral'nyi gosudarstvennyi arkhiv kino-foto-fonodokumentov.]

PART B – CENTRAL STATE ARCHIVES

Stranitsy zhivoi istorii. Ocherk-putevoditel' po Tsentral'nomu gosudarstvennomu arkhivu kino-foto-fonodokumentov SSSR. Prepared by L. D. Aksel'rod, V. P. Mikhailov, V. G. Frolov, and Iu. T. Khodzhaev. Edited by S. S. Ginzburg. Moscow: GAU, 1961. 152 p.
[DLC-PN1993.4.R8; MH-Slav612.135]
> This illustrated, somewhat popularized volume is more a general description of the archive than a technical guide, but provides the only general coverage of the archive published. It describes the holdings in laudatory terms, generally in chronological order, with chapters divided according to the period divisions in the archive, starting with the earliest prerevolutionary materials for 1855-1856 and extending to 1955. No numerical or catalog references are given, nor any bibliography, but a geographical index and short subject index are included.

B-161. Pleshakov, S.
"Tsentral'nyi gosudarstvennyi arkhiv kino-foto- i fonodokumentov SSSR." In *Iz istorii kino. Materialy i dokumenty*, no. 1 (1958), pp. 105-28.
> This article provides a description of the archive holdings, but much less extensive than the guide above. The serial volume, published irregularly by the Cinema History Institute of the Academy of Sciences of the USSR, often contains articles of related interest and draws on materials in the archive.

B-162. Khodorkovskii, V. R.
"Kinodokumenty po istorii sovetskoi kinematografii." *Istoricheskii arkhiv*, 1960, no. 6, pp. 174-77.
> A short survey of TsGAKFFD holdings relevant to the history of the Soviet cinema.

PUBLISHED CATALOGS AND SPECIALIZED DESCRIPTIONS

B-163. [Russia (1923-USSR). Tsentral'nyi gosudarstvennyi arkhiv kino-foto-fonodokumentov.]
Kino i fotodokumenty po istorii Velikogo Oktiabria, 1917-1920. Edited by N. P. Abramov and V. P. Mikhailov. Moscow: Izd-vo AN SSSR, 1958. 354 p.
[DLC-DK265.A534; MH-Slav1728.100.125]
> This volume provides an extensive catalog of the TsGAKFD holdings on the period 1917-1920 covering the Russian Revolution and Civil War. It is divided into separate sections covering film (pp. 19-92) and still photographs (pp. 95-332). It indicates the size, length, and other technical data, and gives the archival catalog number for each entry. Geographic and personal name indexes are included.

B-164. [Russia (1923-USSR). Tsentral'nyi gosudarstvennyi arkhiv kino-foto-fonodokumentov.]
Sovetskaia kinokhronika, 1918-1925 gg. Annotirovannyi katalog. Edited by Iu. A. Poliakova and S. V. Drobashenko. Vol. 1: *Kinozhurnaly.* Moscow: TsGAKFFD, 1965. 152 p.

[DLC-PN1995.9.D6R8]
> Lists newsreels from the period 1918-1925, classified by the year of issue and producing agencies. Gives annotations and technical data about the films, including archival call numbers. Includes personal and geographic name indexes.

165. Khodorkovskii, V. R.
"Kinodokumenty po istorii sovetskogo kino, khraniashchiesia v Tsentral'nom gosudarstvennom arkhive kinofotofonodokumentov (1917-1945)." In *Iz istorii kino. Materialy i dokumenty,* no. 3, pp. 165-206. Moscow: Izd-vo AN SSSR, 1960.
> Catalog description of the history of the Soviet cinema providing technical information and catalog numbers for entries covered.

10. TsENTRAL'NYI GOSUDARSTVENNYI ARKHIV ZVUKO-ZAPISEI (TsGAZ SSSR)

[Central State Archive of Sound Recordings]
   Address: Moscow, B-5, 2-ia Baumanskaia, 3

The Central State Archive of Sound Recordings, established by resolution of the Council of Ministers on 11 November, 1967, is still in the process of formation and has not yet opened as a functioning repository. The establishment of TsGAZ in effect represents the splitting off of the phonographic division of the former Central State Archive of Film, Photo, and Phonographic Documents of the USSR [Tsentral'nyi gosudarstvennyi arkhiv kino-foto-fonodokumentov SSSR– TsGAKFFD, now TsGAKFD]. The main state archival collection of sound recordings which will form the basis for the new archive is still stored in the TsGAKFD complex of buildings and will be transferred to the new archive when sufficient storage areas have been constructed to house the materials. The archive will encompass recordings in the form of tapes and records of an artistic as well as documentary nature; special provisions have been made so that copies of recordings by the all-union recording studio "Melodia," which produces most of the records in the USSR, will be deposited in the archive. The headquarters of TsGAZ are now located in the Lefort Palace which also houses the military history archive TsGVIA, but there are plans for a new building specially constructed for archival use.

The existence of a separate archive of sound recordings will actually not be a new departure in Soviet archival organization because a separate archive for these materials already had an independent existence as the official all-union Central Archive of Sound Recordings [Tsentral'nyi arkhiv zvukozapisei], founded in 1932, until its merger with the state film and photographic archive in 1936 to form the Central Photo, Phonographic, and Film Archive [Tsentral'nyi foto-fono-kinoarkhiv SSSR], which in 1941 was renamed TsGAKFFD, the name that it kept until the subsequent split in 1967.

There has been no published description of this archive or explanation of the extent or organization of its holdings, aside from the official notice of its formation published in *Sovetskie arkhivy*, 1968, no. 1, p. 117. Since it will be receiving the record collections until now stored in TsGAKFD, some further details about their contents can be found in the short descriptive guide to TsGAKFFD, *Stranitsy zhivoi istorii. Ocherk-putevoditel' po Tsentral'nomu gosudarstvenomu arkhivu kino-foto-fonodokumentov SSSR* (Moscow: GAU, 1961) (see B-160).

11. TsENTRAL'NYI GOSUDARSTVENNYI ARKHIV NAUCHNO-TEKHNICHESKOI DOKUMENTATSII SSSR (TsGANTD SSSR)

[Central State Archive of Scientific and Technical Documentation in the USSR]
Temporary Address: Moscow, B-66, Spartakovskaia ulitsa, 5/40

In May of 1964 the Council of Ministers of the USSR passed a resolution calling for a central repository for scientific and technical documentation. The archive is still in the planning stage in Moscow and has not yet opened as a functioning storage and research center, but plans call for the construction of a new building in the Volga area. When completed, it will certainly be one of the most unusual and progressive types of scientific archives in the world.

Plans are under way for the concentration of all types of scientific and technical documents in this archive, with specially trained archivists to handle them. Most specifically, it will receive fonds transferred from TsGAOR and TsGANKh that fit its particular categories. It will not, however, encompass documentation from institutes under the Academy of Sciences, which maintain their own archives, or from the institutional records of the Academy of Sciences itself. Nor will it encompass the specialized scientific reference collections such as the All-Union Geological Fond (Vsesoiuznyi geologicheskii fond) or the Hydrometric Fond of the USSR (Gidrometfond SSSR), although coordination is planned with these other archival institutions.

There has not yet been any published description of the archive, since it is still in the process of formation, but the series of articles on problems of its organization by V. M. Laiko, A. A. Kuzin, and K. I. Puzanov in *Sovetskie arkhivy*, 1967, no. 6, pp. 55-72, gives a good idea of the plans and prospects for this new type of archival repository.

PART C

**ARCHIVES AND MANUSCRIPT COLLECTIONS OF THE
ACADEMY OF SCIENCES OF THE USSR**

PART C

ARCHIVES AND MANUSCRIPT COLLECTIONS OF THE ACADEMY OF SCIENCES OF THE USSR

The extensive archives and manuscript collections of the Academy of Sciences of the USSR have traditionally remained completely independent of the Main Archival Administration. Although their holdings are legally considered part of the State Archival Fond, they have always been administered separately by the Academy and have never been incorporated into the state archival system. However, because of the central importance of the Academy of Sciences in the scientific and cultural life of the nation, both before and since the Revolution, the archives and manuscript repositories under its jurisdiction are of fundamental importance to the research scholar, comprising as they do holdings of large numbers and great variety, many of which go well beyond the immediate activities and purposes of the different institutes or organizations of the Academy responsible for them.

First, on the all-union level, and most directly related to the institution and activities of the Academy itself is the Archive of the Academy of Sciences [Arkhiv Akademii nauk SSSR], with its main headquarters in Moscow and a branch in Leningrad. The Leningrad archive itself was founded in 1728, and contains records dating back to the early eighteenth-century beginnings of the Imperial Academy of Sciences; it remained the central repository of Academy records until the foundation of the Moscow archive in 1936. In 1963 the Moscow branch was designated as the main archive of the Academy, housing the records of the presidium and other Academy files since 1934; the Leningrad archive is now officially its branch, retaining its important historical holdings.

Second, but in the realm of manuscript collections rather than archives, is the rich Manuscript and Rare Book Division of the main Library of the Academy of Sciences [Biblioteka Akademii nauk SSSR–BAN] with its rich collections of medieval manuscripts and incunabula.

Third, many separate institutes under the Academy of Sciences maintain their own archives or have amassed extensive manuscript collections in their libraries or manuscript divisions, many of which have long prerevolutionary roots. Most notable in this category is the Archive of the Leningrad Branch of the Institute of History of the USSR, the Manuscript Division of the Institute of Russian Literature (Pushkinskii Dom), the Manuscript Division and Archive of the Leningrad Branch of the Institute of Oriental Studies, the Archives of the Geographical Society and the Archeological Institute, all in Leningrad, the collection of the Institute of Russian Language, and the Gor'kii Archive and the Manuscript Division of the Institute of World Literature in Moscow. The Tolstoi Archive as part of the Tolstoi Museum in Moscow was originally also under Academy jurisdiction, but it is now separately administered under the Ministry of Culture (see Part E, section 6).

Moreover, all institutes under the Academy of Sciences retain their own institutional records, and several other institutes also house specialized subject-related archives or manuscript collections; hence the present coverage cannot be termed exhaustive. Among the holdings not covered in Part C are the collections under the jurisdiction of the Siberian Branch of the Academy of Sciences of the USSR, most notably those in Ulan Ude and Novosibirsk. The Academy also maintains an extensive photographic archive in Moscow, the Photo Archive of the Laboratory of Photography and Cinematography for Applied Science [Fotoarkhiv Laboratorii nauchno-prikladnoi fotografii i kinematografii—LAFOKI], with an additional archive in connection with the Leningrad branch of the laboratory.

Finally, many of the Academies of Sciences of the different Soviet republics have also developed sizeable archives and manuscript collections of general interest in their associated institutes or as divisions of their principal libraries. However, since these repositories all lie outside of Moscow and Leningrad, information about their holdings will not be included in the present volume.

Academy archives and manuscript collections are all administered separately by the institutions in which they are located. Since 1964, the Academy has made a more concerted effort to coordinate the various phases of its archival work through a special organ founded in that year, the Council on the Organization of Acquisitions and Use of Documentary Materials [Sovet po organizatsii komplektovaniia i ispol'zovaniia dokumental'nykh materialov AN SSSR]. This organ deals with a variety of organizational and methodological problems and further coordinates work of Academy archives with those under the state system, since it exchanges representatives between its own meetings and the "learned council" of the Main Archival Administration. In 1967, for the first time, the council brought together representatives from the many archival repositories under the Academy for a joint conference on archival resources and problems. It has also instituted cooperative conferences, exchanges of information, and other projects with representatives of Academy archives in the other Communist countries of Eastern Europe.

GENERAL LITERATURE

An extensive multi-volume bibliography of publications relating to Academy archival holdings is currently in preparation at the Leningrad branch of the Academy archive, under the direction of Iurii Abramovich Vinogradov; the first volume, entitled *Arkhivy Akademii nauk sotsialisticheskikh stran. Bibliografiia,* vol. 1: *1917-1968* (Leningrad: Izd-vo "Nauka," 1971; 251 p.) covers publications from 1917 to 1968 relating to the central Academy archives of the USSR and other Communist-bloc states.

C-1. [Akademiia nauk SSSR.]
Akademicheskie arkhivy SSSR za 50 let sovetskoi vlasti
(*Trudy 1-go soveshchaniia arkhivistov Akademii nauk SSSR i akademii nauk soiuznykh respublik, 17-23 maia 1967 g.*). Edited by B. V. Levshin. Moscow: Izd-vo "Nauka," 1968. 313 p.
[DLC-CD1711.A65; MH-612.161]

This collection of papers by participants in the 1967 Academy archival
conference published in a small offset edition includes reports from different

manuscript repositories in the Academy system, and a general treatment of
the development of Academy archives by the director of the Archives of the
Academy of Sciences, B. V. Levshin. It provides much more extensive
coverage than the short article by Levshin, "Arkhivy Akademii nauk SSSR,"
in *Sovetskie arkhivy*, 1967, no. 5, pp. 117-21; a German translation of this
latter article appeared simultaneously in the East German archival journal,
"Das Archiv der Akademie der Wissenschaften der UdSSR,"
Archivmitteilungen 17 (1967, no. 5):178-81.

1. ARKHIV AKADEMII NAUK SSSR (AAN)

[Archive of the Academy of Sciences of the USSR]
Address: Moscow, V-333, ulitsa Vavilova, 46

LENINGRADSKOE OTDELENIE [Leningrad Branch]
Address: Leningrad, V-164, Vasil'evskii ostrov, Universitetskaia
naberezhnaia, 1

CONTENTS

The archive proper of the Academy of Sciences of the USSR, now totalling some fifteen hundred fonds, is divided between Leningrad, the former headquarters of the Academy, and Moscow, its current center. Together they contain one of the most significant collections of documentation for the history of science and learning in the country, including as they do not only the institutional records of the Academy since its foundation in 1725 and of its various agencies, but also some 570 fonds of personal papers of individual scientists and scholars. According to the current numbering system, fonds numbered 1−350 and 701 or above are located in Leningrad and those between 351 and 700 are housed in Moscow.

The Leningrad Branch is the oldest archival institution of the Academy, founded in 1728. The organization of the archive in the present building took place after 1929, when papers from various institutes and many defunct institutions traditionally under the Academy were gathered together in the main repository. It remained the central archive of the Academy until in 1963 it formally became the branch archive, with the Moscow repository as the main archival headquarters.

The Leningrad archive is now divided into three main divisions. The first, containing the institutional records of the Academy going back to the eighteenth century, is subdivided into fonds covering the different chancelleries of the governing bodies of the Academy, and fonds originating with the various institutes historically under the Academy in the realms of science, history and ethnography, and linguistics and literature. Of special interest to scholars abroad is the wealth of foreign correspondence among these papers. A second division includes the fonds of individual academicians, members of various institutes under the Academy, and other important scholars and scientists; these are divided into subsections according to their academic or scientific discipline. A third division includes the miscellaneous special documentary collections, including manuscript treaties, maps, scientific drawings, and materials from various Academy-sponsored expeditions.

The Moscow archive of the Academy was originally established in 1936 as a branch of the main archive in Leningrad. As its nucleus it took over the various archival fonds of the then defunct Communist Academy. It has since grown to encompass the main institutional records of the Academy presidium since it moved its headquarters to Moscow in 1934, the files of various Academy institutes in the Moscow area, and many personal fonds of individual academicians and other important scientists and scholars, primarily those associated with Moscow-based institutions. The records of the Academy presidium and its various central chancelleries, although under the jurisdiction of the Academy archive, are now retained at the Academy headquarters [Leninskii prospekt, 14]. Records of ongoing institutes of the Academy are also usually retained in their separate institutional archives for a considerable length of time. The records of defunct or reorganized institutes, however, usually are immediately transferred to the main Academy archive. Such was the case with the records of the Institute of History [Institut istorii AN SSSR], which was reorganized in 1968 and split into the separate Institute of History of the USSR [Institut istorii SSSR AN SSSR] and the Institute of World History [Institut vseobshchei istorii AN SSSR].

WORKING CONDITIONS

The Moscow archive has a small reading room, where catalogs and handwritten inventories are available, but the relative contemporaneity of most of the documents there has meant that few foreign scholars have been admitted.

The earlier historical records in Leningrad have been visited by many foreign researchers and are relatively accessible to specialists whose topics fall into their province. Detailed catalogs and inventories have been prepared for almost all the fonds and are supplemented by the guidance of the archival staff.

GENERAL PUBLISHED DESCRIPTIONS AND SERIALS

For a detailed bibliography of publications issued between 1917 and 1968 regarding the Soviet Academy of Sciences archives, see the relevant section in the new volume under the editorship of Iu. A. Vinogradov, *Arkhivy Akademii nauk sotsialisticheskikh stran. Bibliografiia,* vol. 1: *1917-1968* (Leningrad: Izd-vo "Nauka," 1971).

A recent description of the development of the Academy archives and short reports on various aspects of its organization and publication activities will be found in the volume edited by the archive director, B. V. Levshin, *Akademicheskie arkhivy SSSR za 50 let sovetskoi vlasti* (C-1).

C-2. [Akademiia nauk SSSR. Arkhiv.]
Trudy arkhiva AN SSSR. Moscow/Leningrad: Izd-vo AN SSSR, 1933+.
[DLC-AS262.A6135; MH-LSoc3983.110]

> Most of the general descriptions of the archive and the inventories of special fonds or sections have been published as part of this main archival series of which twenty-three volumes have appeared, up to 1969. Because American library catalogs usually include them as separate monographs, or do not always analyze this series in full, the volumes that comprise the general descriptive series will be listed in this section and those that present inventories of specific fonds or sections of the archives will be included below.

C-3. [Akademiia nauk SSSR. Arkhiv. Obozrenie arkhivnykh materialov.]
Arkhiv Akademii nauk SSSR. Obozrenie arkhivnykh materialov. 6 vols. *Trudy*

arkhiva AN SSSR, vols. 1, 5, 9, 16, 19, and 24. Moscow/Leningrad: Izd-vo AN
SSSR, 1933-1971.
[DLC-AS262.A6135; MH-LSoc3983.110]

Vol. 1: Edited by G. A. Kniazev. *Trudy arkhiva AN SSSR*, vol. 1. Leningrad:
Izd-vo AN SSSR, 1933. 259 p.

An introductory section gives a brief history of the archive and description of
the organization which is now outdated by subsequent rearrangements. Part 1
describes the fonds of the different sections of the institutional archive,
including the fonds of the main and subsidiary chancelleries, and of former
museums, commissions, institutes, and different branches of the Academy.
Part 2 is devoted to short paragraph descriptions of 108 fonds of individual
Academy members or other important scientists or scholars, subdivided
according to their academic or scientific discipline. A third part is devoted to
some of the miscellaneous collections of documents from different
expeditions or projects of the Academy, manuscript works of members, and
maps or other illustrative materials. A final part gives a few notes on some of
the Academy of Sciences collections in other archives under its jurisdiction,
but it is too short to be of much real value and is now significantly outdated
by subsequent rearrangements and more recent publications. Some
bibliographical indications are included with individual entries. The volume
covers holdings roughly to 1930.

Vol. 2: Edited by G. A. Kniazev and L. B. Modzalevskii. *Trudy arkhiva AN
SSSR,* vol. 5. Moscow/Leningrad: Izd-vo AN SSSR, 1946. 391 p.

This volume continues the description of the Academy archive given in
volume 1, covering materials roughly to 1939. The first section describes
more of the fonds relating to various institutes under the Academy. The
second section describes the different archival fonds of the Communist
Academy, which formed the basis for the main Moscow Archive of the
Academy of Sciences. A third section describes 49 additional personal fonds
grouped by discipline. A fourth section supplements descriptions recorded in
the previous volume and describes additional institutional and personal fonds
acquired earlier that were not previously covered.

Vol. 3: Edited by G. A. Kniazev, P. N. Koriakov, and G. P. Blok. *Trudy arkhiva
AN SSSR*, vol. 9. Moscow/Leningrad: Izd-vo AN SSSR, 1950. 142 p.

This volume gives short descriptions of 65 fonds of personal papers of
individual academicians and other scholars and scientists, acquired by the
archive during the Second World War and up to 1948, grouped under the
disciplines which the individuals represent: mathematics-physics, chemistry,
geology-geography, biology, and engineering.

Vol. 4: Edited by G. A. Kniazev, G. P. Blok, and T. I. Lysenko. *Trudy arkhiva
AN SSSR*, vol. 16. Moscow/Leningrad: Izd-vo AN SSSR, 1959. 353 p.

Similar in format to volume 3, this volume gives short descriptions of 112 personal fonds of academicians and other scholars and scientists that were acquired by the archive since World War II, subdivided by the disciplines represented, with sections for physics-mathematics, chemistry, geology-geography, biology, engineering, history, philology, and oriental studies.

Vol. 5: Edited by G. A. Kniazev, E. S. Kuliabko, B. V. Levshin, N. M. Raskin, and A. M. Chernikov. *Trudy arkhiva AN SSSR*, vol. 19. Moscow/Leningrad: Izd-vo AN SSSR, 1963. 188 p.

Similar in format to volumes 3 and 4, this volume gives descriptions of some 65 additional personal fonds now housed in the archives in the fields of mathematics and physics, chemistry, geology and geography, biology, engineering, history-ethnography, economics, and philological sciences. A most helpful appendix gives a cumulative list of the individuals whose papers have been described in the different volumes of the archival *Trudy* together with the volume and page numbers for the descriptions.

Vol. 6: Edited by B. V. Levshin, E. S. Kuliabko, and T. I. Lysenko. *Trudy arkhiva AN SSSR*, vol. 24. Leningrad: Izd-vo "Nauka," 1971. 224 p.

Similar in format to the previous volumes, this most recent supplement covers newly acquired personal fonds in the fields of physics and mathematics, chemistry, geology and geography, medicine and biology, engineering, and history and philology.

INVENTORIES AND SPECIALIZED DESCRIPTIONS–LENINGRAD BRANCH

The following volumes, with the exception of C-9, are all part of the archive's *Trudy* series (C-2), and are often not cataloged separately in libraries. In addition to these actual inventories, about 250 descriptive articles have been published about different fonds or groups of documents; space prohibits their inclusion here, but they will all be listed in the new bibliography of Academy archival publications mentioned above being prepared by Iu. A. Vinogradov.

Institutional Correspondence

C-4. *Uchenaia korrespondentsiia Akademii nauk XVIII veka. Nauchnoe opisanie, 1766-1782.* Compiled by I. I. Liubimenko. Edited by G. A. Kniazev and L. B. Modzalevskii. *Trudy arkhiva AN SSSR*, vol. 2. Moscow/Leningrad: Izd-vo AN SSSR, 1937. 606 p.

Academy Expeditions

C-5. *Materialy dlia istorii ekspeditsii Akademii nauk v XVIII i XIX vekakh. Khronologicheskie obzory i opisanie arkhivnykh materialov.* Compiled by V. F. Gnucheva. Edited by V. L. Komarov, L. S. Berg, et al. *Trudy arkhiva AN SSSR*, vol. 4. Moscow/Leningrad: Izd-vo AN SSSR, 1940. 310 p.

Eighteenth-Century Chemistry

C-6. *Rukopisnye materialy khimikov vtoroi poloviny XVIII v. v arkhive Akademii nauk SSSR. Nauchnoe opisanie.* Compiled by N. M. Raskin. Edited by M. A. Bezborodov, G. A. Kniazev, and N. A. Figurovskii. *Trudy arkhiva AN SSSR*, vol. 15. Moscow/Leningrad: Izd-vo AN SSSR, 1957. 213 p.

Geographical Department

C-7. *Geograficheskii departament Akademii nauk XVIII veka.* By V. F. Gnucheva. Edited by A. I. Andreev, G. A. Kniazev, and L. B. Modzalevskii. *Trudy arkhiva AN SSSR*, vol. 6. Moscow/Leningrad: Izd-vo AN SSSR, 1946. 446 p.

> Includes some materials and documents as well as an inventory of maps in the manuscript division of BAN (see C-23).

Personal Fonds and Materials Relating to Individuals

Leonhard Euler (1707-1783)

C-8. *Rukopisnye materialy L. Eulera v arkhive Akademii nauk SSSR.* Vol. 1: *Nauchnoe opisanie.* Compiled by Iu. Kh. Kopelevich, M. V. Krutikova, G. K. Mikhailov, and N. M. Raskin. Edited by G. A. Kniazev et al. *Trudy arkhiva AN SSSR*, vol. 17. Moscow/Leningrad: Izd-vo AN SSSR, 1962. 427 p.

> A second volume of this publication published in 1965 (*Trudy arkhiva*, vol. 20) contains documents from this archive relating to Euler.

C-9. *Leonard Euler. Perepiska. Annotirovannyi ukazatel'.* Compiled by T. N. Klado et al. Edited by V. I. Smirnov and A. P. Iushkevich. Leningrad: Izd-vo "Nauka," 1967. 391 p.
[MH-S1373.131.25]

> Published under the sponsorship of the Institut Istorii estestvoznaniia i tekhniki AN SSSR, this is an independent publication not in the *Trudy* series. It provides a scholarly catalog of Euler correspondence with detailed annotations and the exact location of items and folio numbers. Of the 2654 letters covered, 2273 are located in the Academy archive in Leningrad; over a hundred are elsewhere in the USSR, and several hundred more are abroad. An appendix contains a list of some of Euler's other papers in the Academy of Sciences in Berlin.

E. S. Fedorov (1853-1919)

C-10. *Rukopisnye materialy E. S. Fedorova v arkhive Akademii nauk SSSR. Nauchnoe opisanie, teksty.* Compiled by I. I. Shafranovskii and N. M. Raskin. Edited by G. A. Kniazev and V. A. Nikolaev. *Trudy arkhiva AN SSSR*, vol. 14. Moscow/Leningrad: Izd-vo AN SSSR, 1957. 215 p.

B. B. Golitsyn (1862-1916)

C-11. *Rukopisi B. B. Golitsyna v arkhive Akademii nauk SSSR.* Compiled by G. P. Blok and M. V. Krutikova. Edited by V. F. Bonchkovskii and G. P. Gorshkov. *Trudy arkhiva AN SSSR*, vol. 10. Moscow/Leningrad: Izd-vo AN SSSR, 1952. 139 p.

A. N. Krylov (1863-1945)

C-12. *Rukopisnoe nasledie akademika Alekseia Nikolaevicha Krylova. Nauchnoe opisanie.* Compiled by M. N. Glagoleva, N. M. Raskin, N. G. Skrynskii, and L. M. Stolin. Edited by V. I. Smirnov. *Trudy arkhiva AN SSSR*, vol. 23. Leningrad: Izd-vo "Nauka," 1969. 333 p.
[MH-S1501.13]

I. P. Kulibin (1735-1818)

C-13. *Rukopisnye materialy I. P. Kulibina v arkhive Akademii nauk SSSR. Nauchnoe opisanie s prilozheniem tekstov i chertezhei.* Compiled by N. M. Raskin and B. A. Mal'kevich. Edited by I. I. Artobolevskii et al. *Trudy arkhiva AN SSSR*, vol. 11. Moscow/Leningrad: Izd-vo AN SSSR, 1953. 734 p.

M. V. Lomonosov (1711-1765)

C-14. *Rukopisi Lomonosova v Akademii nauk SSSR. Nauchnoe opisanie.* Compiled by L. B. Modzalevskii. Edited by G. A. Kniazev. *Trudy arkhiva AN SSSR*, vol. 3. Moscow/Leningrad: Izd-vo AN SSSR, 1937. 403 p.

F. P. Moiseenko (1754-1781)

C-15. *Materialy F. P. Moiseenko v arkhive Akademii nauk SSSR. Opisanie nauchnykh rabot, lichnykh i sluzhebnykh dokumentov, teksty mineralogicheskikh rabot.* Compiled by I. I. Shafranovskii and N. M. Raskin. Edited by G. A. Kniazev and E. K. Lazarenko. *Trudy arkhiva AN SSSR*, vol. 12. Moscow/Leningrad: Izd-vo AN SSSR, 1955. 105 p.

I. P. Pavlov (1849-1936)

C-16. *Rukopisnye materialy I. P. Pavlova v arkhive Akademii nauk SSSR. Nauchnoe opisanie.* Compiled by G. P. Blok and E. S. Kuliabko. *Trudy arkhiva AN SSSR*, vol. 8. Moscow/Leningrad: Izd-vo AN SSSR, 1949. 156 p.

V. F. Shishmarev (1875-1957)

C-17. *Rukopisnoe nasledie V. F. Shishmareva v arkhive Akademii nauk SSSR. Opisanie i publikatsii.* Compiled by M. A. Borodina and B. A. Mal'kevich. Edited by M. A. Borodina, B. V. Levshin, et al. *Trudy arkhiva AN SSSR*, vol. 21. Moscow/Leningrad: Izd-vo "Nauka," 1965. 245 p.
See also F-28.

INVENTORIES—MOSCOW ARCHIVE

I. I. Mechnikov (1845-1916)

C-18. *Rukopisnye materialy I. I. Mechnikova v arkhive Akademii nauk SSSR. Nauchnoe opisanie, teksty.* Compiled by L. K. Kuvanova and M. S. Bastrakova. Edited by G. A.

Kniazev and B. E. Raikov. *Trudy arkhiva AN SSSR,* vol. 18. Moscow/Leningrad: Izd-vo AN SSSR, 1960. 98 p.

K. E. Tsiolkovskii (1857-1935)

C-19. *Rukopisnye materialy K. E. Tsiolkovskogo v arkhive Akademii nauk SSSR. Nauchnoe opisanie.* Compiled by M. Ia. Rzheznikova, I. P. Staroverova, and L. G. Samokhvalova. Edited by B. N. Vorob'ev and B. V. Levshin. *Trudy arkhiva AN SSSR*, vol. 22. Moscow/Leningrad: Izd-vo "Nauka," 1966. 171 p.

2. BIBLIOTEKA AKADEMII NAUK SSSR (BAN)

[Library of the Academy of Sciences of the USSR]

OTDEL RUKOPISNOI I REDKOI KNIGI [Division of Manuscript and Rare Books]
    Address: Leningrad, V-164, Birzhevaia liniia, 1

CONTENTS

Founded in 1714, this library has been part of the Academy of Sciences since 1725. The Manuscript and Rare Book Division is as old as the library itself, having grown out of the personal library and manuscript book collections of Peter the Great, his family, and especially his son Aleksei Petrovich. In the course of the last 250 years, the library, known familiarly by its acronym BAN, has developed into one of the most valuable manuscript repositories in the country, with over 16,000 storage units of medieval manuscript books and a variety of other pre-nineteenth-century manuscript holdings. This division of the library also houses many incunabula and other early printed books.

The original part of the collection from Peter the Great includes navigational and geographical atlases and many volumes relating to technical and military affairs. In the course of the eighteenth century, several important medieval chronicles were added to the division. The extensive manuscript collections of the early historian V. N. Tatishchev and the many materials given by M. V. Lomonosov further enriched the holdings.

At the beginning of the twentieth century the library acquired the invaluable collections of I. I. Sreznevskii, A. I. Iatsimirskii, P. A. Syrku, and part of the N. P. Likhachev collection, along with the manuscripts from the library of V. I. Sreznevskii.

Among the medieval manuscript collections acquired after the Revolution were those of V. G. Druzhinin, F. A. Kalikin, N. K. Nikol'skii, S. G. Stroganov, and of the Vorontsov family. Further additions included an important collection of early legal charters from Pskov, the manuscript book collection of the Imperial Archeographical Commission, the extensive holdings of the Antoniev-Siiskii and Aleksandr-Svirskii monasteries, the important Arkhangel'sk collection, and collections from other northern Russian religious institutions.

Manuscripts in various foreign languages form an important part of the division. These include some extremely valuable Greek and early Latin manuscripts, many interesting early foreign travelers' accounts of Russia, and other Western European manuscripts dating from the twelfth to the eighteenth centuries.

A geographical section contains many early manuscript maps, plans, and other early charts, including the especially rich eighteenth-century collection of the Geographical Department of the Russian Academy of Sciences.

The manuscript division has continued to enrich its holdings, most notably through a series of archeographical expeditions to collect medieval manuscripts in various parts of the Soviet Union.

PART C – ACADEMY OF SCIENCES HOLDINGS

WORKING CONDITIONS

Inventories or detailed descriptions for many of the manuscripts in BAN have been published and are hence readily available for use. Since almost all the holdings are manuscript books or older manuscripts of one type or another, most of them have been fully cataloged; although in cases in which the cataloging was originally done prior to the Revolution, the nomenclature or numbering systems have been changed. In general shelf lists are available to readers.

Because the Manuscript and Rare Book Division is within the major library of the Academy, scholars working there have easy access to published materials from the library holdings. See Appendix 1 for further details. There are facilities for both microfilming and photocopying documents; arrangements are normally made individually with the approval of the library director. Microfilms may be ordered from abroad through the Exchange Division of the library.

PUBLISHED DESCRIPTIONS AND INVENTORIES

Chapters in the general history of BAN each contain sections on the Manuscript Division that provide general historical background about the different collections: [Akademiia nauk SSSR. Biblioteka.] *Istoriia Biblioteki Akademii nauk SSSR, 1714-1964*, by S. P. Luppov et al., edited by M. S. Filippov (Moscow/Leningrad: Izd-vo "Nauka," 1964; 599 p. [DLC-Z820.A64; MH-LSoc3983.116.19]). The general guide to the library provides a brief description of the Manuscript and Rare Book Division: [Akademiia nauk SSSR. Biblioteka.] *Spravochnik-putevoditel' po Biblioteke Akademii nauk SSSR*, compiled by I. F. Grigor'eva, T. M. Koval'chuk, and T. I. Skripkina, edited by G. A. Chebotarev (Moscow/Leningrad: Izd-vo AN SSSR, 1959; 112 p. [DLC-Z820.L5457; MH-LSoc 3983.116.10]); a slightly longer description is found in the general handbook to Academy libraries published the same year: *Biblioteki Akademii nauk SSSR. Spravochnik*, compiled by A. I. Chebotarev (Moscow: Izd-vo AN SSSR, 1959) (see Appendix 1). See also the short note about archeographical expeditions sponsored by BAN written by the former director of the Manuscript and Rare Book Division, A. I. Kopanev, "Arkheograficheskie ekspeditsii kak odin iz istochnikov komplektovaniia fondov rukopisnoi i redkoi knigi Biblioteki AN SSSR," in *Akademicheskie arkhivy SSSR za 50 let sovetskoi vlasti*, edited by B. V. Levshin (C-1), pp. 290-94.

For a comprehensive bibliography of published catalogs of medieval manuscripts in BAN, see the relevant section of *Spravochnik-ukazatel' pechatnykh opisanii slaviano-russkikh rukopisei*, compiled by Iu. K. Begunov et al. (A-14), pp. 71-89. For a discussion of printed catalogs, see the article by A. I. Kopanev, "Pechatnye katalogi rukopisnogo sobraniia Biblioteki Akademii nauk SSSR," *Sovetskaia bibliografiia*, 1964, no. 5, pp. 82-90.

The Manuscript and Rare Book Division of BAN is comprehensively described and many of the fonds are inventoried in several different series, the most important of which will be described below, following the bibliographical guide which lists more fully the literature about the library.

210

C-20. [Akademiia nauk SSSR. Biblioteka.]
Biblioteka Akademii nauk SSSR, 1714-1964. Bibliograficheskii ukazatel'. Compiled
    by E. P. Faidel' et al. Edited by M. S. Filippov. Leningrad, 1964. 308 p.
    [DLC-Z5816.A46A5; MH-LSoc3983.116.21]

        This directory presents a complete bibliography of books and articles
        published by and about the library divisions, including sections covering
        prerevolutionary publications about manuscripts (pp. 106-40) and
        publications since 1917 (pp. 215-36). There is considerable overlap between
        this list and the coverage by Begunov (A-14), pp. 71-89, mentioned above.

C-21. [Akademiia nauk SSSR. Biblioteka.]
Istoricheskii ocherk i obzor fondov rukopisnogo otdela Biblioteki Akademii nauk.
    Vol. 1: *XVIII vek.* By M. N. Murzanova, E. I. Bobrova, and V. A. Petrov. Edited
    by V. P. Adrianova-Peretts. Moscow/Leningrad: Izd-vo AN SSSR, 1956. 484 p.
    [DLC-Z6620 R9 A6; MH-Slav251.277.8]

        An article by M. N. Murzanova on the original fonds of the Manuscript
        Division covers the history of the library of Peter I and surveys the collection
        of manuscript books of Peter I and the book collection of Tsarevich Aleksei
        Petrovich. An article by E. I. Bobrova surveys the foreign manuscript books
        in the collection of Peter I. An article by V. A. Petrov gives a history of the
        manuscript fonds of BAN from 1730 to 1800. Annexes present inventories of
        the libraries of Peter I and of Aleksei, and of the collections of V. N.
        Tatishchev together with that of other eighteenth-century acquisitions.
    Supplement to vol. 1: *Karty, plany, chertezhi, risunki i graviury sobraniia Petra*
    I. Moscow/Leningrad: Izd-vo AN SSSR, 1961. 289 p.
    [DLC-Z6620.R9A62.1961; MH-Slav251.277.8]

        Provides a detailed description and inventory of maps and other graphic
        manuscripts in the collection of Peter I, with detailed indexes.
    Vol. 2: *XIX-XX veka.* By A. I. Kopanev, V. A. Petrov et al. Moscow/Leningrad:
    Izd-vo AN SSSR, 1958. 398 p.
    [DLC-Z6620.R9.A6; MH-Slav251.277.8]

        Gives a history of the manuscript division with a section from 1800 to the
        October Revolution, and a second section for the postrevolutionary period,
        by A. I. Kopanev and V. A. Petrov (pp. 5-76). The next large section surveys
        47 major collections of individuals or institutions (pp. 77-204). Subsequent
        sections survey the holdings in foreign manuscripts (pp. 205-71), and Greek
        manuscripts (pp. 272-84). A final section surveys the A. P. Kartavov
        collection, covering watermarks on Russian papers in the eighteenth and
        nineteenth centuries.

C-22. [Akademiia nauk. Biblioteka. Rukopisnyi otdel.]
Opisanie rukopisnogo otdeleniia Biblioteki Imperatorskoi Akademii nauk.
Part 1: *Rukopisi.* Edited by V. I. Sreznevskii and F. I. Pokrovskii. 2 vols.
St. Petersburg: Tipografiia Imperatorskoi Akademii nauk, 1910-1915.
    Vol. 1: 1) *Knigi sviashchennogo pisaniia i* 2) *Knigi bogosluzhebnye.*

St. Petersburg, 1910. 525 p.

Vol. 2: 3) *Tvoreniia ottsov i uchitelei tserkvi;* 4) *Bogoslovie dogmaticheskoe i polemicheskoe i* 5) *Bogoslovie uchitel'noe.* Petrograd, 1915. 629 p.

[DLC-Z6621.L5527; MH-Slav251.277.10]

[Akademiia nauk SSSR. Biblioteka. Rukopisnyi otdel.]

Opisanie rukopisnogo otdela Biblioteki Akademii nauk SSSR.

Vol. 3, part 1: (*Khronografy, letopisi, stepennye, rodoslovnye, razriadnye knigi*). Compiled by V. F. Pokrovskaia, A. I. Kopanev, M. V. Kukushkina, and M. N. Murzanova. Edited by A. I. Andreev. 2nd edition enlarged. Moscow/Leningrad: Izd-vo AN SSSR, 1959. 708 p.

[DLC-Z6621.L5528; MH-Slav251.277.11]

This is the expanded and corrected second edition of the earlier volume 3, part 1, published in 1930: *Opisanie rukopisnogo otdeleniia Biblioteki Akademii nauk SSSR*, part 1: *Rukopisi*, vol. 3, part 1: 6) *Istoriia*, edited by V. I. Sreznevskii and F. I. Pokrovskii (Leningrad, 1930; 233 p. [MH-Slav251.277.10]).

Vol. 3, part 2: *Istoricheskie sborniki XV-XVII vv.* Compiled by A. I. Kopanev, M. V. Kukushkina, and V. F. Pokrovskaia. Edited by V. A. Petrov. Moscow/Leningrad: Izd-vo "Nauka," 1965. 362 p.

[DLC-Z6621.L5527; MH-Slav251.277.11 (3 pt. 2)]

Vol. 3, part 3: *Istoricheskie sborniki XVIII-XIX vv.* Leningrad: Izd-vo "Nauka," 1971. 420 p.

Vol. 4, part 1: (*Povesti, romany, skazaniia, skazki, rasskazy*). Edited by A. P. Konusov and V. F. Pokrovskaia. Moscow/Leningrad: Izd-vo AN SSSR, 1951. 598 p.

[DLC-Z6621.L5527; MH-Slav251.277.10(4)]

C-23. Aleksandrov, B. V.

"Opisanie rukopisnykh kart XVIII v., khraniashchikhsia v otdele rukopisnoi knigi Biblioteki Akademii nauk SSSR." In *Geograficheskii departament Akademii nauk XVIII veka*, edited by V. F. Gnucheva, *Trudy arkhiva AN SSSR*, vol. 6, pp. 267-412. Moscow/Leningrad: Izd-vo AN SSSR, 1946. (See C-7)

C-24. [Akademiia nauk SSSR. Biblioteka. Otdel rukopisnoi i redkoi knigi.]

Materialy i soobshcheniia po fondam otdela rukopisnoi i redkoi knigi Biblioteki Akademii nauk SSSR. Edited by A. I. Kopanev. Moscow/Leningrad: Izd-vo "Nauka," 1966. 207 p.

[DLC-Z240.A36; MH-Slav251.277.70]

Of special interest for descriptions of manuscripts, see the articles by M. N. Murzanova, "Sobranie Petrovskoi galerei" (pp. 79-89), and by M. V. Kukushkina, "Postupleniia rukopisei v BAN SSSR v 1964 g." (pp. 103-05).

3. ARKHIV LENINGRADSKOGO OTDELENIIA INSTITUTA ISTORII SSSR AN SSSR (LOII)

[Archive of the Leningrad Branch of the Institute of History of the USSR of the Academy of Sciences of the USSR]
    Address: Leningrad, P-110, Petrozavodskaia ulitsa, 7

CONTENTS

The rich holdings of the Archive of the Leningrad Branch of the Institute of the History of the USSR include both significant archival fonds and important manuscript collections divided into Russian and Western European sections. The Russian section of the archive alone includes more than 160 archival fonds and about 86 manuscript collections with close to 181,500 storage units. As the nucleus of this section, about two-thirds of these holdings (103 fonds, containing around 63,800 storage units), were the legacy of the Archeographical Commission of the Imperial Russian Academy of Sciences. In addition, the division also received the bulk of the extensive prerevolutionary N. P. Likhachev collection with some 86 fonds and several subsidiary collections.

There are several major groups of Russian archival fonds housed in the archive. One large section contains archival fonds from a wide variety of local administrative institutions from the sixteenth to the nineteenth century (C-25, pp. 21-123). There is another large section containing manuscript collections from monasteries, bishoprics, churches, and cathedrals (C-25, pp. 124-86). Another section contains fonds from military fiefs and patrimonial estates, some of which include documents dating back to the fourteenth century, but mostly from the seventeenth and eighteenth centuries (C-25, pp. 187-251).

A large proportion of the holdings is made up of a group of some 128 personal archival fonds from families who had important roles in prerevolutionary Russia. The large majority of these documents date from the eighteenth and nineteenth centuries (C-25, pp. 252-336). Perhaps most important in terms of size and interest in this section are the Vorontsov Papers; although they are divided among several major archives (the next largest portion is in TsGADA), the part of them contained in the Institute of History—still in the process of being recataloged—served as the basis for the forty-volume publication, *Arkhiv kniazia Vorontsova*, edited by P. I. Bartenev (Moscow, 1870-1897) (see C-26).

Another section of fonds comes from the organs of central governmental administration, scientific and cultural societies, military institutions, and factories. In most cases there are relatively few documents in individual fonds, although there are sizeable collections from such organizations as the Russian Imperial Historical Society and such units as the eighteenth-century chancelleries of A. D. Men'shikov and B. P. Sheremetev (see C-25, pp. 252-360).

Some of the important Russian collections in this archive include the voluminous collection of pre-1613 acts, a collection of charters and other administrative documents from Chernigov guberniia, a collection of the Archeographical Commission and from archeographic expeditions (especially of P. M. Stroev), and a collection of miscellaneous documents from the Library of the Academy of Sciences, among many other collections of early documents and manuscript books. The collections of P. N. Dobrokhotov, N. G. Golovin, I. A. Shliapkin, M. I. Semevskii, S. M. Solov'ev, V. O. Kliuchevskii, and, as mentioned above, N. P. Likhachev, are among the largest of the many private manuscript collections now housed in the archive (see C-25, pp. 361-450).

There is also a large section of manuscripts from various southern and Western European countries, containing 61 collections and fonds with about 25,000 units. These are grouped by country of origin. The largest groups come from Italy, Germany, France, Poland, and the Papacy (see C-25, pp. 451-506, and C-27).

WORKING CONDITIONS

The location of manuscripts in LOII is quite efficient because of the exceedingly comprehensive nature of the published guide and the large number of published catalogs and inventories available. Published inventories as well as ones in manuscript or typescript are usually shelved in the reading room and are readily available for consultation. There is still some backlog of documents not fully inventoried, but the archivists are generally exceedingly knowledgeable about the contents. Paging usually takes less than an hour, since the manuscripts are close by and arranged for easy access.

Published materials relating to the manuscripts are usually available in the Institute library; if not, arrangements may be made for them to be ordered from BAN. Microfilming and photocopying services are available by arrangement through the Academy of Sciences facilities; microfilm can often be prepared within several weeks for personal delivery in Leningrad.

PUBLISHED GUIDE

The unusually comprehensive and well-annotated guide listed below gives bibliographical references to other descriptive material published earlier. The more recently published short article by P. I. Kozintseva and V. I. Rutenburg, "V Arkhive Leningradskogo otdeleniia Instituta istorii AN SSSR," in *Voprosy istorii*, 1966, no. 2, pp. 160-66, gives a brief general description and lists other published literature.

C-25. [Akademiia nauk SSSR. Institut istorii. Leningradskoe otdelenie. Arkhiv.]
Putevoditel' po arkhivu Leningradskogo otdeleniia Instituta istorii. Compiled by I. V. Valkina, L. G. Katushkina, and G. E. Kochin et al. Edited by A. I. Andreev, A. G. Man'kov, V. A. Petrov, and V. I. Rutenburg. Moscow/Leningrad: Izd-vo AN SSSR, 1958. 603 p.
[DLC-CD1739.L4.A46; MH-LSoc3983.116.5]
    A detailed, comprehensive guide to the LOII collections, with extensive bibliographical references to published inventories or other descriptive

literature, and documentary publications from the holdings. The volume is organized according to the main sections of the archive as described above and has a full index, including an index of names of individuals whose correspondence may be included in one of the fonds described. It includes a supplementary description of the LOII library.

PUBLISHED INVENTORIES AND SPECIALIZED DESCRIPTIONS

A comprehensive bibliography of published inventories or other descriptive literature about the medieval Slavic holdings in LOII is included in the general directory compiled by Iu. K. Begunov et al., *Spravochnik-ukazatel' pechatnykh opisanii slaviano-russkikh rukopisei* (A-14), pp. 59-71.

-26. Petrov, V. A.
"Obzor sobraniia Vorontsovykh, khraniashchegosia v arkhive Leningradskogo otdela Instituta istorii Akademii nauk SSSR." *Problemy istochnikovedeniia* 5 (1956): 102-45.

-27. Rutenburg, V. I.
"Zapadnoevropeiskaia sektsiia arkhiva Instituta istorii AN SSSR." *Voprosy istorii*, 1947, no. 4, pp. 152-54.

-28. Rukhmanova, E. D., and Iu. V. Kurskov.
"Istochniki po istorii russko-skandinavskikh otnoshenii v rukopisnykh sobraniiakh g. Leningrada." *Skandinavskii sbornik*, edited by V. V. Pokhlebkina and L. K. Roots, 3:257-69. Tallin: Estonskoe gosudarstvennoe izd-vo, 1958.
[DLC-DL1.S5; MH-PScan348.4(3)]
> The largest part of the article (pp. 257-65) is devoted to a description of materials in LOII, pertaining to Russian-Scandinavian relations from the sixteenth through the nineteenth century.

-29. Liublinskii, V. S.
"Istochniki po istorii skandinavskikh stran v Leningradskom otdelenii Instituta istorii AN SSSR." *Skandinavskii sbornik* 6 (1963):258-73.
[DLC-DL1.S5; MH-PScan348.4(6)]
> Describes materials from the sixteenth to the nineteenth century, mostly relating to Sweden.

PART C – ACADEMY OF SCIENCES HOLDINGS

4. INSTITUT RUSSKOI LITERATURY (PUSHKINSKII DOM) AKADEMII NAUK SSSR (PD)

[Institute of Russian Literature (Pushkin House) of the Academy of Sciences of the USSR]
RUKOPISNYI OTDEL [Manuscript Division]
FONOGRAMMARKHIV [Phonographic Archive]
    Address: Leningrad, V-164, naberezhnaia Makarova, 4

CONTENTS

Manuscript Division

Pushkinskii Dom dates back to 1905, when it was founded under the Academy of Sciences to house Pushkin's personal library, and as a repository for Pushkin manuscripts and other materials. It was transformed into a major research institute for Russian literature under the Academy of Sciences in 1930, at which time it took its present name (although there have subsequently been slight variations). It is still commonly called Pushkinskii Dom, although the research functions of the institute and the manuscript and library holdings have now gone well beyond the initial purpose. In fact, the Manuscript Division of Pushkinskii Dom has become one of the richest collections of literary manuscripts in the Soviet Union from the prerevolutionary and Soviet periods. Its holdings, which now number over 700 fonds, encompass rich medieval collections as well as a variety of cultural and general political materials, particularly from the prerevolutionary period.

The Manuscript Division is formally divided into five subdivisions, generally reflecting the origin of the materials involved. The first and largest encompasses the majority of literary fonds and autograph literary manuscripts. The second includes manuscript materials transferred from BAN in the 1930's. The third consists of fonds acquired from the Institute of World Literature (IMLI) in Moscow; when the Manuscript Division of IMLI was reorganized in 1951, all its prerevolutionary holdings were transferred to Pushkinskii Dom. The fourth division is devoted to medieval manuscript books and has been the center for the Institute's Division of Early Russian Literature; some medieval manuscripts from IMLI were also deposited in this special division. The fifth division consists of the folklore collection.

Since its foundation, Pushkinskii Dom has built up its collection of papers of and relating to Pushkin, becoming the main center for Pushkin studies, with close to 6,000 storage units of Pushkiniana. Although it thus contains by far the largest group of Pushkin papers, it has not become the centralized exclusive Pushkin archive, comparable to the Tolstoi Archive, as some of its scholars had hoped; a large group of Pushkin papers is also housed in TsGALI in Moscow. In addition to Pushkin, most of the other major prerevolutionary Russian writers are also represented in the holdings of the Manuscript Division, most notably Lermontov, Krylov, Gogol, Nekrasov, Turgenev, Goncharov, Ostrovskii, Dostoevskii, Chekhov, Blok, and Teternikov (Sologub). Many important Soviet writers are also represented, especially from the 1920's and 30's; among the largest fonds are those of Bulgakov, Novikov-Priboi, Zoshchenko, Chapygin, Libedinskii, and Voloshin.

A major collection received from the Onegin Museum in Paris in 1928 included, in addition to manuscripts of Pushkin, Turgenev, and Zhukovskii, a variety of manuscripts and personal papers of important Western European writers and musicians, especially from France. When the Library of the Academy of Sciences (BAN) was reorganized in 1931, many of the archival fonds pertaining to literature and social thought were transferred to Pushkinskii Dom.

Large groups of papers from early socialist writers and revolutionaries such as Bakunin, Belinskii, Herzen, Dobroliubov, Chernyshevskii, and Ogarev are now to be found here, as are papers of many of the Decembrists, including the large fond of S. G. Volkonskii, and the rich archive of the Turgenev brothers. Additional manuscripts of important Russian musicians and artists from a variety of sources, as well as some of foreign artists and composers, have come to the Manuscript Division, broadening the holdings into many fields of cultural history.

The cultural wealth of the repository has been increased by the archives of several important prerevolutionary periodicals such as *Russkaia starina, Vestnik Evropy, Sovremennik,* and *Severnyi vestnik.* There are also many materials pertaining to prerevolutionary newspapers and other cultural journals. Additional holdings of postrevolutionary literary and cultural organizations and journals also abound here.

The large section of the Manuscript Division devoted to medieval Slavic holdings has about 5,000 manuscripts and manuscript books dating from the twelfth to the eighteenth century. Numerous archeographical expeditions undertaken by the early literature section of the literary research institute have resulted in numerous additions in this field.

Another large section is devoted to folklore with a wide variety of holdings. Some materials had been transferred there from the ethnographical institute, and from other repositories to form a more centralized folklore collection under the Academy.

Phonographic Archive

The Phonographic Archive of Pushkinskii Dom houses the richest collection of recorded folk songs in the Soviet Union. It was originally founded in 1931 under the Academy's then constituted Institute of Anthropology, Ethnography, and Archeology, with an impressive collection of folklore sound recordings, the earliest of which date back to the 1890's (see C-33 and C-42). In 1939 this collection, along with other folklore materials, was transferred to Pushkinskii Dom where it became the basis for the Phonographic Archive as presently constituted. The archive has consolidated materials from other institutions as well, including copies of over 15,000 items from the pre-World War II Berlin phonographic archive. The continually expanding archive now includes over 37,000 items—records, tapes, and early cylindrical recordings. Although the bulk of the materials is from the USSR, representing seventy different nationalities, there are many recordings from foreign countries.

PART C – ACADEMY OF SCIENCES HOLDINGS

WORKING CONDITIONS

Access to materials in Pushkinskii Dom has varied considerably in recent years according to the specific topic, and has varied from scholar to scholar. Generally, it would appear that it is less easy to obtain access to recent than to older materials.

Foreign scholars work in the main reading room of the Manuscript Division. There is a special separate reading room for the medieval manuscript section. The Phonographic Archive has its own listening rooms and studio facilities in another part of the building. Comprehensive inventories have been prepared for a large proportion of the fonds in the Manuscript Division in either printed, typewritten, or handwritten form. Many are shelved in the reading room, and others are generally made available on request, although this has not been the case where politically sensitive manuscripts are involved, or those that have not been well studied by Soviet scholars. There is, however, a considerable cataloging backlog; and often it is difficult to obtain information about materials which have not been thoroughly cataloged.

Although there are more extensive card catalogs for staff use, scholars normally have access only to the card catalog in the main reading room. The extent and comprehensiveness of this file varies tremendously with the fond in question. For the well-processed fonds, it even lists by personal name materials by a given individual in fonds other than his own. For such fonds, the catalog has the detailed coverage of a good inventory that can be used as a basis for ordering specific items. For others, references are more general, and the scholar must rely on the archivist to ferret out manuscript materials for him. Except in a few cases where sensitive materials require more careful scrutiny and special permission for use, paging normally proceeds without delay. Manuscripts should usually be requested half a day or a full twenty-four hours in advance of the time desired.

There is an excellent library across the main entrance hall from the Manuscript Division, the resources of which are generally open to scholars working on manuscripts. Requests can usually be made from the manuscript reading room for books to be delivered; direct access to the library is usually possible upon request.

There are very satisfactory facilities for microfilming documents through the Academy of Sciences photographic laboratory. Permission for ordering films, however, varies considerably from case to case and is generally difficult to obtain. In recent years, particularly since 1965, there has been more reluctance to film materials for foreign scholars, particularly unless some exchange arrangement can be worked out in an individual case.

GENERAL PUBLISHED DESCRIPTIONS

There is no general guide to the holdings of the Manuscript Division of Pushkinskii Dom. A survey of the medieval manuscripts was published in 1965; a comprehensive survey of the personal fonds has been in preparation for some time but is not yet ready for publication.

C-30. [Akademiia nauk SSSR. Institut russkoi literatury.]
50 let Pushkinskogo doma. Edited by V. G. Bazanov. Moscow/Leningrad, 1956.
247 p.
[DLC-PG2920.A47; MH-Slav 4350.4810.10]

This jubilee volume describes the history and work of the Institute of Russian
Literature. A section devoted to the Manuscript Division (pp. 28-40) gives a
short general survey of the contents, and mentions some of the major
holdings. The volume also gives a complete bibliography of books and articles
published by Pushkinskii Dom (pp. 167-229); it includes a detailed list of the
articles found in different issues of the Institute serials. It should not,
however, be considered a complete bibliography of descriptive literature
because it does not include prerevolutionary catalogs or other descriptions of
manuscripts not published by the Institute itself. This coverage updates and
replaces the earlier descriptive article by L. M. Dobrovol'skii and L. B.
Modzalevskii, "Rukopisnyi otdel Instituta literatury (Pushkinskogo doma)
Akademii nauk SSSR. Kratkii istoricheskii ocherk," in *Biulleteni
Rukopisnogo otdela Pushkinskogo doma* 1 (1947):5-30. A shorter but more
recent article surveying the development of the Manuscript Division since
1917 by its former director, I. V. Izmailov, is included in *Akademicheskie
arkhivy SSSR za 50 let sovetskoi vlasti* (C-1), pp. 232-43; it is followed by a
short report on bibliographical materials in the division (pp. 244-54), and a
survey by P. P. Shirmakov of the fonds of Soviet writers (pp. 255-64).

C-31. [Akademiia nauk SSSR. Institut russkoi literatury.]
Drevne-russkie rukopisi Pushkinskogo doma (obzor fondov). Compiled by V. I.
Malyshev. Edited by V. P. Adrianova-Peretts. Moscow/Leningrad: Izd-vo "Nauka,"
1965. 230 p.
[DLC-Z6621.L5547; MH-Slav 251.107]

This comprehensive survey of the medieval manuscripts in Pushkinskii Dom
includes a bibliography for many of the collections covered, with notes about
other pertinent publications. More recent acquisitions have been reported
annually by V. I. Malyshev in the journal *Russkaia literatura*: 1966, no. 2, pp.
217-19; 1967, no. 1, pp. 195-97; 1968, no. 2, pp. 201-04; 1969, no. 2, pp.
119-25; and 1970, no. 1, pp. 191-96. A cumulative description of these
acquisitions and a concise survey of the development of the medieval
manuscript section is presented by V. I. Malyshev, "Sobranie drevnerusskikh
rukopisei Pushkinskogo doma (k 20-letiiu ego organizatsii), in *Trudy Otdela
drevnerusskoi literatury Akademii nauk SSSR* 25 (1970):333-38.

C-32. Shapovalova, G. G.
"Fol'klornye fondy rukopisnogo otdela Instituta russkoi literatury AN SSSR
(obzor)." *Sovetskaia etnografiia*, 1963, no. 2, pp. 139-44.
Surveys the holdings of the folklore section.

C-33. "Fonogrammarkhiv Instituta russkoi literatury Akademii nauk SSSR (Pushkinskii dom)." In *Muzykal'nyi Leningrad, 1917-1957* (A-53), pp. 377-81.

> Describes the Soviet Union's richest collection of recorded folk songs and other folklore materials. See also the earlier description of the original section of the collection which had been brought together under the Academy's Institute of Anthropology, Ethnology, and Archeology: E. V. Gippius, "Fonogrammarkhiv Fol'klornoi sektsii Instituta antropologii, etnografii i arkheologii Akademii nauk SSSR," *Sovetskii fol'klor. Sbornik statei i materialov*, no. 4-5 (Moscow/Leningrad: Izd-vo AN SSSR, 1936), pp. 405-14. There is also a briefer description of the holdings at that time in the general coverage of Academy archives published in 1933, *Arkhiv Akademii nauk SSSR. Obozrenie arkhivnykh materialov* (C-3)1:195-99. See the detailed catalog of the early holdings listed below as C-42.

PUBLISHED INVENTORIES AND SPECIALIZED DESCRIPTIONS

For a comprehensive list of catalogs and other descriptive literature covering medieval Slavic manuscripts in Pushkinskii Dom, see the appropriate section of *Spravochnik-ukazatel' pechatnykh opisanii slaviano-russkikh rukopisei*, compiled by Iu. K. Begunov et al. (A-14), pp. 110-18, in addition to the listings under C-31 above.

Serials

C-34. [Akademiia nauk SSSR. Institut russkoi literatury. Rukopisnyi otdel.] *Biulleteni Rukopisnogo otdela Pushkinskogo doma.* 1947-1961.
[DLC-Z6621.M84.A4; MH-PSlav 109.60]

> This major serial put out by the Institute of Literature includes many articles about the Manuscript Division and its individual collections as well as inventories of many fonds. Each issue includes a survey of the new or recent manuscript acquisitions. Because its contents are not normally analyzed in library catalogs, and because of the large number of important descriptions and inventories included, the names of those fonds covered by inventories or surveys in each issue are listed below:

Vol. 1 (1947): A. P. Chekhov, A. N. Veselovskii.

Vol. 2 (1950): M. Iu. Lermontov, V. G. Belinskii, A. I. Herzen, I. S. Turgenev.

Vol. 3 (1952): N. A. Nekrasov, I. A. Goncharov, G. P. Derzhavin.

Vol. 4 (1953): N. A. Nekrasov, A. V. Kol'tsov, I. S. Nikitin; medieval manuscripts received from the Institute of World Literature (IMLI); autograph manuscripts of Czech and Slovak writers.

Vol. 5 (1955): N. P. Ogarev, M. I. Mikhailov, M. Iu. Lermontov.

Vol. 6 (1956): I. A. Krylov, A. S. Pushkin.

Vol. 7 (1957): F. M. Dostoevskii; Polish and Yugoslav autograph manuscripts.

Vol. 8 (1959): A. S. Pushkin, V. M. Garshin, I. A. Bunin.

Vol. 9 (1961): M. E. Saltykov-Shchedrin.

C-35. [Akademiia nauk SSSR. Institut russkoi literatury.]
Ezhegodnik Rukopisnogo otdela Pushkinskogo doma. Leningrad, 1971+.
This new series scheduled to start with a volume for 1970 has a format
somewhat similar to that of the earlier *Biulleteni* with articles pertaining to
different parts of the Manuscript Division holdings.

C-36. [Akademiia nauk SSSR. Institut russkoi literatury.]
Opisanie rukopisei i izobrazitel'nykh materialov Pushkinskogo doma. 7 vols.
Moscow/Leningrad: Izd-vo AN SSSR, 1951-1962.
[DLC-PG2920.A46; MH-Slav251.390]
Volumes 3, 6, and 7 of this series cover only representational material in the
museum collections of Pushkinskii Dom, and hence are not included here.
Vol. 1: *N. V. Gogol'.* Compiled by E. A. Kovalevskaia et al. Edited by B. V.
Tomashevskii. Moscow/Leningrad, 1951. 136 p.
See also the earlier inventory of Gogol' autographs by B. [P.] Gorodetskii,
"Opisanie avtografov N. V. Gogolia v sobranii Instituta literatury Akademii
nauk SSSR," *Literaturnyi arkhiv. Materialy po istorii literatury i
obshchestvennogo dvizheniia* 1(Moscow: Izd-vo AN SSSR, 1938):432-74.
Vol. 2: *M. Iu. Lermontov.* Compiled by A. Iu. Veis et al. Edited by B. V.
Tomashevskii. Moscow/Leningrad, 1953. 365 p.
Vol. 4: *I. S. Turgenev.* Compiled by I. E. Grudinina et al. Edited by B. V.
Shaposhnikov and M. P. Alekseev. Moscow/Leningrad, 1958. 379 p.
Vol. 5: *I. A. Goncharov, F. M. Dostoevskii.* Compiled by A. D. Alekseev et al.
Edited by E. N. Kupreianova. Moscow/Leningrad, 1959. 289 p.

Other Manuscripts of Individuals

N. G. Chernyshevskii (1828-1889)

C-37. [Akademiia nauk SSSR. Institut russkoi literatury.]
*Rukopisi N. G. Chernyshevskogo v sobranii Instituta literatury (Pushkinskogo
doma) Akademii nauk SSSR. Nauchnoe opisanie.* Compiled by K. N. Grigor'ian.
Edited by L. B. Modzalevskii. Moscow/Leningrad: Izd-vo AN SSSR, 1939. 56 p.
[MH-Slav4337.8.837]

D. I. Pisarev (1840-1868)

C-38. [Akademiia nauk SSSR. Institut russkoi literatury.]
Rukopisi D. I. Pisareva v sobranii Instituta. Nauchnoe opisanie. Compiled by K. N.
Grigor'ian. Edited by L. B. Modzalevskii. Moscow/Leningrad: Izd-vo AN SSSR,
1941. 54 p.
[DLC-Z8693.8.A4]

A. S. Pushkin (1799-1837)

C-39. [Akademiia nauk SSSR. Institut russkoi literatury.]
Rukopisi Pushkina, khraniashchiesia v Pushkinskom dome. Nauchnoe opisanie.

PART C – ACADEMY OF SCIENCES HOLDINGS

Compiled by L. B. Modzalevskii and B. V. Tomashevskii. Moscow: Izd-vo AN SSSR, 1937. 395 p.
[DLC-Z6616.P8.A45; MH-Slav4350.4.903]
> Detailed inventory of Pushkin manuscripts in Pushkinskii dom, correlated with published editions.

C-40. [Akademiia nauk SSSR. Institut russkoi literatury.]
Rukopisi Pushkina, postupivshie v Pushkinskii dom posle 1937 goda. Kratkoe opisanie. Compiled by O. S. Solov'eva. Edited by N. V. Izmailov. Leningrad: Izd-vo "Nauka," 1964. 112 p.
[DLC-Z6616.P8.A46; MH-Slav 4350.4.903.5]
> A supplement to C-39 above; compare with the earlier catalog of GLM holdings, B-63.

Pechora Collection

C-41. Malyshev, V. I.
Ust'-tsilemskie rukopisnye sborniki XVI-XX vv. Syktyvkar: Komi knizhnoe izd-vo, 1960. 215 p.
[DLC-Z6620.R9M3; MH-Slav251.256.30]
> Two supplements to this volume have been published by V. I. Malyshev: "Ust'-tsilemskie rukopisi XVII-XIX vv. istoricheskogo, literaturnogo i bytovogo soderzhaniia," *Trudy Otdela drevnerusskoi literatury Akademii nauk SSSR* 17 (1961):561-604; and "Perepiska i delovye bumagi ust'-tsilemskikh krest'ian XVIII-XIX vv.," *ibid.*, 18 (1962):442-57. For additional descriptions of the archeographical expeditions in this area and the manuscripts now in Pushkinskii Dom, see the list given in the volume compiled by Begunov et al. cited above (A-14), pp. 114-16.

Phonographic Archive

C-42. Magad, S. D.
"Spisok sobranii fonogramm-arkhiva fol'klornoi sektsii IAEA Akademii nauk SSSR." *Sovetskii fol'klor. Sbornik statei i materialov*, no. 4-5 (Moscow/Leningrad: Izd-vo AN SSSR, 1936), pp. 415-28.
[DLC-GR190.A5; MH-27231.21.10]

Musical Materials

C-43. "Muzykal'nye fondy Instituta russkoi literatury Akademii nauk SSSR (Pushkinskii dom)." In *Muzykal'nyi Leningrad 1917-1957* (A-53), pp. 374-75.

Materials Relating to the Decembrists

C-44. Danilov, V. V.
"Dekabristskie materialy v rukopisnom otdele Instituta russkoi literatury (Pushkinskogo doma)." In *Dekabristy i ikh vremia. Materialy i soobshcheniia,*

edited by M. P. Alekseev and B. S. Meilakh, pp. 259-79. Moscow/Leningrad: Izd-vo
AN SSSR, 1951.
[DLC-DK212.A64; MH-Slav1255.130]

Archives of Periodicals

C-45. Shtakel'berg, Iu. I.
"Arkhiv 'Russkoi stariny.' " In *K stoletiiu geroicheskoi bor'by 'Za nashu i vashu
svobodu.' Sbornik statei i materialov o vosstanii 1863 g.* (A-44), pp. 292-356.
While principally covering material relating to the Polish uprising of 1863, the
article describes the archive of this important prerevolutionary journal,
especially in regard to papers up to 1870.

5. INSTITUT MIROVOI LITERATURY IMENI A. M. GOR'KOGO AKADEMII NAUK SSSR (IMLI)

[A. M. Gor'kii Institute of World Literature of the Academy of Sciences of the USSR]
ARKHIV GOR'KOGO [Gor'kii Archive]
RUKOPISNYI OTDEL [Manuscript Division]
    Address: Moscow, G-69, ulitsa Vorovskogo, 25a

CONTENTS

The Institute of World Literature, or IMLI, houses two separate manuscript repositories of great interest to scholars interested in twentieth-century literature and the development of Soviet culture.

Gor'kii Archive

Best known through its extensive publication projects and published descriptions is the Gor'kii Archive established in 1937, after Gor'kii's death, as the official repository of all the archival materials and literary manuscripts of and relating to him. This archive, most of which is organized in a single fond, has grown to include more than 100,000 storage units. Most recently the archive has acquired the papers of Gor'kii's first wife and the papers of his lifelong biographer, I. A. Gruzdev, neither of which has as yet been completely inventoried. The archive is the center for Gor'kii studies and publications, and is currently involved in a new comprehensive multi-volume edition of his writings and biographical materials. With its extensive collection of correspondence and other documents, many of which relate only peripherally to Gor'kii, the archive should also prove of interest to scholars interested in many other literary figures, so many of whom were in contact or correspondence with Gor'kii.

Manuscript Division

Less known because there are no published descriptions of the holdings, but also of importance to scholars of Soviet literature, is the Manuscript Division of IMLI. Started as early as 1935, and continuing to be related to the research work of the IMLI staff, this repository now contains close to 500 fonds with approximately 50,000 storage units. In the early years of IMLI the Manuscript Division had significant numbers of papers of and relating to several major prerevolutionary literary figures, and a collection of medieval Slavic manuscripts, but these were all transferred to the Institute of Russian Literature [Pushkinskii Dom] in Leningrad in 1951. Most of the fonds of personal papers in this repository are relatively small, but sizeable fonds are to be found for such well-known literary figures as Sergei Esenin, Eduard Bagritskii, Dem'ian Bednyi, Aleksei Chapygin, Dmitrii Furmanov, Aleksandr Malyshkin, Aleksei Tolstoi, Evgenii Zamiatin, and Petr Zamoiskii.

Also represented in the division's holdings are fonds of important writers' organizations such as MORP (Mezhdunarodnaia organizatsiia revoliutsionnykh i proletarskikh pisatelei [International organization of revolutionary and proletarian writers]), 1931-1935. Particularly because of IMLI's interests in such international organizations, the division possesses a few fragmentary literary manuscripts, correspondence, and biographical materials regarding Western European authors. Many of the fonds of the division have not been fully worked over and cataloged, so it is difficult to appraise precisely their extent and significance.

WORKING CONDITIONS

The manuscript holdings remain a working part of the institute and are not always open to outside researchers, but recently a few foreigners have been given access for specific projects.

PUBLISHED DESCRIPTIONS AND CATALOGS

Manuscript Division

No general survey of the fonds in the Manuscript Division of the institute has been published, nor are inventories or descriptions available of individual fonds. Almost all personal fonds contained in the division are, however, listed in the general guide to personal archival fonds in the Soviet Union, *Lichnye arkhivnye fondy v gosudarstvennykh khranilishchakh SSSR. Ukazatel'* (A-9).

Gor'kii Archive

C-46. Zimina, S. S.
"Arkhiv velikogo pisatelia." *Russkaia literatura*, 1968, no. 2, pp. 3-12.
Gives a recent general survey of the Gor'kii Archive as an introduction to some published materials.

C-47. Zimina, S. S.
"Gor'kogo M. Arkhiv." In *Kratkaia literaturnaia entsiklopediia*, 2 (Moscow, 1964):295-98.
Gives a brief description of the archive and a bibliography of publications from its contents.

C-48. [Akademiia nauk SSSR. Arkhiv A. M. Gor'kogo.]
Opisanie rukopisei A. M. Gor'kogo.
Part 1: *Khudozhestvennye proizvedeniia, literaturno-kriticheskie i publitsisticheskie stat'i.* Edited by I. P. Ladyzhnikov and E. P. Rozmirovich. Moscow: Izd-vo AN SSSR, 1948. 730 p.
[DLC-Z6616.G6.A6; MH-Slav4350.12.929]
This systematic, comprehensive inventory covers Gor'kii's literary and critical manuscripts, all of which are now located in the Gor'kii Archive. It further provides detailed correlations between the manuscripts and the published

versions, and an extensive index. It completely replaces the earlier inventory, which covered these manuscripts when they were still located in a variety of different archives, edited by Sergei Dmitrievich Balukhati: *Opisanie rukopisei M. Gor'kogo*, part 1: *Khudozhestvennye proizvedeniia* (Moscow/Leningrad: Izd-vo AN SSSR, 1936; 263 p.; [DLC-Z6616.G6.B3 (Part 1); MH-Slav 4350.12.904]).

Part 2, intended to cover the correspondence and other documentary or bibliographical material in the Gor'kii Archive, has never been published, but exists in an early, now somewhat outdated, manuscript edition for the use of the staff.

6. LENINGRADSKOE OTDELENIE INSTITUTA VOSTOKOVEDENIIA AKADEMII NAUK SSSR (LOIV AN)

[Leningrad Branch of the Institute of Oriental Studies of the Academy of Sciences of the USSR]
ARKHIV VOSTOKOVEDOV [Archive of Orientalists]
RUKOPISNYI OTDEL [Manuscript Division]
    Address: Leningrad, D-41, Dvortsovaia naberezhnaia, 18

CONTENTS

The Leningrad Branch of the Institute of Oriental Studies houses one of the world's most extensive and valuable collections of oriental manuscripts and, in addition, some rich archives related to various aspects of oriental studies. The present holdings are the outgrowth of long historical development, since the institute is the heir of the world-renowned Asiatic Museum, founded in 1818 under the Imperial Russian Academy of Sciences, which became one of the world's great centers for oriental studies in the latter nineteenth century. Augmented by the manuscript legacy of other prerevolutionary institutions, the Asiatic Museum was reorganized in 1930 and its rich manuscript holdings became part of the Institute of Oriental Studies of the Academy of Sciences of the USSR. In 1950 the Academy of Sciences established an Institute of Oriental Studies in Moscow, and the Leningrad Institute subsequently became its branch. The main branch in Moscow (Armianskii pereulok, 2) has developed a sizeable library, including a special library for Sinology, and retains its own institutional archive, but it has not become a manuscript repository.

The name of the institute was changed in 1960 to the Institute of Asian Peoples [Institut narodov Azii Akademii nauk SSSR–INA], which name it kept for the next nine years until it resumed the original name in 1969. The Manuscript Division and Archive are now administered separately from the library, since the library itself (with over 1,000,000 volumes) is for administrative purposes considered a branch of the main Academy library in Leningrad, BAN.

The Manuscript Division includes about 62,000 storage units in close to fifty different oriental languages, dating as far back as samples of ancient Egyptian papyrus and bronze tablets from the Southern part of the Arabian peninsula. Among the largest collections are those in Arabic languages with over 5,000 manuscripts from the eleventh to the twentieth century, Turkic languages with around 3,500 manuscripts, mostly from the sixteenth to the early twentieth century, a rich group of about 3,000 Persian (and Tadzhik) manuscripts–some dating back to the eleventh century–and over 1,000 Hebrew manuscripts. Other significant collections include Syriac, Ethiopic, Mongolic, Tangut, Tibetan, Manchurian, Chinese, and Japanese language holdings. There are also numerous collections of miscellaneous documents or fragments and a significant group of cartographic materials. Some of the most famous texts are kept in display cases in the exhibition hall.

PART C — ACADEMY OF SCIENCES HOLDINGS

The Archive of Orientalists includes around seventy fonds, mostly personal fonds of important orientalists; there are also some documentary collections arranged by different oriental language groups. Some of the personal fonds of leading Academy orientalists which had originally been deposited in this archive were transferred to the Leningrad Branch of the Archive of the Academy of Sciences.

WORKING CONDITIONS

The Institute of Oriental Studies receives visiting scholars from all over the world, and its manuscripts and archival materials are all accessible. Published catalogs, descriptive literature, and other reference materials about the holdings are available in the large reading room. Separate card catalogs covering most of the language groups in the Manuscript Division are open to visiting scholars. The archive has no systematic catalog, but shelf lists for individual fonds and collections are available. Readers may order other published materials as needed from the large library of the institute.

PUBLISHED GUIDES, GENERAL DESCRIPTIONS, AND BIBLIOGRAPHY

A comprehensive guide to the Institute's holdings is now on press: *Spravochnik-putevoditel' po rukopisnym, arkhivnym i knizhnym fondam Leningradskogo otdeleniia Instituta vostokovedeniia Akademii nauk SSSR*. This includes coverage of the Manuscript Division with descriptions of the holdings in each language group, of the cartographic materials, and of the documentary collections; other sections cover the Archive of Orientalists and the library. Bibliographical supplements include a complete general bibliography of publications relating to the holdings of the institute and its predecessor, the Asiatic Museum; specialized bibliographies cover Armenian and Georgian manuscripts and documents and Moslem manuscripts.

Although it is now outdated as a directory of the holdings, scholars using some of the early collections will want to consult the original description of the Asiatic Museum, which includes detailed descriptions of the manuscript acquisitions during the first half of the nineteenth century: Bernhard [Boris Andreevich] Dorn, *Das Asiatische Museum der kaiserlichen Akademie der Wissenschaften zu St. Petersburg* (St. Petersburg: Buchdrückerei der kaiserlichen Akademie der Wissenschaften, 1846; 776 p.)

Manuscript Division

C-49. Tikhonov, D. I.
"Vostochnye rukopisi Instituta vostokovedeniia Akademii nauk SSSR." *Uchenye zapiski Instituta vostokovedeniia AN SSSR* 6 (1953):3-33.
A general survey of the manuscript holdings, including a short bibliography of earlier general and specialized descriptions.

C-50. "Biblioteka Leningradskogo otdeleniia Instituta narodov Azii Akademii nauk SSSR—Rukopisnyi otdel." In *Vostokovednye fondy krupneishikh bibliotek*

Sovetskogo Soiuza. Stat'i i soobshcheniia. (A-22), pp. 30-59.
Separate sections by different authors describe the manuscript holdings in different language groups and provide basic bibliography of published catalogs or other descriptive literature.

Archive of Orientalists

C-51. Zhuravlev, N. P., and A. M. Muginov.
"Kratkii obzor arkhivnykh materialov, khraniashchikhsia v sektore vostochnykh rukopisei Instituta vostokovedeniia Akademii nauk SSSR." In *Uchenye zapiski Instituta vostokovedeniia AN SSSR* 6 (1953):34-53.
Gives brief descriptions of 56 of the most interesting archival fonds and 15 of the documentary collections which constitute the Archive of Orientalists.

C-52. [Akademiia nauk SSSR. Institut narodov Azii. Leningradskoe otdelenie.]
"Biulleten' Arkhiva vostokovedov." Typescript. No. 1, 1961; no. 2, 1962; no. 3, 1963.
These three parts of the archival bulletin include survey descriptions of many of the archival fonds and collections. There are several bibliographical compilations and inventories. Some of the materials have been reworked and are now awaiting publication; texts of the original typescript bulletins are available in the archive and library of the Institute.

Bibliography
In addition to the specific bibliographies listed below, see the general reference aids for oriental manuscripts included in the general bibliography (Part A, section 7).

C-53. Livotova, O. E.
"Osnovnaia literatura ob Aziatskom muzee—Institute vostokovedeniia Akademii nauk SSSR (1776-1954)." In *Ocherki po istorii russkogo vostokovedeniia* 2 (Moscow: Izd-vo AN SSSR, 1956): 469-511.
[MH-OL225.160.10(2)]
A general bibliography of publications relating to the Institute of Oriental Studies and its predecessor arranged by year of publication to 1954.

C-54. Livotova, Ol'ga Emannuilovna, [and V. B. Portugal'].
Vostokovedenie v izdaniiakh Akademii nauk 1726-1917. Bibliografiia. Moscow: Izd-vo "Nauka," 1966. 143 p.
[DLC-Z3001.L55; MH-Asia28.113]
This comprehensive bibliography includes the various catalogs and other descriptive literature about the holdings of the Asiatic Museum published by the Academy before the Revolution.

C-55. Livotova, O. E.
"Bibliografiia izdanii Aziatskogo muzeia i Instituta vostokovedeniia Akademii nauk SSSR (1917-1958)." In *Ocherki po istorii russkogo vostokovedeniia* 3 (Moscow, 1960): 196-311.

PART C — ACADEMY OF SCIENCES HOLDINGS

[MH-OL225.160.10(3)]
> Similar in format to the preceding, this volume continues the coverage of the publications of the Asiatic Museum and its successor, the Institute of Oriental Studies, through 1958. A supplemental bibliography covering publications during the years 1956-1967 is now on press as a separate publication.

Serials

C-56. [Akademiia nauk SSSR. Institut vostokovedeniia.]
Uchenye zapiski Instituta vostokovedeniia AN SSSR. Moscow/Leningrad, 1950+.
Irregular.
[DLC-DS1.A4225; MH-Asia 1.1]
> Of the many volumes in this major series put out since 1950 by the Institute of Oriental Studies, three volumes (numbers 6, 9, and 16) have been devoted to describing various sections of the manuscript and archival holdings in the institute; only some of the most general of these surveys will be included in the bibliography below.

PUBLISHED INVENTORIES AND SPECIALIZED DESCRIPTIONS

Arabic Manuscripts

C-57. Beliaev, V. I.
"Arabskie rukopisi v sobranii Instituta vostokovedeniia Akademii nauk SSSR."
Uchenye zapiski Instituta vostokovedeniia AN SSSR 6 (1953):54-130.

C-58. [Akademiia nauk SSSR. Institut narodov Azii.]
Katalog arabskikh rukopisei Instituta narodov Azii AN SSSR. 3 vols. Moscow, 1960-1965.
[DLC-Z6621.I6A55; MH-OL 19002.160]
> Vol. 1: *Khudozhestvennaia proza*. Compiled by A. B. Khalidov. Edited by V. I. Beliaev. Moscow: Izd-vo vostochnoi literatury, 1960. 136 p.
> Vol. 2: *Geograficheskie sochineniia*. Compiled by A. I. Mikhailova. Edited by V. I. Beliaev. Moscow: Izd-vo vostochnoi literatury, 1961. 77 p.
> Vol. 3: *Istoriia*. Compiled by A. I. Mikhailova. Edited by P. A. Griaznevich. Moscow: Izd-vo "Nauka," 1965. 199 p.

Armenian Manuscripts

C-59. Orbeli, R. R.
"Sobranie armianskikh rukopisei Instituta vostokovedeniia Akademii nauk SSSR."
Uchenye zapiski Instituta vostokovedeniia AN SSSR 6 (1953): 104-30.

Chinese Manuscripts

C-60. Vorob'eva-Desiatovskaia, M. I., et al.
Opisanie kitaiskikh rukopisei Dun'khuanskogo fonda Instituta narodov Azii. Edited

by L. N. Men'shikov.
[DLC-Z6605.C5.V67; MH-Ch5.116]
Vol. 1: Moscow: Izd-vo vostochnoi literatury, 1963. 774 p.
Vol. 2: Moscow: Izd-vo "Nauka," 1967. 688 p.

Georgian Manuscripts and Documents

-61. [Akademiia nauk SSSR. Institut vostokovedeniia.]
Gruzinskie rukopisi Instituta vostokovedeniia.
[DLC-Z6621.M843.G4(pt. 1); MH-OL46003.71]
Vol. 1: *Istoriia, geografiia, puteshestviia, arkheologiia, zakonodatel'stvo, filosofiia, iazykoznanie, bibliografiia.* Compiled by R. R. Orbeli. Edited by D. I. Tikhonov. Moscow/Leningrad: Izd-vo AN SSSR, 1956. 214 p.
See also the general survey of Georgian manuscripts by R. R. Orbeli, "Sobranie gruzinskikh rukopisei Instituta vostokovedeniia Akademii nauk SSSR," *Uchenye zapiski Instituta vostokovedeniia AN SSSR* 9 (1954):30-66.

-62. Kakabadze, Saurmak Sarkissovich.
Gruzinskie dokumenty Instituta narodov Azii AN SSSR. Moscow: Izd-vo "Nauka," 1967. 512 p.
[MH-OL46113.72]

Hebrew Manuscripts

-63. [Akademiia nauk SSSR. Institut vostokovedeniia.]
Katalog evreiskikh rukopisei sobraniia Instituta vostokovedeniia AN SSSR.
Compiled by I. L. Gintsburg. Edited by A. M. Gazov-Ginzberg i K. B. Starkova.
Moscow: Izd-vo "Nauka," forthcoming.
This detailed catalog of the Hebrew manuscripts of the Institute of Oriental Studies was approved for publication in the early 1960's and is now reportedly in production.

Hindi and Punjabi Manuscripts

-64. Zograf, Georgii Aleksandrovich.
Opisanie rukopisei Khindi i Pandzhabi Instituta vostokovedeniia. Moscow: Izd-vo vostochnoi literatury, 1960. 100 p. [AN SSSR. Institut vostokovedeniia.]
[DLC-Z6621.M843.H5; MH-IndL12.347]
See also the general survey of Hindi holdings by V. S. Vorob'ev-Desiatovskii, "Sobranie indiiskikh rukopisei Instituta vostokovedeniia Akademii nauk SSSR," *Uchenye zapiski Instituta vostokovedeniia AN SSSR* 9 (1954):128-45.

Japanese Manuscripts

-65. Petrova, Ol'ga Petrovna.
[Akademiia nauk. Institut narodov Azii. Rukopisnyi otdel.-MH]

Opisanie iaponskikh rukopisei, ksilografov, i staropechatnykh knig.
[DLC-Z6621.L5545; MH-Jap 43.60]
> Vol. 1: Compiled by O. P. Petrova and V. N. Goregliad. Moscow: Izd-vo
> vostochnoi literatury, 1963. 243 p.
> Vol. 2: *Filologiia.* Compiled by G. D. Ivanova, V. N. Goregliad, and O. P.
> Petrova. Moscow: Izd-vo "Nauka," 1964. 231 p.
> Vol. 3: *Ideologiia.* Compiled by O. P. Petrova and V. N. Goregliad. Moscow:
> Izd-vo "Nauka," 1966. 174 p.
> Vol. 4: Compiled by O. P. Petrova and V. N. Goregliad. Moscow: Izd-vo
> "Nauka," 1969. 172 p. [AN SSSR. Institut vostokovedeniia.]
>> Covers materials relating to science, numismatics, military and naval science.
> Vol. 5: Compiled by V. N. Goregliad. Moscow: Izd-vo "Nauka," 1971. 132 p.
>> Covers materials relating to cartography, art and culture, calligraphy, and
>> architecture, in addition to archival documents.
> Vol. 6: Compiled by V. N. Goregliad and Z. Khanin.
> Moscow: Izd-vo "Nauka," 1971. 192 p.

Korean Manuscripts

C-66. Petrova, Ol'ga Petrovna.
Opisanie pis'mennykh pamiatnikov koreiskoi kul'tury. Edited by D. I. Tikhonov.
[DLC-Z6621.M843K6; MH-Jap4015.5]
> Vol. 1: Moscow/Leningrad: Izd-vo AN SSSR, 1956. 98 p. [AN SSSR. Institut
> vostokovedeniia].
> Vol. 2: Moscow: Izd-vo vostochnoi literatury, 1963. 52 p. [AN SSSR. Institut
> narodov Azii].
>> See also the general survey of Korean holdings by O. P. Petrova, "Sobranie
>> koreiskikh pis'mennykh pamiatnikov Instituta vostokovedeniia Akademii
>> nauk SSSR," *Uchenye zapiski Instituta vostokovedeniia AN SSSR* 9 (1954):
>> 3-29.

Kurdish Manuscripts

C-67. Rudenko, Margarita Borisovna.
Opisanie kurdskikh rukopisei leningradskikh sobranii. Moscow: Izd-vo vostochnoi
literatury, 1961. 125 p.
[DLC-Z6650.K8R8; MH-3263.66.35]
>> This offset publication of the Leningrad Branch of the Institute of Asian
>> Peoples, as the Institute of Oriental Studies was then called, covers some
>> manuscripts there as well as those in the A. D. Jaba Collection in the State
>> Public Library (GPB) in Leningrad. See listing as F-44.

Manchurian Manuscripts

C-68. Volkova, Maiia Petrovna.
Opisanie man'chzhurskikh rukopisei Instituta narodov Azii AN SSSR. Moscow:

Izd-vo "Nauka," 1965. 139 p.
[DLC-Z6621.A34.M35; MH-OL61800.5]

Mongolic Manuscripts

-69. [Akademiia nauk SSSR. Institut vostokovedeniia.]
Mongol'skie, Buriat-mongol'skie i oiratskie rukopisi i ksilografy Instituta vostokovedeniia. Compiled by L. S. Puchkovskii.
[DLC-Z6605.O75.A4; MH-OL61000.5]
> Vol. 1: *Istoriia. Pravo.* Edited by B. I. Pankratov and D. I. Tikhonov.
> Moscow/Leningrad: Izd-vo AN SSSR, 1957. 277 p.
>> See also the general survey of Mongolian holdings by L. S. Puchkovskii,
>> "Sobranie mongol'skikh rukopisei i ksilografov Instituta vostokovedeniia
>> Akademii nauk SSSR," *Uchenye zapiski Instituta vostokovedeniia AN SSSR*
>> 9 (1954):90-127.

Persian and Tadzhik Manuscripts

-70. Akimushkin, O. F., and Iu. E. Borshchevskii.
"Materialy dlia bibliografii rabot o persidskikh rukopisiakh." In *Narody Azii i Afriki*
3 (1963):165-74; 6 (1963):228-41.
> The first part of this article (see A-31) provides a bibliography of the
> published catalogs and descriptive literature regarding the Institute's Persian
> manuscripts. See also A-30.

-71. [Akademiia nauk SSSR. Institut narodov Azii.]
Persidskie i tadzhikskie rukopisi Instituta narodov Azii AN SSSR (Kratkii alfavitnyi katalog). Compiled by N. D. Miklukho-Maklai et al. Edited by N. D.
Miklukho-Maklai. 2 vols. Moscow: Izd-vo "Nauka," 1964. 633 p.
[DLC-Z6621.A34.P4; MH-OL35003.145.5]

-72. [Akademiia nauk SSSR. Institut vostokovedeniia.]
Opisanie tadzhikskikh i persidskikh rukopisei Instituta vostokovedeniia.
[DLC-Z6621.M843.T3; MH-OL35003.145]
> Vol. 1: *Geograficheskie sochineniia.* Compiled by N. D. Miklukho-Maklai. Edited
> by V. I. Beliaev and D. I. Tikhonov. Moscow/Leningrad: Izd-vo AN SSSR, 1955.
> 106 p.

[Akademiia nauk SSSR. Institut vostokovedeniia.]
Opisanie tadzhikskikh i persidskikh rukopisei Instituta narodov Azii.
> Vol. 2: *Biograficheskie sochineniia.* Compiled by N. D. Miklukho-Maklai. Edited
> by I. A. Orbeli and V. I. Beliaev. Moscow: Izd-vo vostochnoi literatury, 1961.
> 168 p.
> Vol. 3: *Istoricheskie sochineniia* is on press.

[Akademiia nauk SSSR. Institut vostokovedeniia.]
Opisanie persidskikh i tadzhikskikh rukopisei Instituta narodov Azii.

Vol. 4: *Persidskie tolkovye slovari (farkhangi)*. Compiled by S. I. Baevskii. Edited by A. N. Boldyrev. Moscow: Izd-vo vostochnoi literatury, 1962. 79 p.

[Akademiia nauk SSSR. Institut narodov Azii.]
Opisanie persidskikh i tadzhikskikh rukopisei.
Vol. 5: *Dvuiazychnye slovari*. Compiled by S. I. Baevskii. Moscow: Izd-vo "Nauka," 1968. 103 p.

Syriac Manuscripts

C-73. Pigulevskaia, N. V.
Katalog siriiskikh rukopisei Leningrada. Published as *Palestinskii sbornik*, vol. 6 (69). Moscow/Leningrad: Izd-vo AN SSSR, 1960. 230 p.
[DLC-D532.5.P3; MH-Asia9202.13]
> Also covers manuscripts in the State Public Library (GPB) in Leningrad, see F-48.

Tangut Manuscripts

C-74. [Akademiia nauk SSSR. Institut narodov Azii.]
Tangutskie rukopisi i ksilografy. Spisok otozhdestvlennykh i opredelennykh tangutskikh rukopisei i ksilografov kollektsii Instituta narodov Azii AN SSSR. Compiled by Z. I. Gorbacheva and E. I. Kychanov. Moscow: Izd-vo vostochnoi literatury, 1963. 171 p.
[DLC-Z6605.T4.A4; MH-OL64100.4]
> See also the general survey of Tangut holdings by Z. I. Gorbacheva, "Tangutskie rukopisi i ksilografy Instituta vostokovedeniia Akademii nauk SSSR," *Uchenye zapiski Instituta vostokovedeniia AN SSSR* 9 (1954):67-89.

Turkic Manuscripts

C-75. Dmitrieva, Liudmila Vasil'evna.
Opisanie tiurkskikh rukopisei Instituta narodov Azii. Compiled by L. V. Dmitrieva, A. M. Muginov, and S. N. Muratov. Edited by A. N. Kononov. Moscow: Izd-vo "Nauka," 1965. 258 p. [AN SSSR. Institut narodov Azii] .
[DLC-Z6621.A34.T83; MH-OL30003.260]

Uigur Manuscripts

C-76. Muginov, Abdulladzhan Muginovich.
Opisanie uigurskikh rukopisei Instituta narodov Azii. Moscow: Izd-vo vostochnoi literatury, 1962. 207 p. [AN SSSR. Institut narodov Azii] .
[DLC-Z6621.A325; MH-2226.8.665] .

7. ARKHIV GEOGRAFICHESKOGO OBSHCHESTVA AKADEMII NAUK SSSR (AGO AN SSSR)

[Archive of the Geographical Society of the Academy of Sciences of the USSR]
Address: Leningrad, tsentr., per. Grivtsova, 10

CONTENTS

The archive of the Geographical Society, although a relatively small and special-ized repository, is one of the oldest Academy archives; it dates back to 1845, when it was founded as a special archive of the Imperial Geographical Society in St. Petersburg. It now contains approximately 95 fonds and 115 sections [*razriady*] with over 50,000 storage units. About 65 of the fonds contain the papers of members of the society; these include P. K. Kozlov, N. N. Miklukho-Maklai, N. M. Przheval'skii, and N. I. Vavilov. Other fonds consist of a wide variety of geo-graphical documentary materials regarding different regions. Documents in the archive date from the sixteenth century to the present, although the largest pro-portion is from the late nineteenth century.

WORKING CONDITIONS

There is a small reading room for manuscript materials next to the archive office on the top floor of the building which has traditionally housed the Geographical Society. The archive has admitted a number of scholars from many foreign coun-tries. Comprehensive catalogs and published literature about the materials are avail-able in the reading room.

PUBLISHED DESCRIPTIONS

C-77. [Akademiia nauk SSSR. Geograficheskoe obshchestvo.]
Russkie geografy i puteshestvenniki. Fondy arkhiva Geograficheskogo obshchestva.
Compiled by T. P. Matveeva, T. S. Filonovich, and L. I. Iarukova. Leningrad: Izd-vo "Nauka," 1971. 175 p.
[no US location reported]
> This recently published guide surveys the 64 personal fonds in the Archive of the Geographical Society, giving pertinent details about the contents of each. Appendices give the contents of smaller personal fonds not described in the guide, a list of the fonds from organizations or institutions, and a list of the documentary collections [*razriady*] described in more detail in the inventory below (C-78). An introductory article surveys publications about the archive and another chronicles its history. This survey largely repeats the material found in the article by T. P. Matveeva, "Arkhiv Geograficheskogo obshchestva za 50 let i perspektivy ego dal'neishei raboty," in *Akademicheskie arkhivy SSSR za 50 let sovetskoi vlasti* (C-1), pp. 265-73, and the earlier article by B. A. Val'skaia, "Iz istorii Uchenogo arkhiva

Geograficheskogo obshchestva SSSR," in *Strany i narody Vostoka* 3 (Moscow, 1964):198-205.

C-78. Zelenin, Dmitrii Konstantinovich.
Opisanie rukopisei Uchenogo arkhiva Imperatorskogo russkogo geograficheskogo obshchestva. 3 vols. Petrograd: Tipografiia A. V. Orlova, 1914-1916. 1279 p. [DLC-Z6621.G354.Z4; MH-Slav251.34]

> These comprehensive inventories of the materials in the Geographical Society archive at the time of the First World War cover a major and certainly one of the most important sections of the present archive. The documents described are organized by 35 guberniias with detailed descriptions of manuscripts from each. These volumes are still used as the most complete location aids for these original collections [*razriady*] from the prerevolutionary archive.

C-79. Droblenkova, N. F., and L. S. Shepeleva.
"Opisanie rukopisnogo sobraniia arkhiva Geograficheskogo obshchestva SSSR." In *Trudy otdeleniia drevnerusskoi literatury Instituta russkoi literatury* 13 (1957):561-68.

> Describes the over 150 medieval manuscript holdings in the archive which date from the sixteenth to the eighteenth century.

C-80. Vereiskii, N. G.
"O rukopisiakh po geologii i geomorfologii, khraniashchikhsia v arkhive Gosudarstvennogo geograficheskogo obshchestva." In *Izvestiia Gosudarstvennogo geograficheskogo obshchestva*, 1935, no. 5, pp. 611-24.

C-81 Zelenin, D. K.
"Obzor rukopisnykh materialov Uchenogo arkhiva Vsesoiuznogo geograficheskogo obshchestva o narodakh SSSR. I. Bashkiry, Besermiane, Bolgary, Vensy, Evrei, Kalmyki, Karely, Komi, Komi-Permiaki." *Sovetskaia etnografiia,* 1941, no. 4, pp. 193-205.

C-82. Zelenin, D. K.
"Obzor rukopisnykh materialov Uchenogo arkhiva Vsesoiuznogo geograficheskogo obshchestva o narodakh Pribaltiki (Latyshi, Litovtsy, Esty)." *Sovetskaia etnografiia*, 1947, nos. 6-7, pp. 254-74.

8. ARKHIV INSTITUTA ETNOGRAFII IMENI N. N. MIKLUKHO-MAKLAIA AKADEMII NAUK SSSR

[Archive of the N. N. Miklukho-Maklai Institute of Ethnography of the Academy of Sciences of the USSR]

Address: Leningrad, Universitetskaia naberezhnaia, 3

The Institute of Ethnography has relatively small and specialized archival holdings numbering some 7,500 storage units, mostly reports and other materials collected in the course of scientific expeditions of the institute and the personal fonds of institute members. Most of the collection postdates the Second World War, since the earlier materials have mostly been transferred to the folklore section of the Manuscript Division and the Phonographic Archive of the Institute of Russian Literature [Pushkinskii Dom]. The holdings now include over 150,000 photographs. They are richest in information about Siberia, but other areas of the USSR are also represented.

There is no published description of the contents.

9. LENINGRADSKOE OTDELENIE INSTITUTA ARKHEOLOGII AN SSSR (LOIA)

[Leningrad Branch of the Institute of Archeology of the Academy of Sciences of the USSR]
RUKOPISNYI ARKHIV [Manuscript Archive]
FOTOARKHIV [Photographic Archive]
    Address: Leningrad, D-41. Dvortsovaia naberezhnaia, 18

CONTENTS

The Academy's Institute of Archeology was founded after the Revolution on the basis of the Imperial Archeological Commission [Imperatorskaia arkheologicheskaia komissiia]. From 1919 to 1926 it was called the Russian Academy of the History of Material Culture [Rossiiskaia akademiia istorii material'noi kul'tury—RAIMK], which in 1926 was renamed the State Academy of the History of Material Culture [Gosudarstvennaia akademiia istorii material'noi kul'tury—GAIMK]. This academy was reorganized in 1937 and became the Institute of the History of Material Culture in the Name of N. Ia. Marr, under the Academy of Sciences [Institut istorii material'noi kul'tury imeni N. Ia. Marra AN SSSR—IIMK]. At that time a branch was established in Moscow, but the archival holdings remained in Leningrad. In 1945, the Moscow section became the main institute, and Leningrad was named the branch. In 1959, IIMK was renamed the Institute of Archeology.

Many of the archival materials were gathered before the Revolution when the Archeological Commission was involved in many forms of cultural activity. The manuscript holdings now include 67 fonds with about 55,000 storage units dating from 1820 to 1968: of these 45 are personal fonds of important archeologists and archivists. Institutional fonds and collections include those from the Russian Archeological Society (1841-1925) and the Moscow Archeological Society (1864-1920). There are many maps and plans as well as other records of archeological activities. Some archival holdings of the institute are now also concentrated in Moscow, particularly the post-Second World War materials relating to activities by the Moscow center.

The institute's extensive Photographic Archive was founded in 1919, and includes many prerevolutionary photographs collected by the Imperial Archeological Commission, the Archeological Institute, and Russian Archeological Society in St. Petersburg. There are also collections from several defunct institutions and numerous personal photographic collections. Not all the materials relate to archeology. The archive now contains over 411,000 photographs, including negatives, prints, slides, and a few films. An extensive card catalog covers the holdings.

PUBLISHED DESCRIPTION
Photographic Archive

C-83. Devel', T. M.

"Obozrenie kollektsii sobraniia fotoarkhiva Instituta istorii material'noi kul'tury im. N. Ia. Marra AN SSSR." *Sovetskaia arkheologiia*, 1950, no. 12, pp. 289-336. Includes a name and geographical index of the holdings which are now contained in the photographic archive of the Institute of Archeology as they were organized in 1950. This covers only about half of the present archive, since the collection totaled 240,000 units at that time.

10. INSTITUT RUSSKOGO IAZYKA AN SSSR (IRIaz)

[Institute of the Russian Language of the Academy of Sciences of the USSR]
RUKOPISNYI OTDEL [Manuscript Division]
   Address: Moscow, G-19, Volkhonka, 18/2

CONTENTS

   The Manuscript Division of the Institute of the Russian Language was organized in 1958 to house a very limited number of manuscripts and early printed books related to the linguistic activities of the institute. There are a number of personal fonds of individuals associated with the work of the institute, although some in this category have been transferred to the main archive of the Academy. There are a number of manuscript books and other texts dating from the fifteenth to the twentieth century. The institute also has many photographic copies of early manuscripts from the eleventh to the seventeenth century.

   Apart from the Manuscript Division, the institute also houses a number of extensive card files related to its various dictionary publications. These files naturally remain a fundamental source for many phases of Russian linguistic studies. There are also a number of sound recordings relating to linguistic studies, organized as a separate sound library; some of these linguistic materials are maintained in Leningrad.

PUBLISHED DESCRIPTION

C-84. [Akademiia nauk SSSR. Institut russkogo iazyka.]
   Lingvisticheskie istochniki. Fondy Instituta russkogo iazyka. Edited by S. I. Kotkov and A. I. Sumkina. Moscow: Izd-vo "Nauka," 1967. 319 p.
   [DLC-PG2074.A36]

   This volume of articles by various members of the institute covers the various linguistic card files which remain from earlier linguistic projects and from the preparation of several important dictionaries of the Russian language. A short section (pp. 244-52) describes the holdings of the Manuscript Division, including the personal fonds, manuscripts, and rare book collections.

PART D–SPECIAL ARCHIVES

PART D - SPECIAL ARCHIVES

Besides the archives and other manuscript repositories under the Academy of Sciences, there are several other archives of all-union importance that are outside the system of the Main Archival Administration. Covered in this part are those of the Communist Party of the Soviet Union, the Ministry of Foreign Affairs, the Ministry of Defense, and the all-union comprehensive film archive, Gosfil'mofond.

1. THE ARCHIVAL SYSTEM OF THE COMMUNIST PARTY OF THE SOVIET UNION

Just as the Communist Party organization generally parallels the organization of state government in the Soviet Union, so a system of Party archives has been developed paralleling state archives on all-union, republic, oblast, and other local administrative levels. Their administration and control are entirely under Party auspices; they accordingly remain completely independent of the state archival system and the Main Archival Administration, although a representative of the Party archival system sits on the Learned Council of GAU, and the Party archives participate in many joint publications and other activities in cooperation with GAU.

Aside from the Central Party Archive under the Institute of Marxism-Leninism in Moscow, the largest Party archives are the Leningrad branch, with over 3,610,000 storage units, and the local Moscow Party archive, with over 1,038,000 storage units, according to figures from the early 1960's. Other particularly large archives include those in Azerbaijan with 857,000, in Georgia with 802,000, in Sverdlovsk with 797,000, and in Novosibirsk with 770,000 storage units.

GENERAL BIBLIOGRAPHY

D-1. Maksakov, Vladimir Vasil'evich.
Organizatsiia arkhivov KPSS (Uchebnoe posobie). Edited by Iu. F. Kononov.
Moscow: MGIAI, 1968. 108 p.
[DLC-JN6598.K7M276]

> The most comprehensive coverage of the history and organization of the
> system of Party archives available, this pamphlet, prepared as a text for the
> archival training institute, gives a general, administratively oriented account;
> it does not, however, serve as an adequate reference aid for users of the
> archives. It is more complete than, and hence supersedes, the earlier article by
> A. A. Solov'ev, "O nekotorykh voprosakh komplektovaniia partiinykh
> arkhivov dokumental'nymi materialami," *Sovetskie arkhivy,* 1967, no. 2,
> pp. 63-70.

PART D – SPECIAL ARCHIVES

a. TsENTRAL'NYI PARTIINYI ARKHIV INSTITUTA MARKSIZMA-LENINIZMA PRI TsENTRAL'NOM KOMITETE KPSS (TsPA IML)

[Central Party Archive of the Institute of Marxism-Leninism of the Central Committee of the Communist Party of the Soviet Union]

Address: Moscow, I-256, Sel'skokhoziaistvennyi proezd, 4

HISTORY AND CONTENTS

The Central Party Archive of the Institute of Marxism-Leninism in Moscow is undoubtedly the single most important archive for the historian or political scientist analyzing almost all phases of life and development of the Soviet Union. Although it will probably remain the most difficult of access to any foreign scholars, especially those not members of the Communist Party, a brief description of its history and contents merits inclusion here.

As currently constituted, the Central Party Archive is an outgrowth of three earlier institutions, and its organization is still determined by their contents: 1) the holdings of the early Institute for History of the Party and the October Revolution (Istpart) and other Party records retained separately; 2) the collection from the original Marx-Engels Institute; and 3) the Lenin Archive.

The Institute for the History of the Party and the October Revolution (Istpart) was established in 1920, and among other activities was empowered to collect documents and published materials relating to the Communist Party and the October Revolution. At the same time, the Archive of the October Revolution [Arkhiv Oktiabr'skoi revoliutsii–AOR] was established, by Lenin's decree, to house all the materials relating to the Revolution, including specifically Party files. Administratively considered the Fourth Division of the State Archive of the RSFSR [IV-e otdelenie Gosudarstvennogo arkhiva RSFSR], this archive was also associated with the Moscow division of the eighth section of the Single State Archival Fond that had originally been organized as a gathering point for many types of printed documentary materials relating to the Revolution. A special division of the archive was set up under the auspices of Istpart for documents relating to the Communist Party. Other Party records were carefully guarded in other storage areas; in 1924, a separate current Party archive was set up in the Kremlin Palace.

A separate Institute of Marx and Engels, established under Party control in 1922, developed a documentary repository for materials relating to Marx and Engels. By the end of 1923, the newly formed Lenin Institute was empowered to gather documents relating to the life and work of V. I. Lenin; this collection was formally established as the Lenin Archive after his death in 1924.

In 1928 the Lenin Institute and the institute of Party history (Istpart) were combined and their archives amalgamated into a Single Party Archive [Edinyi partiinyi arkhiv–EPA], and many of the fonds from the earlier Archive of the October Revolution relating to Party history were transferred there.

Following the formal establishment in 1931 of the Institute of Marx, Engels, and Lenin, a further step in consolidating Party archival materials took place with the formation of the Central Party Archive [Tsentral'nyi Partiinyi arkhiv–TsPA] under

Institute auspices. The archival holdings of the earlier three separate institutions, gradually brought together, augmented by subsequent acquisitions, and thoroughly cataloged in the Central Party Archive, still constitute its three major divisions.

The first division is devoted to the manuscripts and papers of Marx and Engels, either original manuscripts or photocopies from other archives abroad (classified as fond no. 1). These materials have been the basis for massive publication projects, historical studies, and textual criticism under institute sponsorship.

A second major division developed from the original Lenin Archive is devoted to the documentary materials of and pertaining to Lenin. This has become the official center for Lenin studies and the official repository for all the papers of or relating to the great Bolshevik leader. Again, as in the case of Marx and Engels, these materials have been subjected to the greatest possible scholarly and political scrutiny, and a large proportion of them have been published.

TsPA fond no. 2 is devoted to the papers of Lenin himself, including manuscripts of his published works, letters, and other documents, which now total over 30,000 items. Other fonds consist of the papers of members of his family, biographical materials regarding him, including a large collection of letters addressed to him, memoir accounts of him, and other documents relating to his life and activities before, during, and after the Revolution. When it has not been possible to acquire the originals, the archive has obtained photocopies of documents of and about Lenin from archives throughout the Soviet Union and from other parts of the world. The archive also has about four hundred different photographs of Lenin, and a considerable amount of film and sound recordings of his activities and speeches. (For details about the Lenin archive, see D-3.)

A third division of TsPA contains Party records. Separate sections house records of various prerevolutionary activities and publications and documents pertaining to the 1917 October Revolution; it should be noted that many important materials from the year 1917 are to be found in the Leningrad branch of the Party archive. Large sections cover developments during the immediate postrevolutionary years and the Civil War, successive Party congresses, and the records of the Party Central Committee from the time of the Revolution. Fonds are organized along the lines of Party organization. Special Comintern fonds include the records of the successive Communist Internationals. Special fonds relate to foreign Communist parties and contain documents regarding different international socialist movements.

Besides institutional and organizational fonds, the Central Party Archive contains a large number of personal fonds of important Party leaders.

In addition to manuscript materials, the archive includes a large quantity of pictorial documents, films, recordings of speeches, etc., and miscellaneous other materials relating to Party history.

WORKING CONDITIONS

Since its establishment, the Party archive has generally remained closed to foreign scholars and, with few exceptions, to non-members of the Communist Party.

PART D – SPECIAL ARCHIVES

PUBLISHED DESCRIPTIONS

There is no published guide or general directory to the Party archive, and the only available survey listed below is somewhat dated. Aside from the treatment in the general text on Party archives listed above (D-1), a short history of its early development can be found in the article by N. S. Komarov, "K istorii Instituta Lenina i Tsentral'nogo partiinogo arkhiva (1919-1931 gg.)," *Voprosy istorii*, 1956, no. 10, pp. 181-91.

The pre-World War II work of collecting and publishing documents under the Party archive is discussed by T. V. Ivnitskaia in the article, "Arkheograficheskaia deiatel'nost' Instituta Marksa-Engel'sa-Lenina v predvoennye gody," *Trudy MGIAI* 15 (1962):52-80. More recent publication activities are covered by V. V. Anikeev, "O publikatorskoi rabote partiinykh arkhivov," *Voprosy arkhivovedeniia*, 1962, no. 1, pp. 9-16.

D-2. Struchkov, A. A.
"Tsentral'nyi partiinyi arkhiv Instituta Marksizma-Leninizma pri TsK KPSS."
Istoricheskii arkhiv, 1956, no. 4, pp. 188-200.
> The most extensive although now somewhat dated general survey of the most important fonds in the three main divisions of the Central Party Archive. This article is more informative in terms of the holdings than the later one by the same author, "Partiinye arkhivy i ikh rol' v razrabotke istorii KPSS," *Istoricheskii arkhiv*, 1958, no. 6, pp. 162-70.

D-3. Akhapkin, Iu. A.
"Organizatsiia Leninskogo arkhiva." *Voprosy istorii*, 1970, no. 3, pp. 52-65.
> An up-to-date description of the history and contents of the fonds of and relating to Lenin in the Central Party Archive. See also the earlier coverage by T. V. Shepeleva, "Nauchnaia obrabotka i khranenie dokumentov V. I. Lenina v Tsentral'nom partiinom arkhive Instituta marksizma-leninizma pri TsK KPSS." *Istoricheskii arkhiv*, 1961, no. 2, pp. 169-80.

D-4. Grebennikov, M. V., and L. N. Fomicheva.
"Kino-foto-fonodokumenty o V. I. Lenine v Tsentral'nom partiinom arkhive."
Istoricheskii arkhiv, 1960, no. 2, pp. 195-201.

D-5. Kuznetsov, N. I.
"Obzor dokumental'nykh materialov fondov gazet 'Vpered' i 'Proletarii.' "
Istoricheskii arkhiv, 1959, no. 3, pp. 195-99.

D-6. Vorob'eva, O. B.
"Obzor dokumentov Eleonory Marks-Eveling." *Istoricheskii arkhiv*, 1958, no. 2, pp. 185-90.

D-7. Dridzo, V. S.
"Istoriia sozdaniia i kratkii obzor dokumentov fondov N. K. Krupskoi."
Istoricheskii arkhiv, 1960, no. 2, pp. 179-85.

D-8. New acquisitions to the Party archive are summarized periodically in the journal *Voprosy istorii KPSS.* For example, see the following issues since 1958:

1958, no. 2, pp. 217-21.	1963, no. 2, pp. 117-21.
1959, no. 2, pp. 191-95.	1964, no. 3, pp. 114-18.
1960, no. 2, pp. 202-07.	1965, no. 2, pp. 150-55.
1961, no. 3, pp. 164-70.	1966, no. 4, pp. 138-41.
1962, no. 3, pp. 217-22.	1968, no. 3, pp. 150-56.

OTHER LOCAL PARTY ARCHIVES

D-9. Iudin, G. V.

"Partiinyi arkhiv Instituta istorii partii MK i MGK KPSS." *Istoricheskii arkhiv*, 1958, no. 5, pp. 228-31.

Surveys the holdings of the Moscow Party archive which in 1958 contained 1,038,653 storage units.

b. TsENTRAL'NYI ARKHIV VSESOIUZNOGO LENINSKOGO KOMMUNISTI-CHESKOGO SOIUZA MOLODEZHI (TsA VLKSM)

[Central Archive of the All-Union Lenin Communist Youth League]

CONTENTS

Komsomol documents are retained in their own separate archive, although these materials generally fall under Party control. The central holdings include 300,000 storage units; in addition there are local-level fonds retaining Komsomol records throughout the Soviet Union, although in some areas they are amalgamated with the local Party archives.

PUBLISHED DESCRIPTION

-10. Krivoruchenko, V. K.

"Vazhnyi istoricheskii istochnik." *Sovetskie arkhivy*, 1968, no. 4, pp. 16-23.

Describes the archives housing the Komsomol records not only in the Central Archive in Moscow, but also throughout the USSR.

2. ARCHIVES UNDER THE FOREIGN MINISTRY OF THE USSR

The Foreign Ministry is another key high-level governmental organ whose archives are outside the centralized system of state archives. A special archival administration for the Foreign Ministry was first established after the Second World War. Known under its present name since 1958, the Historical-Diplomatic Administration of the Foreign Ministry of the USSR [Istoriko-diplomaticheskoe upravlenie MID SSSR] runs its own archives quite independently of the Main Archival Administration, although the two archival administrations exchange representatives on their "scientific councils."

Before World War II, the so-called Political Archive of the Foreign Ministry [Politicheskii arkhiv MID SSSR] housed postrevolutionary diplomatic records, while earlier diplomatic files remained in other state archives under the control of the Main Archival Administration. But in 1946 all the official diplomatic records going back to the reign of Peter the Great also came under the control of the Foreign Ministry, and a separate prerevolutionary Foreign Ministry archive was established. Thus there are now two archives under the administration of the Foreign Ministry, the contemporary Archive of Foreign Policy of the USSR [Arkhiv vneshnei politiki SSSR], housing postrevolutionary diplomatic records in the main Foreign Ministry building, and a separate historical repository for prerevolutionary records, the Archive of Russian Foreign Policy [Arkhiv vneshnei politiki Rossii].

a. ARKHIV VNESHNEI POLITIKI SSSR (AVP SSSR)

[Archive of Foreign Policy of the USSR]
    Address: Moscow, Smolenskaia ploshchad', 32/34

CONTENTS

As its name implies, the Archive of Foreign Policy of the USSR contains the official records of the Soviet Foreign Ministry since 1917. Following general Soviet archival practice, the documents are organized according to the organization of the ministry itself. This archive contains copies of all diplomatic and consular correspondence with missions abroad and with foreign missions in the Soviet Union, and communications with other branches of domestic government and administration. Party files relating to foreign policy and the Comintern are retained separately in the Central Party Archive, although copies of Party directives to the ministry would presumably be retained in this archive. The extensive publication series now in progress from this archive, so far covering 1917 to 1933, gives a sample of its contents: *Dokumenty vneshnei politiki SSSR*, 16 vols. (Moscow: Izd-vo politicheskoi literatury, 1957-1970).

WORKING CONDITIONS

This archive remains entirely closed to Western scholars, although there has been very limited access to certain files for selected researchers from Communist-bloc countries.

b. ARKHIV VNESHNEI POLITIKI ROSSII (AVPR)

[Archive of Russian Foreign Policy]
    Address: Moscow, Bol'shaia Serpukhovskaia ulitsa, 15

HISTORY AND CONTENTS

The Archive of Russian Foreign Policy, like its contemporary counterpart, contains the official diplomatic records of the Russian Empire, in this case dating from 1721 until 1917. They are organized in several divisions, generally reflecting their origin or the original archive in which they were kept. These include a special division for original treaties, a division housing the records of the eighteenth-century College of Foreign Affairs, and several divisions housing nineteenth- and early twentieth-century records of the Ministry of Foreign Affairs.

Original treaties and similar official state acts are housed separately from the other diplomatic records in special high-security vaults. Almost all of these documents from prerevolutionary years have been published or are available elsewhere in the archive in working copies.

The eighteenth-century division of AVPR consists of the documents from the prerevolutionary Moscow Main Archive of the Ministry of Foreign Affairs [Moskovskii glavnyi arkhiv Ministerstva inostrannykh del], which had remained a depository for official diplomatic documents until the early 1830's. The archive was founded at the time of the establishment of the College of Foreign Affairs in 1720 and took over the records of the earlier office that handled Russian foreign relations, the Posol'skii Prikaz, or Prikaz of Ambassadors, whose archive had the richest documentary repository of pre-Petrine Russia, and the records of several other defunct prikazy from the sixteenth and seventeenth centuries. The eighteenth-century Moscow Archive of the College of Foreign Affairs [Moskovskii arkhiv Kollegii inostrannykh del] remained one of the most important state archives of the period, particularly under the direction of the historian Georg Friedrich Müller and later of N. N. Bantysh-Kamenskii.

After the formation of the Ministry of Foreign Affairs at the time of the administrative reform of 1802, the Moscow archive developed into a purely historical repository, although some diplomatic records continued to be transferred to it from St. Petersburg until the early 1830's. After the Revolution, this archive was amalgamated into the ancient section or Drevlekhranilishche of the Moscow division of the Central Historical Archive, which in 1931 was officially named the State Archive of the Feudal-Serfdom Epoch [Gosudarstvennyi arkhiv feodal'no-krepostnicheskoi epokhi–GAFKE]; in 1941 its name was changed to the Central State Archive of Ancient Acts [Tsentral'nyi gosudarstvennyi arkhiv drevnikh aktov], or TsGADA. Following the Second World War, when the Foreign Ministry formed its own archival administration and took over all prerevolutionary diplomatic records, the fonds pertaining to foreign relations during the eighteenth century that were housed in TsGADA were split and those sections postdating 1720 were transferred to the newly formed AVPR (the sections transferred as described in the 1946 TsGADA guidebook are listed under D-11 below); the earlier records from the archive of the Posol'skii Prikaz and other eighteenth-century files which had been part of the prerevolutionary Moscow MID archive still remain in TsGADA (see Part B, section 6). The general arrangement of these fonds has not been changed since their transfer to AVPR, and the original manuscript inventories (*opisi*) are still used for the identification of individual items.

The nineteenth- and early twentieth-century records now in AVPR fall into three major divisions according to where they had been deposited before the Revolution: 1) holdings of the former St. Petersburg Main Archive of the Ministry of Foreign Affairs [Sankt-Peterburgskii glavnyi arkhiv Ministerstva inostannykh del]; 2) records that had been retained in the chancellery of the Foreign Ministry itself in St. Petersburg; and 3) the archives of different Russian missions abroad.

The St. Petersburg Main Archive of the Ministry of Foreign Affairs was established in the ministerial building in 1834; soon afterwards, many of the records postdating the 1802 formation of the ministry became part of this archive; however, those records that had already been placed in the Moscow archive (and a few files were sent to Moscow dating from as late as the early 1830's) were never moved back to St. Petersburg, and some of the most important diplomatic records were retained in the ministerial chancellery. The archive came under common administration with the State Archive of the Russian Empire [Gosudarstvennyi arkhiv Rossiiskoi imperii] in 1864, and it continued to be the depository for diplomatic records through 1885, after which date almost all files were retained in the chancellery.

Constituted as part of the Second Division of the State Archive of the Russian Federation [Gosarkhiv RSFSR] in 1920, the contents of this archive (parts of it had been evacuated from Petrograd at the time of the Revolution), along with the records that had remained in the chancellery of the Foreign Ministry (see below), were all transferred to Moscow in 1923 and stored in their present location, the building of which had previously been a famous pawn-shop. As a separate repository under the Moscow division of the Central Historical Archive [Moskovskii tsentral'nyi istoricheskii arkhiv], all these nineteenth- and early twentieth-century diplomatic records became part of the Archive of the Revolution and Foreign Policy [Arkhiv revoliutsii i vneshnei politiki]. When this archive was split into two separate archives, although still within the same building, in 1934, the diplomatic records constituted the State Archive of Foreign Policy [Gosudarstvennyi arkhiv vneshnei politiki] under the administration of the all-union state archival administration. With the 1941 archival reorganization this archive became part of the Central State Historical Archive in Moscow [Tsentral'nyi gosudarstvennyi istoricheskii arkhiv v g. Moskve—TsGIAM].

Five years later these records were removed from TsGIAM. When in 1946 the Foreign Ministry took charge of all post-1720 diplomatic records, these files became part of AVPR. Despite these many administrative changes, the records themselves have remained stored in the same location since their arrival in Moscow in 1923, and their internal arrangement has not been changed.

According to the original organization of the St. Petersburg Main Archive of the Ministry of Foreign Affairs, these nineteenth-century diplomatic documents are divided into five basic sections or *razriady*:

> *Razriad I.* Documents of a political character, including correspondence re-
> garding the relations of Russia with the states of the Far East, Near East,
> and the Balkans;
> *Razriad II.* Records of relations with foreign missions in Russia, and records
> of general relations with states of Asia, Europe, and America;
> *Razriad III.* Documents relating to appointments, remuneration, and
> rewards;
> *Razriad IV.* Documents relating to personnel questions;
> *Razriad V.* Records of diplomatic and consular organs of Russia in Turkey
> and in the Balkans, and of missions in Peking, Tokyo, and Tehran.

As can be seen from this plan, the organization did not always follow the structure of the ministry, and often involved some overlapping and confusion; because catalogs and earlier publications had been prepared according to this plan, no attempt has as yet been made to reorganize the documents according to contemporary archival practice.

Another main division of AVPR consists of the records which were retained in the chancellery of the Foreign Ministry during the nineteenth century and the entire body of post-1885 records that had never been transferred to the archive. Since their transfer from Petrograd to Moscow in 1923, these records have remained in the same location and have been subject to the same administration as those from the former St. Petersburg Main Archive as described above. These documents have also been retained in their original organization (although some sections have been now classified into separate fonds) with four basic divisions:

> 1) The chancellery papers [*Fond kantseliarii*] are organized chronologically
> by year with subdivisions for different expeditions (i.e., to different diplo-
> matic posts) and for incoming and outgoing correspondence;
> 2) The Asiatic Department records are subdivided by different *stoly* [desks],
> as the working divisions were called in the nineteenth century;
> 3) The records of the Ministry's Department of Internal Communications com-
> prise files pertaining to the relations of the Foreign Ministry with other
> ministries such as trade and commerce, and those from its judicial and
> ecclesiastical sections and its press and information division;

4) The administrative records of the ministry contain the files from the Ministry's Department of Personnel and Administration.

A final major division of AVPR comprises the records of Russian embassies, consulates, and various other missions abroad. For the most part these had been retained in the country where they were located. Since the Revolution most of the prerevolutionary Russian embassy archives have been recovered, although in countries with which the Soviet Union has not had continuous diplomatic relations, as, for example, in Spain, negotiations have never been concluded for their return to Moscow.

Although most of the official prerevolutionary diplomatic documents are to be found in AVPR, some have found their way into other repositories. For example, the holdings of the former State Archive of the Russian Empire, which are now located in TsGADA (see Part B, section 6), include several sections with high-level diplomatic documents that had originally come from the Foreign Ministry chancellery in the early nineteenth century; these have all been retained according to their original archival organization. Many of the records of foreign trade also contain some diplomatic papers; for the eighteenth century these are mostly retained in TsGADA, while those of the nineteenth and early twentieth centuries are housed in TsGIA SSSR in Leningrad. It should also be noted that, in a period of relatively lax archival practices, foreign ministers or other high officials of the ministry often retained official documents or drafts and copies of official documents among their own personal papers; these have now found their way into a variety of archives, some in the Soviet Union and others abroad. Furthermore, many official diplomatic papers, or copies of them, also are to be found in the archives of the foreign offices of other nations, particularly in the case of those of the major powers with whom Russia conducted diplomatic relations.

Because the records of other foreign powers are so important to the study of Russian diplomatic history, the Soviet Foreign Ministry Archival Administration has been interested in exchange projects that have led to the acquisition and exchange of microfilms with several different repositories. For example, an exchange negotiated with the Swedish state archives brought Swedish microfilms to AVPR and has made available in Sweden some limited films from AVPR pertaining to early Russo-Swedish relations. A similar exchange has been effected with the State Archives of Denmark. And as a lesser example, a small exchange was arranged between AVPR and the Massachusetts Historical Society in connection with the publication of the Adams Papers, involving documents relating to John Quincy Adams' ministry in Russia in the early nineteenth century.

WORKING CONDITIONS

As is the case with foreign office archives in many countries of the world, admission is more selective and research conditions are more difficult than in most other archives. In recent years, however, a few foreign scholars from a number of countries have been admitted for research in AVPR. Preference has in many cases been given to selected scholars from Communist-bloc nations working on problems connected with their own nations' relations with Russia; relatively few Western scholars have been granted access.

Access has been somewhat easier in the case of the eighteenth-century division which had been transferred from TsGADA and AVPR. Use of these documents is facilitated by their published description in the first volume of the 1946 guide to TsGADA (D-11). Scholars working in the first quarter of the nineteenth century are likely to find documents tied up in the hands of the editing commission working on the major documentary publication project for this period (*Vneshniaia politika Rossii XIX i nachala XX veka. Dokumenty rossiiskogo Ministerstva inostrannykh del,* Series I, vols. 1-7 [Moscow: Gosudarstvennoe izd-vo politicheskoi literatury, 1960-1970]); there appears to be considerable reluctance to permit open research in documents not chosen for inclusion or immediately related to the documents included in the publications.

Foreign scholars work in the large archival reading room together with their Soviet colleagues. Card catalogs are not open for public consultation and shelf-lists or prerevolutionary handwritten inventories (*opisi*) are not available for use. Ordinarily, researchers must rely on the archival staff to choose documents; in many cases, only limited files or portions thereof have been available.

Microfilm facilities are available in AVPR, but arrangements are often time-consuming; preference is sometimes given to microfilm exchange arrangements rather than cash transactions.

PUBLISHED DESCRIPTIONS AND CATALOGS

There is no general guide or published description of AVPR, nor is there a complete bibliography of various earlier catalogs and documentary publications from the fonds now located there. However, several publications prepared when its contents were housed in previous locations will still be of some help to researchers.

Eighteenth-Century Documents from the former Moscow Main Archive of the Ministry (before 1802, College) of Foreign Affairs.

The most extensive prerevolutionary description of this archive occurs in a subsection of the chapter on prerevolutionary state archives by V. S. Ikonnikov, "Moskovskii arkhiv Ministerstva inostrannykh del," in *Opyt russkoi istoriografii* (A-83), vol. 1, part 1, pp. 386-413. There is also a brief description of the archive together with an elaborate collection of engravings published at the end of the nineteenth century: [Russia. Ministerstvo inostrannykh del. Moskovskii glavnyi arkhiv.], *Moskovskii glavnyi arkhiv Ministerstva inostrannykh del. Vidy arkhiva i snimki khraniashchikhsia v nem dokumentov, rukopisei i pechatei* (Moscow: Tipografiia G. Lisnera i A. Geshelia, 1898; 8 p. + 23 plates [DLC-Yudin CD1719.M6.1898]); a French edition published simultaneously, *Les archives principales de Moscou du Ministère des affaires étrangères,* is available in the New York Public Library. The prerevolutionary serial publication of the archive, *Sbornik Moskovskogo glavnogo arkhiva Ministerstva inostrannykh del* (7 volumes of which were published in the 1880's), contains several articles about different parts of the archive, including a French commentary, "Renseignements sur les archives de Russie," in volume 1 (1880):2-49, with tables covering some of the categories of foreign office holdings. The most recent treatment of the history of the archive by G. A. Dremina, "Moskovskii arkhiv Kollegii inostrannykh del," in the pamphlet *Iz istorii Tsentral'nogo gosudarstvennogo arkhiva drevnikh aktov SSSR* (see B-75), pp. 23-69, may also prove of some interest to researchers. For more general information and bibliography about this archive, see the section on TsGADA in Part B.

D-11. [Russia (1923-USSR). Tsentral'nyi gosudarstvennyi arkhiv drevnikh aktov.]
Tsentral'nyi gosudarstvennyi arkhiv drevnikh aktov. Putevoditel'. Part 1. Compiled by V. N. Shumilov et al. Edited by S. K. Bogoiavlenskii. Moscow: GAU, 1946. 363 p.
[DLC-CD 1713.A53; MH-Slav610.40]

    This first volume of the general guide to TsGADA (see above, B-70), gives a description of the fonds from the former Moscow Main Archive of the Ministry of Foreign Affairs. After the publication of this guide in 1946, the fonds containing the eighteenth-century records of the College of Foreign Affairs were split up, and the post-1720 records (the College was established in 1720) were transferred to AVPR. As described in pages 22-80, those that were split with post-1720 parts transferred include (in this order) fonds numbered 32, 35, 50, 53, 58, 79, 93, 97, 96, 51, 367, 61, 55, 67, 74, 76, 84, 41, 78, 88, 52, 66, 68, 59, 86, 95, 103, 56, 126, 62, 77, 89; as described on pages 100-101, fonds 369, 155, and 167. Those transferred intact to AVPR, as described on pages 25-80, include fonds numbered 33, 36, 54, 80, 195, 209, 72, 73, 200, 94, 87, 37, 38, 91, 39, 42-45, 47, 83, 75, 71, 92, 48, 49, 70, 60, 85, 81, 57, 69, 378, 105, 90, 34, 65, and 174; as described on pages 98-101, fonds 172, 99, 374, 173, and 157. The guide also lists publications and other descriptive literature relevant to these documents.

D-12. Bantysh-Kamenskii, N. N.
Obzor vneshnikh snoshenii Rossii (po 1800 god).
    Vol. 1: (*Avstriia, Angliia, Vengriia, Gollandiia, Daniia, Ispaniia*). Moscow: Tipografiia E. Lissnera i Iu. Romana, 1894. 303 p.
    Vol. 2: (*Germaniia i Italiia*). Moscow: Tipografiia E. Lissnera i. Iu. Romana, 1896. 271 p.
    Vol. 3: (*Kurliandiia, Lifliandiia, Estliandiia, Finliandiia, Pol'sha i Portugaliia*). Moscow: Tipografiia E. Lissnera i Iu. Romana, 1897. 319 p.
    Vol. 4: (*Prussiia, Frantsiia i Shvetsiia*). Moscow: Tipografiia G. Lissnera i A. Geshelia, 1902. 463 p.
[MH-Slav778.1; MH-L]

    These volumes, although not technically archival catalogs, provide detailed descriptions of the diplomatic records most of which for the years after 1721 are in AVPR; they were prepared (but never published) at the beginning of the nineteenth century by the then director of the Moscow archive, under the title "Sokrashchennoe izvestie o vzaimnykh mezhdu Rossiiskimi monarkhami i evropeiskimi dvorami posol'stvakh, perepiskakh i dogovorakh, khraniashchikhsia v Gosudarstvennoi kollegii inostrannykh del v Moskovskom arkhive s 1481 po 1801 god." Listed also as item B-76.

Documents from the former St. Petersburg Main Archive of the Ministry of Foreign Affairs

There is no archival guide or description covering this division of AVPR, but a short article written in 1938, when it was a separate archive, tells about its organization after the Revolution: A. Iur'ev, "Gosudarstvennyi arkhiv vneshnei politiki i ego politicheskoe znachenie," *Arkhivnoe delo* 47 (1938, no. 3): 116-24. See also the earlier description of this part of the archive when it was combined with the Archive of the Revolution: V. Maksakov, "Arkhiv revoliutsii i vneshnei politiki XIX i XX vv.," *Arkhivnoe delo* 13 (1927):27-41.

D-13. Golder, Frank A.
Guide to Materials for American History in Russian Archives. Publication No. 239 of the Carnegie Institution of Washington.
    Vol. 1: Washington, 1917. 177 p.
    Vol. 2: Washington, 1937. 65 p.
[DLC-CD1718.U6G6; MH-US63.23RR3621.58]
    This publication, described in more detail as item A-46 above, covers documents from the Foreign Ministry archives relating to America; vol. 1, pp. 15-115, covers the years 1783-1853; vol. 2, pp. 1-65, covers the years 1854-1870.

D-14. Goriainov, Sergei M.
1812: Dokumenty Gosudarstvennogo i S.-Peterburgskogo glavnogo arkhivov.
Published by the Ministry of Foreign Affairs. 2 parts in 1 vol. St. Petersburg:
Tipografiia M. A. Aleksandrova, 1912. 562 p. and 182 p.
[MH-L]
    A complete inventory for the documents from 1812 found in the State Archive of the Russian Empire and the St. Petersburg Main Archive of the Ministry of Foreign Affairs. The second part includes selected documents, and a full index.

3. ARKHIV MINISTERSTVA OBORONY SSSR

[Archive of the Ministry of Defense of the USSR]
Address: Moskovskaia oblast', g. Podol'sk, Varshavskoe shosse, 9a

CONTENTS

Although a large percentage of pre-World War II records of the Soviet armed forces, especially the voluminous files of the Red Army during the Civil War and the 1920's, have now been deposited in the Central State Archive of the Soviet Army, TsGASA (see above Part B, section 3), the Ministry of Defense maintains its own independent archive in the town of Podol'sk outside of Moscow.

Most significantly, this archive was constructed to house and administer the voluminous records of the Second World War, and is closely tied in with the official military history projects.

Although it is projected that this archive will eventually become part of TsGASA, for the present and foreseeable future, it remains independent of the Main Archival Administration under the complete control of the Ministry of Defense.

PUBLISHED DESCRIPTIONS

D-15. Rubenkov, G. I.
"Opisanie materialov v Arkhive Ministerstva oborony SSSR." *Voprosy arkhivovedeniia*, 1963, no. 3, pp. 75-78.

> Discusses the work being done to inventory the voluminous documentary legacy of the Second World War.

4. GOSFIL'MOFOND (GFF)

[State Film Archive]
   Address: Moskovskaia oblast', stantsiia Belye Stolby

CONTENTS

Started in 1948, Gosfil'mofond is a centralized repository for the collection and storage of all the artistic, popular science, and other feature films and shorts produced in the Soviet Union. First established under the name All-Union State Motion Picture Archive [Vsesoiuznyi gosudarstvennyi fond kinofil'mov], it was administered by the Ministry of Culture for a number of years, but it is now an organ of the Motion Picture Commission directly under the USSR Council of Ministers. Located on a large estate outside of Moscow, Gosfil'mofond is a center for film research, with an extensive cataloging and publication program. It has several studios that present programs of film classics and other retrospectives, as well as extensive laboratories that have developed advanced techniques for restoration, preservation, and reproduction of early films. Air-conditioned storage vaults have been specially constructed to provide the optimum conditions for preservation.

Gosfil'mofond now receives a negative, positive, and masterprint of every film produced in the Soviet Union, not only from Moscow and Leningrad studios, but also those from all the Soviet republics. The archive has collected several hundred films from the period 1908 to 1917, in addition to the thousands made in the Soviet Union before the Second World War. According to 1970 figures, the archive now holds a total of 35,000 film titles (approximately 85,000 copies), almost all of which are in 35mm. Of these approximately 5,000 are Russian; the rest are in other languages of the Soviet Union or are foreign films obtained on exchange with distribution centers or film archives throughout the world.

Extensive catalogs provide detailed information about each film with indexes and cross reference notes to aid in ready identification of directors, actors, etc., or particular types of footage.

In addition to the films themselves the archive has an extensive collection of close to 200,000 still photographs and 25,000 posters, and a large clipping collection of reviews and articles. There is also a collection of shooting scripts, literary scenarios, and other materials relating to production, and a substantial reference library with film journals, catalogs, and other reference literature relating to motion pictures from all over the world.

This archive, it should be noted, does not handle documentary films, and should thus be carefully distinguished from the Central State Archive of Film and Photographic Documents (TsGAKFD) under the Main Archival Administration located in Krasnogorsk. See the description and bibliography of reference materials for TsGAKFD in Part B, section 9. Individual film studios such as Lenfilm or Mosfilm also maintain their own archives, which presumably retain additional footage shot in the course of production. Television films and video-tape recordings are also retained separately in studio archives.

PUBLISHED DESCRIPTIONS AND CATALOGS

For a comprehensive listing of catalogs and other historical and descriptive literature about Soviet motion pictures, see the section on the USSR in the international film bibliography prepared by Ervin Voiculescu, *Repertoriu mondial al filmografiilor naționale/ Répertoire mondial des filmographies nationales* (Bucharest: Arhivă națională de filme, 1970) (A-57), pp. 71-75. Not all these entries relate directly to Gosfil'mofond, but they will provide a helpful starting point for those interested in its collections.

D-16. Hill, Stephen P.
"Film Archive Work in the USSR." *Film Society Review*, January 1966, pp. 16-21.
> This article presents a general description of the organization and work of Gosfil'mofond, based on the author's visit there and interviews during the 1965 Moscow Film Festival.

D-17. [Vsesoiuznyi gosudarstvennyi fond kinofil'mov.]
Sovetskie khudozhestvennye fil'my. Annotirovannyi katalog. Compiled by N. A. Glagoleva et al. Edited by A. V. Macheret, L. A. Parfenov, O. V. Iakubovich and M. Kh. Zak. 4 vols. Moscow: Gosudarstvennoe izd-vo "Iskusstvo," 1961-1968. [DLC-PN1998.V8(vols.1-3); MH-Thr176.30(vols.1-4)]
> Vol. 1: *Nemye fil'my (1918-1935).* 527 p.
> Vol. 2: *Zvukovye fil'my (1930-1957 gg.).* 784 p.
> Vol. 3: *Prilozheniia.* 307 p.
> Vol. 4: *(1958-1963).* Moscow, 1968. 824 p.
>> The first volume covers 1172 silent films from the period 1918 to 1935, organized chronologically with specifications of each; those held by Gosfil'-mofond are indicated accordingly. The second volume covers 2502 sound films produced between 1930 and 1957 with similar coverage of each. The third volume indexes the first two, providing an alphabetical guide to films by title; lists of directors, actors, etc., in a proper-name index; lists of films by issuing studio, consisting of chronological lists under the different republics of the USSR; and a supplementary list of films produced by private firms during the period 1917-1921. The fourth volume extends the coverage through 1963. This series is the basic catalog of feature films and shorts produced in the Soviet Union, copies of most of which are held by Gosfil'mofond (there are gaps, however, in the early films in GFF).
>> For other types of catalogs, film histories, and critical studies of special types of films, see the bibliography listed above.

PART E
MANUSCRIPT DIVISIONS OF LIBRARIES AND MUSEUMS
IN MOSCOW

PART E

MANUSCRIPT DIVISIONS OF LIBRARIES AND MUSEUM
IN MOSCOW

The richness and variety of manuscript and other types of documentary holdings in libraries and museums of the Soviet Union are difficult to overestimate. Yet because these materials have still largely escaped the centralizing tendencies of Soviet archival development, they are often extremely hard to locate and their riches go unappreciated, especially by foreign scholars. In many ways, the Soviet Union has done more than most nations to locate its manuscript wealth and bring it under state control; however, in the realm of libraries, museums, and smaller repositories that are not under the administration of the Main Archival Administration or of the Academy of Sciences, there is no overall directory, and basic descriptive literature is still usually lacking.

Several of the general and specialized library directories (see Appendix 1) mention the existence and extent of manuscript divisions. But even the most important libraries of the nation, the Lenin Library in Moscow and the Saltykov-Shchedrin Public Library in Leningrad, lack adequate published catalogs or general descriptions of their large and varied manuscript divisions, to the extent that, prior to his arrival, the foreigner is usually very much in the dark about their holdings.

The most important museum in the nation in terms of manuscript and documentary holdings, the State Historical Museum in Moscow, is much better described in publications. However, there is no general directory of museums (even the latest official list, *Spisok gosudarstvennykh muzeev SSSR* [Moscow: Ministerstvo kul'tury SSSR, 1969] is not complete), or even any general coverage of their manuscript holdings. The few printed descriptions or catalogs available have invariably been issued in small editions and often escape adequate bibliographical notice.

Some strides have been made in guiding the researcher to specific types of materials for Moscow repositories. For example, the general directory of personal papers, *Lichnye arkhivnye fondy v gosudarstvennykh khranilishchakh SSSR. Ukazatel'* (A-9), lists the holdings in many museums and libraries throughout the Soviet Union. And the general bibliography of published descriptions of medieval Slavic manuscripts compiled by Iu. K. Begunov et al., *Spravochnik-ukazatel' pechatnykh opisanii slaviano-russkikh rukopisei* (A-14), covers many different types of repositories. As will be seen in Part F below, Leningrad repositories are generally much better covered by location aids than are those in Moscow and other cities. Since the special institute devoted to museum affairs under the Ministry of Culture (Nauchno-issledovatel'skii institut muzeevedeniia i okhrany pamiatnikov istorii i kul'tury) has plans for more comprehensive cataloging efforts, the situation may improve. The present coverage can only include the most important and representative repositories.

Many of the institutions date back well into the nineteenth century, as many of their holdings are carried over from prerevolutionary Russia, bequeathed to the institutions involved by family owners or gathered and guarded by the diligence of the staff. Since the Revolution, many smaller museums or libraries have been consolidated from earlier institutions or established anew. Some are commemorative of specific famous individuals; others are devoted to a specific subject such as music, the theater, communications, or artillery. Others, such as university libraries, house a wide variety of different types of materials.

These repositories usually differ from state archives in that they do not house official records of state institutions, and most particularly do not receive the records of ongoing institutions; hence they are almost entirely historical in orientation. Several general types of holdings are usually found: rich collections of medieval manuscripts from prerevolutionary religious institutions or private collections, miscellaneous documentary collections from a variety of sources, holdings gathered by a particular type of museum or institute relating to its own specialized subject, such as music or military history, and the personal papers (or parts thereof) of important political or cultural leaders.

Libraries and museums in the Soviet Union come under a wide variety of administrations, but a large proportion of those described in this part and the succeeding part on Leningrad institutions are administered by the Ministry of Culture. These institutions often retain a certain degree of administrative autonomy; all remain quite independent of the Main Archival Administration although they cooperate in joint cataloging ventures, publications, and other matters with GAU. Furthermore, since their holdings are all legally part of the State Archival Fond (GAF) GAU reserves the right to appropriate their collections or archival holdings for transfer to state archives, if and when it sees fit to do so.

Although few descriptive publications have appeared in print, scholars often note that these institutions are much better cataloged and easier to use than state archives. In many cases this reflects the fact that their catalogs are generally open to the public; the staff with whom the foreigner deals have been directly involved with the materials, often over a long period; and, perhaps most important, they generally contain a far smaller proportion of restricted materials. In many cases these institutions have come through the Revolution with earlier catalogs intact; with smaller holdings, more extensive and comprehensive cataloging has proceeded apace. In other cases, however, cataloging has notoriously lagged behind. In recent years standardized procedures and forms for cataloging and reference aids have been developed by the Main Archival Administration, and under the guidance of such manuals, older cataloging is being superseded by more modern methods.

The coverage in Part E is limited to institutions in Moscow and the general Moscow region, but no attempt has been made to cover every museum or small manuscript repository. Many other smaller commemorative or specialized museums or other types of libraries may have documentary materials of note, but the lack of any published directory, centralized information, or individual published descriptions has made more comprehensive coverage of other institutions impossible. And since holdings and official names of institutions frequently change in the Soviet Union, only those whose contents could be verified are included.

1. GOSUDARSTVENNAIA ORDENA LENINA BIBLIOTEKA SSSR IMENI V. I. LENINA (GBL)

[V. I. Lenin State Library with the Order of Lenin]
OTDEL RUKOPISEI [Manuscript Division]
    Address: Moscow, tsentr, Prospekt Kalinina, 3
    (Manuscript Division entrance: ulitsa Frunze, 6)

CONTENTS

The Manuscript Division of the Lenin Library was, in effect, started half a century before it became part of the state library. It owes its origin to the substantial collection of early Russian and Slavic manuscripts gathered in the late eighteenth and early nineteenth centuries by the wealthy nobleman N. P. Rumiantsev, which, along with his large library, he left to the public at his death in 1826. Initially set up as the Rumiantsev Museum in St. Petersburg, the collection was later transferred to Moscow to form the basis for the Moscow Public and Rumiantsev Museum [Moskovskii publichnyi i Rumiantsevskii muzei] established in 1862 in the imposing late eighteenth-century Pashkov Palace facing the Kremlin. The manuscript holdings were expanded, along with the library, in the course of the late nineteenth century to become one of the largest and most prestigious repositories of prerevolutionary Russia. With these holdings as its basis, when government power was shifted to Moscow after 1917 the Moscow Publichnaia Biblioteka, as it was then called, was elevated to the position of the most important library in the country; it was renamed the Lenin State Library in 1925, and the manuscript holdings of the Rumiantsev Museum became the library's Manuscript Division.

The Manuscript Division is today still housed in the prerevolutionary building of the Rumiantsev Museum beside the monumental new Lenin Library. Its holdings have grown with the other main library divisions. Although its contents are predominantly in the realm of personal archival fonds and medieval manuscript collections as opposed to the more official or institutional records found in most of the central state archives, they rank with these archives for their significance in all phases of Russian history and culture. As of 1969, the division had some 514 archival fonds, 75 collections of handwritten books and other manuscripts, and 24 miscellaneous documentary collections.

The original collection gathered by and for N. P. Rumiantsev is but one of the best known which came from the Rumiantsev Museum. The largest and most valuable single collection of medieval Russian and Slavic manuscripts is the so-called Museum Collection (fond 178) gathered by the Rumiantsev Museum and later by the Manuscript Division between the years of 1862 and 1947. Those acquired since 1947 have been grouped into the Collection of the Manuscript Division (fond 218). Many other important collections have been added through the years from a variety of sources. The rich collections from the Troitsko-Sergievskii monastery, the Moscow Ecclesiastical Academy, and the nineteenth-century Society of Russian History

263

and Antiquities are among the most significant institutional legacies. Important private manuscript collections of note include those of V. I. Grigorovich, N. S. Tikhonravov, V. M. Undol'skii, E. E. Egorov, and I. Ia. Lukashevich and N. A. Markevich. Others have been acquired by the division from outlying sources such as the Archangel, Kostroma, and Vologda provincial libraries.

The division also contains significant early Chinese, Arabic, Persian, Turkic, Hebrew, and other oriental manuscripts. Several of the collections contain valuable Greek and Western European medieval texts.

Mention of a few of the prominent families from the eighteenth to the twentieth century whose personal papers are to be found here suggests the extent and importance of the archival fonds in the Manuscript Division. Among major prerevolutionary leaders important in government and court circles, the division retains, for example, many of the papers of the Bariatinskii, Golitsyn, Panin, Sheremetev, and of course the Rumiantsev families. Other political figures whose papers are represented include D. A. Miliutin, P. D. Kiselev, M. I. Kutuzov, and K. P. Pobedonostsev. Among early socialist and revolutionary pioneers, the Division contains many papers of Belinskii, Herzen, Ogarev, and several of the Decembrists. Cultural leaders of more conservative Slavophile sympathy are represented by the papers of Aksakov, Cherkasskii, Chicherin, Katkov, Pogodin, and Samarin.

In the literary realm, the division houses major portions of the papers of Gogol', Nekrasov, Dostoevskii, Ostrovskii, Turgenev, Tiutchev, Chekhov, and Korolenko, among others. Papers of artists represented here include those of the painters A. A. Ivanov and A. A. Kiselev, the composer M. Iu. Vel'gorskii, and the music critic S. N. Krugliakov. The papers of the historians Kliuchevskii, Solov'ev, and Granovskii, among others, are also found here.

In addition to the medieval manuscript collections and the personal archival fonds, the Manuscript Division also contains a number of miscellaneous collections of historical and literary documents and famous autographs. Many foreign manuscripts, some with important autographs, form parts of various collections. In addition the Museum Collection of Foreign Autographs includes manuscript documents and letters of foreign origin that are apt to be of particular interest to Western readers.

WORKING CONDITIONS

Expectant readers, aware of the simple procedure for gaining immediate access to the Lenin Library reading rooms by presenting a passport at the registration office and filling out the requisite form, should be warned that admission to the Manuscript Division, like admission to other archives, is much more difficult and involved, and cannot be obtained by simple application at the library itself. For official exchange participants, access to this repository is relatively easy and permission usually comes with minimal delay following application through the foreign department of the Soviet institution with which the foreigner is affiliated. Occasionally post-doctoral foreign scholars who are not official exchange participants have been able to arrange access, but such applications, with a letter from the visitor's embassy to the Cultural Section of the Foreign Ministry (sometimes presented through the Ministry of Culture), are apt to take considerable time.

Working conditions are generally easier for readers here than in state archives, largely because of the extensive public card catalogs and readily available inventories. Card catalogs cover over two-thirds of the archival fonds, with separate detailed author and subject files housed in the room immediately adjacent to the main reading room off the entrance hall; these even include many cross-references to individuals mentioned in letters and other documents. Cataloged earlier with code letter designations, the archival fonds have recently all been assigned fond numbers and the cataloging is being changed accordingly.

Inventories are readily available in the reading room for almost all of the fonds in the Manuscript Division; those not on the shelves are usually brought out on request with the exception of a few for inadequately cataloged materials.

Medieval manuscripts, although many are well-known individually, are commonly cataloged under the names of the collections of which they form part; these are usually named for the collector or their early locations. Although many still retain their original cataloging, the collections now have all been given fond numbers in the Manuscript Division; some are gradually being recataloged and indexed.

Paging is normally exceptionally prompt, and documents requested in the evening are usually ready for use by opening-time the following morning. Delays are apt to involve uncataloged materials, sensitive documents, or manuscripts being reserved for a Soviet reader.

The Manuscript Division has a small library of its own, mostly on open shelves in the reading room and in the adjoining hall and entrance foyer, with publications relating to the holdings along with other basic reference works; included here is an exceptionally large collection of Soviet archival guides and published manuscript catalogs covering materials throughout the Soviet Union. Books from the main Lenin Library stacks can be ordered for use in the Manuscript Division and held indefinitely on a special shelf for the borrower (usually limited to five at a time per person). Periodicals and newspapers can also normally be borrowed when required. See Appendix 1 for information about other parts of the library.

Photocopying and microfilming service is also usually available upon written application to the division director. Sometimes severe restrictions as to the number of frames have been imposed (often limited to 40 or 50 frames). The actual filming (of varying quality), in positive copy, is done by the photo-duplication division of the library off the courtyard in the rear of the building. Recently, for orders involving only a few pages, a new rapid copy service has been introduced.

For a further description of the card catalogs and the cataloging system used in the Manuscript Division, see the article by G. I. Dovgallo, "Spravochnyi apparat otdela rukopisei," in *Zapiski otdela rukopisei* 25 (1962):464-86.

GENERAL PUBLISHED DESCRIPTIONS AND BIBLIOGRAPHY

The Manuscript Division has never published a comprehensive or systematic guide to its holdings, with a complete bibliography of available inventories, etc., although such a publication would certainly be most helpful for readers. Information about the holdings must accordingly come from a wide variety of sources. Of particular importance are the specialized types of manuscript directories and bibliographies of catalogs included in the General Bibliography above, Part A. Except as otherwise indicated, the specialized lists below include only those catalogs published as separate volumes since 1917, and articles published since 1962 which are not included in the comprehensive bibliographical article (E-1).

E-1. Safronova, G. F.
"Fondy i deiatel'nost' otdela rukopisei Gosudarstvennoi biblioteki SSSR imeni V. I. Lenina. Bibliografiia 1836-1962." *Zapiski otdela rukopisei* 25 (1962):487-520 (see E-3).

> Although now somewhat outdated, this article gives the most complete bibliography of publications pertaining to the Manuscript Division and is a starting point for readers trying to locate more extensive descriptions of various fonds. It analyzes the contents of each issue of the published *Zapiski* of the Manuscript Division (1938-1961), together with the issues of the earlier periodical series of the museum and library. It includes general literature about the Manuscript Division as well as relevant sections of more general guides to the library as a whole, inventories or catalogs of manuscript collections, catalogs of manuscripts of personal archival fonds, and thematic collections and documentary publications with materials from the division. The last six pages consist of a most helpful alphabetical index for the collections (pp. 513-15) and for the archival fonds (pp. 515-19), which gives their fond numbers and references to earlier bibliographical entries pertaining to individual fonds, thus providing an efficient directory to published descriptions of the division holdings. This bibliography largely supersedes the earlier and less comprehensive one given in the 1954 issue of the same series: I. A. Tyzhnova, "Ukazatel' izdanii otdela rukopisei Gos. biblioteki SSSR im. V. I. Lenina (1918-1953)," *Zapiski otdela rukopisei* 16 (1954):251-62. There is no more recent cumulative compilation of this type, although the annual reports of the library (E-4) contain lists of publications related to the Manuscript Division. Because of the comprehensive nature of its coverage and the general availability of this volume, the lists below will contain only more recent publications that were not included, and the most important earlier separate monographic volumes.

E-2. Zimina, V. G.
"Otdel rukopisei za 100 let." In [Moscow. Publichnaia biblioteka.], *Istoriia Gosudarstvennoi ordena Lenina biblioteki SSSR imeni V. I. Lenina za 100 let, 1862-1962,* edited by F. S. Abrikosova, K. R. Kamenetskaia, and E. V. Seglin,

pp. 246-71. Moscow: Izdanie Biblioteki Moskvy, 1962. 279 p.
[DLC-Z820.M8357; MH-B8889.8.161F]

> This chapter of the elaborate, large-format centennial history of the library
> gives the fullest short description of the Manuscript Division available.
> Acquisitions and publication highlights appear generally in chronological
> order as part of the summary history of the division. Some brief descriptions
> of significant parts of the holdings are also included. Bibliographical
> footnotes list most of the division publications, including catalogs,
> inventories, and other descriptive materials as well as documentary
> publications. This article largely supersedes the earlier articles by Konshina
> and Georgievskii in the 80-year commemorative volume put out by the
> library (*Vosem'desiat let na sluzhbe nauki i kul'tury nashei rodiny*, edited by
> N. N. Iakovlev [Moscow, 1943; 248 p.]), but for bibliographical purposes it
> does not replace the article by F. F. Safronova above (E-1).

SERIAL PUBLICATIONS

E-3. [Moscow. Publichnaia biblioteka. Otdel rukopisei.]
Zapiski otdela rukopisei. 1938+.
[DLC-Z6620.R9M6; MH-Slav740.15]

> Issues come out annually and contain lengthy descriptions of individual fonds
> or groups of manuscripts, articles about the activities of the division, and
> publications of edited texts from the manuscript holdings. It is of particular
> value for the often complete inventories of fonds or collections included,
> and for the extensive descriptions of new manuscript acquisitions. A
> cumulative bibliography of the articles was included in a bibliography of
> the division publications in volume 16 (1954) and a more comprehensive
> one was published in volume 25 (1963) (see E-1); the latter includes a
> complete listing of the table of contents of each issue, and of other library
> series which also contain important articles about materials in the Manuscript
> Division.

E-4. [Moscow. Publichnaia biblioteka.]
Gosudarstvennaia ordena Lenina biblioteka SSSR imeni V. I. Lenina v 1947 godu.
Moscow: GBL, 1949.
[DLC-Z820.M845; MH-B8889.8.147]

> Subsequent volumes through 1965 have been published annually, usually
> coming out a couple of years after the title year. Each usually contains a
> short article summarizing developments in the Manuscript Division and
> gives a bibliography of publications issued by the division or related to it.
> These bibliographies are later integrated into the cumulative lists published
> in *Zapiski* (E-3), but the *Zapiski* series does not always publish all the most
> recent bibliography. The coverage for 1966 and 1967 is combined in a
> volume published in 1969; the coverage for the years 1968-1970 will be
> combined into a single larger volume.

PART E – MOSCOW LIBRARIES AND MUSEUMS

PUBLISHED CATALOGS AND DESCRIPTIONS OF SLAVIC MANUSCRIPT COLLECTIONS

For the most comprehensive bibliography of descriptions and catalogs of medieval Slavic manuscripts in the division published before 1960, see the handbook compiled by Iu. K. Begunov et al., *Spravochnik-ukazatel' pechatnykh opisanii slaviano-russkikh rukopisei* (A-14), pp. 124-42. Only a few of the most important recent publications are listed below.

The division has not published a general description of these collections, but the typescript survey (E-5) available in the reading room remains the most important substitute.

E-5. Dovgallo, G. I., I. M. Kudriavtsev, and M. N. Kuz'minskaia, compilers.
"Sobraniia otdela rukopisei (kratkie obzory)." Moscow: GBL, 1958. 284 p.
Typescript.
> Although it covers only 48 of the manuscript collections in the Division, it is the most important single reference tool for these holdings; in addition to detailed surveys of the contents of the individual collections, it gives further bibliographical indications about catalogs, descriptions, or unpublished inventories. Unfortunately, it is available only in the division's reading room, and in the reading room of the Manuscript Division of the Saltykov-Shchedrin Public Library in Leningrad.

E-6. Tikhomirov, N. B.
"Katalog russkikh i slavianskikh pergamennykh rukopisei XI-XII vekov, khraniashchikhsia v otdele rukopisei Gosudarstvennoi biblioteki SSSR imeni V. I. Lenina."
> Part 1: "XI vek." *Zapiski otdela rukopisei* 25 (1962):143-83.
> Part 2: "XII vek." *Ibid.* 27 (1965):93-148.
> Part 3: "Dopolnitel'naia (XII i kon. XII-nach. XIII vv.)." *Ibid.* 30 (1968):87-156.

E-7. [Moscow. Publichnaia biblioteka. Otdel rukopisei.]
Muzeinoe sobranie rukopisei. Opisanie. Vol. 1: *No. 1-3005.* Edited by I. M. Kudriavtsev. Moscow: GBL, 1961. 524 p.
[DLC-Z6621.M853; MH-Slav251.277.9]

E-8. [Moscow. Publichnaia biblioteka. Otdel rukopisei.]
Sobraniia D. V. Razumovskogo i V. F. Odoevskogo. Arkhiv A. V. Razumovskogo. Opisaniia. Edited by I. M. Kudriavtsev. Moscow: GBL, 1960. 261 p.
[DLC-ML136.M78P86; MH-Slav 251.277.40]

E-9. [Moscow. Publichnaia biblioteka. Otdel rukopisei.]
Sobranie I. Ia. Lukashevicha i N. A. Markevicha. Opisanie. Compiled by Ia. N. Shchapov. Edited by I. M. Kudriavtsev. Moscow: GBL, 1959. 144 p.
[DLC-Z6621.M854; MH-Slav251.277.7]

2-10. Ivanina, L. I.
"Troitskii sbornik materialov po istorii zemlevladeniia russkogo gosudarstva XVI-XVII vv." *Zapiski otdela rukopisei* 27 (1965):149-63.

OTHER SPECIALIZED DESCRIPTIONS

Western Manuscripts
For Greek manuscripts see A-37; for Latin manuscripts see A-40.

2-11. Zhitomirskaia, S. V.
"Zapadnoe srednevekov'e v rukopisiakh Gosudarstvennoi biblioteki SSSR im. V. I. Lenina." *Srednie veka* 10 (1957):285-305.

2-12. Gerasimova, Iu. I.
"Vospominaniia Filippo Balatri—Novyi inostrannyi istochnik po istorii petrovskoi Rossii (1698-1701)." *Zapiski otdela rukopisei* 27 (1965):164-90.

Theater and Music Materials

2-13. Volkova, E. P.
"Materialy k istorii russkogo dramaticheskogo i muzykal'nogo teatra v otdele rukopisei Gosudarstvennoi biblioteki SSSR imeni V. I. Lenina (XVII v.—1930e gody)." In *Teatr i muzyka. Dokumenty i materialy,* edited by A. D. Alekseev and I. F. Petrovskaia (A-51), pp. 72-90.

PUBLISHED DESCRIPTIONS OF ARCHIVAL FONDS

Most of the personal archival fonds acquired by the division before 1960 are listed in the general directory of personal fonds, *Lichnye arkhivnye fondy v gosudarstvennykh khranilishchakh SSSR. Ukazatel'.* (A-9).

2-14. [Moscow. Publichnaia biblioteka. Otdel rukopisei.]
Kratkii ukazatel' arkhivnykh fondov otdela rukopisei. Compiled by E. N. Konshina and N. K. Shvabe. Edited by P. A. Zaionchkovskii and E. N. Konshina. Moscow: GBL, 1948. 253 p.
[DLC-Z6621.M84R8; MH-B8889.8.175]
> This helpful directory lists the archival fonds which had come into the Division through 1945. Coverage is alphabetical under the name of the individual or institution concerned. A short paragraph about the fond includes the dates and types of manuscripts and number of storage units contained, but falls short of a comprehensive description. Bibliographical citations refer to fuller descriptions available in many cases. The directory is now 25 years out of date, for both fonds covered and the related bibliographical citations. Based on the old system of code-letter cataloging, it does not give the fond numbers now in use for the archival fonds. Despite

these limitations it remains the only available coverage of its type; hence, until a more recent and complete guide is published, scholars must depend on this volume for the archival fonds except for the few for which a more complete description is available elsewhere. An augmented and up-to-date manuscript version of this volume is available in the reading room in a loose-leaf binder.

Memoirs, Diaries, and Travel Accounts

E-15. [Moscow. Publichnaia biblioteka. Otdel rukopisei.]
Ukazatel' vospominanii, dnevnikov i putevykh zapisok XVIII-XIX vv. (iz fondov otdela rukopisei). Compiled by S. V. Zhitomirskaia et al. Edited by P. A. Zaionchkovskii and E. N. Konshina. Moscow: GBL, 1951. 224 p.
[DLC-Z6621.M855; MH-Slav 241.277.25]

This exceedingly thorough directory of manuscript memoirs, diaries, and travel accounts in the archival fonds of the Division is a key reference tool for scholars using this type of material. The copy in the Division reading room has incorporated manuscript corrections.

Personal Papers

N. S. Angarskii (1879-1943)

E-16. Ivanova, L. M.
"Arkhiv N. S. Angarskogo [N. S. Klestov]." *Zapiski otdela rukopisei* 28 (1966):4-44.

G. Bakalov (1873-1939)

E-17. Goriainov, A. N.
"Neopublikovannyi bibliograficheskii trud G. Bakalova 'Revoliutsionnaia kniga Bolgarii.'" *Zapiski otdela rukopisei* 27 (1967):147-57.

V. G. Belinskii (1811-1848)

E-18. [Moscow. Publichnaia biblioteka. Otdel rukopisei.]
Rukopisi i perepiska V. G. Belinskogo. Katalog. Compiled by R. P. Matorina. Edited by N. L. Brodskii. Moscow: GBL, 1948. 42 p.
[DLC-Z6616.B45.M6; MH-Slav4336.2.935]

V. D. Bonch-Bruevich (1873-1955)

E-19. Zhitomirskaia, S. V., L. V. Gapochko, and B. A. Shlikhter.
"Arkhiv V. D. Bonch-Bruevicha." *Zapiski otdela rukopisei* 25 (1962):7-79.

V. Ia. Briusov (1873-1924)

E-20. Konshina, E. N.
"Perepiska i dokumenty V. Ia. Briusova v ego arkhive." *Zapiski otdela rukopisei* 27 (1965):5-42.

E-21. Konshina, E. N.
"Tvorcheskoe nasledie V. Ia. Briusova v ego arkhive." *Zapiski otdela rukopisei* 25 (1962):80-142.

Bulgakov Family (18th-19th Centuries)

E-22. Gerasimova, Iu. I.
"Arkhiv Bulgakovykh. Materialy Ia. I. i I. M. Bulgakovykh." *Zapiski otdela rukopisei* 30 (1968):4-86.

E-23. Gerasimova, Iu. I.
"Arkhiv Bulgakovykh. Materialy A. Ia. i K. Ia. Bulgakovykh." *Zapiski otdela rukopisei* 31 (1969):5-85.

A. P. Chekov (1860-1904)

E-24. [Moscow. Publichnaia biblioteka. Otdel rukopisei.]
Arkhiv A. P. Chekova. Annotirovannoe opisanie pisem k A. P. Chekhovu. Compiled by E. E. Leitnekker. Edited by N. L. Meshcheriakova. 2 vols.
Vol. 1: (A-K). Moscow: Gos. sotsial'no-ekonomicheskoe izd-vo, 1939. 115 p.
Vol. 2: (L-Ia). Moscow: Gos. sotsial'no-ekonomicheskoe izd-vo, 1941. 95 p.
[DLC-Z8165.4.M6(1&2); MH-Slav4337.2.807(1&2)]

E-25. [Moscow. Publichnaia biblioteka. Otdel rukopisei.]
Rukopisi A. P. Chekhova. Opisanie. Compiled by E. E. Leitnekker. Moscow: Gos. sotsial'no-ekonomicheskoe izd-vo, 1938. 124 p.
[DLC-Z6616.C47.M6; MH-Slav4337.2.830]

V. G. Chertkov (1854-1936)

E-26. Klibanov, A. I.
"Materialy o religioznom sektantstve v posleoktiabr'skii period v arkhive V. G. Chertkova." *Zapiski otdela rukopisei* 28 (1966):45-95.

F. M. Dostoevskii (1821-1881)
See the general inventory, *Opisanie rukopisei F. M. Dostoevskogo*, listed as (A-11) above.

D. A. Furmanov (1891-1926) and Wife (d. 1941)

E-27. Chugakova, M. O.
"Arkhiv D. A. i A. N. Furmanovykh." *Zapiski otdela rukopisei* 29 (1967):113-46.

N. V. Gogol' (1809-1852)

E-28. [Moscow. Publichnaia biblioteka. Otdel rukopisei.]
Rukopisi N. V. Gogolia. Katalog. Compiled by G. P. Georgievskii and A. A.
Romodanovskaia. Moscow: Sotsekgiz, 1940. 127 p.
[DLC-Z6616.G58.M6; MH-Slav4341.1.920]
   A supplement to this catalog has been published in *Zapiski otdela rukopisei*
   19 (1957):37-46.

A. I. Herzen (Gertsen) (1812-1870)

E-29. [Moscow. Publichnaia biblioteka. Otdel rukopisei.]
Opisanie rukopisei A. I. Gertsena. Compiled by A. V. Askariants and E. V.
Kemenova. Edited by B. P. Koz'min. 2nd edition. Moscow: GBL, 1950. 159 p.
[DLC-Z6616.H53M6.1950]

I. Ia. Iakovlev (1848-1930)

E-30. Butina, K. I.
"Arkhiv I. Ia. Iakovleva." *Zapiski otdela rukopisei* 31 (1969):86-114.

V. G. Korolenko (1853-1921)

E-31. [Moscow. Publichnaia biblioteka. Otdel rukopisei.]
*Opisanie rukopisei V. G. Korolenko. Khudozhestvennye proizvedeniia,
literaturno-kriticheskie stat'i, istoricheskie i etnograficheskie raboty; zapisnye
knizhki, materialy k proizvedeniiam.* Compiled by R. P. Matorina. Moscow: GBL,
1950. 223 p.
[MH-Slav4345.4.880(1)]

E-32. Fedorova, V. M.
Opisanie pisem V. G. Korolenko. Edited by S. V. Zhitomirskaia. Moscow: GBL,
1961. 659 p.
[DLC-Z6616.K6F4; MH-Slav4345.4.880(2)]

M. Iu. Lermontov (1814-1841)

E-33. Andronikov, I. L.
"Rukopisi iz Fel'dafinga." *Zapiski otdela rukopisei* 26 (1963):5-33.

N. A. Nekrasov (1821-1877)

E-34. [Moscow. Publichnaia biblioteka. Otdel rukopisei.]
Rukopisi N. A. Nekrasova. Katalog. Compiled by R. P. Matorina. Moscow:
Sotsial'no-ekonomicheskoe izd-vo, 1939. 79 p.
[DLC-Z8617.45.M6; MH-Slav4348.1.840]

V. I. Nevskii [V. I. Krivobokov] (1876-1939)

E-35. Gapochko, L. V.
"Arkhiv V. I. Nevskogo." *Zapiski otdela rukopisei* 29 (1967):5-122.

N. P. Ogarev (1813-1877)

E-36. [Moscow. Publichnaia biblioteka. Otdel rukopisei.]
Opisanie rukopisei N. P. Ogareva. Compiled by A. V. Askariants. Edited by Ia. E. Cherniak. Moscow: GBL, 1952. 206 p.
[DLC-Z6616.O3.M6; MH-Slav1460.8.800]

V. P. Orlov-Davydov (1809-1882) Family

E-37. K. A. Malkova.
"Arkhiv Orlovykh-Davidovykh." *Zapiski otdela rukopisei* 32 (1971):5-60.

A. N. Ostrovskii (1823-1886)

E-38. [Moscow. Publichnaia biblioteka. Otdel rukopisei.]
Rukopisi A. N. Ostrovskogo. Katalog. Compiled by N. P. Kashin. Moscow: Gos. sotsial'no-ekonomicheskoe izd-vo, 1939. 51 p.
[DLC-Z6616.O8.M6; MH-Slav4349.1.890]

L. M. Reisner (1895-1926)

E-39. Zhitomirskaia, S. V.
"Arkhiv L. M. Reisnera." *Zapiski otdela rukopisei* 27 (1965):43-92.

N. A. Rubakin (1862-1946)

E-40. Ivanova, L. M., A. B. Sidorova, and M. V. Charushnikova.
"Arkhiv N. A. Rubakina." *Zapiski otdela rukopisei* 26 (1963):63-206.

D. N. Shipov (1851-1920)

E-41. Zeifman, N. V.
"Arkhiv D. N. Shipova." *Zapiski otdela rukopisei* 31 (1969):115-42.

D. L. Tal'nikov [D. L. Shpital'nikov] (1882-1961)

E-42. Blagovolina, Iu. P.
"Arkhiv D. L. Tal'nikova." *Zapiski otdela rukopisei* 31 (1969):143-76.

I. S. Turgenev (1818-1883)

E-43. Matorina, R. P.
"Opisanie avtografov I. S. Turgeneva." In *I. S. Turgenev. Sbornik,* edited by N. L. Brodskii, pp. 171-219. Moscow, 1940.

A. M. Vereshchagin (1810-1873)

E-44. Gladysh, I. A., and T. G. Dinesman.
"Arkhiv A. M. Vereshchagina." *Zapiski otdela rukopisei* 26 (1963):34-62.

2. NAUCHNAIA BIBLIOTEKA IMENI A. M. GOR'KOGO MOSKOVSKOGO GOSUDARSTVENNOGO UNIVERSITETA IMENI M. V. LOMONOSOVA

[A. M. Gor'kii Research Library of Moscow State University in the name of M. V. Lomonosov]
OTDEL REDKIKH KNIG I RUKOPISEI [Division of Rare Books and Manuscripts]
Address: Moscow, tsentr, Prospekt Karla Marksa, 20

CONTENTS

The Division of Rare Books and Manuscripts in the main library of Moscow University is located in its original building in the center of the city. The relatively small manuscript holdings number about 500 items, including about 200 Slavic manuscripts, 4 Greek, and 6 Latin texts; oriental texts include 15 Chinese, Mongolian, and Tibetan manuscripts, 10 Persian, 7 Turkish and Tatar, and 6 Arabic manuscripts. In addition there are some miscellaneous literary manuscripts and some documentary collections from private libraries of professors and others associated with the university in the nineteenth and early twentieth centuries.

The archives of Moscow University, although housed in the same building, are not connected with the library. They currently contain only postrevolutionary records and personal fonds deposited there after 1917. In the early 1960's all the prerevolutionary records and personal papers of professors (except for some library and documentary collections) were transferred to the local state archive, now officially called the Central State Archive of the City of Moscow [Tsentral'nyi gosudarstvennyi arkhiv goroda Moskvy—TsGAgM], formerly named the State Historical Archive of Moscow oblast [Gosudarstvennyi istoricheskii arkhiv Moskovskoi oblasti]. (For a description of these records, see the published *Putevoditel'* [G-7], fond 418, 1799-1917, pp. 216-17, 328.)

PUBLISHED DESCRIPTIONS

General

2-45. Mel'nikova, N. N.
"Rukopisi i redkie knigi v fondakh Nauchnoi biblioteki." In *Opyt raboty Nauchnoi biblioteki MGU,* 1957, no. 5, pp. 11-39.
A general survey of the Rare Book and Manuscript Division holdings.

Medieval Slavic Manuscripts

2-46. [Moscow. Universitet. Biblioteka.]
Slaviano-russkie rukopisi XIII-XVII vv. v fondakh Nauchnoi biblioteki imeni A. M. Gor'kogo Moskovskogo Gosudarstvennogo universiteta. Opisanie. Compiled by E. I. Koniukhova. Edited by A. M. Sakharov. Moscow: Izd-vo MGU, 1964. 102 p.
[DLC-Z6627.M8658; MH-Slav251.277.65]

A detailed catalog of the medieval Slavic manuscripts. For earlier descriptive publications regarding the medieval Slavic holdings see the bibliography compiled by Iu. K. Begunov et al., *Spravochnik-ukazatel' pechatnykh opisanii slaviano-russkikh rukopisei* (A-14), pp. 161-62. See particularly the extensive earlier catalog prepared by V. N. Peretts, *Rukopisi biblioteki Moskovskogo universiteta, samarskikh bibliotek i muzeia i minskikh sobranii* (Leningrad, 1934), pp. 13-29.

Greek Manuscripts

E-47. Fonkich, B. L.
"Grecheskie rukopisi Biblioteki Moskovskogo universiteta," *Vestnik drevnei istorii,* 1967, no. 4, pp. 95-103.
Inventories the four Greek manuscripts.

Oriental Manuscripts

E-48. Kleinman, G. A.
"Vostochnye fondy Nauchnoi biblioteki im. A. M. Gor'kogo Moskovskogo Gosudarstvennogo universiteta im. M. V. Lomonosova," in *Vostokovednye fondy krupneishikh bibliotek Sovetskogo Soiuza* (A-22), pp. 202-18.
For the coverage of manuscripts, see pp. 212-16; the rest of the article covers printed books and other materials.

3. GOSUDARSTVENNYI ISTORICHESKII MUZEI (GIM)

[State Historical Museum]
OTDEL RUKOPISEI [Manuscript Division]
OTDEL PIS'MENNYKH ISTOCHNIKOV [Division of Written Sources]
    Address: Moscow, K-25, Krasnaia ploshchad', No. 1/2
    (Manuscript reading room entrance on side of building facing the Kremlin)

CONTENTS

The State Historical Museum, in its elaborate building facing Red Square in Moscow, contains the nation's third largest holdings of early Slavic manuscripts as well as a sizeable number of more recent archival fonds which make it of prime interest to scholars of Russian history and culture. The museum itself was founded in 1873 as the Russian National Museum; the present building and the manuscript collection date from the early 1880's. Renamed the Imperial Russian Historical Museum in honor of the heir to the throne in 1881, the museum took the name of Emperor Alexander III in 1895. After 1917 it was called the Russian Historical Museum until given its present name in 1929. Now administered by the Ministry of Culture, the museum includes collections and exhibits of all types of historical and archeological relics and has vast research, educational, and publication programs in which it cooperates with museums throughout the country.

There are two quite separate divisions of the museum which handle manuscript materials. The rich medieval Russian and Slavic collections are principally to be found in the actual Manuscript Division [Otdel rukopisei] which now contains approximately 22,000 file numbers. Even before the Revolution the museum functioned as a repository for medieval manuscripts with such significant collections as those of A. I. Bariatinskii, I. A. Vakhrameev, I. E. Zabelin, and A. D. Chertkov; two of the largest to be added before the Revolution were the E. V. Barsov collection acquired in 1912 and the P. I. Shchukin collection received in 1915.

The Manuscript Division greatly increased its holdings after the Revolution when it acquired many collections from individuals and from important religious institutions, most notably the collection from the Moscow Synod, which includes many manuscripts from cathedrals and monasteries in the Moscow region, as well as a large collection of Greek manuscripts (see E-49, pp. 12-32). Other large collections added after 1917 include those of A. I. Khludov, A. S. Uvarov, and N. P. Vostriakov. The museum has also acquired several rich collections of early Slavic manuscript books, and of manuscripts from various non-Russian parts of the Slavic world. Its holdings in Greek manuscripts, dating from the ninth to the fourteenth centuries A.D., total 551 storage units, making it the second largest repository in this category in the Soviet Union.

Manuscript holdings in the Division of Written Sources [Otdel pis'mennykh istochnikov] fall principally into the category of prerevolutionary archival fonds, totalling some 460 fonds and collections with over 43,000 storage units. Formerly referred to as the museum archive, this division includes many significant literary, scientific, and other post-seventeenth-century cultural manuscripts. It has a particularly rich group of over 300 private archives from many notable families and institutions important in the governmental, economic, and cultural life of prerevolutionary Russia (see E-52); although a few date back to the sixteenth and seventeenth centuries and a few extend beyond the revolutionary years, the largest bulk of material dates from the late eighteenth and nineteenth centuries. The division also has an important collection of charters, especially interesting ones from the seventeenth century. The several extensive private collections of historical sources and autographs gathered in the nineteenth century contain a wide variety of documents from different origins, greatly enriching the division's holdings (see E-51).

The Historical Museum also has a very well-endowed Map Division [Otdel kartografii] with a rich collection of early manuscript maps (see E-54–E-56).

WORKING CONDITIONS

Scholars consulting manuscripts in the Division of Written Sources use the small office on the top floor. Since it can accommodate only a few readers at a time, admission is often difficult to arrange. An excellent card catalog covers almost all of the archival fonds, with author and subject categories. As a most helpful feature, entries include not only main personal-name subject headings for the fonds themselves, but also important cross references to persons in other fonds. Complete inventories (either handwritten or typed) have been prepared for most of the archival fonds and are promptly brought to scholars on request.

Working hours are limited in the Historical Museum and paging often takes several days (since it is carried out only at special times), but the staff is usually very cooperative in helping the researcher plan his time so that he may know when materials will be ready for him to use.

Scholars using the Manuscript Division proper use the large reading room shared with the Division of Rare Books. There are published catalogs for most of the early manuscripts, which are shelved in the reading room, and also extensive card catalogs.

There is a library in the museum which has many general reference materials as well as publications relating to the archival fonds and manuscript collections.

PUBLISHED GUIDES AND DESCRIPTIONS

The manuscript holdings in the Historical Museum are well surveyed in publications. A comprehensive survey of the Manuscript Division and one for the Division of Written Sources were both published in 1958 and an extensive guide to the personal archival fonds in the latter division was issued in 1967.

A series of articles devoted to the general history of the Historical Museum give considerable coverage of the development of the manuscript holdings, although they will not be of immediate importance to scholars using the materials: the prerevolutionary period is covered by A. M. Razgon, "Rossiiskii Istoricheskii muzei. Istoriia ego osnovaniia i deiatel'nosti (1872-1917 gg.)," in [Moscow. Nauchno-issledovatel'skii institut muzeevedeniia.], *Ocherki istorii muzeinogo dela v Rossii*, part 2 (Moscow: Izd-vo "Sovetskaia Rossiia," 1960; *Trudy Nauchno-issle-dovatel'skogo instituta muzeevedeniia*), pp. 224-99. Successive articles by A. B. Zaks bring the coverage up to 1957: "Iz istorii Gosudarstvennogo istoricheskogo muzeia (1917-1941 gg.)," in *ibid.*, part 2, pp. 300-79, and "Iz istorii Gosudarstvennogo istoricheskogo muzeia (1941-1957 gg.)," in *ibid.*, part 3 (Moscow, 1961), pp. 5-54.

The museum publishes several different serials which contain articles or monographs about various aspects of the museum, its exhibitions and holdings, but these have scant relevance for readers using the manuscripts.

Manuscript Division

A comprehensive bibliography of published descriptions, catalogs, and inventories (listed under the name of the collection by order of their publication date) of individual collections of medieval Slavic manuscripts in the division is provided in the general compilation by Iu. K. Begunov et al., *Spravochnik-ukazatel' pechatnykh opisanii slaviano-russkikh rukopisei* (A-14), pp. 143-61.

-49. [Moscow. Gosudarstvennyi istoricheskii muzei.]
Sokrovishcha drevnei pis'mennosti i staroi pechati. Obzor rukopisei russkikh, slavianskikh, grecheskikh, a takzhe knig staroi pechati Gosudarstvennogo istoricheskogo muzeia. Compiled by M. V. Shchepkina and T. N. Protas'eva. Edited by M. N. Tikhomirov. Pamiatniki kul'tury, vol. 30. Moscow: Izd-vo "Sovetskaia Rossiia," 1958. 87 p.
[DLC-DK30.A1832.vol.30; MH-Slav251.277.14]
> For each of the 27 main collections of medieval manuscripts and 7 collections of early books covered, the commentary provides a brief history of the collection, a survey of the contents, and a bibliography of published catalogs and related literature.

-50. Shchepkina, M. V. et al.
"Opisanie pergamentnykh rukopisei Gosudarstvennogo istoricheskogo muzeia."
> Part 1: "Russkie rukopisi." *Arkheograficheskii ezhegodnik za 1964 god,* pp. 135-234.
> Part 2: "Rukopisi bolgarskie, serbskie, moldavskie." *Arkheograficheskii ezhegodnik za 1965 god*, pp. 273-309.

Division of Written Sources

-51. [Moscow. Gosudarstvennyi istoricheskii muzei.]
Pis'mennye istochniki v sobranii Gosudarstvennogo istoricheskogo muzeia. Part 1. Compiled by S. Sakovich. Moscow, 1958. 110 p.
[DLC-uncataloged; MH-Slav251.277.30]

Presenting a comprehensive survey of the subject contents of the archival fonds and other documentary collections, this key handbook to the Division of Written Sources should be the starting point for the scholar contemplating work there. It contains chapters by different authors on the fonds from landed estates (*Votchinnye fondy*), the collection of seventeenth-century charters (*Zhalovannye gramoty*), fonds of eighteenth- and nineteenth-century scientific and cultural leaders, private collections of historical sources made in the nineteenth century, materials on the history of the nineteenth-century Russian revolutionary movements, and documentary materials from the early twentieth century. A list of the personal fonds in the division is given at the end.

E-52. [Moscow. Gosudarstvennyi istoricheskii muzei. Otdel pis'mennykh istochnikov.] *Putevoditel' po fondam lichnogo proiskhozhdeniia Otdela pis'mennykh istochnikov Gosudarstvennogo istoricheskogo muzeia.* Compiled by E. I. Bakst et al. Edited by I. S. Kalantyrskaia. Moscow: Izd-vo "Sovetskaia Rossiia," 1967. 388 p. [DLC-Z2506.M894; MH-Slav612.100.20]

The guide, an excellent model of its type, surveys the extensive private archives, mostly of eminent prerevolutionary Russian leaders, in the Division of Written Sources. Careful annotations covering 95 percent of the holdings give biographic identification of individuals, the number of storage units and dates included, and a summary of the fond contents, including lists of individuals to whom letters are addressed, etc. The additional 5 percent of the fonds, mostly too small to merit individual attention, are listed at the end. Extensive geographic, personal-name, and subject indexes aid in ready location of the contents.

E-53. Kalantyrskaia, I. S.
"Materialy po istorii russkogo teatra XVIII-XX vv. v Otdele pis'mennykh istochnikov Gosudarstvennogo istoricheskogo muzeia." In *Teatr i muzyka. Dokumenty i materialy* (A-51), pp. 91-104.

Cartographic Division

E-54. Navrot, M. I.
"Katalog rukopisnykh istoricheskikh kart XVIII-XX vv. khraniashchikhsia v fondakh Gosudarstvennogo istoricheskogo muzeia." [Geograficheskoe obshchestvo SSSR. Moskovskii filial.] *Istoriia geograficheskikh znanii i istoricheskaia geografiia. Etnografiia* 2 (1967):17-19.
[MH-Geog115.5]

Brief description of maps and the existing catalogs in GIM, presented in the form of an abstract of a more extensive oral presentation.

E-55. Navrot, M. I.
"Katalog gravirovannykh kart Rossii XVI-XVIII vv. i reproduktsii s nikh, khraniashchikhsia v Otdele istoricheskoi geografii i kartografii Gosudarstvennogo

istoricheskogo muzeia." [Geograficheskoe obshchestvo SSSR. Moskovskii filial.] *Istoriia geograficheskikh znanii i istoricheskaia geografiia. Etnografiia* 4 (1970):39-43.
[MH-Geog115.5]
 Brief description of engraved maps in the GIM collection.

E-56. Navrot, M. I.
"Katalog gravirovannykh i rukopisnykh kart Sibiri XVI-XVII vv., khraniashchikhsia v sektore kartografii Istoricheskogo muzeia." [Geograficheskoe obshchestvo SSSR. Moskovskii filial.] *Istoriia geograficheskikh znanii i istoricheskaia geografiia. Etnografiia* 5 (1971):34-38.
 Brief description of sixteenth and seventeenth century maps of Siberia in GIM with coverage of available catalogs.

4. GOSUDARSTVENNYI LITERATURNYI MUZEI (GLM)

[State Literary Museum]
OTDEL RUKOPISEI [Manuscript Division]
  Address: Moscow, G-2, ulitsa Vesnina, 9/5 kv. 1

CONTENTS

The main exhibits and administration of the State Literary Museum are located at Ulitsa Dimitrova, 38, but the Manuscript Division now occupies an apartment of the fifth floor of the building that houses the small Lunacharskii Museum. It contains over 210 fonds, with over 30,000 storage units. Writers best represented in the present holdings of predominantly personal fonds, all acquired after the Second World War, include S. A. Esenin, M. V. Isakovskii, S. V. Mikhalkov, A. A. Blok, I. S. Turgenev, A. P. Chekhov, and V. G. Korolenko; there is also a substantial group of papers of various members of the Orlov family (1811-1899). In addition to the literary holdings the Manuscript Division has an important folklore collection from the nineteenth and twentieth centuries of about 134,650 items.

The present relatively small size and minor importance of the museum's Manuscript Division contrasts sharply with its position before the Second World War, when its illustrious holdings were among the most significant literary repositories in the ·Soviet Union. The State Literary Museum was officially founded in 1934 on the basis of the consolidation of the holdings of the Literary Museum of the Lenin Library, a special library subsidiary which had hitherto been a gathering point for literary manuscripts and personal fonds, and the holdings of the former Central Museum of Belles Lettres, Criticism, and Journalism [Tsentral'nyi muzei khudozhestvennoi literatury, kritiki i publitsistiki]. Occupying the building across from the Lenin Library that now houses the Kalinin Museum, the State Literary Museum became the largest and richest repository of literary manuscripts in the Soviet Union. The Gor'kii papers were transferred out to the special Gor'kii Archive (see Part C, section 5) in the late 1930's. The museum virtually ceased to exist as a manuscript repository when its remaining fonds were all transferred to the Central State Literary Archive [Tsentral'nyi gosudarstvennyi literaturnyi arkhiv], the present-day TsGALI, after it was established in 1941. It was only in the 1950's and 1960's that the Manuscript Division again began acquiring literary fonds, but these holdings are now largely subsidiary to the exhibiting function of the Literary Museum, and the Manuscript Division remains minor as a repository for important literary fonds.

WORKING CONDITIONS

Readers work in the small reading room adjacent to the division office and storage area. Unpublished inventories are available for almost all fonds, and there is a card catalog of personal names.

PUBLISHED DESCRIPTIONS

A general description of the division is in preparation but as yet there has been no published survey, except for the folklore holdings. Almost all the personal fonds in the division are listed in the general directory of personal archives, *Lichnye arkhivnye fondy v gosudarstvennykh khranilishchakh SSSR. Ukazatel'* (A-9). For the earlier publication work of the museum containing inventories of some of its earlier holdings, see section 5 of Part B, covering TsGALI. For a sketch of the history of the museum and background of the present holdings, see K. M. Vinogradova, "Gosudarstvennyi literaturnyi muzei (1921-1960 gg.)," in *Voprosy raboty muzeev literaturnogo profilia*, published as [Moscow. Nauchno-issledovatel'skii institut muzeevedeniia.] *Trudy* 6 (1961):51-93.

E-57. Mints, S. I.

"Fol'klornyi arkhiv Gosudarstvennogo literaturnogo muzeia (Moskva)." *Sovetskaia etnografiia*, 1963, no. 3, pp. 148-53.

> Gives detailed descriptions of the important fonds with folklore materials and the separate folklore collections.

5. GOSUDARSTVENNAIA BIBLIOTEKA-MUZEI V. V. MAIAKOVSKOGO (BMM)

[V. V. Maiakovskii State Library and Museum]
    Address: Moscow, Zh-4, pereulok Maiakovskogo, 15/13

CONTENTS

This museum and library dedicated to the poet V. V. Maiakovskii contains a large part of his manuscripts and other personal papers, but it is not a centralized gathering point as are the Gor'kii and Tolstoi Archives. A large portion of his papers are now located in TsGALI, but some are scattered in various other repositories.

PUBLISHED DESCRIPTIONS

There is no separate description of the museum holdings, but detailed information about the whereabouts of Maiakovskii's papers, and an inventory of some sections of them, are available in the two-volume publication:

E-58. [Russia (1923-USSR). Tsentral'nyi gosudarstvennyi arkhiv literatury i iskusstva.]
    V. V. Maiakovskii. Opisanie dokumental'nykh materialov.
    Vol. 1: *"Okna" Rosta i gravpolitprosveta 1919-1922 gg.* Compiled by K. N.
    Suvorova. Edited by V. D. Duvakina. Moscow: GAU and TsGALI, 1964. 287 p.
    Vol. 2: *Rukopisi. Zapisnye knizhki. Zhivopis'. Risunki. Afishi. Programmy.*
    Zapisi golosa. Compiled by V. A. Arutcheva et al. Edited by N. V.
    Reformatskaia. Moscow: GAU, TsGALI, and BMM, 1965. 303 p.
    [DLC-Z8542.9.R87; MH-Slav4565.41.1(vols. 1&2)]
        Listed also as item A-13 and B-67.

6. GOSUDARSTVENNYI MUZEI L. N. TOLSTOGO

[L. N. Tolstoi State Museum]
OTDEL RUKOPISEI [Manuscript Division]
  Address: Moscow, G-34, Kropotkinskaia, 21

CONTENTS

  The Manuscript Division of the State Tolstoi Museum, located in an Academy of Sciences building a block beyond the museum itself (Kropotkinskaia, 11), is the central repository for all Tolstoi manuscripts, personal papers, and other biographical materials. There are now 63 fonds with over 200,000 storage units, dating from the beginning of the nineteenth century to the present and covering not only Lev Nikolaevich but also members of his family, friends, and acquaintances. The division is the center for research and publication projects regarding Tolstoi.

PUBLISHED INVENTORIES AND DESCRIPTIONS

E-59. [Moscow. Gosudarstvennyi muzei L. N. Tolstogo.]
Opisanie rukopisei khudozhestvennykh proizvedenii L. N. Tolstogo. Compiled by
V. A. Zhdanov, E. E. Zaidenshnur, and E. S. Serebrovskaia. Edited by V. A.
Zhdanov. Moscow: Izd-vo AN SSSR, 1955. 634 p.
[DLC-Z6616.T6M6; MH-Slav4354.2.936]
    Covers the literary manuscripts in the Tolstoi Museum arranged in
    chronological order.

E-60. [Moscow. Gosudarstvennyi muzei L. N. Tolstogo.]
Opisanie rukopisei statei L. N. Tolstogo. Literatura, iskusstvo, nauka, pedagogika.
Compiled by E. E. Zaidenshnur and E. S. Serebrovskaia. Edited by V. A. Zhdanov.
Moscow: Izd-vo "Sovetskaia Rossiia," 1961. 279 p.
[DLC-Z6616.T6M62; MH-Slav4354.2.936.5]

E-61. Tolstoi, Lev Nikolaevich.
Ukazateli k Polnomu sobraniiu sochinenii L. N. Tolstogo. Alfavitnyi ukazatel'
proizvedenii. Alfavitnyi ukazatel' adresatov. Alfavitnyi ukazatel' imen
sobstvennykh. Khronologicheskii ukazatel' proizvedenii. Moscow: Izd-vo
"Khudozhestvennaia literatura," 1964. 667 p.
[DLC-PG3365.A1.1928 Index; MH-Slav4354.2.8.1]
    This index and directory to Tolstoi's collected writings also provides a guide
    to the manuscripts of these materials, all of which are to be found in the
    Manuscript Division of the Tolstoi Museum.

E-62. [Moscow. Gosudarstvennyi literaturnyi muzei.]
L. N. Tolstoi. Rukopisi, perepiska i dokumenty. Compiled by A. V. Askariants et
al. Edited by N. N. Gusev. *Biulleteni Gosudarstvennogo literaturnogo muzeia*, no. 2.
Moscow: Zhurnal'no-gazetnoe ob"edinenie, 1937. 236 p.
[DLC-Z6616.T9M6.no 2]

PART E – MOSCOW LIBRARIES AND MUSEUMS

This early catalog was prepared while these materials were housed in the State Literary Museum, but they have since all been transferred to the Tolstoi Museum.

7. GOSUDARSTVENNYI TsENTRAL'NYI MUZEI MUZYKAL'NOI KUL'TURY IMENI M. I. GLINKI (GTsMMK)

[M. I. Glinka State Central Museum of Musical Culture]
   Address: Moscow, K-9, Georgievskii pereulok, 4

CONTENTS

The State Central Museum of Musical Culture in Moscow is undoubtedly one of the largest and richest specialized repositories for manuscripts relating to music in the world. Its 320 fonds total over 171,000 storage units with documentary materials relating to the history of musical culture in the USSR. A large portion of the manuscript holdings were originally housed in the library of the Moscow Conservatory, but were transferred here within the last ten years; the museum is continuing to enrich its holdings with manuscripts acquired from other sources to serve as a centralized repository for this type of material. Most of the fonds contain both manuscript musical scores and the personal papers of noted composers; some of the largest include portions of the personal archives of Chaikovskii, Rakhmaninov, Musorgskii, Rimskii-Korsakov, Shostakovich, Skriabin, and Prokofiev. There are also personal fonds of noted conductors, music critics, folklorists, and historians or theoreticians of music. Important institutional fonds include the archive of the Moscow Conservatory and the Russian Musical Society. The museum is now housed in small quarters behind the Gosplan headquarters off Prospekt Marksa, but a larger new building is under construction with more modern facilities for housing the manuscript riches and for museum exhibitions.

PUBLISHED DESCRIPTION

As yet there is no published general description, and only one specialized catalog has been issued.

-63. [Moscow. Gosudarstvennyi tsentral'nyi muzei muzykal'noi kul'tury.]
Avtografy P. I. Chaikovskogo v fondakh Gosudarstvennogo tsentral'nogo muzeia muzykal'noi kul'tury imeni M. I. Glinki. Katalog-Spravochnik. Compiled by B. V. Dobrokhotov and V. A. Kiselev. Edited by V. A. Kiselev. Moscow, 1956. 78 p. [DLC-ML134.C42.M65; MH-Music Library]
   Covers all categories of Chaikovskii manuscripts including both musical scores and personal letters. See also A-10, B-41, and E-64.

PART E – MOSCOW LIBRARIES AND MUSEUMS

8. GOSUDARSTVENNYI DOM-MUZEI P. I. CHAIKOVSKOGO

[State Museum and Home of P. I. Chaikovskii]
Address: Moskovskaia oblast', g. Klin, ulitsa Chaikovskogo, 48

CONTENTS

Located in the house where the composer last lived, this museum contains the largest fond of Chaikovskii's personal papers and musical scores, although many of his manuscripts and papers are scattered in other repositories.

PUBLISHED DESCRIPTION

E-64. [Klin, Russia. Dom-muzei P. I. Chaikovskogo.]
Avtografy P. I. Chaikovskogo v arkhive Doma-Muzeia v Klinu. Spravochnik. Edited by E. V. Korotkova-Leviton.
Vol. 1: Compiled by K. Iu. Davydova, E. M. Orlova, and G. R. Freindling. Moscow/Leningrad: Gosudarstvennoe muzykal'noe izd-vo, 1950. 96 p.
Vol. 2: Compiled by K. M. Davydova. Moscow: Gosudarstvennoe muzykal'noe izd-vo, 1952. 332 p.
[DLC-ML134.C42K5; MH-Music Library]
The first volume includes a short description of the archive and subdivisions covering 1) manuscript musical scores, and 2) memoirs and diaries. The second volume covers manuscript letters and other autographs. For additional information on Chaikovskii manuscripts see the detailed manuscript lists at the end of each entry in the general volume, *Muzykal'noe nasledie Chaikovskogo. Iz istorii ego proizvedenii* (A-10).

9. GOSUDARSTVENNYI TsENTRAL'NYI TEATRAL'NYI MUZEI IMENI A. A. BAKHRUSHINA (GTsTM)

[A. A. Bakhrushin State Central Theatrical Museum]
  Address: Moscow, Zh-54, ulitsa Bakhrushina, 31/12

CONTENTS

The State Central Theatrical Museum, founded by A. A. Bakhrushin in 1894, is the oldest of various Soviet theatrical museums and contains one of the richest archival repositories in the field of Russian theatrical history; the holdings, which now total over 100,000 storage units, mostly dating from the late nineteenth and early twentieth centuries (80 percent of the manuscripts are prerevolutionary), grew out of Bakhrushin's personal collection of theatrical art started at the end of the nineteenth century. The Manuscript Division, which was organized as such in 1935, contains about 400 personal fonds of noted theatrical figures—directors, artistic directors, dramatists, theatrical administrators, actors, critics, and composers. A second section contains institutional fonds of several different theaters, theatrical groups, and theatrical journals. A third section consists of various collections of theatrical materials—autograph collections, playbills, tickets, diaries, theatrical scrapbooks, etc.

The museum's Photo-Negative Division now contains over 300,000 items, including about 200,000 photographs and 100,000 negatives; most of these pictures are from contemporary theatrical productions. The museum is also very rich in printed materials relating to the theater, including a division with over 300,000 theatrical posters.

Although this museum has the status of the Central Theatrical Museum, it should be noted that many other Moscow theaters maintain their own museums, libraries, and collections of manuscript and photographic materials relating to their productions.

WORKING CONDITIONS

The small reading room for the Manuscript Division is open for research on Wednesdays, although arrangements can often be made for foreigners on limited visits to work at other times.

PUBLISHED DESCRIPTION

E-65. Miasnikova, E. S.
  "Mesto rukopisnykh fondov v deiatel'nosti teatral'nogo muzeia." In *Teatral'nye muzei v SSSR*, pp. 108-23. Published as [Moscow. Nauchno-issledovatel'skii institut muzeevedeniia] *Trudy Nauchno-issledovatel'skogo instituta muzeevedeniia i okhrany pamiatnikov istorii i kul'tury*, vol. 23. Moscow, 1969.
    This brief description is more current than the earlier article by
    A. Fridenberg, "Rukopisnye materialy, khraniashchiesia v GTsTM," in

Trudy Gosudarstvennogo tsentral'nogo teatral'nogo muzeia im. A. A. Bakhrushina (Moscow/Leningrad:Iskusstvo, 1941), pp. 175-307.

10. MUZEI MOSKOVSKOGO KhUDOZHESTVENNOGO AKADEMICHESKOGO TEATRA (MKhAT)

[Museum of the Moscow Academic Art Theater]
Address: Moscow, K-9, Proezd Khudozhestvennogo teatra, 3a

CONTENTS

The Manuscript Division of the Moscow Art Theatre Museum (MKhAT) is located together with the museum on the fourth floor of the building next door to the theater. It contains some 350 archival fonds with over 100,000 storage units, covering the history of the theater since its foundation in 1888. The majority of the fonds are organized around the personal papers of individual actors, directors, or others associated with the theater; the most interesting personal fond is that of Stanislavskii, the great majority of whose papers are located in this archive. Also included are many photographic resources, as well as collections of costume and stage designs, and administrative materials from the theater. A large library contains many scripts, prompt-books, and published reference works.

PUBLISHED DESCRIPTION

66. Mikhal'skii, F.
"Rukopisnye fondy muzeia Moskovskogo Khudozhestvennogo teatra." In
Teatral'nye muzei v SSSR, pp. 124-38. Published as [Moscow.
Nauchno-issledovatel'skii institut muzeevedeniia] *Trudy
Nauchno-issledovatel'skogo instituta muzeevedeniia i okhrany pamiatnikov istorii i
kul'tury*, vol. 23. Moscow, 1969.
    This largely replaces the earlier article by V. M. Novoselova,
    "Dokumental'nye materialy po istorii khudozhestvennogo teatra v arkhive
    muzeia MKhAT," in *Trudy MGIAI* 10 (Moscow, 1957):199-213.

11. GOSUDARSTVENNAIA TRET'IAKOVSKAIA GALEREIA (GTG)

[State Tret'iakov Gallery]
    Address: Moscow, Zh-17, Lavrushinskii pereulok, 10

CONTENTS

The Manuscript Division of the State Tret'iakov Gallery contains almost 100 fonds, most of which consist of private papers of important Russian artists, including I. S. Ostroukhov, V. D. Polenov, I. E. Repin, V. A. Serov, and the Botkin family. One of the most important personal fonds is that of P. M. Tret'iakov, whose personal collection of Russian art gathered during the last half of the nineteenth century which, when presented to the city of Moscow in 1892, formed the basis for this museum. The division also contains the institutional archives of the gallery which are rich in correspondence with leading Russian artists and art connoisseurs. A separate Division of Drawings and Engravings contains more purely artistic manuscript materials.

PUBLISHED DESCRIPTION

There is no published description of the Manuscript Division holdings, but inventories have been prepared for most of the fonds and there is an excellent card catalog available for scholarly consultation. Almost all of the personal fonds are listed in the two-volume directory of private papers, *Lichnye arkhivnye fondy v gosudarstvennykh khranilishchakh SSSR. Ukazatel'* (A-9).

12. GOSUDARSTVENNYI MUZEI IZOBRAZITEL'NYKH ISKUSSTV IMENI A. S. PUSHKINA (GMII)

[A. S. Pushkin State Museum of Fine Arts]
   Address: Moscow, G-19, Kropotkinskaia ulitsa, 12/2

CONTENTS

The Pushkin Museum of Fine Arts devoted to non-Russian (predominantly Western) art in Moscow has several different divisions with manuscript holdings. The Manuscript Division itself has approximately 35 fonds with around 30,000 storage units. Here are to be found the records of the museum administration going back to its early foundation in the nineteenth century as an art museum under Moscow University. About two-thirds of the fonds consist of personal papers of different individuals associated with the museum; one of the largest is that of the first director, Professor I. V. Tsvetaev. In addition to these archival holdings, there are some valuable manuscripts to be found in the Division of Ancient Near East Art of the museum. The Division of Drawings and Engravings contains a rich collection of drawings and other graphic materials.

PUBLISHED DESCRIPTIONS

67. Ernshtedt, Petr Viktorovich.
Koptskie teksty Gosudarstvennogo muzeia izobrazitel'nykh iskusstv imeni A. S. Pushkina. Leningrad: Izd-vo AN SSSR, 1959. 215 p.
[DLC-Z6621.M8443C6; MH-FA57.1.70]

68. Vodo, N. N.
"Stoletie graviurnogo kabineta." In [Moscow. Gosudarstvennyi muzei izobrazitel'nykh iskusstv.] *50 let Gosudarstvennomu muzeiu izobrazitel'nykh iskusstv imeni A. S. Pushkina. Sbornik statei.*, pp. 14-29. Moscow: Izd-vo Akademii khudozhestv, 1962.
[DLC-N3321.A92; MH-FA57.1.74]

69. Rubinshtein, R. I.
"Sobranie rukopisei Otdela drevnego Vostoka GMII im. A. S. Pushkina." In *ibid.*, pp. 52-58.

13. GOSUDARSTVENNYI NAUCHNO-ISSLEDOVATEL'SKII MUZEI ARKHI-TEKTURY IMENI A. V. SHCHUSEVA

[State Scientific-Research Museum of Architecture in the Name of A. V. Shchusev]
OTDEL NAUCHNYKH FONDOV [Division of Scientific Fonds]
OTDEL NAUCHNOI FOTOTEKI [Division of Scientific Photographs]
   Address: Moscow, tsentr, Prospekt Kalinina, 5
   (location of holdings—Donskaia ploshchad', 1)

CONTENTS

This research museum administered by the State Commission for Civil Construction is the largest center in the Soviet Union for the collection and care of documents and photographs relating to architecture and city-planning. The museum itself is located near the Lenin Library on Prospekt Kalinina, but the manuscript collections are located in the former Donskoi monastery. The so-called Division of Scientific Fonds holds over 70,000 sheets of architectural drawings, plans, blueprints, and engineering calculations. In addition to the sections for the history of prerevolutionary and Soviet architecture, the museum also has a special section devoted to architectural engravings and lithographs. Its Division of Scientific Photographs has a file of over 300,000 negatives and over 400,000 photographs, making it one of the most impressive collections of its type in the world. The museum from time to time receives the personal papers of important architects, but after these have been inventoried and the materials of interest to the special museum collections removed, the rest of the fonds are transferred to TsGALI.

There is no published description of the holdings.

14. MUZEI ISTORII I REKONSTRUKTSII g. MOSKVY

[Museum of the History and Reconstruction of Moscow]
    Address: Moscow, K-12, Novaia ploshchad', 12

CONTENTS

This museum, which dates back to the city museum founded in Moscow in 1896, has some limited manuscript holdings supplementing the fonds in the Moscow city archive (TsGAgM). It contains maps, early guides, and some miscellaneous manuscript materials about Moscow's history and culture.

There is no published description of the manuscript holdings.

15. TsENTRAL'NYI GOSUDARSTVENNYI ORDENA LENINA MUZEI REVOLIUTSII SSSR

[Central State Museum of the Revolution of the USSR with the Order of Lenin]
Address: Moscow, ulitsa Gor'kogo, 21

CONTENTS

This large museum devoted to the history of the Revolution contains a number of miscellaneous manuscript materials of interest as well as copies of documents from other archives.

There is no published description of the manuscript holdings.

16. TsENTRAL'NYI MUZEI VOORUZHENNYKH SIL SSSR

[Central Museum of the Armed Forces of the USSR]
Address: Moscow, ploshchad' Kommuny, 2

CONTENTS

Originally founded in 1919 as the Museum of the Red Army [Muzei Krasnoi Armii], it was renamed the Central Museum of the Soviet Army [Tsentral'nyi muzei Sovetskoi Armii] after World War II; the present name dates from the end of 1964.

During the fifty years of its existence, the museum has developed an extensive Documentary Fond [Dokumental'nyi fond] with over 100,000 storage units. The wide variety of documentary materials relating to military affairs and the development and activities of the Soviet Army include a number of personal papers of such military leaders as T. M. and M. V. Frunze, D. A. Furmanov, F. I. Tolbukhin, and I. D. Cherniakhovskii, among others.

The museum has also collected a large photographic archive [Fotonegativnyi fond] with over 200,000 negatives, photographs, and photograph albums.

Most of these archival materials are related to the exhibitory functions of the museum, but they may prove of interest to researchers interested in military affairs, particularly in light of the limited access to state military archives.

PUBLISHED DESCRIPTION

There is no published guide to the archival materials in the museum, but they are briefly described in the general guide to the exhibits, *Tsentral'nyi muzei Vooruzhennykh sil SSSR. Putevoditel'* (Moscow: Voennoe izd-vo Ministerstva oborony SSSR, 1965; 215 p.), pp. 210-11.

Some of the documents and military handbills in the museum are described in the series, *Soobshcheniia i materialy Tsentral'nogo muzeia Sovetskoi Armii*, 1962, part 2.

17. GOSUDARSTVENNAIA PUBLICHNAIA ISTORICHESKAIA BIBLIOTEKA RSFSR

[State Public Historical Library of the RSFSR]
    Address: Moscow, tsentr, Starosadskii pereulok, 9

CONTENTS

Among its rare book and incunabula collections, the State Public Historical Library has a small number of early manuscript books of some note. These do not, however, form a manuscript division of any size or significance. Hence the library will be of more importance to foreign scholars for its catalogs and printed holdings (see Appendix 1).

PUBLISHED DESCRIPTION

E-70. Malyshev, V. I.
"Rukopisi Gosudarstvennoi publichnoi istoricheskoi biblioteki." *Voprosy istorii,* 1953, no. 2, pp. 125-27.
    Brief survey of the manuscript holdings.

18. STAROOBRIADCHESKAIA OBSHCHINA PRI ROGOZHSKOM KLADBISHCHE

[Old Believer Society at Rogozhskii Cemetery]
    Address: Moscow, ulitsa Voitovicha

CONTENTS

The library of one of the most important Old Believer groups in the Moscow region has maintained a small collection of approximately 100 early manuscripts.

Its most valuable holdings which had formed part of the original collection, however, have been transferred to the Manuscript Division of the Lenin Library, where they are maintained as a separate fond (no. 247).

PUBLISHED DESCRIPTION

-71. Malyshev, V. I.
    "Drevnerusskie rukopisi Rogozhskogo kladbishcha. Pis'mo iz Moskvy." *Russkie novosti* (Paris), 14 September 1962, p. 4.
        A brief survey of the holdings.

PART F
MANUSCRIPT DIVISIONS OF LIBRARIES AND MUSEUMS IN LENINGRAD

PART F

MANUSCRIPT DIVISIONS OF LIBRARIES AND MUSEUMS
IN LENINGRAD

The manuscript wealth in Leningrad libraries, museums, and other repositories not associated with the systems of the Academy of Sciences or of the Main Archival Administration is at least as great and varied as that in Moscow, if not more so. The general nature of these repositories and the types of materials contained are similar to those described in the introduction to the Moscow section above. Fortunately, preparation of basic location aids for these materials has proceeded much further in Leningrad than in Moscow.

However, the largest and most important single institution in this category, the Manuscript Division of the Saltykov-Shchedrin State Public Library, still has no general guide to its holdings and bibliographical compilations of published catalogs and surveys are far from adequate.

In the fall of 1970 the Manuscript Division of the State Public Library issued a small general directory of manuscript repositories in Leningrad: *Rukopisnye fondy leningradskikh khranilishch. Kratkii spravochnik po fondam bibliotek, muzeev, nauchno-issledovatel'skikh i drugikh uchrezhdenii*, compiled by A. S. Myl'nikov (A-8). In a mimeographed format of limited availability, it covers all the repositories listed here in Part F as well as some of those listed in Part C above that are under the administration of the Academy of Sciences. It also includes a few additional institutions whose limited holdings (under 300 storage units) were not judged to be of sufficient size or interest to foreign readers to merit inclusion here in Part F. In a few cases, it gives slightly more detailed descriptions than the present survey, but its bibliographical coverage, particularly for the larger institutions, is much scantier.

The various general and specialized library directories (see Appendix 1) are helpful in listing manuscript divisions in different types of libraries and usually indicate working hours and other information.

As in the case of Moscow repositories, personal papers in many Leningrad institutions are listed in the general directory of personal fonds, *Lichnye arkhivnye fondy v gosudarstvennykh khranilishchakh SSSR. Ukazatel'* (A-9), and medieval holdings are covered in the directory compiled by Iu. K. Begunov et al., *Spravochnik-ukazatel' pechatnykh opisanii slaviano-russkikh rukopisei* (A-14). A few additional collections of Slavic manuscripts in Leningrad are covered in the article by V. G. Putsko, "Maloizvestnye rukopisnye sobraniia Leningrada," in *Trudy Otdela drevnerusskoi literatury Akademii nauk SSSR* 25 (1970):345-48. Greek manuscripts in different Leningrad repositories are well cataloged in the series of articles by E. E. Granstrem, "Katalog grecheskikh rukopisei leningradskikh khranilishch" (A-38). And several different types of oriental manuscripts are also covered in general descriptive literature (see the general bibliography, Part A, section 7).

Leningrad is particularly rich in documentary materials relating to music and the theater; despite the fact that these materials are spread out over a wide variety of local institutions, they are much easier to locate than similar materials in Moscow thanks to such general surveys as the article by I. F. Petrovskaia, "Dokumenty o teatre i muzyke v arkhivakh, muzeiakh i bibliotekakh Leningrada," in the volume *Teatr i muzyka. Dokumenty i materialy* (A-51), pp. 5-23, and the earlier more systematic coverage in the section "Biblioteki i muzei," in *Muzykal'nyi Leningrad, 1917-1957* by I. V. Golubovskii (A-53), pp. 351-428. The short pamphlet published in 1940 by A. M. Brianskii, *Teatral'nye biblioteki, muzei i arkhivy Leningrada* (A-56) is also still of limited use in this area.

1. GOSUDARSTVENNAIA ORDENA TRUDOVOGO KRASNOGO ZNAMENI PUBLICHNAIA BIBLIOTEKA IMENI M. E. SALTYKOVA-SHCHEDRINA (GPB)

[M. E. Saltykov-Shchedrin State Public Library with the Order of the Red Banner of Labor]

OTDEL RUKOPISEI [Division of Manuscripts]

Address: Leningrad, D-69, Sadovaia ulitsa, 18

HISTORY AND CONTENTS

The Manuscript Division of the Saltykov-Shchedrin State Public Library in Leningrad houses among the world's richest collections of Slavic, Western, and oriental manuscripts; its early manuscripts, together with its more than 1,000 modern archival fonds, total over 300,000 storage units. Unlike the Lenin Library, which was the outgrowth of a private collection and became a state public library in 1862, this distinguished institution, from its opening in 1814 (it had originally been established by order of Catherine the Great) has had the status of a national public library and a legal depository for all books published in Russia.

At the time of the library's public opening, its importance as a manuscript repository was already established. The library of the Zaluski brothers, which was brought from Warsaw to St. Petersburg in 1795 to become one of the foundation collections of the new Imperial Public Library [Imperatorskaia Publichnaia biblioteka], was very rich in manuscripts, especially early Western manuscript books and other Western manuscripts. (Most of this collection was returned to Poland after the Treaty of Riga in 1921 and perished in the Second World War.) In 1805 the extensive manuscript collection of Petr P. Dubrovskii, mostly gathered in Europe during the upheavals of the French Revolution, was purchased for the library, extending the variegated basis of the holdings with its 100 oriental, 20 Greek, 50 Russian, and 700 Western manuscript books and over 15,000 historical documents, mostly from France, dating from the thirteenth through the eighteenth century.

The Manuscript Depository, (or Depo manuskriptov) as it was then called, was the object of special imperial interest and expenditure during the nineteenth century, and grew both in early manuscripts and modern documentary legacies. By the Revolution it ranked second to the Bibliothèque Nationale in Paris among world libraries in terms of the extent and value of its manuscript holdings. Although in the Soviet Union its volume of printed books is now numerically outranked by the Lenin Library in Moscow, the Leningrad Public Library has maintained the primacy of its Manuscript Division.

The library's holdings of medieval Russian and Slavic manuscripts are undoubtedly the most important in the world. The "Ostromir Gospel," which was written in 1056-1057 and is the oldest extant Russian, i.e., Church Slavonic, manuscript and the most famous single illuminated volume in the division, was presented to the library by Alexander I in 1806. Another famous early Russian manuscript, the Laurentian Chronicle [Lavrent'evskaia letopis'] of 1377, the oldest part of the so-called Russian Primary Chronicle, was presented in 1811.

The medieval holdings of the library were enriched during the early nineteenth century by the acquisition of the noted private collections of P. K. Frolov in 1816 and of F. A. Tolstoi in 1830, the latter consisting of some 1,300 manuscript books and historical documents. In 1852 the library acquired the extensive collection of over 2,000 manuscript books and historical documents gathered by the noted historian M. P. Pogodin; this included a number of more modern materials along with famous Russian and foreign autographs, as well as medieval Russian and Slavic manuscripts.

Further extensive growth of the Russian holdings came in the 1850's and 60's when the imperial collections from the Hermitage Library were transferred to the Public Library (other parts of the Hermitage collection were transferred after the Revolution); this meant the addition of many different types of foreign materials as well as such famous early Russian manuscripts as the 1076 *Izbornik Sviatoslava* and the law code (*Sudebnik*) of Ivan IV. Among the most important acquisitions in the nineteenth century, a large part of the collection of Bishop Porfirii Uspenskii augmented the Slavic holdings as well as the Greek and Orientalia sections; the early twentieth century saw the acquisition of such extensive Slavic collections as that of A. A. Titov.

After the Revolution the Manuscript Division became the heir to the inestimable manuscript riches of several important religious institutions, including 1,575 volumes of manuscript books from the Cathedral of Saint Sophia [Sofiiskii Sobor] in Novgorod and 1,402 manuscript books from the Kirillo-Belozerskii monastery; these were acquired together with the famous first two collections of the St. Petersburg Ecclesiastical Academy [Sankt-Peterburgskaia Dukhovnaia Akademiia]. The division also acquired the large collection of the Solovetskii monastery and the Society of Friends of Ancient Literature [Obshchestvo liubitelei drevnei pis'mennosti], along with numerous smaller institutional and private collections. In addition to the nation's richest holdings of medieval Slavic manuscript books, the Manuscript Division has acquired from many of these collections Russian historical documents dating from the thirteenth to the eighteenth century and numbering in the tens of thousands.

The Manuscript Division now contains over half the Greek manuscripts in the Soviet Union. Their number and importance, totalling as they do around 1,000 manuscripts or fragments, make the Public Library one of the most impressive repositories of Greek texts outside Greece. The most important of these are religious texts, including a sixth-century codex of the Gospels and a Psalter dating from 862.

The extent and variety of Western European manuscripts and documentary materials in the Leningrad Public Library are greater than those in any other Soviet repository. The most important collections came to Russia during the late eighteenth and early nineteenth centuries. Although not technically part of the Manuscript Division, the extensive personal library of Voltaire with his own marginalia and the many materials he collected for Catherine the Great, form a special collection in the library. Also from the same period, the Manuscript Division houses a large collection of Diderot's personal papers, including many of his manuscript works, which had been purchased for Catherine the Great. The collection of the Russian diplomat P. P. Dubrovskii, which at first formed a special museum, has remained the most extensive collection of Western materials in the division with about 700 medieval manuscript books and over 15,000 historical documents and famous autographs from all over Europe; the most important are the materials from France, including about 13,000 documents from the Bastille archive and a number of materials from the monasteries of St. Germain des Prês and of St. Antoine des Champs. The Zaluski collection also had a number of Western manuscripts, but most of these were returned to Poland after World War I. The Vaksel' and Sukhtelen collections are also especially rich in foreign autographs, along with many letters of statesmen and literary figures, and other important texts. Many important Western manuscripts came into the division with the acquisition of the imperial Hermitage collection. Some of the most notable early manuscripts in the division include texts of Cicero, a fifth-century parchment codex of the works of Saint Augustine, an early text of Bede's *Historia ecclesiastica*, and a number of legal codices and other religious and literary texts. Historical documents from the Middle Ages and Italian Renaissance include papal bulls and municipal charters. Documents and manuscripts of more modern periods number in the tens of thousands; the bulk of them are from France, although almost every nation on the Continent is represented in the holdings.

After the Leningrad Branch of the Institute of Oriental Studies, the Public Library has the second most valuable and extensive holdings of oriental manuscripts in the Soviet Union. Ancient papyri from the Libyan Era of the tenth and ninth centuries B.C. are among its oldest manuscripts. The largest number of manuscripts in any language group are those in Tadzhik and Persian (around 1,000), Arabic (around 800), Turkic (around 400), and Chinese (about 250). Indian Buddhist texts in the Pali language written on palm leaves, fifth-century Syriac manuscripts, important famous Hebrew, Mongolian, and Georgian texts, and manuscripts in the Armenian, Chaldean, and Samaritan languages, to name a few of the materials represented, give some indication of the extent, richness, and variety of the oriental holdings.

Within the realm of post-seventeenth-century Russian materials, more than 1,000 archival fonds contain personal papers of prominent leaders in all phases of the political, social, and cultural life of the nation. In addition to personal fonds, there are many collections of historical or cultural manuscripts, and autographs. Collections made by the Manuscript Division itself are so classed; others, brought together by private individuals or societies, came to the division in whole or part and still bear the names of their collectors, as for example the P. L. Vaksel' collection. The personal archives of Glinka, Rimskii-Korsakov, Musorgskii, Rubinshtein, Borodin, and other composers, along with other extensive music collections, make the library the richest single repository for Russian musicology. Most of the great Russian writers of the eighteenth, nineteenth, and early twentieth centuries are represented by significant numbers of literary manuscripts—holographs of Krylov's

Fables, of Gogol's *Dead Souls*, and Turgenev's *Fathers and Sons*, are but a few of the prominent examples. There are numerous materials from many of the Decembrists, letters by Herzen and Chernyshevskii and other nineteenth-century reformers and revolutionaries; the Plekhanov House collection, maintained as an auxiliary branch of the Manuscript Division, includes Plekhanov's personal archive and library with more than 8,000 volumes and 6,000 manuscripts.

WORKING CONDITIONS

The Manuscript Division has a large reading room located on the ground floor of the main library building, and its exhibition, office, and storage areas are adjacent.

Permission to work in the Manuscript Division must normally be arranged in advance by written request through the academic institution with which the foreign scholar is affiliated in the Soviet Union. In some instances, post-doctoral scholars not affiliated with an official exchange program have been able to arrange access for short periods of research. There have been no reports of delays or difficulties in obtaining permission for exchange participants, except when uncataloged fonds or those with special restrictions are involved. Normally there have been no restrictions on the use of medieval materials, although some collections are still inadequately cataloged. Restrictions on modern fonds may be applied to a few sensitive materials, and there has been occasional reluctance to permit a foreign scholar to work with unpublished literary manuscripts.

Advance preparation for research as well as actual work in the Manuscript Division is often difficult because of the lack of a published guide or comprehensive annotated bibliography of available descriptive literature. But the help of the experienced staff and the available catalogs in the reading room make the location of materials in the division relatively easy. What problems arise usually stem from the large cataloging backlog, since at present only about 70 percent of the holdings have been thoroughly inventoried; this situation often makes it difficult for the scholar who might wish to probe the lesser-known riches of the division.

Some catalog discrepancies may give readers problems, since the division has been changing over to standard Soviet procedures from the various systems that had been employed in the past. In most cases, when materials have been cataloged earlier, even if they were previously housed in another institution, their original cataloging has stayed with them and is still used for their identification. Because of various rearrangements and shifts of materials among institutions, there are some discrepancies between old catalogs and the documents actually still available; in most cases, however, the reference copy of the catalog in the reading room has been marked accordingly.

A card catalog for many of the personal archival fonds is available in the reading room, with some cross-references to correspondents whose letters may be found among fonds other than their own. For the fonds covered, it is of tremendous assistance in locating materials; due to the cataloging backlogs, however, the catalog is far from complete and does not include all the fonds inventoried. There is also a card file listing the different archival fonds or manuscript collections under the names by which they are commonly known; this file provides a fairly comprehensive indicator of the holdings in the division and shows whether or not an inventory is available for the fond in question.

Inventories may be handwritten, typed, mimeographed, or in some cases printed, but there is no published bibliography or directory of them. Many of the published inventories or other descriptive surveys have appeared in or as supplements to the periodical organs of the Manuscript Division; others have been published by the library or occasionally by outside scholars as separate publications. The published ones are available along the inside wall of the reading room, as are many of the recently completed ones which have been put out in mimeographed form. (Most of these are also available in Moscow in the reading room of the Lenin Library Manuscript Division.) Normally, for fully inventoried fonds, the inventories [*opisi*] are promptly and freely made available, although there have been some complaints by scholars in the past about delays in obtaining handwritten ones.

Manuscripts normally should be ordered half a day to a day ahead. Paging delays usually involve fonds not fully cataloged or manuscripts being used by or being reserved for the use of other scholars.

The Manuscript Division maintains a full stock of basic reference books, and other published materials may be freely ordered from the main stacks of the library for use in the manuscript reading room. Ordered books or periodicals may be reserved indefinitely for use by readers there. Microfilming procedures and availability differ according to the materials in question. Usually there is a reluctance to film unpublished literary manuscripts, or entire sets of documents, especially if publication is contemplated. Sometimes it has been possible to place a straight order, to be paid for in rubles, for a small number of frames. But in most cases the division operates only on the basis of exchange of microfilm of desired manuscript materials in foreign libraries for microfilm of materials in the division.

For notes about working conditions and access to the published books and periodicals in the library, see Appendix 1.

GENERAL PUBLISHED DESCRIPTIONS AND BIBLIOGRAPHY

The Manuscript Division is badly in need of a comprehensive guide with a complete bibliography of literature about its holdings and/or different sections of its holdings; but unfortunately such a publication remains in the planning stage. Because of the lack of adequate bibliographies, the present compilation will be more extensive than in the case of other repositories, but where more specialized bibliographies are available, it will only serve as a supplement to, or list some of, the most comprehensive and important publications. An annotated list of the different catalogs published in recent decades in mimeographed form by the division is included as a supplement to the general directory of Leningrad manuscript fonds, *Rukopisnye fondy leningradskikh khranilishch* (A-8), pp. 68-91. For a prerevolutionary description, including a comprehensive bibliography of catalogs and other finding aids, see V. S. Ikonnikov, *Opyt russkoi istoriografii* (A-83), vol. 1, part 1, pp. 781-841.

F-1. Morachevskii, N. Ia., and Iu. P. Ivkov.
"Obzor bibliograficheskikh izdanii Gos. publichnoi biblioteki za 1917-1957 gg."
Trudy GPB 4 (7) (1957):177-274.
[DLC-Z820.L564; MH-B8888.7.12.5]

> This bibliography of limited value lists only officially published catalogs of
> manuscripts issued by the library since the Revolution (pp. 194-200), and
> briefly lists contents of other library serial publications. See also the shorter
> but more recent coverage by A. S. Myl'nikov, "Pechatnye katalogi i obzory
> rukopisnykh fondov Gosudarstvennoi publichnoi biblioteki im. M. E.
> Saltykova-Shchedrina," *Arkheograficheskii ezhegodnik za 1968 god*, pp.
> 455-57.

F-2. [Leningrad. Publichnaia biblioteka.]
*Istoriia Gosudarstvennoi ordena Trudovogo Krasnogo Znameni publichnoi
biblioteki imeni M. E. Saltykova-Shchedrina.* Edited by V. M. Barashenkov, Iu. S.
Afanas'ev, A. S. Myl'nikov, et al. Leningrad: Lenizdat, 1963. 435 p.
[DLC-Z820.L5713; MH-B8888.7.65F]

> Each chronological section of this large-format 150th anniversary volume has
> a chapter on the Manuscript Division, presenting a summary of major
> acquisitions and publication activities. The rich bibliographical footnotes
> listing catalogs and documents published by the division make it more
> helpful than the general bibliography (F-1), particularly since they cover the
> nineteenth century. More details on the prerevolutionary make-up of the
> division and on early published catalogs can be found in the section of
> Ikonnikov, *Opyt russkoi istoriografii* (A-83), vol. 1, part 1:781-841, and in
> the centenary volume published in 1914, [Leningrad. Publichnaia
> biblioteka.], *Imperatorskaia Publichnaia biblioteka za sto let (1814-1914)*
> (Petrograd, 1914; 841 p. [DLC-Z820.L57.1914; MH-B8888.7.15F]).

F-3. Golubeva, Olga.
"The Saltykov-Shchedrin Library, Leningrad." *The Book Collector* 4 (Summer,
1955): 99-109.

> This general description of the library by a staff member devotes most of its
> space to the Manuscript Division, with some shorter coverage of rare books
> and incunabula. The bibliographical footnotes are a helpful guide to some
> further descriptive literature and catalogs. It is generally more useful than the
> chapter by Arundell Esdaile, "Leningrad: The Saltykov-Shchedrin Library,"
> in *National Libraries of the World: Their History, Administration and Public
> Service*, 2d rev. ed. by R. H. Hill (London: The Library Association, 1957;
> [DLC-Z721.E74.1957]).

F-4. [Leningrad. Publichnaia biblioteka. Otdel rukopisei.]
*Kratkii otchet rukopisnogo otdela za 1914-1938 gg. so vstupitel'nym istoricheskim
ocherkom.* Edited by T. K. Ukhmylova and V. G. Geiman. Leningrad: GPB, 1940.
302 p.
[DLC-Z6621.L559; MH-Slav251.256.2]

Although now somewhat dated, this most important single volume on the division gives a brief history to 1938 and a fairly comprehensive directory of fonds acquired between 1917 and 1938. In the part covering medieval Russian manuscripts it briefly describes 8 collections from prerevolutionary religious institutions and antiquarian societies, 13 made by private individuals, and several other special collections. In the second part devoted to archival fonds it describes the papers of 13 societies and organizations, 5 literary organizations, and 120 individuals. Other sections cover Greek, Western, and oriental manuscripts. A complete index covers proper names of individuals and organizations. The more recent article "Komplektovanie fondov otdela rukopisei Gosudarstvennoi publichnoi biblioteki v 1917-1941 gg.," in *Trudy GPB* 8 (11) (Leningrad, 1960):267-87, also describes the acquisitions during these years but provides neither indexes, bibliography, nor catalog numbers.

F-5. [Leningrad. Publichnaia biblioteka. Otdel rukopisei.]
Kratkii otchet o novykh postupleniiakh za 1939-1946 gg. Edited by A. I. Andreev. Leningrad: GPB, 1951. 162 p.
[DLC-Z6621.L558; MH-Slav251.256.2]
    Continues the preceding volume through 1946.

F-6. [Leningrad. Publichnaia biblioteka. Otdel rukopisei.]
Kratkii otchet o novykh postupleniiakh za 1947-1949 gg. Edited by A. I. Andreev. Leningrad: GPB, 1952. 131 p.
[DLC-Z6621.L558; MH-Slav251.256.2]
    Continues the preceding volumes through 1949.

F-7. [Leningrad. Publichnaia biblioteka. Otdel rukopisei.]
Kratkii otchet o novykh postupleniiakh za 1950-1951 gg. Edited by V. G. Geiman. Leningrad: GPB, 1953. 142 p.
[no US location reported]
    Continues the preceding volumes through 1951.

F-8. [Leningrad. Publichnaia biblioteka. Otdel rukopisei.]
Novye postupleniia v otdele rukopisei (1952-1966). Kratkii otchet. Edited by R. B. Zaborova and A. S. Myl'nikov. Moscow: Izd-vo "Kniga," 1968. 200 p.
[DLC-Z6621.L5592; MH-Slav251.256.2]
    Continuing the preceding volumes through 1966, this volume replaces the yearly compilations in various serial publications of the library. It first describes 89 personal fonds that were acquired in these years, and then covers the many other collections of manuscripts, handwritten books, and documents relating to a variety of cultural, political, and scientific subjects arranged generally in thematic order. Extensive personal and geographic name indices are included.

Serial Publications

In addition to the library serials listed below, the library also issues a mimeographed serial, "Informatsionnyi biulleten' Gosudarstvennoi publichnoi biblioteki," which contains articles about the Manuscript Division, but which is not available outside of the USSR.

F-9. [Leningrad. Publichnaia biblioteka.]
Otchet imperatorskoi Publichnoi biblioteki za 1850 g.[-za 1913 g.]
[DLC-Z820.L565; MH-B8888.7.10]

> Published in St. Petersburg between the years 1851 and 1917 (the final volume covered the year 1913), this series included many descriptions of archival fonds and manuscript collections in the Manuscript Division of the library. Many of the years had supplementary volumes with extensive inventories of some of the fonds and collections.

F-10. [Leningrad. Publichnaia biblioteka.]
Sbornik. Vols. 1-3. Leningrad, 1953-1955.
[DLC-Z6621.L5576 (only vols. 2 and 3); MH-B8888.7.12]

> Superseded by *Trudy* (F-11) and similar to it in format and contents.

F-11. [Leningrad. Publichnaia biblioteka.]
Trudy. Vols. 1-12 (4-15). Leningrad, 1957-1964. (abbreviated as *Trudy GPB*)
[DLC-Z820.L564; MH-B8888.7.12.5]

> Superseded *Sbornik* above (F-10) and continued its numbering in parentheses. Four volumes were issued in 1957, 3 in 1958, none in 1959, and annual volumes from 1960 through 1964. They include general articles about library affairs and different divisions or collections. Scattered issues have important descriptions or inventories of manuscripts. This series should not be confused with the unnumbered irregular monographic volumes entitled *Trudy [otdela rukopisei]* issued by the Manuscript Division. A volume containing library articles for the years 1964-1969 is in preparation.

F-12. [Leningrad. Publichnaia biblioteka.]
Gosudarstvennaia publichnaia biblioteka im. M. E. Saltykova-Shchedrina v [1954 g.] Leningrad, 1955+.
[DLC-Z820.L5643; MH-B8888.7.19]

> This series started as annual reports, but since 1962-1963 has been issued biennially. Of special interest to users of the Manuscript Division as they list published general descriptions and catalogs, including those issued in small numbers in mimeographed form, and include the tables of contents of other library serial publications. Since the 1959 issue they have also included detailed lists of acquisitions of the Manuscript Division.

INVENTORIES AND SPECIALIZED DESCRIPTIONS

The present list will include the mimeographed publications of the division that are often not differentiated in Soviet bibliographies; however, copies of these are available only in a few key research centers, including the reading room of the Manuscript Division of the Lenin Library in Moscow, and are not available for export. An annotated bibliography of these is included in *Rukopisnye fondy leningradskikh khranilishch* (A-8), pp. 68-91.

Medieval Slavic Manuscripts

A comprehensive bibliography of descriptions and catalogs of medieval Slavic manuscripts of the division is available in the general directory compiled by Iu. K. Begunov et al., *Spravochnik-ukazatel' pechatnykh opisanii slaviano-russkikh rukopisei* (A-14), pp. 90-109. Since it covers articles that appeared in the prerevolutionary library *Otchet* along with other catalogs, and even those for collections only subsequently transferred to the library, it is the best starting place for locating such publications prior to 1961; except for general publications its entries will not be repeated below.

`-13. Al'shits, D[aniil] N[atanovich].
Istoricheskaia kollektsiia Ermitazhnogo sobraniia rukopisei. Pamiatniki XI-XVII vv. Opisanie. Edited by A. S. Myl'nikov. Moscow: Izd-vo "Kniga," 1968. 158 p.
[DLC-Z6621.L5563; MH-Slav251.256.40]
> An inventory of 434 manuscripts, covering the early part of the collection that came to GPB from the Hermitage. It does not replace nor should it be confused with the earlier mimeographed "Katalog russkikh rukopisei Ermitazhnogo sobraniia," compiled by D. N. Al'shits and E. G. Shapot (Leningrad, 1960; 381 p.) which covers 816 manuscripts, including the eighteenth and nineteenth century materials in the collection. See also the earlier survey of the collection published in *Trudy GPB* 5 (1958):167-84.

`-14. [Leningrad. Publichnaia biblioteka. Otdel rukopisei.]
Opisanie russkikh i slavianskikh pergamennykh rukopisei. Rukopisi russkie, bolgarskie, moldavovlakhiiskie, serbskie. Compiled by E. E. Granstrem. Edited by D. S. Likhachev. Leningrad: GPB, 1953. 129 p.
[MH-B8888.7.55; DDO]
> General description of 471 medieval Slavic parchment manuscripts.

-15. Geiman, V. G., and E. E. Granstrem, compilers.
"Katalog drevnerusskikh gramot, khraniashchikhsia v otdele rukopisei Gos. publichnoi biblioteki im. M. E. Saltykova-Shchedrina v Leningrade, 1647-1660 gg." Part 5. Leningrad: GPB, 1960. 248 p. Mimeographed.
> Four earlier parts of this catalog have been published serially in a variety of locations: Part 1, compiled by A. I. Andreev, was first published in *Letopis' zaniatii Arkheograficheskoi komissii za 1919-1922 gg.*, 32 (Petrograd, 1923):1-46, and then issued separately; Part 2, compiled by V. G. Geiman, is published as a supplement to F-5, pp. 114-62; Parts 3 and 4, compiled by V. G. Geiman and E. E. Granstrem are published as supplements to F-6, pp. 79-113, and F-7, pp. 87-142. The fifth part as listed here was issued in

mimeographed form and is hence not widely available. Details of these and other printed catalogs covering the Division's collection of early Russian charters are listed by Begunov (A-14), pp. 101-102.

Greek Manuscripts

See also the general catalog of Greek manuscripts in Leningrad by E. E. Granstrem (A-38).

F-16. Granstrem, E. E.
"Grecheskie rukopisi Gosudarstvennoi publichnoi biblioteki im. M. E. Saltykova-Shchedrina." *Trudy GPB* 2 (5) (1957):211-37.

F-17. [Leningrad. Publichnaia biblioteka.]
Catalogue des manuscrits grecs de la Bibliothèque Impériale publique. Compiled by E. de Muralt. St. Petersburg: Imprimerie de l'Académie Impériale des Sciences, 1864. 100 p.
[DLC-Z6621.L56G7; MH-B3700.2.5]
> Published supplements to this original catalog of the Greek manuscript holdings are listed by M. Richard in his general directory, *Répertoire des bibliothèques et des catalogues de manuscrits grecs* (A-37), pp.132-34; *Supplément* 1:30-31; Richard's notes on the GPB holdings with details about Greek manuscripts in different collections and an appraisal of the typewritten inventory are recorded in his "Rapport sur une mission d'étude en URSS (5 octobre-3 novembre 1960)," *Bulletin d'information de l'Institut de recherche et d'histoire des textes* 10 (1961):51-53.

Eastern European Materials (non-Russian)

See also items F-14, F-16, and F-23.

F-18. Kopreeva, T. N.
"Obzor pol'skikh rukopisei Gosudarstvennoi publichnoi biblioteki (Sobranie P. P. Dubrovskogo)." *Trudy GPB* 5 (8) (1958):137-65.
> In addition to this survey of Polish materials see the brief notes about the library's Polish holdings in the article by Edmund Rabowicz, "Polonica oświeceniowe w bibliotekach i archiwach ZSRR," in *Miscellanea z doby Oświecenia. Archiwum literacke* 5 (1960):553-55.

F-19. Myl'nikov, A. S.
"Cheshskie i slovatskie rukopisi Gosudarstvennoi publichnoi biblioteki. Obzor." *Trudy GPB* 5 (8) (1958):119-36.

F-20. Rozov, N. N.
"Iuzhnoslavianskie rukopisi Gosudarstvennoi publichnoi biblioteki. Obzor." *Trudy GPB* 5 (8) (1958):105-18.

Western European Manuscripts

General

F-21. Voronova, T. P.

"Western Manuscripts in the Saltykov-Shchedrin Library, Leningrad." *The Book Collector* 5 (Spring 1956):12-18.

This survey of Western holdings by a staff specialist, with extensive bibliographical footnotes to inventories and other relevant literature, updates the earlier survey by A. D. Liublinskaia, "Zapadnye rukopisi v Leningradskoi publichnoi biblioteke," in *Sovetskaia nauka,* 1940, no. 9, pp. 96-107.

F-22. Mnukhina, R. S.

"Istochniki po istorii novogo vremeni v otdele rukopisei Leningradskoi Gosudarstvennoi publichnoi biblioteki im. M. E. Saltykova-Shchedrina." In [Leningrad. Universitet.] *Vestnik. Seriia istorii, iazyka i literatury* 14 (1962):135-39.

Surveys holdings for non-Russian history of interest to foreign historians; lists many bibliographies and articles of relevance to the documents.

F-23. [Leningrad. Publichnaia biblioteka. Otdel rukopisei.]

Katalog pisem i drugikh materialov zapadnoevropeiskikh uchenykh i pisatelei XVI-XVIII vv. iz sobraniia P. P. Dubrovskogo. Compiled by E. V. Bernadskaia and T. P. Voronova. Edited by M. P. Alekseev. Leningrad: GPB, 1963. 105 p. [DLC-Z6621.L56.D8; MH-Slav251.256.15]

Gives a detailed listing of 308 items in the Dubrovskii collection with classification numbers, dates, pagination, language, and bibliographical references. Following a long historical introduction, the contents are arranged by country of origin—Netherlands, Germany, France, Italy—and there is also some correspondence of A. D. Kantemir and J. A. Zaluski. Includes summary table of contents in German, French, and English. For an earlier general description of this collection, see the article by T. V. Luizova, "Sobranie rukopisei P. P. Dubrovskogo v Gosudarstvennoi publichnoi biblioteke imeni M. E. Saltykova-Shchedrina," *Voprosy istorii,* 1952, no. 8, pp. 150-54.

Latin and Other Medieval Manuscripts

For a detailed bibliography of descriptions and catalogs including some manuscript inventories of Latin manuscripts in GPB, see Kristeller, *Latin Manuscript Books Before 1600* (A-40), pp. 136-38, 263-64; all the items listed by Kristeller will not be repeated here. See additional entries under French and Italian manuscripts below.

F-24. [Leningrad. Publichnaia biblioteka.]

Les manuscrits latins du Ve au XIIIe siècle conservés à la Bibliothèque Impériale de Saint-Pétersbourg. Description, textes inédits, reproductions autotypiques.

Compiled by Dom Antonio Staerk. 2 vols., in folio. St. Petersburg: Franz Krais,
1910. 320 p. 140 plates.
[DLC-Z6621.L56L3.1910; MH-D651.70]
> The second volume consists of facsimiles. Many of the manuscripts described
> are from the Dubrovskii and the Zaluski collections; most of the latter were
> returned to Warsaw after 1918 and perished during World War II.

F-25. [Leningrad. Publichnaia biblioteka.]
Les anciens manuscrits latins de la Bibliothèque Publique de Leningrad. Compiled
by O. A. Dobiash-Rozhdestvenskaia.
> Part 1: *V-VII siècles.* Published as *Srednevekov'e v rukopisiakh Publichnoi*
> *biblioteki. Analecta Medii Aevi*, vol. 3. Leningrad, 1929. 64 p.
> [MH-ML9.25.11]
> Part 2: "Rukopisi VIII-nach. IX vv." (with general title in Russian: "Drevneishie
> latinskie rukopisi Publichnoi biblioteki. Katalog." Leningrad: GPB, 1965. 153 p.
> Mimeographed.
>
> The second volume in the library *Occidentalia* series includes several articles
> related to Western manuscripts, *Srednevekov'e v rukopisiakh Publichnoi*
> *biblioteki. Analecta Medii Aevi*, vol. 2 (Leningrad, 1927; 200 p.)

F-26. Laborde, Alexandre de.
Les principaux manuscrits à peintures conservés dans l'ancienne Bibliothèque
Impériale publique de Saint-Pétersbourg. 2 vols. Paris: Société française de
reproductions de manuscrits à peintures, 1936-1938. 196 p. unbound. 86 plates.
[MH-Fogg Museum; DDO]
> This detailed catalog was prepared before World War I; not all of the
> illuminated manuscripts included remain in Leningrad. See also item F-30 for
> the French manuscripts covered, some of which are now available on
> microfilm in Paris.

F-27. Luizova, T. V.
"Rannegoticheskie rukopisi Gosudarstvennoi publichnoi biblioteki im. M. E.
Saltykova-Shchedrina." *Trudy GPB* 1 (4) (1957):237-64.

French Manuscripts

F-28. Shishmarev, V. F.
"Frantsuzskie rukopisi Gosudarstvennoi publichnoi biblioteki." In *Rukopisnoe*
nasledie V. F. Shishmareva v arkhive Akademii nauk SSSR. Opisanie i publikatsii.
Published as *Trudy arkhiva AN SSSR* 21 (1965):75-134 (see C-17).
> Presents detailed description and some texts of French manuscripts in
> Dubrovskii and Zaluski collections.

F-29. Voronova, T. P.
"Frantsuzskie srednevekovye rukopisnye knigi v sobranii Gosudarstvennoi
publichnoi biblioteki im. M. E. Saltykova-Shchedrina. (Iz istorii srednevekovykh
bibliotek i kollektsii)." *Srednie veka* 22 (1962):258-66.

Describes the medieval manuscript books with extensive bibliographical footnotes, including references to earlier catalogs.

F-30. Brayer, Edith.
"Manuscrits français du moyen âge conservés à Leningrad." *Bulletin d'information de l'Institut de recherches et d'histoire des textes*, 1958, no. 7, pp. 23-33.
A list of 75 medieval French manuscripts in the Manuscript Division of GPB, correlated with the earlier catalogs of Laborde (F-26) and Bertrand (F-31) and indicating those for which microfilms are available in Paris.

F-31. Bertrand, M. Gustave.
Catalogue des manuscrits français de la bibliothèque de Saint-Pétersbourg. Paris: Imprimerie nationale, 1874. 227 p. Reprinted from *Revue des sociétés savantes,* 5th series, 6 (1873):373-599.
[MH-B2700.2.10]
Catalog is arranged by subjects. Many of the manuscripts in the Zaluski collection were returned to Warsaw after World War I and were subsequently destroyed in World War II; the reference copy in the Manuscript Division reading room is marked accordingly. See also the notes on the medieval manuscripts contained in this volume in the list in item F-30.

F-32. "Dokumenty iz bastil'skogo arkhiva. Annotirovannyi katalog." Compiled by A. D. Liublinskaia. Leningrad: GPB, 1960. 327 p. Mimeographed.
Includes an extensive index. For a description of the fate of the Bastille Archive (a part of which is now in the Dubrovskii collection of GPB) after the fall of the Bastille, see the article by A. D. Liublinskaia, "Bastiliia i ee arkhiv," in *Frantsuzskii ezhegodnik. Stat'i i materialy po istorii Frantsii. 1958* (Moscow: Izd-vo AN SSSR, 1959), pp. 104-26.

F-33. Caussy, Fernand.
Inventaire des manuscrits de la Bibliothèque de Voltaire conservés à la Bibliothèque Impériale publique de Saint-Pétersbourg. Paris, 1913. Geneva: Slatkine Reprints, 1970. 96 p.
[DLC-Z6621.L562V63.1970]
Gives a detailed inventory of the contents of 13 volumes of correspondence, 5 volumes of notes and manuscripts for Voltaire's *Histoire de Russie sous Pierre le Grand*, a volume of memoranda, and a volume of copies of his letters to Madame d'Epinay. A final section covers documents from other collections in the GPB Manuscript Division. A detailed inventory of the printed books in Voltaire's library, now still intact in GPB, includes a supplementary list of manuscript notes included in the books, and gives some information about marginalia: [Leningrad. Publichnaia biblioteka. Biblioteka Vol'tera.], *Biblioteka Vol'tera. Katalog knig/Bibliothèque de Voltaire. Catalogue des livres,* edited by M. P. Alekseev and T. N. Kopreeva (Leningrad: Izd-vo AN SSSR, 1961; 1166 p. [DLC-Z997.V83L4]). See also the published original catalog of the library, *Voltaire's Catalogue of his Library at Ferney*, edited by

George R. Havens and Norman L. Torrey (Geneva: Institut et musée Voltaire, 1959; 258 p.; Publications de l'Institut et musée Voltaire. *Studies on Voltaire and the Eighteenth Century*, vol. 9; [DLC-PQ2105.A258.vol.9] . See also the article by V. S. Liublinskii, "Nasledie Vol'tera v SSSR," *Literaturnoe nasledstvo* 29/30 (1937):3-200, especially the section "Vol'terovskie materialy v sovetskikh sobraniiakh," pp. 162-200; most of the materials listed are in GPB, but a few miscellaneous other documents are included.

F-34. Tourneux, Maurice.
"Les manuscrits de Diderot conservés en Russie. Catalogue." *Archives des missions scientifiques,* 3rd series, 12 (Paris, 1885):439-74.
[DLC-AS162.F8]
Describes the 32 volumes of Diderot manuscripts from the imperial collection in the Hermitage transferred to GPB in the 1860's. Also covers a few other miscellaneous manuscripts. Volume 17 of the manuscripts of Diderot's works (missing at the time of the Tourneux catalog) has been subsequently analyzed in detail by Johan Viktor Johansson, *Etudes sur Denis Diderot. Recherches sur un volume manuscrit conservé à la bibliothèque publique de l'Etat à Leningrad* (Göteborg: Wettergren and Kerbers/ Paris: Champion [1927] ; 209 p.) An up-to-date appraisal of the Diderot holdings by an American scholar is presented by Arthur Wilson, "Leningrad, 1957: Diderot and Voltaire Gleanings," *French Review* 31 (1958):351-63.

Italian Manuscripts
See also the Latin entries and some of the general descriptive literature listed above.

F-35. Bernadskaia, E. V.
"Ital'ianskaia rukopisnaia kniga v sobranii Gosudarstvennoi publichnoi biblioteki im. M. E. Saltykova-Shchedrina v Leningrade." *Srednie veka* 30 (1967):251-60.
Gives a brief description of the 250 Italian manuscript books in GPB, dating from the 5th to the 18th century.

F-36. Bernadskaia, E. V.
"Arkhiv venetsianskogo izdatelia A. Kaladzhera v Leningrade." In *Rossiia i Italiia. Iz istorii russko-ital'ianskikh kul'turnykh i obshchestvennykh otnoshenii,* edited by S. D. Skazkin et al., pp. 51-56. Moscow: Izd-vo "Nauka," 1968.
[DLC-DK67.5.I8R6; MH-Ital 467.192]
Brief description of the papers of the abbot D. Angelo Calogerà (1699-1766) which include over 12,000 letters addressed to him.

Scandinavian Documents

F-37. Rukhmanova, E. D., and Iu. V. Kurskov.
"Istochniki po istorii russko-skandinavskikh otnoshenii v rukopisnykh sobraniiakh g. Leningrada." In *Skandinavskii sbornik* 3, edited by V. V. Pokhlebkina and L. K.

Roots, pp. 257-69. Tallin: Estonskoe gosudarstvennoe izd-vo, 1958.
[DLC-DL1.S5; MH-PScan 348.4(3)]

> Materials in the Manuscript Division of GPB are covered on pp. 265-69. See
> also the listing under item C-28 for the coverage of LOII in this article.

Autograph Collections
See also F-23

-38. "Katalog sobraniia avtografov M. P. Pogodina." Compiled by N. A. Dvoretskaia.
Leningrad: GPB, 1960. 128 p. Mimeographed.

-39. Naidich, E. E.
"Avtografy russkikh pisatelei v sobranii P. L. Vakselia. Obzor." *Sbornik GPB* 3
(1955):89-102.

Oriental Manuscripts
See further printed literature in the general directories covering specific oriental
language groups in Part A, section 7, above.

-40. Demidova, M. I., and G. I. Kostydova.
"Fondy rukopisei i pechatnykh izdanii na iazykakh narodov vostoka v
Gosudarstvennoi publichnoi biblioteke im. M. E. Saltykova-Shchedrina." In
Vostokovednye fondy krupneishikh bibliotek Sovetskogo soiuza (A-22),
pp. 156-71.

> Gives a general description of the oriental holdings in GPB. The coverage of
> the Manuscript Division (pp. 163-71) gives details about the holdings in
> different language groups and provides a starting bibliography of published
> catalogs.

-41. [Leningrad. Publichnaia biblioteka.]
*Catalogue des manuscrits et xylographes orientaux de la Bibliothèque Impériale
publique de St. Pétersbourg.* Compiled by B. A. Dorn. St. Petersburg: Imprimerie
de l'Académie Impériale des sciences, 1852. 719 p.
[DLC-Z6621.L56.O7.1852; MH-OL85.215]

> This monumental catalog has never been superseded by a more
> comprehensive, up-to-date version; it includes, of course, only the oldest parts
> of the oriental holdings in the division. Supplemental descriptions of
> additions coordinated with this catalog are listed in the general directory of
> oriental holdings by J. D. Pearson (A-23).

Egyptian Papyri

42. Evgenova, V. I.
"O drevneegipetskikh papirusakh sobraniia Gosudarstvennoi publichnoi biblioteki
im. M. E. Saltykova-Shchedrina." *Trudy GPB* 2 (5) (1957):5-16.

Coptic Manuscripts

F-43. Elanskaia, A. I.
Koptskie rukopisi Gosudarstvennoi publichnoi biblioteki imeni M. E. Saltykova-Shchedrina. Leningrad: Izd-vo "Nauka," 1969. 151 p. *Palestinskii sbornik*, vol. 20 (83).
[DLC-DS32.5P3; MH-Asia9202.13(83)]

Kurdish Manuscripts

F-44. Rudenko, Margarita Borisovna.
Opisanie kurdskikh rukopisei leningradskikh sobranii. Moscow: Izd-vo vostochnoi literatury, 1961. 125 p.
[DLC-Z6650.K8R8; MH-3263.66.35]
This offset edition published by the Leningrad Branch of the Institut narodov Azii (now Institut vostokovedeniia) covers the A. D. Jaba collection in GPB and a few other manuscripts in the Institute of Oriental Studies in Leningrad (see C-67). For an earlier description of the Jaba collection see M. B. Rudenko, "Kollektsiia A. D. Zhaba (Kurdskie rukopisi)," in *Trudy GPB* 2 (5) (1957):165-84.

Hebrew Manuscripts

F-45. [Leningrad. Publichnaia biblioteka.]
Catalog der hebräischen und samaritanischen Handschriften der Kaiserlichen Öffentlichen Bibliothek in St. Petersburg.
Vol. 1: *Catalog der hebräischen Bibelhandschriften der Kaiserlichen Öffentlichen Bibliothek in St. Petersburg.* Compiled by A[braham] Harkavy and H. L. Strack. St. Petersburg: C. Ricker/ Leipzig: J. C. Hinrichs, 1875. 297 p. In German.
Vol. 2: *Opisanie samaritanskikh rukopisei khraniashchikhsia v imperatorskoi Publichnoi biblioteke.* Compiled by A[braham] Harkavy (Garkavi). St. Petersburg: Tipografiia imperatorskoi AN, 1875. 536 p. In Russian.
DLC-Z6621.L56H4.1875; microfilm 21526Z; MH-OL3003.215]

F-46. Gurland, Johan Hayyim.
Kurze Beschreibung der mathematischen, astronomischen und astrologischen hebräischen Handschriften der Firkowitsch'schen Sammlung in der Kaiserlichen Öffentlichen Bibliothek zu St. Petersburg. St. Petersburg: Buchdruckerei der Kaiserlichen Akademie der Wissenschaften, 1866. 57 p.
[DLC-Z6621.S22H4.1866]
An identical Russian edition was published simultaneously: Gurliand, Iona. *Kratkoe opisanie matematicheskikh, astronomicheskikh i astrologicheskikh evreiskikh rukopisei iz kollektsii Firkovichei, khraniashchiesia v imperatorskoi Publichnoi biblioteke v S. Peterburge.* St. Petersburg: Tipografiia imperatorskoi AN, 1866. 59 p. "Novye pamiatniki evreiskoi literatury v S. Peterburge," vol. 2. The catalog covers manuscripts in the first Firkovich collection.

F-47. Katsh, Abraham I.

The Antonin Genizah in the Saltykov-Shchedrin Public Library in Leningrad. New York: Institute of Hebrew Studies, 1963. 17 p. Reprinted from the Leo Jung Jubilee volume, 1962.

[DLC-Z6621.L56.H45; MH-Heb744.469]

   Describes and inventories the Antonin collection.

Syriac Manuscripts

F-48. Pigulevskaia, N. V.

Katalog siriiskikh rukopisei Leningrada. Published as *Palestinskii sbornik,* vol. 6 (69). Moscow/Leningrad: Izd-vo AN SSSR, 1960. 230 p.

[DLC-D532.5.P3; MH-Asia9202.13]

   Also covers manuscripts in the Leningrad Branch of the Institute of Oriental Studies (see C-73).

Arabic, Persian, and Turkic Manuscripts

F-49. [Leningrad. Publichnaia biblioteka.]

Die Sammlung von morgenländischen Handschriften, welche die Kaiserliche Öffentliche Bibliothek zu St. Petersburg im Jahre 1864 von Hrn v. Chanykov erworben hat. Compiled by B[oris Andreevich] Dorn. St. Petersburg: Buchdrückerei der kaiserlichen Akademie der Wissenschaften, 1865. 93 p.

[DLC-Z6621.L5607.1865]

   Covers the Khanykov collection of Persian, Turkic, and Arabic manuscripts.

Indian Manuscripts

F-50. [Leningrad. Publichnaia biblioteka.]

Katalog indiiskikh rukopisei Rossiiskoi Publichnoi biblioteki. Sobranie I. P. Minaeva i nekotorye drugie. Compiled by N. D. Mironov. Vol. 1: Petrograd: Izdanie Rossiiskoi AN, 1918. 288 p.

[DLC-Z6621.L56I5.1918]

   Only one volume was published.

F-51. Beskrovnyi, V. M.

"Indiiskie rukopisi, napisannye v Rossii." In *Sbornik GPB* 3 (1955):157-70.

Central Asian Khanate Archives

   The catalogs of the archives of the Khanates of Khiva and Kokand which were prepared by the GPB Manuscript Division will be listed under the Central State Historical Archive of the Uzbek SSR, where the documents are now housed; with the transfer of these fonds to Tashkent, microfilms of the documents were retained by GPB.

Materials for Modern Russian History

F-52. "Katalog rukopisnykh materialov o voine 1812 g." Compiled by L. A. Mandrykina, T. P. Voronova, and S. O. Vialova. Leningrad: GPB, 1961. 169 p. Mimeographed.

F-53. [Leningrad. Publichnaia biblioteka. Otdel rukopisei.]
Opisanie rukopisnykh materialov po istorii dvizheniia dekabristov. Compiled by E. P. Fedoseeva. Edited by S. B. Okun. Leningrad: GPB, 1954. 100 p.
[DLC-Z6621.L56R85; MH-Slav1255.220]

F-54. "Katalog rukopisnykh materialov po sotsial'no-ekonomicheskoi istorii imperializma v Rossii." Compiled by M. Ia. Stetskevich. Leningrad: GPB, 1960. 60 p. Mimeographed.

F-55. *Istoriia Leningrada. Katalog rukopisei.* Compiled by V. I. Pishvanova and T. P. Glushkov. Edited by A. I. Andreev. Leningrad: GPB, 1954. 124 p.
[no US location reported]

F-56. Borodkina, L. M.
"Obzor rukopisnykh planov Peterburga XVIII v. i nachala XIX v." *Sbornik GPB* 2 (1954):235-68.
See also F-63.

Materials for Ukrainian History

F-57. Stetskevich, M. Ia.
"Obzor materialov po istorii krest'ianstva Ukrainy perioda vtoroi revoliutsionnoi situatsii (po fondu revizii senatora A. A. Polovtsova)." *Trudy GPB* 12 (15) (1964):219-27.
See also item F-78.

Literary and Theater Materials

F-58. Zaborova, R. B., I. A. Konopleva, and N. N. Rozov.
"Materialy po istorii russkoi literatury v rukopisnykh fondakh GPB." *Trudy GPB* 12 (15) (1964):157-98.

F-59. Rozov, N. N.
"Materialy po istorii russkogo dramaticheskogo teatra v rukopisnykh fondakh Gosudarstvennoi publichnoi biblioteki imeni M. E. Saltykova-Shchedrina v Leningrade (XVII v.—1940e gody)." In *Teatr i muzyka. Dokumenty i materialy.* (A-51), pp. 57-71.
General survey of holdings.

Music Materials

F-60. [Leningrad. Publichnaia biblioteka. Otdel rukopisei.]
Muzykal'nye sokrovishcha rukopisnogo otdeleniia Gosudarstvennoi publichnoi biblioteki imeni M. E. Saltykova-Shchedrina (Obzor muzykal'nykh rukopisnykh

fondov). Compiled by Andrei Nikolaevich Rimskii-Korsakov. Leningrad: GPB, 1938. 111 p.
[DLC-ML136.L25R57]

Includes French résumé, pp. 95-99. See also the short description of the music holdings in GPB in *Muzykal'nyi Leningrad* (A-53), pp. 351-55.

Art and Architecture Materials

61. Fomicheva, E. I.
"O nekotorykh rabotakh russkikh khudozhnikov v fondakh Otdela rukopisei Publichnoi biblioteki." *Trudy GPB* 12 (15) (1964):199-214.

62. [Leningrad. Publichnaia biblioteka. Otdel rukopisei.]
Opisanie arkhitekturnykh materialov. Moskva i Moskovskaia oblast'. Compiled by E. P. Fedoseeva. Edited by G. G. Grimm. Leningrad: GPB, 1956. 88 p.
[DLC-NA1197.M6L4]

63. *Opisanie arkhitekturnykh materialov. Leningrad i prigorody.* Compiled by E. P. Fedoseeva. Edited by G. G. Grimm. Leningrad: GPB, 1953. 144 p.
[no US location reported]

See also F-56.

64. "Katalog materialov po arkhitekture SSSR." Compiled by E. P. Fedoseeva. Edited by G. G. Grimm. 3 vols. Leningrad: GPB, 1960. 273 p.; 171 p.; 95 p. Mimeographed.

Materials Relating to Library Science

65. Sirotova, A. V.
"Obzor materialov po bibliotekovedeniiu khraniashchikhsia v russkikh fondakh otdela rukopisei GPB im. M. E. Saltykova-Shchedrina." *Trudy GPB* 12 (15) (1964):145-56.

Personal Archival Fonds

M. A. Balakirev (1836-1910)

66. "Tvorcheskoe nasledie M. A. Balakireva. Katalog proizvedenii." Compiled by A. S. Liapunova. 3 vols. Leningrad: GPB, 1960. 198 p.; 164 p.; 312 p. Mimeographed.

V. G. Belinskii (1811-1848)

67. *Rukopisi V. G. Belinskogo. Opisanie.* Compiled by R. B. Zaborova. Edited by N. Ia. Morachevskii. Leningrad: GPB, 1952. 31 p.
[no US location reported]

PART F — LENINGRAD LIBRARIES AND MUSEUMS

N. L. Benois (1813-1898)

F-68. "Katalog arkhitekturnykh materialov iz arkhiva N. L. Benua." Compiled by E. P. Fedoseeva. Leningrad: GPB, 1965. 187 p. Mimeographed.

    See also the short published survey of the N. L. Benois papers by G. G. Grimm and E. P. Fedoseeva, "Obzor fonda arkhitektora N. L. Benua," in *Trudy GPB* 12 (15) (1964):215-18.

N. A. Dobroliubov (1836-1861)

F-69. [Leningrad. Publichnaia biblioteka. Otdel rukopisei.]
Arkhiv N. A. Dobroliubova. Opis'. Compiled by E. E. Naidich. Edited by N. Ia. Morachevskii. Leningrad: GPB, 1952. 35 p.
[DLC-Z6616.D65.L4]

F. M. Dostoevskii (1821-1881)

F-70. "Rukopisi F. M. Dostoevskogo. Katalog." Compiled by R. B. Zaborova. Leningrad: GPB, 1963. 66 p. Mimeographed.

    See also the comprehensive survey of Dostoevskii manuscripts, A-11.

A. K. Glazunov (1865-1936)

F-71. Liapunova, A. S.
"Rukopisnoe nasledie A. K. Glazunova. Obzor." *Sbornik GPB* 3 (1955):103-21.

M. I. Glinka (1804-1857)

F-72. [Leningrad. Publichnaia biblioteka. Otdel rukopisei.]
Rukopisi M. I. Glinki. Katalog. Compiled by A. S. Liapunova. Edited by V. M. Bogdanov-Berezovskii. Leningrad: GPB, 1950. 100 p.
[MH-Mus2790.15.50]

    An earlier catalog of Glinka manuscripts in GPB was published in 1898 by N. Findeizen.

F-73. Liapunova, A. S.
"Opis' arkhiva M. I. Glinki." *Sbornik GPB* 2 (1954): 187-234.

    Inventories his personal archival fond, and hence complements item F-72.

S. N. Glinka (1776-1847)

F-74. "Rukopisi S. N. Glinki. Katalog." Compiled by E. P. Fedoseeva. Leningrad: GPB, 1963. 22 p. Mimeographed.

N. V. Gogol' (1809-1852)

F-75. *Rukopisi N. V. Gogolia. Opisanie.* Compiled by R. B. Zaborova. Edited by N. Ia. Morachevskii. Leningrad: GPB, 1952. 58 p.
[no US location reported]

I. A. Goncharov (1812-1891)

76. [Leningrad. Publichnaia biblioteka. Otdel rukopisei.]
Rukopisi I. A. Goncharova. Katalog s prilozheniem neopublikovannoi stat'i.
Compiled by B. N. Ravkina. Edited by S. D. Balukhatyi. Vol. 1, Leningrad: GPB,
1940. 44 p.
[DLC-Z6616.G59L4]

A. I. Herzen (Gertsen) (1812-1870)

77. "Rukopisi A. I. Gertsena. Katalog." Compiled by I. A. Konopleva. Edited by R. B.
Zaborova. Leningrad: GPB, 1966. 41 p. Mimeographed.

M. Iu. Lermontov (1814-1841)

78. [Leningrad. Publichnaia biblioteka. Otdel rukopisei.]
Rukopisi M. Iu. Lermontova. Opisanie. Compiled by A. I. Mikhailova. Edited by
B. M. Eikhenbaum. Leningrad: GPB, 1941. 76 p.
[MH-Slav4346.3.806]

N. A. Nekrasov (1821-1877)

79. [Leningrad. Publichnaia biblioteka. Otdel rukopisei.]
Rukopisi N. A. Nekrasova. Katalog. Compiled by A. N. Mikhailova. Edited by N. K.
Piksanov. Leningrad: GPB, 1940. 60 p.
[DLC-Z6616.N4L4]

A. N. Ostrovskii (1823-1886)

80. [Leningrad. Publichnaia biblioteka. Otdel rukopisei.]
Rukopisi A. N. Ostrovskogo. Opisanie. Compiled by A. N. Mikhailova. Edited by
E. E. Naidich. Leningrad: GPB, 1956. 32 p.
[DLC-Z6616.O8L4; MH-Slav4349.1.950]

G. V. Plekhanov (1856-1918)

81. Kurbatova, I. N.
"Materialy arkhiva G. V. Plekhanova." *Voprosy filosofii,* 1964, no. 2, pp. 138-44.
Surveys the manuscript holdings of the special "Plekhanov House" collection,
affiliated with the Manuscript Division, which includes the library and most
of the personal papers of the noted early Russian Marxist. A four-volume
catalog of the library was prepared in mimeographed form by the Manuscript
Division in 1965, compiled by N. A. Dmitrieva et al., and edited by I. N.
Kurbatova.

A. A. Polovtsov (Polovtsev) (1832-1910)

82. "Katalog fonda revizii senatora A. A. Polovtseva Kievskoi i Chernigovskoi gubernii

1880-1881 gg." Compiled by M. Ia. Stetskevich. Leningrad: GPB, 1960. 376 p.
Mimeographed.

See also the materials covered by item F-56.

A. N. Pypin (1833-1904)

F-83. "Katalog fonda A. N. Pypina." Compiled by R. B. Zaborova and V. F. Petrova.
Leningrad: GPB, 1962. 259 p. Mimeographed.

M. E. Saltykov-Shchedrin (1826-1889)

F-84. [Leningrad. Publichnaia biblioteka. Otdel rukopisei.]
Rukopisi M. E. Saltykova-Shchedrina. Opisanie. Compiled by E. E. Naidich. Edited
by N. Ia. Morachevskii. Leningrad: GPB, 1954. 32 p.
[DLC-Z6616.S13L4]

N. K. Schilder (Shil'der) (1842-1902)

F-85. [Leningrad. Publichnaia biblioteka.]
*Opis' bumag N. K. Shil'dera postupivshikh v 1903 godu v Imperatorskuiu
Publichnuiu biblioteku.* Compiled and edited by V. V. Maikov. Published as
supplement to *Otchet Imperatorskoi Publichnoi biblioteki* (St. Petersburg, 1910).
[MH-Slav251.256.3]

M. M. Speranskii (1772-1839)

F-86. "Katalog fonda M. M. Speranskogo (No. 731)." Compiled by M. Ia. Stetskevich.
Leningrad: GPB, 1962. 422 p. Mimeographed.

V. V. Stasov (1824-1906)

F-87. [Leningrad. Publichnaia biblioteka.]
Vladimir Vasil'evich Stasov. Materialy k bibliografii. Opisanie rukopisei. Compiled
by E. N. Viner and S. M. Babintsev et al. Moscow: Gosudarstvennoe izd-vo
kul'turno-prosvetitel'noi literatury, 1956. 283 p.
[DLC-8834.7.L4; MH-FA828.73.35]

A. V. Suvorov (1729-1800)

F-88. [Leningrad. Publichnaia biblioteka. Otdel rukopisei.]
Opisanie sobraniia rukopisnykh materialov A. V. Suvorova. Compiled by L. A.
Mandrykina. Edited by S. N. Valk. Leningrad, 1955. 303 p.
[DLC-Z6616.S8L4; MH-Slav1043.2.22]

L. N. Tolstoi (1828-1910)

F-89. "Rukopisnye materialy otnosiashchiesia k L. N. Tolstomu. Katalog." Compiled by
R. B. Zaborova. Leningrad: GPB, 1966. 64 p. Mimeographed.

I. S. Turgenev (1818-1883)

90. [Leningrad. Publichnaia biblioteka. Otdel rukopisei.]
    Rukopisi I. S. Turgeneva. Opisanie. Compiled by R. B. Zaborova. Edited by M. P.
    Alekseev. Leningrad: GPB, 1953. 143 p.
    [DLC-Z6616.T9L4; MH-Slav4354.3.800.3]

M. N. Zagoskin (1789-1852)

91. "Katalog fonda M. N. Zagoskina." Compiled by I. A. Konopleva. Leningrad: GPB,
    1960. 28 p. Mimeographed.

PART F – LENINGRAD LIBRARIES AND MUSEUMS

2. NAUCHNAIA BIBLIOTEKA IMENI A. M. GOR'KOGO LENINGRADSKOGO GOSUDARSTVENNOGO UNIVERSITETA IMENI A. A. ZhDANOVA

[A. M. Gor'kii Research Library of Leningrad State University in the name of A. A. Zhdanov]

OTDEL REDKIKH KNIG I RUKOPISEI [Division of Rare Books and Manuscripts]
Address: Leningrad, V-164, Universitetskaia naberezhnaia, 7/9
VOSTOCHNYI OTDEL [Oriental Division]
Address: Leningrad, V-164, Universitetskaia naberezhnaia, 11

CONTENTS

Manuscript holdings of Leningrad State University are under the administration of the university library. Russian documentary holdings and early manuscripts from the Slavic world and Western Europe are to be found in the Division of Rare Books and Manuscripts, and the oriental collections are housed in the branch library of the university's Oriental Faculty.

The special collection of Mendeleev Papers is housed in the separate Mendeleev Museum and Archive under the university (see F-100).

As in the case of Moscow University, the prerevolutionary archive–both institutional records and most of the personal fonds of Leningrad University–has been transferred to the local state historical archive, Leningradskii gosudarstvennyi istoricheskii arkhiv (LGIA); the published survey of these materials is listed under this archive in Part G (see G-17).

Division of Rare Books and Manuscripts

The Division of Rare Books and Manuscripts located within the main Leningrad University Library shares its main reading room. It houses a small but valuable group of early Slavic and Russian manuscripts and other documents dating from the fourteenth to the twentieth century and totaling about 11,000 storage units. There are also 18 Greek and 5 Latin manuscripts. The medieval materials are mostly religious and juridical texts. There are some literary and historical manuscripts from the eighteenth and nineteenth centuries, a few personal papers of university professors including a few technical texts, and copies of some university lectures; the most valuable single documentary fond is the rich archive of the early nineteenth-century literary society: Arkhiv Vol'nogo obshchestva liubitelei slovesnosti, nauk i khudozhestv.

Oriental Division

The Oriental Division of the Library, attached to the Oriental Faculty of the university, houses its own manuscripts as a separate subdivision. Its holdings, the first of which were acquired in the early nineteenth century, now include 50,000 storage units of oriental manuscripts and xylographs. The Chinese and Japanese collections are the largest. There are also significant East Asian manuscript holdings in Manchurian, Tibetan, Mongolian, and Korean languages. The earliest manuscripts in ancient Indian languages date back to the ninth and tenth centuries. The division has over 800 Arabic and close to 600 Persian and Tadzhik manuscripts, and many important texts in Turkic languages. Many of the holdings have come from the private collections of noted orientalists who have served in the past as professors in the university's noted Oriental Faculty.

PUBLISHED DESCRIPTIONS

Division of Rare Books and Manuscripts

A detailed catalog of the manuscript holdings in this division was prepared in the 1930's by V. Peretts; it was never published, but a manuscript copy is available for consultation in the reading room.

92. Shustorovich, E. M.
"Slaviano-russkie rukopisi biblioteki imeni A. M. Gor'kogo Leningradskogo gosudarstvennogo universiteta." *Vestnik Leningradskogo universiteta*, vol. 14. *Seriia istorii, iazyka i literatury* 3 (1963):110-15.
A general survey of medieval Slavic manuscripts.

93. Mur'ianov, M. F.
"Piat' rukopisei korpusa Iustiniana v sobranii Leningradskogo universiteta." *Vizantiiskii vremennik* 27 (1967):306-309.
Describes the 5 Latin manuscripts among the LGU holdings.

Oriental Division

94. Abramov, A. T.
"Vostochnyi otdel Nauchnoi biblioteki im. A. M. Gor'kogo Leningradskogo ordena Lenina gosudarstvennogo universiteta im. A. A. Zhdanova." In *Vostokovednye fondy krupneishikh bibliotek Sovetskogo soiuza. Stat'i i soobshcheniia* (A-22), pp. 218-28.

95. Tagirdzhanov, A. T.
"Rukopisnyi fond vostochnogo fakul'teta LGU i ego izuchenie." In *Iranskaia filologiia. Trudy nauchnoi konferentsii po iranskoi filologii (24-27 ianvaria 1962 g.),* pp. 156-62. Leningrad: Izd-vo LGU, 1964.
[MH-OL35038.56]

96. Romaskevich, A. A.
"Spisok persidskikh, turetsko-tatarskikh i arabskikh rukopisei biblioteki Petrogradskogo universiteta." In *Zapiski Kollegii Vostokovedov* 1 (Leningrad, 1925):353-71.
[IU]
See also the earlier compilation by C. Salemann and V. Rosen in *Zapiski*

Vostochnogo otdela Russkogo arkheologicheskogo obshchestva 2 (1887) and
3 (1888), and issued separately, 1888, 50 p.

Arabic Manuscripts

F-97. Beliaev, V. I., and P. G. Bulgakov.
"Arabskie rukopisi sobraniia Leningradskogo gosudarstvennogo universiteta." In
[Leningrad. Universitet.] , *Pamiati akademika Ignatiia Iulianovicha Krachkovskogo.
Sbornik statei*, pp. 21-34. Leningrad: Izd-vo LGU, 1958.
[DLC-PJ26.K7; MH-OL271.2]

Persian and Turkic Manuscripts

F-98. Tagirdzhanov, A. T.
"Tadzhiksko-persidskie i tiurkskie rukopisi Vostochnogo fakul'teta LGU." *Vestnik
Leningradskogo universiteta*, vol. 12, no. 8, *Seriia istorii, iazyka i literatury*
2 (1957): 63-69.
Brief survey of the holdings.

F-99. [Leningrad. Universitet. Biblioteka. Vostochnyi otdel.]
*Opisanie tadzhikskikh, persidskikh i tiurkskikh rukopisei Vostochnogo otdela
Biblioteki LGU.* Compiled by A. T. Tagirdzhanov. Vol. 1: Leningrad: Izd-vo LGU,
1962. 514 p.
[DLC-Z6621.L57T38; MH-OL35003.150]
See also the supplementary pamphlet listing 177 Tadzhik and Persian
manuscripts and 76 manuscripts in Turkic languages: A. T. Tagirdzhanov,
*Spisok tadzhikskikh, persidskikh i tiurkskikh rukopisei Vostochnogo otdela
biblioteki LGU* (Moscow: Izd-vo "Nauka," 1967. 19 p.)

3. MUZEI-ARKHIV D. I. MENDELEEVA PRI LENINGRADSKOM GOSUDAR-STVENNOM UNIVERSITETE IMENI A. A. ZhDANOVA

[Museum and Archive of D. I. Mendeleev at Leningrad State University in the name of A. A. Zhdanov]

Address: Leningrad, V-164, Universitetskaia naberezhnaia, 7/9

CONTENTS

This small museum under the administration of Leningrad State University contains almost all of the personal papers of D. I. Mendeleev along with his personal library, including many interesting marginalia. There are also personal fonds of several members of his family, students, and other assistants, bringing the total number of storage units to around 14,000. The museum collects photocopies of materials relating to Mendeleev from other repositories in the Soviet Union and abroad.

PUBLISHED DESCRIPTIONS

The holdings are briefly mentioned in the short guide to the museum: *Muzei D. I. Mendeleeva. Putevoditel',* compiled by R. B. Dobrotin, I. N. Filimonova, and Iu. V. Rysev (Leningrad, 1969; 48 p.).

100. [Leningrad. Universitet. Muzei-arkhiv D. I. Mendeleeva.]
Arkhiv D. I. Mendeleeva. Avtobiograficheskie materialy. Sbornik dokumentov.
Preface by M. D. Mendeleev. Vol. 1. Leningrad: Izd-vo LGU, 1951. 207 p.
[DLC-QD22.M43L4]

> Along with the publication of a short autobiographical piece from the archive, this volume gives lists of some of the different materials, including a list of the manuscripts of Mendeleev's writings and the volumes of his correspondence.

4. GOSUDARSTVENNAIA TEATRAL'NAIA BIBLIOTEKA IMENI A. V. LUNA-CHARSKOGO (LTB)

[A. V. Lunacharskii State Theatrical Library]
OTDEL RUKOPISEI [Division of Manuscripts]
    Address: Leningrad, D-11, ulitsa Zodchego Rossi, 2

CONTENTS

The State Theatrical Library in Leningrad has an extremely rich manuscript division with materials pertaining to the prerevolutionary Russian theater, subdivided into three principal sections. The first, and undoubtedly the most important, section includes prompt copies of every play produced in Russia from 1756 to 1917, totaling some 54,579 storage units. Some 42,000 items make up the censorship fond containing the archive of the drama censor, with the texts and records of plays submitted. A second division contains a copy of plays in foreign languages performed in Russian theaters from the sixteenth through the nineteenth century. The third, or "epistolary," division is comprised of close to 3,000 storage units of personal letters of theatrical personalities, mostly from the late nineteenth and early twentieth centuries; a comprehensive card catalog is available to identify the writers and recipients. The library also has a division of theatrical art which houses considerable illustrative material regarding the theater, including set and costume designs and other production sketches, etc., dating mostly from the end of the nineteenth and the beginning of the twentieth centuries.

PUBLISHED DESCRIPTION

F-101. Nelidov, Iu. A.
"Leningradskaia teatral'naia biblioteka im. A. V. Lunacharskogo." *Teatral'noe nasledie. Sbornik pervyi,* pp. 9-44. Leningrad: Gosudarstvennyi Akademicheskii teatr dramy, 1934. 278 p.
[DLC-PN2720.T38]

    Other parts of the volume have additional information about aspects of the library holdings. Of particular note is the article covering rare editions of plays and promptbooks by A. N. Ostrovskii. See also the more recent but much briefer mention of the library's holdings in the general article by I. F. Petrovskaia in *Teatr i muzyka. Dokumenty i materialy* (A-51).

5. LENINGRADSKII GOSUDARSTVENNYI TEATRAL'NYI MUZEI

[Leningrad State Theatrical Museum]
RUKOPISNYI OTDEL [Manuscript Division]
   Address: Leningrad, ploshchad' Ostrovskogo, 6

CONTENTS

   Founded in 1918, the Leningrad State Theatrical Museum has developed one of the nation's largest and most important holdings related to the history of the theater and musical culture in the Soviet Union and abroad. As its basis are the museum collections of the Aleksandrinskii, the Mariinskii, and the Mikhailovskii theaters. It has also become the repository for a large number of private papers of people active in theater and music, as well as other related documents of theatrical and music history, with about 13,000 storage units dating from the 1780's to the present. It has a particularly rich collection of theatrical art— drawings of stage and costume designs, theatrical engravings and lithographs, and a large collection of theatrical photographs; these holdings date from the mid-eighteenth century to the present. The museum also has a sound recording section where it has collected many different types of theatrical and musical recordings.

PUBLISHED DESCRIPTIONS

102. Kochetov, A. N.
   "Istoriia i osnovnye napravleniia deiatel'nosti Leningradskogo gosudarstvennogo teatral'nogo muzeia." *Teatr i dramaturgiia. Trudy Nauchno-issledovatel'skogo instituta teatra, muzyki i kinematografii* 1:434-41. Leningrad, 1959.
   [DLC-PN2724.L47]

103. "Muzykal'nye kollektsii teatral'nogo muzeia." In *Muzykal'nyi Leningrad* (A-53), pp. 395-400.

   See also the brief coverage of theatrical as well as music materials in the article by I. F. Petrovskaia in *Teatr i muzyka. Dokumenty i materialy* (A-51), pp. 9-10, 17-18.

6. LENINGRADSKII GOSUDARSTVENNYI INSTITUT TEATRA, MUZYKI I KINEMATOGRAFII

[Leningrad State Institute of Theater, Music, and Cinematography]
ARKHIV RUKOPISNYKH I PERVOPECHATNYKH MATERIALOV [Archive of Manuscript and Early Printed Materials]

Address: Leningrad, tsentr, Isaakievskaia ploshchad', 5

CONTENTS

The rich music manuscript materials now organized as the archive of the Leningrad State Institute of Theater, Music, and Cinematography came from a variety of sources and have had a complicated organizational history. Plans for the museum which gathered them together were started in 1902 and called for a vast museum covering many different phases of musical culture and musicology; its prerevolutionary development owed much to the Petersburg Society of Music Lovers. After the Revolution the museum was first named the State Music Museum, but after it came under the administration of the Leningrad Philharmonic in 1921 it took the name Music History Museum [Muzykal'no-istoricheskii muzei] and acquired the holdings of the former memorial museums for Glinka and Rubinshtein. In 1932 the music museum was put under the administration of the Hermitage, but in 1940 was reorganized under the Scientific Research Institute of Theater and Music [Nauchno-issledovatel'skii institut teatra i muzyki]; at this time the collections of musical instruments were organized as the institute's Museum of Musical Instruments, and the manuscript holdings were organized as the Historiographical Cabinet [Istoriograficheskii kabinet]. In 1944 a separate Rimskii-Korsakov Museum and Archive [Muzei-arkhiv N. A. i A. N. Rimskikh-Korsakovykh] was established under the same Institute. More recently these latter two institutions, both of which had considerable archival holdings, were combined under what came to be called the Scientific Research Division of the Leningrad State Institute of Theater, Music, and Cinematography. Some of the Museum holdings, including some of its manuscript material, however, were transferred to the Rimskii-Korsakov memorial museum in Tikhvin, not far from Leningrad.

The present archival holdings consist of about 50 fonds with close to 50,000 storage units, dating from the eighteenth century to the present, and related to musical history and culture. The largest single fond is that of Rimskii-Korsakov, the contents of which were once housed in the separate museum; other large fonds include those of Glinka and Borodin. There is also a special collection of early musical scores that had formed part of the personal library of the Empress Elizaveta Alekseevna, wife of Alexander I.

PUBLISHED DESCRIPTION

A full description of the archival holdings of the institute has been prepared and should be published soon.

104. "Istoriograficheskii kabinet Nauchno-issledovatel'skogo instituta teatra i muzyki." In *Muzykal'nyi Leningrad* (A-53), pp. 400-405.

"Muzei-Arkhiv N. A. i A. N. Rimskikh-Korsakovykh." In *ibid.*, pp. 405-10.

The holdings described in these two sections have now been consolidated into the institute's archive. These descriptions remain at present the most extensive literature about the holdings. For a brief mention of the early manuscripts included in the holdings, see V. G. Putsko, "Maloizvestnye rukopisnye sobraniia Leningrada," in *Trudy Otdela drevnerusskoi literatury AN SSSR* 25 (1970):345-46.

7. BIBLIOTEKA DVORTSA RABOTNIKOV ISKUSSTV IMENI K. S. STANI-SLAVSKOGO PRI LENINGRADSKOM OTDELENII VSEROSSIISKOGO TEA-TRAL'NOGO OBSHCHESTVA (VTO)

[Library of the Palace of Artistic Workers in the Name of K. S. Stanislavskii of the Leningrad Branch of the All-Russian Theatrical Society]
   Address: Leningrad, Nevskii prospekt, 86

CONTENTS

The very limited manuscript holdings of the Leningrad Branch of the All-Russian Theatrical Society were organized in 1946 and now contain about 1,500 storage units containing materials dating from the 1930's to the present. The materials pertain to successive Leningrad theatrical seasons and meetings and conferences relating to the theater; they include theatrical programs and various biographical materials of theatrical personalities.

There is no published description of the holdings.

8. TsENTRAL'NAIA MUZYKAL'NAIA BIBLIOTEKA GOSUDARSTVENNOGO AKADEMICHESKOGO TEATRA OPERY I BALETA IMENI S. M. KIROVA

[Central Music Library of the S. M. Kirov State Academic Theater of Opera and Ballet]

Address: Leningrad, ulitsa Zodchego Rossi, 2

CONTENTS

The library, which originated as the library of musical scores of the St. Petersburg Imperial Theater, now has one of the largest collections of Russian manuscript musical scores, especially of opera and ballet. There are autograph scores by almost all the important Russian composers and a considerable variety of letters and other personal papers of composers and musicians. The holdings total in the vicinity of 350,000 storage units.

The library has separate card catalogs, one covering letters and autographs and another covering scores or librettos.

PUBLISHED DESCRIPTION

105. "Tsentral'naia muzykal'naia biblioteka ordena Lenina Akademicheskogo teatra opery i baleta imeni S. M. Kirova." In *Muzykal'nyi Leningrad*, by I. V. Golubovskii, (A-53), pp. 366-68.

> This is the most extensive published description aside from the additional brief coverage in the general article by I. F. Petrovskaia in *Teatr i muzyka. Dokumenty i materialy* (A-51), pp. 10-11, 21-22.

9. BIBLIOTEKA LENINGRADSKOI GOSUDARSTVENNOI KONSERVATORII IMENI N. A. RIMSKOGO-KORSAKOVA

[Library of the Leningrad State Conservatory in the name of N. A. Rimskii-Korsakov]

RUKOPISNYI OTDEL [Manuscript Division]

    Address: Leningrad, tsentr, Teatral'naia ploshchad', 3

CONTENTS

The Manuscript Division of the Leningrad Conservatory Library houses close to 6,000 storage units of musical scores—autographs and copies—and letters of musical leaders of the nineteenth and early twentieth centuries, and a few items from the eighteenth and early nineteenth centuries. There are particularly valuable manuscript scores by Borodin, Glazunov, Musorgskii, and Rimskii-Korsakov, as well as a few scores by foreign composers. Notable groups of letters are available signed by Borodin, Glazunov, Liadov, Rimskii-Korsakov, A. N. Serov, and Rubinshtein. The division also houses the large archive of the late nineteenth-century "Patronage Council for the Encouragement of Russian Composers and Musicians" [Popechitel'nyi sovet dlia pooshchreniia russkikh kompozitorov i muzykantov].

PUBLISHED DESCRIPTION

F-106. "Biblioteka ordena Lenina Konservatorii imeni N. A. Rimskogo-Korsakova." In *Muzykal'nyi Leningrad* by I. V. Golubovskii (A-53), pp. 359-65.

    The manuscript materials are covered on pp. 362-64. This is the only brief description available about the holdings aside from the even briefer coverage in the general article by I. F. Petrovskaia in *Teatr i muzyka. Dokumenty i materialy* (A-51), pp. 11-12. The lesser-known early manuscripts in the library are mentioned in the article by V. G. Putsko, "Maloizvestnye rukopisnye sobraniia Leningrada," in *Trudy Otdela drevnerusskoi literatury AN SSSR* 25 (1970):346.

10. NOTNAIA BIBLIOTEKA LENINGRADSKOGO KOMITETA PO RADIO-VESHCHANIIU I TELEVIDENIIU

[Musical Score Library of the Leningrad Committee for Radio Broadcasting and Television]

> Address: Leningrad, D-11, Malaia Sadovaia, 2

CONTENTS

The library began collecting original musical scores of Leningrad composers as early as 1924, but the bulk of the present holdings, which total some 50,000 storage units, dates from the Second World War. Included are all types of musical scores that have been used for radio and television.

There is no published description of the holdings.

11. GOSUDARSTVENNYI RUSSKII MUZEI (GRM)

[State Russian Museum]
SEKTOR RUKOPISEI [Manuscript Section]
    Address: Leningrad, D-11, Inzhenernaia ulitsa, 4

CONTENTS

The Manuscript Division of this major museum of Russian art contains unusually rich holdings of approximately 150 personal fonds of Russian artists and individuals connected with the museum. They total approximately 13,000 storage units. Almost all of these date from the nineteenth and twentieth centuries and contain personal materials and correspondence. Among the largest are those of A. N. Benois, M. V. Doduzhinskii, and K. S. Petrov-Vodkin. The division also houses the institutional archives of the museum from its foundation in 1898 to the present.

More purely artistic manuscript materials are retained in the museum's division of drawings and engravings. The museum also has a few important medieval Slavic manuscripts, especially those forming part of its exhibits of illuminated manuscripts.

There is no published description of the manuscript holdings of the museum, but the personal archival fonds are listed in the general directory of personal archives, *Lichnye arkhivnye fondy v gosudarstvennykh khranilishchakh SSSR. Ukazatel'* (A-9).

12. GOSUDARSTVENNYI ERMITAZH

[State Hermitage]
Address: Leningrad, D-65, Dvortsovaia naberezhnaia, 34

CONTENTS

Several different divisions of the Hermitage have manuscript holdings of some interest, although most of those which remain in the museum are for exhibition use. The main, voluminous historical collection, traditionally known as the Hermitage collection, has now all been transferred to the Saltykov-Shchedrin State Public Library (see above, section 1). The Rare Book Division of the library of the Hermitage now contains an assorted group of about 134 manuscripts, the earliest of which is an eleventh-century edition of Cicero, the latest from the nineteenth century. They include some architectural drawings, travel accounts, and a variety of other texts; the largest number are in French, and only a few are in Russian.

Other divisions of the museum also contain manuscript holdings of some importance. Of particular note are some of the oriental manuscripts, medieval illuminated manuscript books, and some early papyrus and Coptic texts. The division of drawings has a small group of Latin illuminated manuscripts with a handwritten list.

PUBLISHED DESCRIPTIONS

107. Ernshtedt, P. V.
Koptskie teksty Gosudarstvennogo Ermitazha. Moscow/Leningrad: Izd-vo AN SSSR, 1959.
[DLC-Z6621.L56C6; MH-FA57.1.70]

108. Kriuger, O. O., and M. G. Bystikova.
"Neizdannye papirusy i drugie teksty Gosudarstvennogo Ermitazha." *Vestnik drevnei istorii*, 1965, no. 2, pp. 103-06.

109. Izmailova, T. A.
"Armianskie illiustrirovannye rukopisi Gosudarstvennogo Ermitazha. Katalog." In *Trudy gosudarstvennogo Ermitazha* 10 (1969):110-41; *Kul'tura i iskusstvo narodov vostoka*, vol. 7.
Catalog-type description of Armenian illuminated manuscripts in the Hermitage. Text in Russian and French.

13. GOSUDARSTVENNAIA INSPEKTSIIA PO OKHRANE PAMIATNIKOV LENINGRADA GLAVNOGO ARKHITEKTURNO-PLANIROVOCHNOGO UPRA-VLENIIA LENINGRADSKOGO GORODSKOGO SOVETA DEPUTATOV TRU-DIASHCHIKHSIA

[State Inspection for the Preservation of Monuments of Leningrad of the Main Architectural Planning Administration of the Leningrad City Soviet of Workers' Deputies]

NAUCHNO-ARKHITEKTURNYI KABINET [Scientific Architectural Office]
    Address: Leningrad, D-11, ulitsa Zodchego Rossi, 1/3

CONTENTS

This central office of architecture and city-planning for the city of Leningrad has been gathering manuscript materials relating to its activities since 1938. Here are to be found a wide collection of architectural drawings, restoration plans, and similar materials relating to architectural monuments of Leningrad.

There is no published description of the holdings.

14. GOSUDARSTVENNYI MUZEI VELIKOI OKTIABR'SKOI SOTSIALISTI-CHESKOI REVOLIUTSII

[State Museum of the Great October Socialist Revolution]
OTDEL FONDOV [Division of Fonds]
   Address: Leningrad, P-46, ulitsa Kuibysheva, 4

CONTENTS

This museum, devoted to the history of the October Revolution, has very limited manuscript holdings of about 2,000 storage units about that revolution and its leaders. These include some biographical and memoir materials, copies of personal documents, photographs, and some correspondence. It also has a few materials relating to the revolutionary movement before October. Almost all of the manuscript holdings are related to the museum's exhibition functions and are of relatively minor research interest.

There is no published description of the holdings.

15. GOSUDARSTVENNYI MUZEI ETNOGRAFII NARODOV SSSR

[State Ethnographical Museum of the Peoples of the USSR]
SEKTSIIA RUKOPISEI [Manuscript Section]
Address: Leningrad, D-11, Inzhenernaia ulitsa, 4/1

CONTENTS

Although the manuscript holdings of this large ethnological museum are subsidiary to the museum's exhibition functions, it has many materials which merit attention. Its holdings, totalling approximately 20,000 storage units, are organized into 8 different fonds: 1) prerevolutionary materials, mostly relating to the work of the ethnological section of the Russian Museum before 1917; 2) materials relating to the work of the ethnographical division of the museum from 1917 to 1934, and of the separate ethnographical museum from 1934 to the present; 3) the collection of A. S. Teploukhov, mostly relating to archeological expeditions; 4) the collection of A. N. Pypin, mostly relating to folklore bibliography; 5) materials from the former Museum of the Peoples of the USSR; 6) the personal papers of the ethnographer A. A. Makarenko; 7) materials from the "Ethnographical Bureau" of Prince V. N. Tenishev, mostly relating to the peasants of Central Russia during the 1890's; and 8) illustrative materials, including a large photographic archive. This museum should not be confused with Leningrad's other ethnographical museum under the Institute of Ethnography of the Academy of Sciences (those manuscript holdings are covered above in Part C, section 8).

PUBLISHED DESCRIPTIONS

There is no general description of the holdings.

F-110. Nachinkin, N.
"Materialy 'Etnograficheskogo biuro' V. N. Tenisheva." *Sovetskaia etnografiia,* 1955, no. 1, pp. 159-63.
Detailed description of the materials in this seventh section of the museum's manuscript holdings, mostly dating from the late nineteenth century.
Additional information about the project of V. N. Tenishev is included in the study by S. A. Tokarev, *Istoriia russkoi etnografii (Dooktiabr'skii period)* (Moscow: Izd-vo "Nauka," 1966), pp. 403-06.

16. GOSUDARSTVENNYI MUZEI ISTORII RELIGII I ATEIZMA

[State Museum of the History of Religion and Atheism]
RUKOPISNYI OTDEL [Manuscript Division]
    Address: Leningrad, D-88, Kazanskaia ploshchad', 2

CONTENTS

The library of the main Leningrad anti-religious museum in the impressive Kazan Cathedral on Nevskii Prospekt was originally established in 1932 under the auspices of the Academy of Sciences. In the course of the years it gathered a significant collection of early Russian manuscript books, mostly of a religious character. These were reorganized in 1953 under the Manuscript Division, together with several collections of personal papers. The holdings now total in the vicinity of 25,000 storage units dating from the fifteenth century to the present, although the number of manuscript books is relatively small.

PUBLISHED DESCRIPTIONS

A description of the manuscript holdings has been prepared and is to be published soon in the museum's serial publication.

111. Emeliakh, L. I.
"Starinnye rukopisnye knigi Muzeia istorii religii i ateizma Akademii nauk SSSR."
Trudy Otdela drevnerusskoi literatury Akademii nauk SSSR 13 (1957):556-60.
    A list of the early manuscript books published when the museum was still under the Academy of Sciences.

17. MUZEI ARKTIKI I ANTARKTIKI ARKTICHESKOGO I ANTARKTI-CHESKOGO NAUCHNO-ISSLEDOVATEL'SKOGO INSTITUTA

[Museum of the Arctic and Antarctica of the Arctic and Antarctic Scientific Research Institute]

Address: Leningrad, ulitsa Marata, 24-a

CONTENTS

The manuscript holdings of this institute devoted to studies of the Arctic and Antarctica include a variety of materials relating to these regions dating from the eighteenth century to the present in the Russian, English, Norwegian, and Japanese languages. The bulk of the materials stems from various Russian expeditions and includes maps, reports, journals, and photographs. Additional materials pertain to ethnographic studies of tribes in the Northern regions of Russia.

There is no published description of the holdings.

18. TsENTRAL'NYI MUZEI SVIAZI IMENI A. S. POPOVA

[Central Museum of Communications in the name of A. S. Popov]
Address: Leningrad, ulitsa Soiuza, per. Podvel'skogo, 4

CONTENTS

This museum under the administration of the Ministry of Communications possesses limited but varied documentary holdings, totaling approximately 2,000 storage units, related to the development of postal, radio, and telegraphic services, and various other materials relating to communications. Included here is the personal archive of A. S. Popov, who developed radio in Russia, as well as the personal papers of several other pioneers in the history of Russian communications.

PUBLISHED DESCRIPTION

-112. *Materialy po istorii sviazi v Rossii XVIII-nachala XX vv. Obzor dokumental'nykh materialov.* Compiled by F. I. Bunina et al. Edited by N. A. Mal'tseva. Leningrad: GAU, 1966. 335 p.
[DLC-HE8214.M3; MH-Slav3085.500.60]
There is no separate description of the museum's manuscript holdings, but some coverage of them is included in this general survey, which also covers materials in TsGIA SSSR and LGIA (see under items B-137 and G-18).

19. LENINGRADSKII INSTITUT INZHENEROV ZhELEZNODOROZHNOGO TRANSPORTA IMENI AKADEMIKA V. N. OBRAZTSOVA (LIIZhT)

[Leningrad Institute of Railroad Transport Engineers in the name of Academician V. N. Obraztsov]

NAUCHNO-TEKHNICHESKAIA BIBLIOTEKA [Scientific-Technical Library]
Address: Leningrad, Moskovskii prospekt, 9

CONTENTS

The library of the Institute of Railroad Transport Engineers has a variety of manuscript holdings totaling about 1,000 storage units, dating from approximately 1740 to 1910. The materials, all of which were gathered before the Revolution, not only relate to railroads, but also include a variety of documents relating to travel, architectural engineering, bridge construction, natural sciences, and biographical or technical historical studies.

PUBLISHED DESCRIPTION

F-113. *Rukopisnyi fond biblioteki LIIZhTa. Katalog.* Compiled by I. V. Shkliar.
Leningrad: LIIZhT, 1969. 223 p. Offset edition.
[no US location reported]
A detailed catalog of the manuscript holdings of the library.

20. LENINGRADSKII MUZEI ZhELEZNODOROZHNOGO TRANSPORTA PRI LENINGRADSKOM INSTITUTE INZHENEROV ZhELEZNODOROZHNOGO TRANSPORTA IMENI V. N. OBRAZTSOVA

[Leningrad Museum of Railroad Transportation of the Leningrad Institute of Railroad Transport Engineers in the name of Academician V. N. Obraztsov]
BIBLIOTEKA [Library]
  Address: Leningrad, Sadovaia ulitsa, 50

CONTENTS

The Library of the Museum of Railroad Transport has manuscript holdings totaling approximately 7,500 storage units related to the development and construction of railroads in the USSR. The materials date from the early nineteenth century to the present and include the personal fonds of several pioneers in railway development. This library should not be confused with the Institute's Scientific-Technical Library prerevolutionary manuscript holdings (see previous entry) which are described in a detailed published catalog (F-113).

There is no published description of the holdings.

21. VOENNO-ISTORICHESKII MUZEI ARTILLERII, INZHENERNYKH VOISK I VOISK SVIAZI

[Military History Museum of the Artillery, Corps of Engineers, and Signal Corps]
ARKHIV [Archive]
> Address: Leningrad, Park Lenina, d. 7

CONTENTS

As currently constituted this museum dates only from 1963, when the Artillery History Museum [Artilleriiskii-istoricheskii muzei] absorbed the former Central Historical Museum of Military Engineering [Tsentral'nyi istoricheskii voenno-inzhenernyi muzei]. The predecessors of the Artillery History Museum, however, date back to the eighteenth century, and many of its holdings to the time of Peter the Great.

The Artillery History Museum established its formal archive in 1872, at which time many files relating to the history of artillery in Russia were transferred to it from the archive of the Army's artillery command [Arkhiv Glavnogo artilleriiskogo upravleniia]. The holdings now total close to 200,000 storage units dating from the seventeenth century to the present, covering various phases of the development of artillery, military history, and military technology. They include 32 institutional fonds, 43 personal fonds, and 5 collections relating to the history of military affairs.

PUBLISHED DESCRIPTIONS

F-114. [Leningrad. Artilleriiskii istoricheskii muzei.]
Putevoditel' po istoricheskomu arkhivu muzeia. Compiled by A. P. Lebedianskaia, E. V. Rozenbetskaia et al. Edited by I. P. Ermoshin. Leningrad, 1957. 235 p.
[no US location reported]
> A general directory of the archival fonds in the museum, only slightly outdated by more recent acquisitions.

F-115. [Leningrad. Artilleriiskii istoricheskii muzei.]
Katalog arkhivnykh dokumentov po Severnoi voine 1700-1721 gg. Compiled by E. V. Rozenbetskaia. Edited by I. P. Ermoshin et al. Leningrad, 1959. 433 p.
[DLC-Z2508.L4; Slavic microfilm 3660Z; MH-Slav632.66]
> A detailed catalog of the archival holdings relating to the Northern War covering the years 1700-1721.

F-116. [Leningrad. Artilleriiskii istoricheskii muzei.]
Arkhiv russkoi artillerii. Compiled by D. P. Strukov. Edited by N. E. Brandenburg. Vol. 1 *(1700-1718 gg.)* St. Petersburg: Tipografiia Artilleriiskogo zhurnala, 1889. 410 p.
[MH-Slav632.65.5F]
> This detailed catalog of holdings relating to the period 1700-1718 was the

only volume in the projected series published before the Revolution. It covers materials transferred to the museum from the archive of the Main Artillery Administration in 1873, among others.

-117. Chernukha, V. G.

"Materialy arkhiva Artilleriiskogo istoricheskogo muzeia o voennykh deistviiakh 1863 g. na Ukraine." In *K stoletiiu geroicheskoi bor'by 'Za nashu i vashu svobodu.' Sbornik statei i materialov o vosstanii 1863 g.*, pp. 280-91. Moscow: Izd-vo "Nauka," 1964.

See item A-44. Describes materials relating to the Polish rebellion of 1863 in the museum.

22. VOENNO-ISTORICHESKII MUZEI A. V. SUVOROVA

[A. V. Suvorov Military History Museum]
   Address: Leningrad, ulitsa Saltykova-Shchedrina, 43

CONTENTS

The museum has limited manuscript materials relating to military history dating from the eighteenth century to the present. The earlier manuscript holdings were collected in the late nineteenth and early twentieth centuries and were acquired by the museum with its foundation in 1904. Included here are some materials relating to the career of A. V. Suvorov (1729-1800).

There is no published description of the holdings.

23. TsENTRAL'NYI VOENNO-MORSKOI MUZEI

[Central Naval Museum]
RUKOPISNO-DOKUMENTAL'NYI FOND [Manuscript-Documentary Fond]
    Address: Leningrad, Vasil'evskii ostrov, Pushkinskaia ploshchad', 4

CONTENTS

The manuscript holdings of the Central Naval Museum, located in the building of the former St. Petersburg Stock Exchange, now total approximately 32,000 storage units dating from the end of the seventeenth century to the present. They include a variety of materials pertaining to the history of the prerevolutionary Russian navy and the Soviet fleet.

There is no published description of the holdings.

24. VOENNO-MEDITSINSKAIA AKADEMIIA IMENI S. M. KIROVA

[Military Medical Academy in the name of S. M. Kirov]
FUNDAMENTAL'NAIA BIBLIOTEKA [Fundamental Library]
   Address: Leningrad, Pirogovskaia naberezhnaia, 3

CONTENTS

The manuscript holdings of the library of the Military Medical Academy include about 2,000 storage units dating from the eighteenth to the beginning of the twentieth century. They include materials pertaining to various aspects of the development of medicine in Russia and abroad, and most specifically to the history of the Military Medical Academy. Almost all of these were accumulated before the Revolution.

There is no published description of the holdings.

25. LENINGRADSKAIA DUKHOVNAIA AKADEMIIA

[Leningrad Ecclesiastical Academy]
BIBLIOTEKA [Library]
    Address: Leningrad, Obvodnyi kanal, 17

CONTENTS

    The library of the Orthodox seminary in Leningrad includes a small collection of slightly over 150 manuscripts dating from the sixteenth through the nineteenth century. These are predominantly religious in character but also include a few literary and historical manuscripts. This collection was started after the seminary was opened in 1946. It should not be confused with the extensive collection of the prerevolutionary St. Petersburg Ecclesiastical Academy, all of which is now housed in the Manuscript Division of the Leningrad Public Library (GPB).

PUBLISHED DESCRIPTION

8. Putsko, V. G.
"Maloizvestnye rukopisnye sobraniia Leningrada," in *Trudy otdela drevnerusskoi literatury* 25 (1970):346-48.
    Brief general description and list of some of the most important manuscripts by category.

PART G
REPUBLIC AND LOCAL STATE ARCHIVES
IN MOSCOW AND LENINGRAD

PART G

REPUBLIC AND LOCAL STATE ARCHIVES
IN MOSCOW AND LENINGRAD

In addition to the central state archives of the USSR covered above in Part B, there are several other state archives located in Moscow and Leningrad under the administration of the Main Archival Administration (GAU) which are of fundamental historical importance to scholars. These fall in the category of republic, oblast, or city-level archives which in general are excluded from coverage in this volume. However, because they are located in Moscow and Leningrad, they will be described here briefly.

Included in Moscow are 1) the Central State Archive of the RSFSR [Tsentral'nyi gosudarstvennyi arkhiv RSFSR], containing most of the post-1923 records of the Russian Federated Republic; 2) the State Archive of the Moscow Oblast [Gosudarstvennyi arkhiv Moskovskoi oblasti–GAMO], containing post-1923 oblast records; and 3) the Central State Archive of the City of Moscow [Tsentral'nyi gosudarstvennyi arkhiv g. Moskvy–TsGAgM], containing prerevolutionary historical records for the Moscow area and postrevolutionary records relating to the city of Moscow.

Leningrad now has three such archives: 4) the Leningrad State Archive of the October Revolution and Socialist Development [Leningradskii gosudarstvennyi arkhiv Oktiabr'skoi revoliutsii i sotsialisticheskogo stroitel'stva–LGAORSS], containing files beginning with October 1917; 5) the Leningrad State Historical Archive [Leningradskii gosudarstvennyi istoricheskii arkhiv–LGIA], containing prerevolutionary materials from the Leningrad area; and 6) the Leningrad State Archive of Film, Phonographic, and Photographic Documents [Leningradskii gosudarstvennyi arkhiv kinofonofotodokumentov–LGAKFFD]. A fourth local archive–for literature and art–was established in 1969 and is still in the process of formation.

GENERAL PUBLISHED DIRECTORY–LENINGRAD

G-1. [Leningrad (Province). Upravlenie vnutrennikh del. Arkhivnyi otdel.]
Leningradskie gosudarstvennye oblastnye arkhivy. Kratkii spravochnik. Compiled by V. A. Zubkov et al. Edited by P. V. Vinogradov. Leningrad, 1960. 135 p.
[DLC-CD1735L4.A55; MH-Slav3161.5.25]
> Describes LGIA and LGAORSS, with a numbered list of many of their fonds, and lists the district *(raion)* and city archives of Leningrad oblast.

GENERAL DESCRIPTION–MOSCOW

There is no comparable directory for Moscow. For the historical background of regional archives in Moscow, see the article by V. Derbina and A. Abramson, "Arkhivy Moskovskoi oblasti za 20 let," *Arkhivnoe delo* 47 (1938, no. 3):204-12.

G-2. *Arkhivnoe delo Moskovskoi oblasti. Sbornik materialov.* Vol. 2/3.
Moscow: Moskovskoe oblastnoe arkhivnoe upravlenie, 1932. 144 p.
[no U.S. location reported.]

PART G – REPUBLIC AND LOCAL STATE ARCHIVES

This volume contains a number of helpful articles on early archival developments in the region as well as surveys of some records (now to be found in GAMO and TsGAgM) for factory history and labor movements (pp. 51-98), and of Civil War materials (pp. 99-114).

1. TsENTRAL'NYI GOSUDARSTVENNYI ARKHIV RSFSR

[Central State Archive of the RSFSR].
Address: Moscow, G-59, Berezhkovskaia naberezhnaia, 26

CONTENTS

The Central State Archive of the Russian SFSR was founded in 1957 as a repository for the republic-level records of the RSFSR since its formation in 1923. It moved into its present specially constructed building at the end of 1964. This archive now contains about 500 fonds with over 800,000 storage units dating from 1923 to 1954. Previously, these files had been kept in TsGAOR (see Part B, section 1). Some RSFSR records still remain there, most particularly those of the Ministry (formerly the People's Commissariat) of Internal Affairs, because there has not been a separate ministry for the RSFSR; many court records also remain in TsGAOR.

Although this RSFSR archive in Moscow is the repository for the majority of republic-level records, there is a second Central State Archive of the RSFSR in Tomsk (Tsentral'nyi gosudarstvennyi arkhiv RSFSR Dal'nego vostoka), formed in 1943, which houses both pre- and postrevolutionary records relating to the Far Eastern areas; documents retained there, however, are limited to those originating in that area.

WORKING CONDITIONS

There is a regular reading room in the new building. However, the archive generally remains closed to foreign readers, and any limited files they might see would normally be shown them in the foreigners' reading room at GAU headquarters.

PUBLISHED DESCRIPTIONS

There is no published guide to this archive. In addition to the short description and note about new acquisitions listed below, researchers interested in the organization and scope of the archive might consult the short article by A. N. Gavrilov and V. S. Kozlov, "Nekotorye voprosy komplektovaniia Tsentral'nogo gosudarstvennogo arkhiva RSFSR dokumental'nymi materialami," in *Voprosy arkhivovedeniia,* 1963, no. 2, pp. 38-42. Also of interest regarding the administration of the archive, but of no value as a finding aid for readers, is the longer mimeographed handbook for archival use, *Spravochnik o sostave i soderzhanii dokumental'nykh materialov Tsentral'nogo gosudarstvennogo arkhiva RSFSR* (Moscow, 1959; 146 p. [MH-Film]).

G-3. Belov, I. I., and A. N. Gavrilov.
"Tsentral'nyi gosudarstvennyi arkhiv RSFSR." *Istoricheskii arkhiv,* 1960, no. 6, pp. 156-65.

Briefly describes the foundation, organization, and some of the contents of the Central State Archive of the Russian SFSR. See also the note on subsequent acquisitions by V. S. Kozlov, "Novye postupleniia v Tsentral'nyi gosudarstvennyi arkhiv RSFSR," *Voprosy istorii,* 1962, no. 8, pp. 163-65.

2. GOSUDARSTVENNYI ARKHIV MOSKOVSKOI OBLASTI (GAMO)

[State Archive of Moscow Oblast]
Address: Moscow, M-452, Azovskaia ulitsa, 3

CONTENTS

This archive was established in its present form during the reorganization of archives in the Moscow region during the mid-1960's on the basis of the former State Archive of the October Revolution and Socialist Development of Moscow Oblast [Gosudarstvennyi arkhiv Oktiabr'skoi revoliutsii i sotsialisticheskogo stroitel'stva Moskovskoi oblasti—GAORSS MO]. The archive had been originally organized as a separate institution in 1930 and was subsequently known as the State Archive of the October Revolution of Moscow Oblast [Gosudarstvennyi arkhiv Oktiabr'skoi revoliutsii Moskovskoi oblasti—GAORMO]. Now located in a new building constructed for its use in the southern outskirts of Moscow, it contains materials pertaining to the Moscow oblast since its formation in 1922. The earlier fonds are in the Moscow city historical archive (TsGAgM). It now numbers close to 5,000 fonds with 1,500,000 storage units. It also has a branch archive in Bronnitsa, which serves as a depository for materials from several different districts.

WORKING CONDITIONS

Although this archive is not officially closed to foreigners, there are no reports of foreign scholars having used the holdings as they are presently constituted. Presumably, to the extent limited access might be possible, materials would be brought to the foreigners' reading room in GAU headquarters for use.

PUBLISHED DESCRIPTIONS

Presumably most of the fonds relating to the October Revolution in Moscow and the Moscow region have been transferred to TsGAgM; hence the description of them prepared when they were housed in the former GAORMO is listed below as item G-10.

G-4. [Moscow (Province). Gosudarstvennyi arkhiv Oktiabr'skoi revoliutsii i sotsialisticheskogo stroitel'stva.]
Gosudarstvennyi arkhiv Oktiabr'skoi revoliutsii i sotsialisticheskogo stroitel'stva Moskovskoi oblasti. Kratkii spravochnik. Compiled by Iu. Ia. Vlasov, A. I. Kardash, and N. V. Fomicheva. Edited by A. E. Grishanov. Moscow: GAU, 1962. 77 p. [MH-Slav3162.5.245]

> Published before the recent reorganization of Moscow archives, this guide is the basic finding aid for GAMO, although readers should not be confused by the archive's former name in the title. A few of the pre-1923 records listed in this volume and some of those relating to the city of Moscow are presumably now to be found in TsGAgM (see below).

G-5. Davydova, L. I., and L. I. Datsenko.
"Obzor fondov sovnarkhozov Moskvy i Moskovskoi oblasti. (Novoe postuplenie v GAORSS MO, 1922-1932 gg.)." *Istoricheskii arkhiv,* 1960, no. 3, pp. 172-85.

> Covers fonds for the economic council, but probably those relating to the city of Moscow will be transferred to the newly organized TsGAgM (see below).

G-6. *Moskovskaia raboche-krest'ianskaia inspektsiia (Obzor fondov RKI za 1918-1934 gg.).* Compiled by L. I. Davydova, and L. I. Datsenko. Edited by A. E. Grishanov and B. D. Kargaeva. Moscow: GAU, 1966. 166 p. [MH-Slav 1705.300.115]

> This mimeographed volume gives specific references to holdings relating to the inspection agencies for workers and peasants during the years 1918-1934; a list of the fonds in GAMO appears on pages 127-30.

3. TsENTRAL'NYI GOSUDARSTVENNYI ARKHIV goroda MOSKVY (TsGAgM)

[Central State Archive of the City of Moscow]
 Address: Moscow, K-9, ulitsa Ogareva, 15

CONTENTS

The Central State Archive of the City of Moscow was established in its present form in 1963 during the reorganization of Moscow regional archives. In the previous organization, 1917 had been a strict dividing-line, and all the fonds relating to the Moscow region predating 1917 had made up the State Historical Archive of Moscow Oblast [Gosudarstvennyi istoricheskii arkhiv Moskovskoi oblasti–GIAMO]. GIAMO had originally been organized in 1930 on the basis of the Moscow guberniia archive.

This large and exceptionally rich historical archive was the main repository for records from Moscow and Moscow guberniia from the end of the eighteenth century to October 1917. As organized in the 1950's and described in the 1961 published guide (G-7), the holdings are divided into a number of different categories. A large group includes the fonds of administrative and political organizations, comprising mostly the official records of Moscow guberniia and city. A second group includes some fonds of military administrative organs, a third of courts and justice, and a fourth of various institutions of society. Financial and other commercial institutions and factories form additional categories as do fonds regarding regional transport, communications, health, and other social service agencies. The records of educational institutions (including the extensive files of Moscow University), publishing houses, monasteries, and other religious organizations are gathered in different sections, and there are some family fonds of personal origin.

GIAMO as such was liquidated in the mid-1960's, but its holdings became the basis of the new TsGAgM. However, TsGAgM is a more comprehensive archive than its predecessor, as it also houses the postrevolutionary records of Moscow city, such as those of the City Soviet and other administrative organs. A new building is under construction for this archive on Profsoiuznaia ulitsa, and the archive is at present still in the throes of physical reorganization.

WORKING CONDITIONS

Because of the recent reshuffling and the construction of the new building, the archive is presently open only for limited access. Until it is resettled there are apt to be considerable delays for readers who might want to consult its holdings. At present, foreign readers do not work in the archive building itself, but use materials which are brought into the foreigners' reading room at GAU headquarters.

PUBLISHED GUIDE

For some of the postrevolutionary fonds relating to the city of Moscow, see G-4 above. For an historical survey of the development of Moscow oblast archives see the article by V. Derbina and A. Abramson, "Arkhivy Moskovskoi oblasti za 20 let," *Arkhivnoe delo* 47 (1938, no. 3): 204-12, and G-2.

G-7. [Moscow (Province). Gosudarstvennyi istoricheskii arkhiv.]
Gosudarstvennyi istoricheskii arkhiv Moskovskoi oblasti. Putevoditel'. Compiled by L. I. Gaisinskaia et al. Edited by S. O. Shmidt. Moscow: GAU, 1961. 345 p.
[DLC-CD1735.M6A52; MH-Slav 3162.5.110]

> A detailed guide to those holdings of TsGAgM which formed part of the former GIAMO. The guide provides the only general published finding aid, with descriptions of the different fonds in the categories described above. There are unfortunately no bibliographical references to other surveys or related publications for any of the fonds.

PUBLISHED SPECIALIZED DESCRIPTIONS

G-8. [Tsentral'nyi gosudarstvennyi arkhiv g. Moskvy.]
Iz istorii fabrik i zavodov Moskvy i Moskovskoi gubernii (konets XVIII-nachalo XX v.). Obzor dokumentov. Edited by V. A. Kondrat'ev and V. I. Nevzorova. Moscow, 1968. 335 p.
[DLC-HC 337.M6T8; MH-Slav 3162.5.225]

> A detailed description with appended lists of holdings for individual factories. On factory materials in TsGAgM, see also the earlier article, "Obzor dokumental'nykh materialov po istorii fabrik i zavodov khraniashchikhsia v gosudarstvennykh arkhivakh Moskovskoi oblasti," in *A. M. Gor'kii i sozdanie istorii fabrik i zavodov. Sbornik dokumentov i materialov v pomoshch' rabotaiushchim nad istoriei fabrik i zavodov SSSR* (A-41), pp. 326-44.

G-9. Feinberg, I. M.
"Dokumental'nye materialy Gosudarstvennogo istoricheskogo arkhiva Moskovskoi oblasti o revoliutsionnykh sobytiiakh 1905-1907 gg." *Istoricheskii arkhiv,* 1955, no. 6, pp. 197-203.

> Detailed description of different fonds containing materials relating to revolutionary activities now located in TsGAgM.

G-10. Gar'ianova, O. A.
"Dokumental'nye materialy Moskovskogo tsenzurnogo komiteta v Gosudarstvennom istoricheskom arkhive Moskovskoi oblasti. (Obzor materialov fonda za 1798-1865 gg.)." *Trudy MGIAI* 4 (1948): 179-97.

> Description of censorship materials now in TsGAgM.

G-11. [Moscow (Province). Gosudarstvennyi arkhiv Oktiabr'skoi revoliutsii Moskovskoi oblasti.]
Oktiabr' 1917 goda v Moskve i Moskovskoi gubernii. Obzor dokumentov Gosudarstvennogo arkhiva Oktiabr'skoi revoliutsii i sotsialisticheskogo stroitel'stva Moskovskoi oblasti. Compiled by L. I. Davydova and T. N. Dolgorukova. Edited

by G. D. Kostomarov, V. A. Kondrat'ev, and L. I. Iakovlev. Moscow: GAU and GAORMO, 1957. 174 p.
[DLC-DK265.8.M6A55]

> This volume was prepared by the former GAORMO, but presumably many of the materials covered have now been transferred to TsGAgM. A general description of the holdings is followed by a chronological table of documents with citations of items as well as fond numbers. There is also brief mention of documents regarding the October Revolution in TsGAOR SSSR (including the former TsGIAM), TsGVIA, and some originally housed in GIAMO.

G-12. Matveeva, E. A.

> "Gosudarstvennyi istoricheskii arkhiv Moskovskoi oblasti." In *Materialy k istorii russkogo teatra v gosudarstvennykh arkhivakh SSSR*, edited by I. F. Petrovskaia (A-52), pp. 202-10.

> Surveys the records of several Moscow theaters now housed in TsGAgM (at the time of writing called GIAMO).

4. LENINGRADSKII GOSUDARSTVENNYI ARKHIV OKTIABR'SKOI REVO-LIUTSII I SOTSIALISTICHESKOGO STROITEL'STVA (LGAORSS)

[Leningrad State Archive of the October Revolution and Socialist Development]
Address: Leningrad, ulitsa Voinova, 34

CONTENTS

The Leningrad State Archive of the October Revolution and Socialist Develop-ment, or LGAORSS, as it is presently called, is the central repository for records originating in Leningrad oblast since 1917. The basis of its holdings dates back to 1923, when many records of local origin were being consolidated under the then constituted Petrograd Guberniia Archival Bureau [Petrogradskoe gubernskoe arkhivnoe biuro] —after 1924 the Leningrad Guberniia Archival Bureau. After the organization of Leningrad oblast in 1927, the local records were managed by the oblast archival administration.

The forerunner of LGAORSS was established as a distinct institution in 1936 under the name Leningrad Oblast Archive of the October Revolution [Leningrad-skii oblastnoi arkhiv Oktiabr'skoi revoliutsii—LAOR]; in 1941 this archive was combined with the military archive [Leningradskii oblastnoi voennyi arkhiv] and the local photographic archive to form the State Archive of the October Revolution of Leningrad Oblast [Gosudarstvennyi arkhiv Oktiabr'skoi revoliutsii Leningradskoi oblasti—GAORLO]. Its name was later changed to the State Archive of the October Revolution and Socialist Development of Leningrad Oblast [Gosudarstvennyi arkhiv Oktiabr'skoi revoliutsii i sotsialisticheskogo stroitel'stva Leningradskoi oblasti—GAORSS LO], which name it retained until the late 1960's.

The archive currently has over 5,500 fonds with close to 3,000,000 storage units, comprising not only the central governmental records of Leningrad guberniia from 1917 to 1927, and Leningrad oblast after 1927, but also files from a wide range of local institutions. Separate divisions house records of 1) local government, including organs of administration and justice; 2) economic institutions; 3) scientific and cultural establishments; 4) trade unions; and 5) military institutions. There was a separate division for film and sound recordings, but these now constitute a separate archive (see LGAKFFD below). Although most of the records postdate October 1917, there are some important holdings from the period from February to October 1917. As noted above in Part D, all local Communist Party records are housed separately in the local Party archive in Smolnyi Institute. There is a second oblast-level state archive in Vyborg (Leningradskii gosudarstvennyi arkhiv v g. Vyborge—LGOAV).

WORKING CONDITIONS

There have been no reports of Western scholars using materials from this archive. To the extent that limited documents may be available, they would most likely be brought to the foreigners' reading room at TsGIA SSSR, in which building the main offices of the oblast archival administration are housed.

PUBLISHED DESCRIPTIONS

In addition to the 1962 guide listed below, the archive is described, and its fonds listed in some detail, in the general directory of Leningrad regional archives listed above (G-1), pp. 47-71, and 82-130. A recent article about the organization of the archival holdings does not provide any additional information for readers, but it does give some indications about the history of the archive: A. I. Nosova, "Osnovnye etapy komplektovaniia dokumental'nymi materialami Leningradskogo gosudarstvennogo arkhiva Oktiabr'skoi revoliutsii i sotsialisticheskogo stroitel'stva," in *Problemy arkhivovedeniia i istorii arkhivnykh uchrezhdenii* (A-82), pp. 41-49. On the relationship of this archive to other local archives in the Leningrad oblast, see the article by B. M. Shakhov, "Iz istorii raionnykh i gorodskikh gosudarstven- nykh arkhivov Leningradskoi oblasti," in *ibid.*, pp. 229-41.

G-13. [Leningrad (Province). Gosudarstvennyi arkhiv Oktiabr'skoi revoliutsii i sotsialisti- cheskogo stroitel'stva.]
Gosudarstvennyi arkhiv Oktiabr'skoi revoliutsii i sotsialisticheskogo stroitel'stva Leningradskoi oblasti. Kratkii putevoditel'. Compiled by M. V. Kiselev et al. Edited by P. V. Vinogradov. Leningrad, 1962. 183 p.
[DLC-CD1735.L38A54; MH-Slav 3161.5.65]

A short description of the holdings of the postrevolutionary Leningrad oblast archive which is now called LGAORSS. The film and photographic materials listed on pp. 72-81 are now part of a separate photographic archive (see below). Unfortunately the guide does not provide any bibliography of the surveys and other published descriptions of materials in the archive.

G-14. Zubkov, V. A., and Iu. S. Tokarev.
"Gosudarstvennyi arkhiv Oktiabr'skoi revoliutsii i sotsialisticheskogo stroitel'stva Leningradskoi oblasti (GAORSS LO)." In *Oktiabr'skoe vooruzhennoe vosstanie v Petrograde. Sbornik statei* (A-42), pp. 367-81.

Brief survey of the materials relating to the October Revolution in Petrograd in LGAORSS.

G-15. Serdnak, R. V.
Section on LGAORSS in "Perechni dokumentov i materialov po istorii russkogo sovetskogo teatra 1917-1921 gg., khraniashchikhsia v TsGAOR SSSR, TsGASA, TsGALI SSSR, LGAORSS." In *Sovetskii teatr. Dokumenty i materialy. Russkii sovetskii teatr 1917-1921 gg.,* edited by A. E. Lufit, et al., pp. 432-63. Leningrad: Izd-vo "Iskusstvo," 1968. (See A-55.)

Covers a particularly extensive body of materials because the records of many Petrograd cultural institutions of the period were not transferred to TsGALI SSSR, as was the case with Moscow institutions.

5. LENINGRADSKII GOSUDARSTVENNYI ISTORICHESKII ARKHIV (LGIA)

[Leningrad State Historical Archive]
    Address: Leningrad, Pskovskaia ulitsa, 18

CONTENTS

Until it assumed its present name in the late 1960's, the Leningrad State Historical Archive (LGIA) had been known officially as the State Historical Archive of Leningrad Oblast [Gosudarstvennyi istoricheskii arkhiv Leningradskoi oblasti], or GIALO. It was first established in 1936 on the basis of the holdings brought together since the Revolution by the guberniia archival bureau. It houses the records of state and other local institutions in St. Petersburg and the surrounding guberniia from the late eighteenth century to 1917; a few fonds, especially from religious institutions, date back to an earlier period. From the most recent reports, many of the pre-nineteenth-century fonds have been transferred to TsGADA in Moscow. Because of the national significance of many institutions in the region of the imperial capital, LGIA is undoubtedly one of the richest and historically most important regional archives in the Soviet Union.

In addition to official guberniia records, LGIA houses a wide variety of local administrative and court files. It has brought together the remaining records of factories, banks, and other commercial and financial enterprises in the region. It retains the records of the local educational district, of schools and other educational establishments, and of St. Petersburg University. It has collected the remaining files of various social, cultural, and religious organizations and institutions. It also houses many private records and the personal papers of families and estates in the region, so that it is a prime research center for all aspects of local history and the social and cultural life of the prerevolutionary capital.

Many of the fonds relating exclusively to literature and art will presumably be transferred to the recently created special oblast archive of literature and art, currently in the process of formation.

WORKING CONDITIONS

Foreign readers have been given access to various records in LGIA. Requests for admission here are often slower in being processed than is true for the central state archives, and, perhaps because there have been relatively few foreigners admitted, working conditions have been somewhat more restricted. In most cases, materials have been brought to readers in the foreigners' reading room in the TsGIA SSSR building, which also houses the offices of the oblast archival administration. A few foreign readers have been permitted to work at the archive itself although, as in other state archives, inventories and card catalogs are not normally available to them.

PUBLISHED DESCRIPTIONS

In addition to the short 1960 guide listed below, the archive is described and its major fonds listed in the general directory of Leningrad regional archives (G-1), pp. 9-46. The short report by K. I. Iudina, "Iz opyta raboty po sozdaniiu skhemy sistematicheskogo kataloga Leningradskogo gosudarstvennogo istoricheskogo arkhiva," in *Problemy arkhivovedeniia i istorii arkhivnykh uchrezhdenii* (A-82), pp. 105-13, gives a good idea of the extensive work being done on the archival catalog. An additional article in this same volume reports on the use of the archive's records for regional studies: E. S. Eshurina, "Ispol'zovanie dokumental'nykh materialov Leningradskogo gosudarstvennogo istoricheskogo arkhiva v kraevedcheskikh tseliakh," *ibid.,* pp. 160-69.

16. [Leningrad (Province). Gosudarstvennyi istoricheskii arkhiv.]
Gosudarstvennyi istoricheskii arkhiv Leningradskoi oblasti. Kratkii putevoditel'.
Compiled by A. Kh. Gorfunkel' and L. E. Streltsova. Edited by P. V. Vinogradov.
Leningrad, 1960. 107 p.
[DLC-CD1735.L4A53; MH-Slav 3161.5.50]
> This regrettably short guide lists the holdings under different organizational categories by fond number. It includes the dates covered by the fonds and the number of storage units but for the most part gives no further description or bibliographical data.

University Records

17. [Leningrad. Universitet.]
Materialy po istorii Leningradskogo universiteta, 1819-1907. Obzor arkhivnykh dokumentov. Compiled by A. Kh. Gorfunkel', L. A. Nikulina, and S. N. Semanov. Edited by S. N. Valk. [Leningrad] : LGU and GIALO, 1961. 123 p.
[DLC-Z5055.R9L4; MH-Educ 5233.34]
> Surveys the records of LGU which were transferred to LGIA from the university archive.

Communications

8. "Obzor dokumental'nykh materialov po istorii sviazi Leningradskogo gosudarstvennogo istoricheskogo arkhiva." In *Materialy po istorii sviazi v Rossii XVIII-nachala XX vv. Obzor dokumental'nykh materialov,* compiled by F. I. Bunina et al., and edited by N. A. Mal'tseva, pp. 183-93. Leningrad: GAU, 1966.
[DLC-HE8214.M3; MH-Slav3085.500.60]
> See also F-112 and B-137.

PART G – REPUBLIC AND LOCAL STATE ARCHIVES

Factory Records

See the coverage of factory records in LGIA in the appendices of the volume listed as A-41, *A. M. Gor'kii i sozdanie istorii fabrik i zavodov. Sbornik dokumentov i materialov v pomoshch' rabotaiushchim nad istoriei fabrik i zavodov SSSR.*

Revolutionary Movements

G-19. Bondarevskii, V. E.
"Gosudarstvennyi istoricheskii arkhiv Leningradskoi oblasti (GIALO)." In *Oktiabr'skoe vooruzhennoe vosstanie v Petrograde. Sbornik statei* (A-42), pp. 426-34.

Music Culture

G-20. Kaleis, A. S.
"Arkhiv Russkogo muzykal'nogo obshchestva." In *Teatr i muzyka. Dokumenty i materialy* (A-51), pp. 24-56.

Theater History

G-21. Tsaregradskaia, L. I.
"Gosudarstvennyi istoricheskii arkhiv Leningradskoi oblasti." In *Materialy k istorii russkogo teatra v gosudarstvennykh arkhivakh SSSR,* edited by I. F. Petrovskaia (A-52), pp. 196-201.

> Because most of the records of prerevolutionary theaters in St. Petersburg have been deposited in this archive (formerly called GIALO), it is a particularly rich repository, as this survey of holdings makes clear.

6. LENINGRADSKII GOSUDARSTVENNYI ARKHIV KINOFONO-FOTODOKUMENTOV (LGAKFFD)

[Leningrad State Archive of Film, Phonographic, and Photographic Documents]
    Address: Leningrad, Muchnoi pereulok, 2

CONTENTS

The present Leningrad State Archive of Film, Phonographic, and Photographic Documents goes back to 1930, when it was set up as a special division of the state oblast archive. For many years it remained a special division of LGAORSS, but in 1966 was established as a separate archive to house documentary films, photographs, and sound recordings. Many of the materials come from the Leningrad branch of Tass, but other institutional files have also been incorporated into this archive. It now houses over 500,000 photographs relating to the history of Leningrad from 1853 to the present.

PUBLISHED DESCRIPTION

There is no adequate guide to the archive, but many of its holdings which were originally part of LGAORSS are described briefly in the guide to that archive published in 1962 (G-13), pp. 72-81. See the brief description published at the time the archive became an independent repository: L. Zevakina, "Novyi arkhiv v Leningrade," *Sovetskie arkhivy,* 1966, no. 6, p. 117. See also the short recent report on the organization of the archival holdings: L. A. Zevakina, "Opredelenie istochnikov komplektovaniia fotodokumentami Leningradskogo gosudarstvennogo arkiva kinofonofotodokumentov," in *Problemy arkhivovedeniia i istorii arkhivnykh uchrezhdenii* (A-82), pp. 50-56.

APPENDICES

APPENDIX 1
RESEARCH IN LIBRARIES

Since the library resources in most state archives are limited, scholars will find that they need to use the large public or Academy libraries for the bulk of their research in published materials and for their general reference and bibliographical needs. The five most important libraries in this respect in Moscow and Leningrad will be introduced briefly below together with bibliographical data. These institutions with their extensive holdings and abundant reference services are the best starting points for most researchers.

Visiting scholars attached to universities or to research institutes under the Academy of Sciences will also want to explore the more specialized libraries attached to these institutions. These libraries usually have the advantage of conveniently organized collections for their particular discipline. They often permit scholars associated with them to draw books for outside use, and they are often able to provide rapid interlibrary loan services from associated libraries.

At the end of this section an annotated list of directories of Soviet libraries will suggest sources of information about other libraries, their holdings and reference services.

1. GOSUDARSTVENNAIA ORDENA LENINA BIBLIOTEKA SSSR IMENI V. I. LENINA (GBL)

[V. I. Lenin State Library with the Order of Lenin]
Address: Moscow, tsentr, Prospekt Kalinina, 3

Claiming to be the largest library in the world, with over twenty million volumes of books and periodicals, the Lenin Library is the official depository for every book published in the Soviet Union and for academic dissertations. The library was formed on the basis of the holdings of the prerevolutionary Moscow Public and Rumiantsev Museum [Moskovskii publichnyi i Rumiantsevskii muzei], established in 1862. The original museum building, the late-eighteenth-century Pashkov Palace, now houses the Manuscript Division, the dissertation catalogs, and other special sections, while the library itself occupies the imposing postrevolutionary building constructed specially for the purpose in the center of Moscow facing the Kremlin.

A reader's ticket is required for admission to the library. This can be readily obtained on completion of special forms and presentation of a passport at the special office to the right of the main entrance. Tickets are issued for the period of validity of the foreigner's visa (a tourist visa is sufficient here) and are subject to renewal. This ticket is not valid, however, for admission to the Manuscript Division without a special additional stamp, obtained through a much more complicated application procedure (see above, Part E, section 1).

Foreign readers are assigned to the Scientific Reading Room Number One, where paging and catalog searching services will be provided for them. They may avail themselves of the general public card catalogs and the detailed subject catalogs on the third floor, which contain cards analyzing individual issues of many periodicals.

377

Paging normally takes at least several hours, so it is often most convenient to order volumes a day or two in advance.

The special catalogs of dissertations have been moved to the old building of the library near the Manuscript Division. These catalogs are open, but special permission is required to read a dissertation. The lengthy abstract *(avtoreferat)*, however, is always available by simple call slip.

Some reference books and general works, including a collection of archival guides, are available on open shelves on the main floor of the library between the card catalogs and Reading Room Number One. A more extensive collection of bibliographic and reference materials—including archival guides and catalogs—is available in the separate bibliographic reading room (the stacks are usually open), located adjacent to the main reference office. The library reference office has a well-trained staff with specialists in a number of different fields who are prepared to answer questions and assist with bibliographic or other reference problems.

The library publishes a short guide, periodically revised, with a brief survey of the holdings and reference facilities: [Moscow. Publichnaia biblioteka.], *Putevoditel' po Gosudarstvennoi biblioteke SSSR imeni V. I. Lenina,* by M. M. Klevenskii (Moscow, 1959; 198 p.). For additional descriptive literature see the bibliography in Part E, section 1, above, and especially the centennial history of the library, *Istoriia Gosudarstvennoi ordena Lenina biblioteki SSSR imeni V. I. Lenina za 100 let, 1862-1962,* edited by F. S. Abrikosova, K. R. Kamenetskaia, and E. V. Seglin (Moscow: Izdanie Biblioteki Moskvy, 1962; 279 p.) (see E-2). The section on the Lenin Library in the Horecky volume listed below is the most complete description of the library in English.

2. FUNDAMENTAL'NAIA BIBLIOTEKA PO OBSHCHESTVENNYM NAUKAM AKADEMII NAUK SSSR (BON)

[Fundamental Library of Social Sciences of the Academy of Sciences of the USSR]
    Address: Moscow, G-19, ulitsa Frunze, 11

Scholars visiting under the auspices of the Academy of Sciences are likely to find working conditions somewhat easier in this small library than in the larger and more crowded Lenin Library. Its holdings of postrevolutionary publications are quite extensive, since it was initially the library of the Socialist Academy of Social Sciences and later of the Communist Academy until 1936. However, it is comparatively weak in prerevolutionary publications.

The library has particularly extensive reference services, since it is the headquarters for the Academy's Institute of Scientific Information [Institut nauchnoi informatsii], which handles many of the Academy's bibliographic projects and publications in the field of social sciences and humanities.

Scholars attached to institutes under the Academy of Sciences are often able to borrow books from this library on interlibrary loan through associated institute libraries.

3. GOSUDARSTVENNAIA PUBLICHNAIA ISTORICHESKAIA BIBLIOTEKA RSFSR

[State Public Historical Library of the RSFSR]
   Address: Moscow, Starosadskii pereulok, 9

Although far smaller in holdings than the Lenin Library or the Academy library in Moscow mentioned above, this facility is particularly recommended to historians because of its specialized reference collections. Its extensive subject card catalogs include periodical articles from the prerevolutionary period to the present. It has specialized holdings and reference services covering the auxiliary historical sciences, including archival affairs, and a comprehensive and readily available collection of archival guides, published catalogs, and other archival reference aids.

Admission is obtained, as in the case of the Lenin Library, by application and presentation of a passport and visa. Due to its smaller size, paging is much more rapid than in the Lenin Library and working conditions are generally less crowded.

4. GOSUDARSTVENNAIA ORDENA TRUDOVOGO KRASNOGO ZNAMENI PUBLICHNAIA BIBLIOTEKA IMENI M. E. SALTYKOVA–SHCHEDRINA (GPB)

[M. E. Saltykov-Shchedrin State Public Library with the Order of the Red Banner of Labor]
   Address: Leningrad, D-69, Sadovaia, 18

Ranking with the Lenin Library as one of the largest libraries in the world, the State Public Library in Leningrad (familiarly called the *Publichka)* is also an official depository for all Soviet publications. The library first opened in 1814, having been founded originally by the order of Catherine the Great, and before the Revolution always had the status of a national public library and legal depository for all books published in Russia. Although fire destroyed some of its earlier holdings in the nineteenth century, its prerevolutionary collections still outrank those in the Lenin Library, especially those materials published prior to 1860.

Admission is readily obtained by presentation of a passport (a tourist visa is sufficient here) and completion of the special forms for a reader's ticket. As in the Lenin Library, however, admission to the Manuscript Division requires a more elaborate application procedure (see above, Part F, section 1). Foreign readers are assigned to the main scientific reading room where they may avail themselves of the extensive reference and bibliographic services of the well-trained staff.

The library has put out a short general guide to its holdings which may be helpful in introducing visitors to its organization and facilities. The 1956 edition of this guide is now available in English translation: [Leningrad. Publichnaia biblioteka.], *Guide to the M. E. Saltykov-Shchedrin State Public Library,* trans. Raymond H. Fisher (Los Angeles, 1963; 48 p.; UCLA Occasional Papers, no. 14); a later and slightly expanded Russian edition was published in Leningrad in 1962. For additional descriptive literature see the bibliography for the coverage of the

Manuscript Division in Part F above, and especially the 150-year anniversary history of the library [Leningrad. Publichnaia biblioteka.], *Istoriia Gosudarstvennoi ordena Trudovogo Krasnogo Znameni publichnoi biblioteki imeni M. E. Saltykova-Shchedrina,* edited by V. M. Barashenkov et al. (Leningrad: Lenizdat, 1963; 435 p.) (F-2).

5. BIBLIOTEKA AKADEMII NAUK SSSR (BAN)

[Library of the Academy of Sciences of the USSR]
    Address: Leningrad, V-164, Birzhevaia liniia, 1.

Originally founded in 1714, BAN has been the main library of the Academy of Sciences since its establishment in 1725. It is now one of the largest and most important libraries in the USSR. Its location on Vasil'evskii Island, near many of the Academy facilities and Leningrad University, makes it particularly convenient for researchers. Although less comprehensive than the Leningrad Public Library in its holdings, it has the advantage for visiting scholars of extensive bibliographic and other reference services, and its smaller size permits faster paging and less crowded working conditions. Admission is by arrangement through the foreign division of the Academy of Sciences or through the Academy-related institution with which the foreign scholar is affiliated.

The general published guide to the library will be helpful in explaining the organization and facilities: [Akademiia nauk SSSR. Biblioteka], *Spravochnik-putevoditel' po Biblioteke Akademii nauk SSSR,* compiled by I. F. Grigor'eva, T. M. Koval'chuk, and T. I. Skripkina (Moscow/Leningrad: Izd-vo AN SSSR, 1959; 112 p.). More details about these and other publications regarding the library are listed above in Part C under the coverage of the library's Manuscript and Rare Book Division.

DIRECTORIES OF SOVIET LIBRARIES

[Kniaziatova, V. A.]
Biblioteki SSSR obshchestvenno-politicheskogo, filologicheskogo i iskusstvovedcheskogo profilia. Spravochnik. Compiled by V. A. Kniaziatova and N. P. Kuz'mina. Edited by I. Iu. Bagrova, M. I. Rabei, et al. Moscow: Izd-vo "Kniga," 1969. 344 p. A publication of GBL.
[DLC-Z819.A1K55; MH-B8825.80]
    This is the most important single directory of Soviet libraries for scholars in the humanities and social sciences. It systematically covers 1,506 different institutions throughout the Soviet Union from the largest state public libraries and libraries under the all-union and republic Academies of Sciences to the libraries of film studios and local memorial museums, giving the addresses, phone numbers, statistics about the different categories of holdings, indications about catalogs, bibliographical services, and other pertinent information. It is of particular importance to scholars using archives

since it covers libraries in many (but not all) state archives; further, it often gives indications about manuscript holdings in many other libraries, although its coverage in this realm is regrettably somewhat uneven.

Biblioteki SSSR. Spravochnik. Estestvennye i fizikomatematicheskie nauki.
Compiled by N. K. Davidenkova. Edited by A. I. Mankevich. Leningrad: BAN, 1967. 403 p.
[no U.S. location reported.]
> Similar in format to the preceding entry and its companion volume in the same series, this directory covers libraries for the physical, mathematical, and natural sciences, systematically throughout the Soviet Union. In terms of the general state public libraries and libraries of the Academy of Sciences, there is some overlap with the preceding volume, but in this one information is oriented toward the scientific holdings and reference facilities.

Biblioteki Moskvy. Spravochnik. Edited by I. Iu. Bagrova et al.
Compiled by V. A. Kniaziatova and N. P. Kuz'mina. Moscow: Izd-vo "Kniga," 1967. 240 p.
[DLC-Z819. M65B5; MH-B8889.8.187]
> This comprehensive directory of 746 Moscow libraries includes libraries in archives and museums as well as many research or other scientific and technical collections. It indicates the size of the holdings and types of materials included as well as data about special services or collections. It thus replaces and updates the 1931 volume which covered special libraries in Moscow: *Spetsial'nye biblioteki Mosvky. Spravochnik.*

[Leningrad. Publichnaia biblioteka.]
Biblioteki Leningrada. Spravochnik. Compiled by S. M. Babintsev. Edited by B. M. Tolochinskaia and I. A. Fedorovskii. Moscow: Izd-vo "Kniga," 1964. 158 p.
[DLC-Z819.L55; MH-Slav3203.1.342]
> Similar in format to the Moscow directory, this smaller volume lists 277 libraries in Leningrad (120 of these are local public libraries, including 40 children's libraries). It replaces the more extensive but now virtually unavailable 1948 edition compiled by V. I. Granskii and B. I. Itskovich and edited by G. G. Firsov.

[Moscow. Publichnaia biblioteka.]
Biblioteki RSFSR (bez Moskvy i Leningrada). Spravochnik. Compiled by Iu. P. Balasheva et al. Edited by I. Iu. Bagrova et al. Moscow: Izd-vo "Kniga," 1964. 276 p.
[DLC-Z819.M715; MH-B8825.58]
> On the same lines as the two preceding volumes, this handbook completes the coverage of libraries in the Russian Federation.

[Akademiia nauk SSSR. Biblioteka.]
Biblioteki Akademii nauk SSSR. Spravochnik. Compiled by A. I. Chebotarev.

Moscow: Izd-vo AN SSSR, 1959. 323 p.
[DLC-Z819.A56; MH-LSoc3983.72.8]

> This directory gives comprehensive coverage of the libraries under the USSR
> Academy of Sciences, although subsequent changes in organization and
> holdings have already made it somewhat outdated. For its coverage of
> manuscript collections in these libraries, see Part C above.

[Moscow. Universitet. Biblioteka.]
Biblioteki vysshikh uchebnykh zavedenii SSSR. Spravochnik. Compiled by E. Z.
Levinson. Edited by R. T. Ablova. Moscow: Izd-vo MGU, 1964. 442 p.
[DLC-Z819.M8; MH-B8825.57]

> The first chapter covers university libraries throughout the USSR. Subsequent
> chapters list libraries of other institutions subdivided according to subject
> specialties. The volume includes an index by city and also gives some brief
> notes about the manuscript holdings and bibliography of published catalogs
> for different university libraries.

Horecky, Paul Louis.
Libraries and Bibliographic Centers in the Soviet Union. Indiana University
Publications, Slavic and East European Series, no. 16. Bloomington, Indiana, 1959.
287 p.
[DLC-Z819.H6; MH-B8825.10]

> Although naturally less comprehensive than the Soviet directories listed
> above, this volume provides the most extensive English-language coverage of
> the subject.

Ruggles, Melville J., and Raynard C. Swank.
Soviet Libraries and Librarianship. Chicago: American Library Association, 1962.
147 p.
[DLC-Z819.R77; MH-B8825.45]

> This report of the visit of a delegation of U. S. librarians to the Soviet Union
> during May and June of 1961 gives a helpful list of main libraries and a
> bibliography of previous writings about Soviet libraries in English.

APPENDIX 2
REFERENCE AIDS FOR PALEOGRAPHY
AND ANCILLARY HISTORICAL DISCIPLINES

Surveys of Soviet methodological approaches and publications in a number of auxiliary historical disciplines are included in the first volumes (1968 and 1969) of the new Soviet series, *Vspomogatel'nye istoricheskie distsipliny* (see A-77 above), sponsored by the Leningrad Branch of the Archeographical Commission of the Academy of Sciences and edited by the distinguished historian S. N. Valk. Scholars working with various types of Slavic manuscripts will find this series most welcome.

Edward L. Keenan's article, "Recent Discussions of Paleography and Diplomatics," in *Kritika* 6 (Winter 1970): 55-77, presents a critique of several articles in the first volume of this series in relation to other Soviet work in these fields. His observations substantiate the need for extensive training in auxiliary disciplines, particularly for scholars in the medieval field.

The article by Daniel C. Waugh in the same issue of *Kritika,* "Soviet Watermark Studies—Achievements and Prospects," exposes the relative neglect of filigranology and makes some pertinent recommendations about further efforts in this field.

For Slavic diplomatics, the most recent Soviet publication by S. M. Kashtanov, *Ocherki russkoi diplomatiki* (Moscow: Izd-vo "Nauka." 1970; 502 p. [DLC-CD69. R9K38; MH-Slav 602.43.5]), includes many bibliographic references to earlier works.

Soviet publications in the field of paleography have been most recently surveyed in the article by M. V. Kukushkina, "Sovetskaia paleografiia," in *Vspomogatel'nye istoricheskie distsipliny* 1(1968):73-94, which is a good starting point for further bibliography, taken together with the commentary by Edward Keenan mentioned above. For a more extensive treatment of Soviet work in the field together with prerevolutionary publications, see the book by L. P. Zhukovskaia, *Razvitie slaviano-russkoi paleografii (V dorevoliutsionnoi Rossii i v SSSR)* (Moscow, 1963). See also the selected earlier publications mentioned with annotations by David Djaparidzé in his introduction to *Mediaeval Slavic Manuscripts: A Bibliography of Printed Catalogues* (A-15), pp. 1-14. The following list includes some of the best known and most substantial texts on Russian paleography, differing as they do in coverage and approach:

Beliaev, I. S.
Prakticheskii kurs izucheniia drevnei russkoi skoropisi dlia chteniia rukopisei XV-XVIII stoletii. 2nd edition. Moscow: Sinodal'naia tipografiia, 1911. 99 p.
[MH-Arc1163.3.2.]
> This edition is somewhat expanded from the first edition of 1907, a copy of which is available in the Library of Congress.

Cherepnin, L. V.
Russkaia paleografiia. Moscow: Gosudarstvennoe izd-vo politicheskoi literatury, 1956. 616 p.
[DLC-Z115.R9.C53; MH-Arc1163.3.55]

This edition largely replaces the earlier volume that Cherepnin prepared in collaboration with N. S. Chaev, *Russkaia paleografiia* (Moscow: GAU, 1946; 212 p.; *Uchebnye posobiia po vspomogatel'nym istoricheskim distsiplinam,* vol. 1 [MH-Arc 1163.3.45].)

Karskii, E. F.
Slavianskaia kirillovskaia paleografiia. 6th edition. Leningrad: Izd-vo AN, 1928. 494 p.
[DLC-Z115.2.K32]

> This is the final definitive edition of the volume which first appeared in Warsaw as a publication of the author's lectures: *Ocherk slavianskoi kirillovskoi paleografii iz chitannykh v Imperatorskom Varshavskom universitete* (Warsaw: Tipografiia Varshavskogo uchebnogo okruga, 1901; 518 p.; [DLC-Z115.R9.K18]).

Nikolaeva, A. T.
Russkaia paleografiia (konspekt kursa). Moscow: MGIAI, 1956. 61 p.
[DLC-Z115.R9N5]

> Less substantial and basically repetitive of the other handbooks listed.

Paleograficheskii al'bom. Uchebnyi sbornik snimkov s rukopisei russkikh dokumentov XIII-XVIII vekov. Compiled by V. A. Petrova. Edited by S. N. Valk. Leningrad: Izd-vo LGU, 1968. 94 p.
[MH-Arc 1163.3.95]

Shchepkin, Viacheslav Nikolaevich.
Russkaia paleografiia. Moscow: Izd-vo "Nauka," 1967. 244 p.
[DLC-Z115.2.S5; MH-Arc1163.3.4]

> This edition with introduction by P. I. Avanesov is essentially a republication, with a bibliography of the author's publications and a few other minor additions, of the original edition, *Uchebnik russkoi paleografii* (Moscow: Izdanie Obshchestva Istorii i drevnostei Rossiiskikh pri Moskovskom universitete, 1918; republished Gosudarstvennoe izd-vo, 1920 [MH-Arc 1163.3.5]).

Tikhomirov, Mikhail Nikolaevich, and Anatolii Vasil'evich Murav'ev.
Russkaia paleografiia. Moscow: Izd-vo "Vysshaia shkola," 1966. 288 p.
[DLC-Z115.5.R8T5; MH-Arc1163.3.85]

GLOSSARY OF ARCHIVAL TERMS

For brief coverage of the most important Soviet archival terms and their meanings, see the recent *Kratkii slovar' arkhivnoi terminologii* (Moscow/Leningrad: GAU, VNIIDAD, MGIAI, 1968; 58 p.) to which the present glossary is much indebted. For extensive treatment of Russian historical terms in English, see the recent *Dictionary of Russian Historical Terms from the Eleventh Century to 1917*, compiled by Sergei G. Pushkarev, and edited by George Vernadsky and Ralph T. Fisher, Jr. (New Haven, 1970; 199 p.). Only a small number of more commonly used terms are included below, in particular those not likely to be found in standard Russian-English dictionaries, and those with special meanings in Soviet archival literature. For further discussion of some terms involved in Soviet archival arrangement and reference publications, see the section on procedural information above and some of the Soviet archival textbooks cited there. For brief definitions and equivalent usage in major Western languages, see *Elsevier's Lexicon of Archive Terminology: French, English, German, Spanish, Italian, Dutch*, compiled by the International Council on Archives (Amsterdam/New York, 1964; 83 p.)

akt (pl. *akty*): official document, act. The formal official record of a deed or transaction, originating from state, ecclesiastic, or private sources. Although there is considerable scholarly dispute about the exact categories of documents that should be designated *akty*, the term usually refers to prerevolutionary (and generally pre-nineteenth century) documents prepared according to established formulae or juridical norms, such as treaties, contracts, deeds, or the like.

aktovaia kniga: act book, register. A volume in which official decisions or resolutions of juridical or civic authorities were entered. Most commonly found in the *povety* [districts or townships] within the Grand Duchy of Lithuania and (after 1569) the Polish-Lithuanian state.

arkheografiia: (1) The scholarly work of collecting, identifying, cataloging, describing, and publishing manuscripts or other historical sources; traditionally used with reference to medieval manuscript books or other early historical documents, e.g., in connection with the work of the Archeographical Commission (from 1834) or archeographical expeditions. (2) The methodology of the publication of historical sources; used in Soviet archive literature today with reference to official documentary publication programs.

arkhiv: archive(s) (Note: Although the word is usually used in the plural in English, for the purposes of this volume, because a distinction between singular and plural is often necessary, the Russian [and German] use of the singular form has been observed.) (1) A special institution devoted to the care, permanent storage, and public reference use of official non-current records and other documentary materials. In strict Western usage and in Russian before 1917, the word usually implied the storage of *official* state records, but in Soviet usage archives also serve as collecting agencies which house business, church, and private records, personal papers, films, manuscript collections, and miscellaneous documentary collections as well. (See *kollektsiia*.) (2) The preserved records of an institution, organization, or family as a result of its normal activities. In this sense the term is often used synonymously with *fond* (see below). It may contain printed as well as manuscript materials. (3) An area within the creating agency where the non-current records are temporarily stored. In prerevolutionary usage, when records tended to remain stored within and in the custody of their creating agencies, the term referred to that part of the institution devoted to the retention of records. (4) A temporary storage center, usually *vedomstvennyi arkhiv* (see below).

arkhivovedenie: archival affairs (German, *Archivwissenschaft*). Generally used in the sense of a special discipline devoted to the study of archival theory and practice, and of the organization, administration, and history of archival institutions.

avtograf: autograph. (1) An original document. (2) A manuscript written in the hand of the author. (3) A signed document the special value of which is based on the authenticity of the signature or autograph it bears.

chernovik: draft. The initial or an early version of a manuscript as opposed to its final form; may be used with reference to a typewritten as well as handwritten text (see *kontsept*).

delo (pl. *dela*): item, unit. A basic classification unit within archives constituting the smallest thematic unit-division within a fond referring to a single item of business. A major type of *edinitsa khraneniia* (see below); although in cases where a *delo* consists of several different files, each of these may be assigned a separate number as an *edinitsa khraneniia*.

diplomatika: diplomatics. An auxiliary historical discipline devoted to the analysis of documents in terms of their customary format or the formal elements present in their texts. These vary in different areas or periods, and are thus of importance for determining the date, origin, and authenticity of texts.

edinitsa khraneniia (abbr. *ed.khr.*): storage unit. The smallest physical unit division within a fond bearing a separate item number. It may consist of an individual manuscript or group of related documents, a film, or a bound volume of documents. In the case of many state textual records, such a unit coincides with an individual *delo* (see above) and is referred to as such.

faksimile: facsimile. An exact copy which reproduces the physical features of the original. Traditionally an exact copy made by hand, but now generally a photographic reproduction of the original.

filigran: watermark (see *vodianoi znak*).

filigranovedenie, filigranografiia: filigranology. The scientific study of watermarks (*vodianye znaki* or *filigrani*), usually with the object of dating or authenticating texts written or printed on paper from the fourteenth century onwards.

fil'moteka: a film library. (1) A systematic collection of motion pictures. (2) The area in which motion picture films are stored in an archive.

fond or *arkhivnyi fond:* fond. (Note: The term "fond" has been anglicized in this book, because it has no precise English equivalent.) The basic organizational grouping within all Soviet repositories; broadly corresponds to, but should be distinguished from, the "record group" or "archive group" of American and British terminology. Individual archival fonds comprise the records, or the complex of documentary materials, of an institution or organization, or of one of its major structural divisions, produced in the exercise of its institutional functions or activities. The concept is also used with reference to the natural accumulation of papers of an individual or family (i.e., *lichnyi fond*, or *famil'nyi fond*). Since all documents or manuscripts in archives and other repositories are now divided into fonds and assigned fond numbers, a number of earlier documentary or manuscript collections are also classified as fonds, and maintained intact as such, although these are clearly "collections" (see *kollektsiia*) rather than naturally accumulated records. According to Soviet practice, an archival fond should remain undivided in a single repository; (see *provenientsprintsip*); in many cases, however, when parts of institutional records or family papers have through the years been subdivided or broken up, they are usually not reintegrated, although an attempt is often made to secure microfilms or other reproductions of the dispersed sections. (See section 1, note 1, in the procedural information above.)

fonoteka: phonographic library. (1) A systematic collection of sound recordings. (2) The area in which phonograph records or other types of sound recordings are stored in an archive or other institution.

fototeka: photographic library. (1) A systematic collection of photographs. (2) The area in which photographs are stored in an archive or other institution.

gramota (pl. *gramoty*): a deed, charter, or official document. Rarely used for post-eighteenth-century documents. Often used loosely to include any written document, particularly with reference to Muscovite Russia. (See the Pushkarev historical dictionary for definitions of many types of *gramoty* used in Muscovite Russia.)

inkunabul: incunabulum, incunable. A book printed before 1501. Sometimes loosely applied to early printed books of the post-incunable period.

istochnikovedenie: The study of the nature, classification, availability, and use of historical sources. In Soviet usage often classified as a separate auxiliary historical discipline. Many of the studies published under this rubric are of considerable importance for scholars using unpublished archival materials, but the term covers studies of published documents and of other types of historical sources as well.

GLOSSARY

kartoteka: card catalog.

kartochnaia opis': An inventory (see *opis'*) prepared in the form of a card catalog, in which each *edinitsa khraneniia* is recorded on index cards.

katalog: catalog. A comprehensive enumeration (published, in manuscript, or in card form) of individual items in a collection or fond or on a specialized subject, etc., as distinct from a more generalized *putevoditel'* or *obzor*. Used more often for manuscript or documentary collections in distinction to an *opis'* [inventory] for archival fonds, although the terms are used interchangeably in some manuscript repositories. When a catalog of a manuscript collection includes more detailed scholarly description, it is usually termed an *opisanie* (see below). When the term is used in state archives it usually implies a card catalog.

khranilishche, or *arkhivokhranilishche*: stacks, or archival stacks. The area in an archive in which records are actually stored.

kollektsiia, arkhivnaia kollektsiia, or *kollektsiia dokumental'nykh materialov*: collection, archival collection, or collection of documentary materials. An artificially assembled group of individual documents, dossiers, or other units. The items may have been assembled by theme or type, geographical or chronological origin, or merely by the individual or institution that brought them together. The term *kollektsiia* can be used with reference to a group of medieval or oriental manuscript books, but such a collection more traditionally bears the name *sobranie* (see below). A *kollektsiia* is thus technically distinguished from a fond (see *fond* above), but for convenience collections are now usually assigned fond numbers, and are often loosely referred to as fonds.

kontsept: draft. The original or preliminary version of a document, usually in the handwriting of the author, as opposed to the later official copy in the hand of a scribe. The term is usually used with reference to official texts before the advent of typing, although it can also be used with reference to literary manuscripts or other preliminary drafts, as opposed to a later version. (See also *chernovik*.)

konvoliut: convolute; collection. A group of manuscripts or other documents of miscellaneous origin bound together in a single volume. Usually used with reference to early manuscripts, but also may be applied to any volume comprising several disparate parts such as a bound group of pamphlets. The Russian term *sbornik* (see below) is often used instead of this more technical Western term.

kratkii spravochnik: short handbook. A specific type of finding aid which includes less detail than does an archival *putevoditel'* (see below). For an archive, it would usually provide a brief description of the holdings and some of the most important fonds, and possibly a list of the numbers and names of fonds.

laminatsiia: lamination. The process of bonding or permanently uniting superimposed layers of paper, plastic, or other materials, usually for the purposes of preservation of damaged or permanently important documents or manuscripts.

lichnyi fond: personal fond. Personal papers of a private individual.

list (abbr. *1.*, pl. *11.*): folio, leaf, sheet. A leaf of a manuscript book or bound volume of documents, or an individual sheet within a file folder or dossier. Individual folios within an *edinitsa khraneniia* are usually numbered consecutively on the recto if they do not carry an original numeration. The verso or second page of the leaf is cited as the *oborotnaia storona* (abbr. *ob.*). To be distinguished from *stranitsa*, or page.

list ispol'zovaniia: A record sheet inserted in every archival storage unit in Soviet state archives, on which a reader must record his name and the use he is making of the materials.

manuskript: manuscript. The use of the Latin term is rare in Soviet archival practice, and is used only in the context of an early medieval text, especially a manuscript book. (See *rukopis'* below).

miniatiura: miniature. The illustrations or illuminations in a medieval manuscript or book.

nauchno-spravochnyi apparat: reference apparatus. The term is used in connection with the reference services of state archives and in speaking of the complex of published and unpublished finding aids, catalogs, and other reference materials.

oborotnaia storona (abbr. *ob,*): verso. The left-hand page of a bound volume or the second page of an individual sheet or document.

obzor: survey. A general published description of archival materials usually with reference to a specified theme or group of documents, as opposed to a more detailed and systematic *opis'* or *katalog*. Usually described as an *obzor fonda* when the coverage is limited to the materials in a specific fond, or as an *obzor dokumental'nykh materialov*, when the coverage includes materials on a special subject from a number of different fonds.

opis': inventory. The basic finding aid or shelf list for an archival fond or documentary collection, describing consecutively the physical or structural nature of each storage unit *(edinitsa khraneniia)* within a fond and the number of individual items or folios contained therein, together with their basic substantive elements such as date, author, and functional origin. The term *opis'* may also be used for a published inventory or catalog taking for its basis the original *opis'* of the fond or parts thereof; it implies the coverage by number, usually accompanied by a brief description, of the individual items within the fond, and hence is to be differentiated from the more generalized survey found in an archival *putevoditel'*. For some types of collections or descriptive purposes, the term *opis'* is used interchangeably with *katalog* or *opisanie* (compare these entries); these latter terms are more traditionally used with reference to manuscript collections.

opisanie: descriptive catalog, description. The exact technical connotation of the term has varied in different periods and in different institutions; because the word has the general meaning "description" in Russian, it is sometimes used loosely to connote only a very generalized, *obzor* type of description. Usually, however, it is employed with reference to a detailed description of the individual units in a manuscript or documentary collection or (more rarely) of an archival fond. A published *opisanie* may often be limited to materials on a special subject, or of a special type, or to the analytical description of a single manuscript or small group of documents. In some manuscript repositories the term is used interchangeably with *katalog* or with *opis'*, but when a distinction is implied, an *opisanie* usually means a more detailed scholarly description of individual manuscripts with reference to their physical form, characteristics, and basic content. (See also *opis'* and *katalog*, and the section on procedural information.)

paleografiia: paleography. The study of handwriting and of the representation of different written letters of the alphabet in different periods and locations. Considered one of the auxiliary historical disciplines, paleography is particularly important to the dating, decipherment, and internal criticism of medieval handwritten texts and inscriptions. (See Appendix 2 for selected literature on this subject.)

provenientsprintsip: provenance (German, *Provenienzprinzip*). Principle of organization of archival records whereby materials are preserved in the order in which they were produced or received by their creating agency or according to their original internal arrangement. As an extension of this principle, archivists use the French term *respect des fonds*, to indicate that archival fonds should be retained without interfering with the original record-keeping system and without subdividing materials from a single source (see *fond*).

putevoditel': guide. A type of archival finding aid published by Soviet repositories that gives systematic coverage of the contents of a single archive or major section thereof. Following major subdivisions of the given archive, the *putevoditel'* provides a brief description of the major, and usually a list of the minor, fonds with precise data about their institutional origin, size, dates, and major contents. Although it may list various subdivisions and specific units within the fonds, it does not give item numbers—and hence does not replace an inventory or *opis'* from the point of view of the researcher.

razriad: section, division. (1) A division in some prerevolutionary archives into which documentary materials were arranged for classification and cataloging purposes; usually *razriady* were established without respect to the fond, or institutional origin, or creating agency of the documents. (2) In some institutions, as a holdover from repositories of prerevolutionary origin the term is used as a synonym for *kollektsiia* in the case of collections of documents from varied sources brought together on a geographical or subject basis.

rukopis': manuscript. (1) A document written by hand. (2) A manuscript written in the hand of the author, as in the original draft of a literary or musical composition; an autograph (see above). (3) An early manuscript book, rarely referred to by the Latin derivative *manuskript*. (4) The handwritten or typewritten (sometimes *mashinopis'*) text from which the published version is prepared.

sbornik: collection, convolute. A group of texts of miscellaneous origin, bound or otherwise kept together. With reference to early manuscripts, used in the sense of a convolute (sometimes russified *konvoliut*), i.e., a bound volume containing documents of disparate origins, as opposed to a single continuous text (see *konvoliut*). Also used in the case of published collections of texts of miscellaneous origin or authorship in a single volume or group of volumes.

skrepa: The signature of a scribe or secretary (of the eighteenth and early nineteenth centuries) or of a *diak* (fifteenth through seventeenth century) attesting the authenticity of the text and form of an official document. Before the eighteenth century such a signature would be endorsed in each sheet of a series of documents or a *stolbets* (see below), attesting in addition its proper order in relation to others.

sobranie: collection. A group of manuscripts or documents brought together and assembled artificially by an individual or institution, usually from diverse sources or points of origin. Often used as a synonym for *kollektsiia* (see above), except that the term *sobranie* is used more frequently with reference to collections of medieval or oriental manuscripts, and is almost invariably used when Slavic manuscript books are in question. Distinguished from *sbornik* (see above).

sprava: The signature of a responsible official on the verso of the last sheet of an important document authenticating the correctness of the final text; mostly used prior to the eighteenth century.

sstav: A single sheet of a *stolbets*, or the point at which two sheets are glued together.

stolbets (stolp): A roll or register used in Muscovite *prikazy* formed by glueing together individual documents from a single section of a bureau or office. In the nineteenth century a number of the extant *stolbets* from some of the *prikazy* were cut apart and bound together in volumes to provide for easier archival storage.

stolpik: A relatively small *stolbets* (see above) usually containing documents relating to a more limited matter, which were not affixed to the general *stolbets* of the bureau in question.

vedomstvennyi arkhiv: temporary archive. A record-storage center to which various non-current institutional records from neighboring areas are transferred for description and appraisal, or for temporary storage before those destined for permanent preservation are transferred to permanent state archives.

vodianoi znak: watermark. A design impressed in paper in the course of its manufacture and visible when the paper is held up to the light. Sometimes referred to as *filigran*.

AUTHOR-TITLE INDEX

This index includes the titles of all books (italicized) and articles (in quotation marks) listed in the bibliographical sections as finding aids or other reference literature, together with their authors, compilers, and/or editors.

References throughout are to code numbers and not pages, hence items in introductory sections, footnotes, or textual passages are not included.

AUTHOR–TITLE INDEX

SUBJECT INDEX

This index includes the names of individuals, institutions, collections, and geographic entities, as well as principal subject categories. Titles and names occurring in bibliographic citations, however, are covered only in the previous author-title index. Generally, institutions are listed under the key word of the name in English translation, but in the interest of space and convenience, a number of major repositories are listed under the acronyms by which they are commonly known in the Soviet Union. Entries for defunct archival repositories include "see also" references to the present-day repository housing the majority of the records involved. References are to page numbers throughout this index.

STUDIES OF THE RUSSIAN INSTITUTE

PUBLISHED BY COLUMBIA UNIVERSITY PRESS

THAD PAUL ALTON, *Polish Postwar Economy*

JOHN A. ARMSTRONG, *Ukrainian Nationalism*

ABRAM BERGSON, *Soviet National Income and Product in 1937*

HARVEY L. DYCK, *Weimar Germany and Soviet Russia, 1926-1933: A Study in Diplomatic Instability*

RALPH TALCOTT FISHER, JR., *Pattern for Soviet Youth: A Study of the Congresses of the Komsomol, 1918-1954*

MAURICE FRIEDBERG, *Russian Classics in Soviet Jackets*

ELLIOT R. GOODMAN, *The Soviet Design for a World State*

DAVID GRANICK, *Management of the Industrial Firm in the USSR: A Study in Soviet Economic Planning*

THOMAS TAYLOR HAMMOND, *Lenin on Trade Unions and Revolution, 1893-1917*

JOHN N. HAZARD, *Settling Disputes in Soviet Society: The Formative Years of Legal Institutions*

DAVID JORAVSKY, *Soviet Marxism and Natural Science, 1917-1932*

DAVID MARSHALL LANG, *The Last Years of the Georgian Monarchy, 1658-1832*

GEORGE S.N. LUCKYJ, *Literary Politics in the Soviet Ukraine, 1917-1934*

HERBERT MARCUSE, *Soviet Marxism: A Critical Analysis*

KERMIT E. MC KENZIE, *Comintern and World Revolution, 1928-1943: The Shaping of Doctrine*

CHARLES B. MC LANE, *Soviet Policy and the Chinese Communists, 1931-1946*

JAMES WILLIAM MORLEY, *The Japanese Thrust into Siberia, 1918*

ALEXANDER G. PARK, *Bolshevism in Turkestan, 1917-1927*

MICHAEL BORO PETROVICH, *The Emergence of Russian Panslavism, 1856-1870*

OLIVER H. RADKEY, *The Agrarian Foes of Bolshevism: Promise and Default of the Russian Socialist Revolutionaries, February to October, 1917*

OLIVER H. RADKEY, *The Sickle Under the Hammer: The Russian Socialist Revolutionaries in the Early Months of Soviet Rule*

ALFRED J. RIEBER, *Stalin and the French Communist Party, 1941-1947*

ALFRED ERICH SENN, *The Emergence of Modern Lithuania*

ERNEST J. SIMMONS, editor, *Through the Glass of Soviet Literature: Views of Russian Society*

THEODORE K. VON LAUE, *Sergei Witte and the Industrialization of Russia*

ALLEN S. WHITING, *Soviet Policies in China, 1917-1924*

PUBLISHED BY TEACHERS COLLEGE PRESS

HAROLD J. NOAH, *Financing Soviet Schools*

PUBLISHED BY PRINCETON UNIVERSITY PRESS

PAUL AVRICH, *The Russian Anarchists*
PAUL AVRICH, *Kronstadt 1921*
LOREN R. GRAHAM, *The Soviet Academy of Sciences and the Communist Party, 1927-1932*
PATRICIA K. GRIMSTED, *Archives and Manuscript Repositories in the USSR: Moscow and Leningrad*
ROBERT A. MAGUIRE, *Red Virgin Soil: Soviet Literature in the 1920's*
T.H. RIGBY, *Communist Party Membership in the U.S.S.R., 1917-1967*
RONALD G. SUNY, *The Baku Commune, 1917-1918*
JOHN M. THOMPSON, *Russia, Bolshevism, and the Versailles Peace*
WILLIAM ZIMMERMAN, *Soviet Perspectives on International Relations, 1956-1967*

PUBLISHED BY CAMBRIDGE UNIVERSITY PRESS

JONATHAN FRANKEL, *Vladimir Akimov on the Dilemmas of Russian Marxism, 1895-1903*
EZRA MENDELSOHN, *Class Struggle in the Pale: The Formative Years of the Jewish Workers' Movement in Tsarist Russia*

PUBLISHED BY THE UNIVERSITY OF MICHIGAN PRESS

RICHARD T. DE GEORGE, *Soviet Ethics and Morality*